THE
ALPINE JOURNAL
2020

Joe Brown (1930-2020), arguably the greatest British climber of his or any other generation. His obituary appears on p330. *(John Cleare)*

THE
ALPINE JOURNAL
2020

The Journal of the Alpine Club

A record of mountain adventure
and scientific observation

Editor: Ed Douglas

Production: Rosie Edwards

Volume 124

Number 368

Supported by the
MOUNT EVEREST FOUNDATION

Published by
THE ALPINE CLUB

© 2020 by the Alpine Club

THE ALPINE JOURNAL 2020
Volume 124 No 368

www.alpine-club.org.uk

Address all editorial communication to the Hon Editor:
Alpine Club, 55 Charlotte Rd, London, EC2A 3QF
email: journal.editor@alpine-club.org.uk

Address all sales and distribution communications to:
Cordee, 11 Jacknell Rd, Dodwells Bridge Ind Est, Hinckley, LE10 3BS

Back numbers:
Apply to the Alpine Club, 55 Charlotte Rd, London, EC2A 3QF or, for
1969 to date, apply to Cordee, as above.

First published in 2020 by The Alpine Club
Typeset by Rosie Edwards, Vertebrate Publishing
Printed and bound by Novoprint SA, Barcelona

A CIP catalogue record for this book is available from The British Library

ISBN 978-0-9569309-9-6

Front cover: Victor Saunders engulfed in spindrift climbing a variant on the
Migot spur of the Aiguille du Chardonnet. Saunders reflects on our knowledge of avalanches on page 89. *(Ben Tibbetts)*

Endpapers
Front: On the first ascent of Link Sar, Karakoram. *(Graham Zimmerman)*
Back: Night sky in the Karakoram, advance base on Link Sar. *(Graham
Zimmerman)*

Foreword

News of the death of Anne Sauvy came too late for this year's In Memoriam but there was a generous tribute on the Club's website from Robin Campbell. 'Her short mountain fiction was of outstanding quality, and celebrated the better side of mountaineering: its romantic heart, the companionship of the rope, and the beauty of the high Alps.' Anne's ability as a writer spoke, and will continue to speak for itself. Campbell's observations about the 'better side of mountaineering' are a timely reminder of what so many of us value about life in the mountains in a year when much of it has been unexpectedly taken away.

It's much too early to assess fully the problems and changes wrought by the Covid-19 pandemic. Economic damage around the world has been a heavy price and it has sometimes felt that the best things in life – art, theatre, music, eating out, travel and alpinism – are those most affected. We must consider ourselves the luckiest ones. In Nepal, the consequence of lockdown was a spike in infant mortality as fewer women received the healthcare they needed giving birth. Migrant Nepali workers in India were forced to return home but found the border initially shut against them. Those in the Gulf and Malaysia were marooned and often suffered the worst infection rates. Villagers at home relying on their wages found themselves suddenly impoverished. And that's before we consider the impact of a cancelled tourism season.

The impact in the Alps was also dramatic but developed economies have more resources to protect the vulnerable. Here the debate has been about the kinds of tourism that have crowded resorts in recent years. The impact of social media on travel, the selfie posted on Instagram and then on to the next location, has been well observed. I saw a television interview with a museum worker at the Uffizi in Florence who seemed delighted at the new socially distanced version of his workplace, lamenting the fashion for people to zoom round the museum snapping pictures of themselves with 'The Birth of Venus' or whatever and then scarpering. Now they would take their time and appreciate what they were looking at with more depth. And then, days later, the director of the Uffizi, Eicke Schimdt was in trouble for posting an image of Instagram influencer Chiara Ferragni in cut-off jeans next to Boticelli's masterpiece, comparing her and her status to Venus herself. Throw in a Tik Tok meme about the Uffizi's Medusa, and you can see the conundrum: how to bring young people through the doors without turning the whole process into a two-dimensional, half-digested marketing exercise.

Something similar pertains in the world of mountain sports. Consumerism requires us to crave the novel: gear, experiences, destinations, new crags and so forth. The things we possess become transitory and disposable.

I want to direct you to Rob Collister's piece in this year's *Alpine Journal* about cleaning up Cwm Hetiau, (the 'cwm of hats', lost from the heads of tourists), a little known and much-abused corner of Snowdon. News reports of thoughtless campers around the country abandoning tents and garbage in beauty spots surged when lockdown ended and those with a need to party and a lack of options chose the countryside.

Personal responsibility is a hallmark of the mountaineering life. Every herring, as Tilman said, must hang by its own tail. Yet we also know after long experience of the mountains, that the sense of wellbeing and reward from the patient accumulation of experience and knowledge is something to be valued, not a tedious chore. And that friendship is a central part of that process. Older people sometimes agonise about what younger people want and how to give it to them. Although it is now quite a while ago, I distinctly remember when young of having only a vague notion of what I wanted, beyond experiencing the world as widely as possible. Lucky for me, there wasn't the same pressure as there is now on young people: housing costs, student loans and a challenging jobs market. But the same principle applies: the more you dwell over something as complicated as alpinism, or art, or anything worthwhile, the greater the rewards and the more those experiences offer as you age.

With that in mind, it's encouraging to read this year's Alpine Club Library report, which is full of positive steps to secure the future of mountaineering heritage and share it more widely. One of the immediate consequences of Covid-19 has been a shrivelling of resources for this sort of thing. The Alpine Club always has and I hope always will hold a central position in bringing the extraordinary story of mountaineering before the public and the determination to share this work with similarly placed clubs and organisations is commendable.

I want to thank all those who give up their time to make the *Alpine Journal* happen, particularly assistant editor Rod Smith for his work on the obituaries and our area correspondents. The diversity of subjects in this volume is indicative of the range and depth of what we do, something that should encourage us for what may prove a difficult future.

Ed Douglas

Contents

AREA NOTES

This year's frontispieces celebrate the bicentennial of the publication of *Views in the Himala Mountains* by the Scottish artist James Baillie Fraser (1783-1856), among the earliest European artistic interpretations of the Himalaya. See page 121 for Robin Campbell's article on Fraser and his work. Plate numbers are Fraser's. All images are courtesy of the British Library Board.

Pakistan

Plate 4. *'The Ridge and Fort of Jytock [Jaitak]'*

TOM LIVINGSTONE

The Great Game

Acclimatising under the immense north wall of Koyo Zom (6872m).
(Tom Livingstone)

Ally and I sat in an empty hotel restaurant, the morning silence linger-
ing peacefully under the high-vaulted ceiling. I looked around: empty
tables and half-tucked chairs filled the room. The space felt overwhelming,
like we'd stepped into a cathedral. I shifted in my seat and thought suddenly
of our long, cold bivouacs. The day before we'd been surreally teleported to
safety from one of the most intense alpine climbing experiences of my life.
Eight days in the mountains, a hard new route and then as we descended
to base camp, almost home, a sudden accident. The last 28 hours had been
spent caring for Ally as the blood on his head dried. I could still smell it
on my clothes. Now, we were floating on a sea of empty restaurant tables.
I looked around at the endless space again. How did we get here?

*

Pakistan has a bad reputation. Terrorism is rife and there are riots on the
streets, or so people assumed when I told them I was returning to the
mountains in the far north. I saw their eyebrows rise and the surprise on
their faces. 'Is it safe?' they'd ask. It didn't help that I'd be within a few
miles of the Afghan border.

Will Sim had 're-discovered' the Hindu Raj region. Years of political instability and tension had closed this mountainous, and remote area to foreigners. Until eight years ago, the Taliban had occupied the nearby Swat valley. The Hindu Raj remained hidden, submerged in mystery and a lack of information. But Will's curiosity and research secured a permit for autumn 2019, and he invited John Crook, Uisdean Hawthorn, Ally Swinton, and me to join.

Our objective was the impressive Koyo Zom (6872m). Like a medieval fortress in the wilds of Asia, its bulk looks towards the plains of Afghanistan, China and Tajikistan. An enormous, square north face is capped by seracs, and a snowy summit pyramid sits like a crown. The seracs look terrifying, and you can immediately see why the only ascents have climbed the easier, east face. In 1968, a team of Austrians made the first ascent; British climbers repeated this route in 1974. Since then, the mountain – and region – had remained dormant.

Arriving in the heat and hustle of Islamabad on 1 September, our team of five Brits was joined by four Pakistanis, who organised the logistics, cooking and life in base camp. Imran, Mohsin, Nabeem and Eshaan were as excited as we were to explore a different region of Pakistan since most of their work was in the Karakoram range.

We reached base camp on our sixth day. Lying on the warm, scraggy grass surrounded by porter loads, it was easy to forget the dusty, bumpy days riding in Jeeps. We'd rumbled up desolate valleys, rattling like bags of bones on the rough track. As we journeyed further into the mountains, villages shrank in size and frequency to isolated hamlets. Great fields of abundant crops became strips of simple subsistence farms. We waved to everyone and offered a *salaam alaikum*. Intense stares instantly cracked into friendly smiles, handshakes offered in return.

Every evening we arrived at a local guesthouse and stretched our aching bodies in the sun. But when it suddenly dipped behind the ridgeline, the light and warmth was snuffed out like a thumb on a candle. Dusk rushed up the valley. Stars began to pinprick the sky. The moon, clear and bright, grew fatter every night. It was a sliver when we arrived in Islamabad. Now it had swelled into a pockmarked disc.

On our final day of driving up the remote Yarkhun valley a few hours from the Afghan border, we passed tin-roofed houses with mud walls from which children and chickens rushed out as our Jeeps roared by. Weathered men simply watched, emotionless, at the ghostly dust clouds swirling in our wake.

At last, we saw our mountain: Koyo Zom. Instantly recognisable, we whooped and then jabbered at the reality after months of anticipation. Seracs loomed over the entire north face, and we all agreed the most attractive option was the right-hand skyline, which rose to a vast, pale yellow headwall.

At sunset, as the face melted from blood-orange to gold, we knew we'd found a worthy mountain. It looked 'nails for breakfast': bowing walls nearly a mile high, and the headwall glowing, daring us on. We couldn't stop

Above: Ally Swinton, Tom Livingstone, Will Sim, John Crook and Uisdean Hawthorn.

Left: A porter from the Yarkhun valley in northern Chitral district carrying gas to base camp. *(Tom Livingstone)*

pointing. 'Wow! Maybe left from the icefield… then up and right, following a ramp-line?' But we were also intimidated at the thought of the summit being over 3,300m higher than our base camp. As the now full moon shimmered over the summit, we ducked into our tents for the night. I can think of few more exciting, addictive and dangerous things than launching yourself onto an intimidating mountain. Koyo Zom looked just the poison.

We spent several days lying in a tent with a headache, but our two groups, Ally and I versus the rest, bantered back and forth. Sudoku, chess and the occasional meal broke the monotony. Ideally, for acclimatisation, you want to sleep 1,000m lower than your objective's summit. Since Koyo Zom was

Bivy on the initial icefield. *(Tom Livingstone)*

6,872m and the nearby mountains only 5,500m, we decided to 'crag' the start of our planned route on the right-hand skyline, the north-west face. We'd sleep at the necessary altitude, get a good idea of the initial icefield and take a closer look at the headwall.

Unfortunately, Will and Uisdean were ill and stayed at base camp. It was almost inevitable that some of our team would get sick, but we still felt for them; it was unfortunate to miss out on crucial acclimatisation. John, Ally and I spent a cold night at the top of the icefield, breathing heavily at 5,880m. Since we quickly hit hard ice and rock, we created a snow ledge using a purpose-built hammock to catch debris beneath us. The moon shone like a comforting beacon, so bright in fact that we woke early, thinking it was dawn.

Returning to base camp after several nights away, we gorged on the comforts of 'home'. The sun warmed our stiff muscles as we stretched out on our mattresses between each meal. Imran changed Ally's name to 'Ally Boom Boom' – best not ask why – and Uisdean became 'Steve' because his name was too hard for Imran to pronounce.

Mohsin cooked delicious dishes of curries, dhal, vegetables, chicken and goat. We played cricket, until we lost all the balls. Uisdean took up speed-sudoku. Will and Ally passed a book back and forth. John fumed at his Kindle having deleted the second half of his story. I began cutting labels out of my jackets. We spent hours playing cards. Somehow I was 'shithead' more often than not.

The weather remained mostly settled; these were some of the best conditions I'd ever experienced on a trip. But as the leaves on stunted trees began to turn fiery red, we knew cold temperatures and autumn snows were approaching. We could now see the moon during the day, too, arcing faintly through the sky over Koyo Zom.

*

Stupendous rock climbing on the steep headwall above the icefield.
(Tom Livingstone)

On expeditions, you reach a terrible moment when you know it's time to climb. In the months before a trip, the concept of alpine climbing is far in the future. During acclimatisation, you're still learning the mountain's moods: you watch how clouds boil around the peak; you see where snow sticks to the face; and you stare as sunshine and shadow reveal new features. Climbing is ignored because so much can happen between now and then; the team, weather and conditions all need to align. But eventually, the moment arrives.

Livingstone leading up the headwall. *(Ally Swinton)*

All five of us sat down for breakfast on Sunday 22 September, and a weather forecast flashed on the Garmin InReach Mini. 'Sunshine and good weather continues.' The carefree atmosphere quietly slipped out the door on the breeze, and our long-buried thoughts of climbing surfaced: who felt acclimatised, the right-hand line and what alternatives existed. A mix of psyche and anxiety began to bubble. The left-hand skyline of Koyo Zom also shone, appearing to have more moderate climbing along a complex ridge. Ally and I were motivated for the right-hand line but the climbing looked tricky: there was a possibility it was simply too hard, or we would be unlucky. I reckoned we had a 50% chance of climbing this line. At least the headwall looked relatively safe from objective hazards. Will, John and Uisdean chose the left-hand, north-east ridge: it looked fantastic, it would hopefully be easier and it would offer them more time to acclimatise. I shared Will's views about wanting to climb *something*. We'd been on a trip to the Indian Himalaya the year before and not climbed a single pitch.

Base camp resembled a garage sale as we packed, micro-debating for hours what gear to take. We clutched scraps of paper full of scribbled lists and by the evening Ally and I had two enormous rucksacks ready. I cursed the weight of our double rack of cams, set-and-a-half of wires, set of pegs, pair of rock shoes, double sleeping bag, single-skin tent and gas stove, but we couldn't trim anything more.

The following day we shouldered our packs and walked to advance base camp, 1,000m higher. We drifted apart, lost in anticipation. *Would the route go? Would the weather hold? What would the climbing be like?* The crux of many alpine routes seems to be in the mind and this is often the hardest part to control.

Before dawn next morning, after hurriedly wishing the others good luck as they rushed towards the left-hand line, Ally and I slogged up the glacier to the right. We spent several painful hours kicking and punching up the icefield to our previous highpoint and bivy. It was a monstrous 1,300m of altitude gain from ABC, but it was the only way to gain a day with some potential bad weather forecast for the weekend.

Our backpacks appeared like fat, red snail-shells, but at least we could eat more to lose weight. Although the sun had spilled onto the face, I still gritted my teeth as blood returned to my toes. At the bivy, our snow ledge had retained its large, undercut sofa-shape from our acclimatisation night here. We wrapped the hammock around it again and snuggled into the double sleeping bag.

On the second day, Ally led several brilliant mixed pitches up a chimney-gully system. Piece by piece, pitch by pitch, we answered more of our questions, filling in the blanks we'd noted when scanning the face. Everything climbed differently to how we'd expected. Ally thrutched up granite corners, then hauled the bags, which scraped in protest and caught on every nubbin of rock. Although Ally and I had never climbed together before, we seemed to have an easy, relaxed partnership, based on the necessity of 'up'. His smooth Scottish accent also gave me confidence.

I took over, aiming for a snow ridge. I unpeeled my down jacket and synthetic trousers to climb frozen-in spikes and flakes of rock. 'It's like dry tooling with your hands!' I shouted down. Convenient holds were like ladder rungs, albeit with a lot of 'junk pro', which led to an icy tongue flowing from the ridge.

As the sun melted into the horizon, we pitched our tent on the ridge's narrow spine. I snapped photos of Ally in a truly Greater Ranges setting. It felt like we were the only people on Earth and in the distance, jagged 7,000m mountains jutted up like wonky teeth. Although I was concerned we'd finished late and would burn out, I was too pleased with the bivy and too tired to care.

Ally took the breakfast pitches again, front-points screeching against the rock as we chimneyed higher. Finally, we bumped into the headwall's most impressive and intimidating feature: a 90m section of vertical and overhanging rock dotted with roofs and protruding fins. Ally had dubbed it 'The Cathedral'. It reminded me of Mt Alberta in the Canadian Rockies and I wasn't sure which was worse. Like a fox caught in headlights, we froze, hanging on a creaking belay to crane our necks.

Without aid-climbing gear and a portaledge, we'd be here all week unless we found an easier way. Ally urged us on and I was happy to have a look but also doubtful it would go. I'd only aided a couple of moves before, so a few pitches seemed daunting. But once I'd frigged up a crack to the first belay, my confidence returned and I eagerly changed into rock shoes. I could see a line of holds leading out right, towards a groove cutting through the top

Mixed ground at the top of
the headwall. *(Tom Livingstone)*

of the headwall. 'I think it'll go,' we shouted to each other.

It felt like climbing at Gogarth's Main Cliff, a place I'm very fond of, and I began to relish our wild yet somehow familiar position. I chucked the occasional rock over my shoulder, captivated as it spun for seconds before clattering down to the glacier. The sun washed over us now and I tiptoed and smeared in my shoes: this was far better than double boots and crampons. I ripped off my gloves, crimping and pinching and bridging between giant fins, revelling at the thought of rock climbing at 6,200m. Before long, however, I was sitting on a cam and breathing heavily. My body had remembered exactly where we were.

At the final belay, with easier ground in sight, I whooped with delight. This was alpine climbing at its finest. I hadn't expected us to make it through the headwall, but we'd been granted a subtle passage to the upper part of the mountain. It was a pure joy to climb. A few hours later, we'd chopped a small snow ledge and began to spoon as dusk overtook us. It was another long, cold night, but the stars and moon kept spinning around us. eventually fading into another dawn.

Ally led off, and soon we'd popped out above the headwall. We enjoyed the easier ground but were still a long way from the true summit, which was further back from the peak we'd seen from base camp. We both checked into our altitude pain caves. A lying-down bivy, only our second so far, passed in a fatigued haze but I remember getting up in the night to see incredible flashes of lightning from a distant storm. It was as if the sky was tearing itself apart, huge white explosions illuminating thunderheads and boiling clouds. I watched the moon and the storm until sleep welcomed me back.

On the fifth day, we endured a bitter cold on the summit slopes, cocooned in all our jackets. Hoping to see the tracks of Will, Uisdean and John, we pushed on, but figured they must have turned back when we found none. Ally and I were completely alone, a pair that had become a single being.

Sucking in all the air we could manage, and hyperventilating when we couldn't, we finally reached the summit around 1pm. I reflected on what had been one of the best, most enjoyable alpine routes I'd ever climbed. Our shouts of triumph were lost to the mountains in the distance. White-capped fangs rose from dark brown valleys as we looked across Pakistan to China, Tajikistan and Afghanistan. We abseiled and down-climbed the mountain's east face that afternoon, slumping onto the Pechus glacier.

The following day, we walked down the broad glacier towards base camp. Sleep-deprived, hungry, but with all the climbing behind us and the end virtually in sight we stomped along through the snow with about 20m of rope separating us. I began to weave around gaping crevasses, occasionally crawling over sagging snow-bridges, like ploughing through a minefield. The snow hadn't frozen overnight. I held my breath in nervous expectation of suddenly falling into a slot; these crevasses looked like monstrous, soulless depths.

Then, whilst exploring an alternative route, Ally plunged through the snow, vanishing completely. A bridge had broken. The rope whipped through

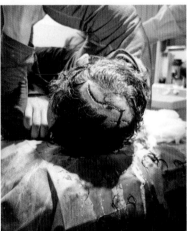

Top: Livingstone and Swinton on the summit. Above: On the final glacial descent, Swinton suffered a head injury following a crevasse fall, necessitating a helicopter rescue. *(Tom Livingstone)*

my gloved hands. The soft snow helped me to hold the fall after 15m or 20m, or else Ally had clattered to a stop. The adrenaline had my heart nearly thumping out of my chest. I could barely move, let alone pull Ally up hand over hand. And I was terrified of being dragged after him. Unable to find any ice, I set up a buried axe belay and began to haul him out using a 3:1 system. Each time I crawled back to the axe, I eyed it dubiously, praying it would hold.

For some reason, I expected Ally to be fine when he slumped over the lip of the crevasse. Then I registered the blood from his head, the grimace on his face, and the limp from his leg. Ally had put his helmet on while he was in the crevasse to protect him from some big icicles raining down on him.

Will Sim, John Crook and Uisdean Hawthorn attempted a long new route via the north-east ridge, reaching 6,000m in four days. *(Uisdean Hawthorn)*

The force of these had broken his helmet into three pieces and he'd used his sleeping mat. I quickly put our only bandage on his head and sliced open his trousers, hoping my fingers wouldn't meet a sharp bone and soft, wet flesh. Thankfully, the leg was only badly bruised.

I tried to think clearly. It was around 10am. We were in a remote region of Pakistan. The only photo I'd seen of our descent route showed it to be a gnarly, long glacier, which would take all day to travel if we were fit and lucky. Ally was in shock, shivering and bleeding from his head. We were out of gas and food, save for a few bars and nuts. I knew Ally needed more medical attention than the single bandage and painkillers I could offer him. After a few minutes' thought, I pressed the SOS button on our Garmin InReach Mini.

Over the next day and a half, I did what anyone would do: caring for Ally as I'm sure he would for me. I was glad he remained conscious throughout, but during that first afternoon he seemed very faint and cold. I was really concerned, fearing the worst. It was quite an experience to spoon Ally throughout the night, listening to his breathing, already irregular from the altitude. When his breath paused for a few seconds, then more seconds, I'd give him a nudge, my own breath held, waiting for his next.

At some point in the night, Ally suggested we called our new route the 'Great Game', a nod to the power plays of Central Asia during the 19th century. We'd read about them as we travelled through Chitral on our journey into the mountains. The name sounded fitting.

By noon the following day, Ally's condition had improved, and he even tried to hobble a few metres. As he returned to the tent, I heard the distinct *'chop-a-chop-a-chop'* of helicopter rotors: what a beautiful sound! The Pakistani helicopter crew loaded Ally on board at around 1pm and then came back for me 45 minutes later, flying to a small village where the air force had established a small fuel dump. Here the helicopters refuelled before flying on to Gilgit, which we reached around 5pm or so.

The whole team were reunited in Islamabad a few days later. We enjoyed a final meal with our agent and team, recounting wild stories of helicopters and hospitals, of Will and John waiting in a nearby airbase to rescue us as Uisdean packed up base camp to drive through the night. After breakfast in the hotel restaurant in Gilgit, Ally and I had been driven to Islamabad. As we spilled onto the street, the moon shone over the city, a full lunar cycle completed during our month in the mountains, as we played the Great Game on Koyo Zom.

Summary

North-west face of Koyo Zom (6877m), *The Great Game* (ED+, 1500m), Ally Swinton and Tom Livingstone. Attempt on north-east ridge of Koyo Zom (6877m), four days to 6,000m, Will Sim, Uisdean Hawthorn and John Crook.

Acknowledgments

This trip was supported by: the Montane Alpine Club Climbing Fund, the Austrian Alpine Club, the BMC, Firepot Food and Trail Butter. Thanks also to Jon Griffith, Ruth Bevan, the Pakistani army, the 'Fearless Five' pilots, Garmin InReach, the UK Foreign Office, the UK Rapid Response Unit, GEOS IERCC, the British embassies in both Islamabad and Karachi, Global Rescue, and our in-country agent Jasmine Tours and team.

MARK RICHEY & STEVE SWENSON

The First Ascent of Link Sar

The south-east face of Link Sar (7041m). *(Graham Zimmerman)*

From 31 July to 8 August 2019, Graham Zimmerman, Steve Swenson, Chris Wright and Mark Richey made the first ascent of Link Sar (7041m) in the central Pakistani Karakoram via its 3,400m south-east face. Having been the objective of at least nine expeditions, the first ascent of this peak has been a highly sought-after prize for the climbing community. The team called their route the *South-east Face* and graded it M6+, WI 4, 90°, 2300m, although the grade does a poor job of portraying a challenge that the Karakoram veteran Swenson called 'one of the most complex and difficult routes I have ever climbed.'

Swenson originally attempted the route in 2001 with George Lowe, Joe Terravecchia, Steve Larson, Andy Tuthill and Eric Winkleman. It was an amazing opportunity for the team since the face lies very near the contested border between Pakistan and India (known as the Actual Ground Position Line or AGPL), and the eastern aspects of the mountain had not been permitted since the mid 1980s when the Siachen conflict broke out. The team did not make it very high on the peak but their attempt inspired Swenson to return and he made repeated efforts over the following decade to get another permit for the peak with no success.

Approaching via the Kondus valley. *(Steve Swenson)*

Over the following years, several attempts were made on the peak's western aspect via the Charakusa valley. And in 2015, Swenson and Zimmerman, along with Scott Bennett, made the first ascent of nearby Changi Tower (6500m) via its *North Ridge* (M6, 5.10, A2, 1200m) and from its summit caught an excellent view of the massive south-east face of Link Sar, supplying better information about the best way to climb the route and further spurring motivation to attempt the mountain.

In 2017, it looked like the area was once again opening to climbing; Swenson and Zimmerman were finally given a permit to access Link Sar's south-east face. They also invited Wright on the expedition as he and Zimmerman had formed a strong partnership in the mountains of Alaska. During this two-and-a-half-month expedition, the team experienced atrocious weather and after multiple attempts reached only 5,900m. Despite this failure, the team made a myriad of observations of the face's immense complexities, providing them with the information they needed to make an ascent safe from the many objective hazards littering the wall.

In 2019, these three climbers, alongside Mark Richey, with whom Swenson won a Piolet d'Or in 2012 for the first ascent of Saser Kangri II in the eastern Karakoram, returned to the south-east face. They left home on 4 June. The approach to the peak is made via the Kondus valley and then up the Kaberi glacier. A road runs adjacent to the glacier up to the location of

Advance base, strongly supplied because of a low base camp.
(Graham Zimmerman)

the same base camp (3600m) used on the 2001 and 2017 attempts. They arrived there on 10 June.

From experience, they knew one of the primary cruxes of the route was acclimatisation. The Kondus valley is one of the deepest in the Karakoram and its walls are precipitously steep. On most 7,000m peaks, a nearby easier 6,000m peak would be used to acclimatise before starting on the primary objective. No such peak exists in the Kondus so the team was forced to use the lower portions of their route on the south-east face. To help with this, they set up an advance base camp at the top of the meadows that make up the bottom 1,100m of the face, hiring five local porters for whom they established a via ferrata of fixed ropes on a series of easy but exposed low fifth class slabs to ensure their safety while making the ascent to ABC.

The team had ABC established by 4 July but were then forced to wait for conditions on the mountain to improve. The 2018-19 winter in the Karakoram was one of the snowiest on record, making the mountain very dangerous, a fact emphasised by a large wet-slab avalanche observed low on the mountain from ABC on 7 July. Thankfully, the weather in early to mid July was clear and very warm, allowing for conditions to improve considerably and the team was able to climb to 6,000m on the peak via the route pioneered in 2017. After spending a couple of nights at this altitude the team considered themselves sufficiently acclimatised to attempt the route.

Wright launching into the lower mixed crux at the start of the first night on route. *(Graham Zimmerman)*

On the morning of 31 July, the team started their alpine-style attempt on the route from advanced base camp at 7.30am. During the cool morning hours, they climbed steep snow and glacial terrain to a camp at 5,100m where they spent the afternoon resting before launching on the lower crux of the route in the early evening. Climbing at night was a necessity due to the intense heat at that altitude on the south-east aspect. The crux section of the route involved 10 sustained pitches of climbing up to M6+ that even in the middle of the night were in very warm, wet and subsequently challenging conditions. Arriving at an excellent and safe bivy at 5,900m around 9.30am, they once again stopped to wait out the heat of the day and recover from climbing through the night.

The following morning, they departed just before dawn. Above the second camp was a serac barrier that was both a cause for concern in terms of overhead hazard and a considerable challenge to circumnavigate. It is important here to note that this serac wall had changed significantly from when the team observed it in 2017 and presented a major surprise. Luckily, the team was able to find a way around the right-hand side of the wall with minimal exposure and well-formed WI4 ice climbing. After 100m of easier climbing, the team found themselves at another large and safe bivouac at 6,200m, situated below the final difficult band of mixed rock and ice climbing.

Top left: Above the second camp was a serac barrier that was both a cause for concern in terms of overhead hazard and a considerable challenge to circum-navigate. *(Graham Zimmerman)*

Above left: Looking up from the slope above camp three. *(Steve Swenson)*
Above right: Above camp three. *(Graham Zimmerman)*

At this point, the team hunkered down for a forecasted 36 hours of bad weather that arrived in the mid afternoon of 3 August, their third day on the route. On 5 August, at 3 am, they departed in poor weather relying on the clearing that was forecast. An hour above camp, they were forced to stop as they were facing technical mixed climbing in weather that had still not im-proved. In order to stay warm and get out of the blowing snow, they dug a snow cave where they waited until 9am. When the weather finally cleared and they were able to continue, three excellent pitches of ice and mixed ground led to a large snow fin that involved five pitches of very challenging and unpro-tectable snow climbing and one pitch of steep but solid serac ice.

At sunset, they finally reached a good bivy site at about 6,700m. Starting at sunrise on 5 August, the team left their tents in place and launched for the summit. An excellent pitch of alpine ice led to the top of a corniced ridge they started traversing. Two pitches along the ridge, Graham triggered a small slab avalanche, a part of which poured over the belay where the rest of the team was standing. The volume of the slide wasn't large enough to harm the belay but it did sweep Graham off his feet and he fell for about 30m or 40m behind a snow ridge and over a cliff. The lead ropes rope caught him and fortunately he was not hurt, climbing back up to re-join the team. After spending some

Above: The final summit slopes.
(Steve Swenson)

Left: Technical climbing above
camp three. *(Steve Swenson)*

time to regroup, we decided to continue but Wright took the lead given that Graham was shaken by his fall. Three more pitches of challenging snow climbing intermixed with short sections of ice and mixed terrain and steep unconsolidated snow led to a final belay 50m below the summit. Even so, the nature of the climbing gave the team little confidence in their ability to reach the summit, though it loomed just overhead. In the final few feet to the summit Wright gave the lead to Richey after an excellent effort. Mark, who has a deep background in the steep challenging snow conditions of Peru, then set off up the final metres, packing a deep trench into the steep unconsolidated snow that was over his head. He reached the summit at sunset.

As can be imagined, the team was elated. The route had taken six days of hard climbing during which they ascended over 30 technical pitches and covered roughly 8,000ft vertically from their advanced base camp and about 11,300ft from base camp proper.

On 8 August, nine days after departing, the team arrived back at advanced base camp. The descent off the peak had taken three days because of making anchors in the bad snow conditions and the need to wait out the heat of the day.

This first ascent of Link Sar had taken a maximal physical and mental effort from the entire team. It required all their collective experience and strength. They are proud to report that the intense decision making required to make the ascent safely came from a very democratic, discussion-

Graham Zimmerman on the summit. *(Steve Swenson)*

oriented decision-making process without which they do not feel that they would have reached the top of this elusive and beautiful summit.

Finally, it is important to note that the expedition was undertaken adhering to strict environmental standards, deep respect for the communities of the Karakoram, and that the carbon footprint incurred by the expedition has been calculated and will be offset with the help of Protect Our Winters.

Acknowledgments

The team would like to first and foremost thank their families and friends for supporting them in the endeavour to climb this peak. They would also like to thank their sponsors and those who provided them funding for the expedition: American Alpine Club, Mount Everest Foundation, British Mountaineering Council, New Zealand Alpine Club,

Additionally, the team would like to thank Jim Woodmency for his excellent weather forecasting. They would also like to thank those in Pakistan who helped them make this trip happen, namely Nazir Sabir Expeditions, Alpine Adventure Guides, Captain Umair Tariq and their dear friends and local staff, Hajji Rasool, Nadeem and Fida Ali.

North America

Plate 12. '*Assemblage of Hill Men*'

SIMON RICHARDSON

Coastal Ranging

Mark Robson on the summit ridge of Peak 5910. The triangular Peak 5919
lies just left of centre. The route of ascent was the east ridge that bounds
the left side of the triangular face. *(Simon Richardson)*

'You've got a bit of a thing about coastal ranges,' Malcolm Bass told me
when he heard that Mark Robson and I were off to the Stikine Icecap.
It was a remarkably perceptive comment: sometimes others know you better
than you know yourself. I delight in playing on home ground in Scotland
where the variable Atlantic weather occasionally results in the elusive perfect
Scottish winter conditions. And in recent years I've tended to visit mountains
that are close to the sea that have a strong maritime influence such as Senja
Island in Norway, the east coast of Greenland and South Georgia.

As well as the visual interplay of sea and mountains, I find coastal ranges
particularly attractive because of the consistency of the snow. Rapidly changing weather results in thaw and freeze and there is nothing more satisfying
than climbing perfect névé interspersed with the odd pitch of soft squeaky
ice. It is perfect mountain travel: fast, efficient and aesthetic. True to form,
my mountaineering adventures in 2019 followed a coastal theme with memorable trips to south-east Alaska and the Coast Mountains of British Columbia in Canada. In between, and by way of contrast, I also climbed a route in
the Canadian Rockies.

Simon Richardson on the summit ridge of Hyder Peak. *(Mark Robson)*

Hyder Peak

The Stikine Icecap straddles the USA-Canada border and lies between the Stikine river and the coastal waters of Frederick Sound in south-east Alaska. Spectacular granite peaks rise from a myriad of glaciers that cover an area equivalent in size to Wales. It is one of the wildest and least known mountain ranges in the world and would be the perfect alpinist's playground if it were not for the weather, which is truly atrocious. To the west lies the Gulf of Alaska: a malevolent, tempestuous sea responsible for most of the precipitation that strikes the Pacific coast of North America. Consequently the Stikine is one of the wettest places on Earth and has been described as a 'rain icecap'.

Unsurprisingly, this makes climbing in the Stikine extremely challenging, and climbers rarely visit. The Devil's Thumb (9077ft) is the most celebrated mountain in the area, and sees two or three attempts a year. The rest of the range is almost completely neglected despite being full of tempting possibilities. For example, approximately 25km to the north-west of the Devil's Thumb at the head of the North Baird glacier lies the impressive Oasis Peak (7925ft), an imposing granite monolith that has only been summited once.

Mark Robson is the perfect partner for a remote and committing adventure. His understated modesty and quiet confidence hides a remarkable breadth of experience from a one-day ascent of El Capitan to paragliding the length of the Alps, and from pioneering remote sea stacks in Scotland to multi-day adventure races. We have shared many adventures together over the years and were keen to visit the Stikine. Our plan was to make the second ascent of Oasis Peak via a new route from the north. This had been attempted a couple of times in the 1970s, but our tactic was to visit in the spring hoping to find more stable snow, ice and mixed climbing conditions than those encountered by the previous teams in mid summer.

We flew onto the North Baird glacier from the fishing village of Petersburg on 30 April. As far as we could tell, we were the first climbing expedition to visit the glacier for over 40 years. Unfortunately, as soon as we arrived it was immediately clear that any technical climbing was unlikely. All the mountains were heavily snowed up, draped with enormous cornices and unstable snow mushrooms. But more significantly, it was not freezing at night and there were (literally) hundreds of avalanches: so much for our dreams of hard névé and soft squeaky ice. After a week we abandoned all thoughts of climbing Oasis Peak and moved our camp down to where we could access the north arm of the North Baird glacier.

Finally, the weather improved enough for us to climb through the icefall guarding entry to the North Arm. We were probably the first mountaineers ever to visit this part of the icecap and were surrounded by over a dozen unclimbed summits. The big prize was Hyder Peak (7180ft), which lay 8km away at the head of the adjacent Dawes glacier. This massive and isolated mountain, with a steep rocky summit triangle, lies on the western edge of the range and was one of the highest unclimbed peaks in south-east Alaska.

We'd spotted Hyder Peak from a distance earlier in the trip and thought it looked low-angled enough to ascend on skis, which were the only viable form of travel in the bottomless wet snow. Daybreak on 10 May found us post holing up steep mountainside with our skis strapped to rucksacks. As we gained altitude the snow finally began to firm up and we wondered why on earth we were carrying skis at all: the lower slopes had been far too steep to ski, whilst up here it was very exposed with a drop of 600m to the glacier below and the crust too icy for skins. Finally, a plateau opened up ahead of us for almost two kilometres. On safer terrain at last, we clipped into our bindings and made rapid progress towards the summit triangle.

Having stashed our skis, I took the lead, punching steps up the steep front face. There was avalanche debris all around us and it felt a spooky place. The sun was now rising quickly in the sky and the stability of the slope was about to deteriorate fast.

'What's our turn around time, Simon?'

'Eight o'clock: we've got 45 minutes.'

I ran out 60m of rope and pushed on further. The summit tower was draped in unstable cornices and I decided that just reaching the final ridge would have to do, but at the last moment for some inexplicable reason, I started climbing directly towards the summit. I led up increasingly steep snow and eventually found a belay on a rocky outcrop. Mark took over and climbed tricky mixed ground onto the summit ridge, which was draped with spectacularly curled snow formations. He was close to the top, but the way ahead looked impossible. We'd passed our 8am time limit and the pressure was on.

Mark traversed left across a 30cm blanket of snow that appeared incredibly to be glued to a near-vertical rocky slab, which led to the final section of ridge. Soon after, he was perched on the airy summit. I came up and without hesitating we started our abseil descent. The return across the plateau on skis was fun; the pressure was off momentarily, and in front of us was an endless expanse of unclimbed mountains. The lower section was not so enjoyable. We skied for as long as we dared, and then ploughed a trench through thigh-deep snow that sloughed off and didn't stop sliding until it hit the glacier hundreds of metres below. By 11.30am we were down. We spent the afternoon relaxing in the sunshine, relieved and delighted to have summited.

Overall, we only had three days when it was not raining but we were also successful in making first ascents of Peak 5910, Peak 5720, Peak 5800 and the shapely Peak 5919. Snow conditions remained soft throughout, avalanches took place constantly and we experienced considerable cornice difficulties.

Despite all of these challenges, it was an extremely rewarding expedition. The climbing was often very exciting and picking safe lines and negotiating the beautiful corniced summit ridges made it very exacting. We had one huge cornice collapse but fortunately both of us stayed upright on the solid side of the fracture line. And above all, when the rain stopped and the fog lifted, we were treated to some of the most beautiful and pristine mountain landscapes either of us had ever seen.

The north face of Mount Phillips. The north spur takes the dividing line between light and shade. *(John Scurlock)*

Mount Phillips

I first met Canadian climber Ian Welsted on the international winter climbing meet in Scotland in January 2016. The weather was typically Scottish with rapidly fluctuating temperatures, high winds and varying amounts of snow. Conditions were challenging: few routes were in nick and just surviving on the hill was a challenge in itself. Ian and his fellow Canadian Raphael Slawinski took this in their stride and made some superb ascents. My already high assessment of Canadian alpinism was considerably enhanced.

Roll forward nearly two years to November 2017. I was attending the Banff Mountain Film Festival. Ian was keen to reciprocate the hospitality of the Scottish meet and offered to take me climbing after the event. Needless to say I jumped at the chance. My track record in the Canadian Rockies was limited to a handful of well-known routes and climbing with Ian was too good an opportunity to miss. It was snowing heavily in town and winter was already in full swing, so we decided to attempt an unclimbed gully on the north flank of Storm Mountain (3158m).

It was dark when we reached the top of the 500m route. To our surprise we had come across a nut and couple of pegs in its upper half, so our 'un-climbed' gully was not a new climb after all. Halfway up, Ian inadvertently dislodged a huge block that struck me a glancing blow. I was a little shaken but unhurt although Ian was impressed that I wanted to continue. He in-correctly assumed this was toughness, determination and drive, but it was nothing of the sort. I had just been lucky. Our desire to complete the climb

Above: Ian Welsted climbing the north face of Mount Phillips. *(Simon Richardson)*

Right: Ian Welsted approaching the summit of Mount Phillips. *(Simon Richardson)*

together highlighted a quiet confidence and a shared appetite for adventure and commitment. We agreed to climb together in the Coast Mountains in summer 2019.

We thought mid July would be the optimum time but before leaving home I became concerned that a large high-pressure system anchored over Alaska was directing unsettled weather over Canada's western mountains. I'd recently come across John Scurlock's beautiful image of the north side of Mount Phillips in the Canadian Rockies on the Internet. A quick Google search revealed that Mount Phillips was a 3,246m peak just to the north of Mount Robson. Even better, Phillips' 600m north face appeared to be unclimbed. The sharp-cut north spur dividing the north-east and north-west faces of the mountain was a compelling feature that simply had to be climbed. Almost on a whim, I printed off the photo hours before I boarded the plane to Calgary.

When I showed the photo to Ian he was similarly inspired; the route appeared to be an objectively safe option as the delayed Rockies spring transitioned into summer. The weather had been poor in the Rockies too, but we hoped to take advantage of cool conditions on the back of a passing front.

On 21 July, loaded with four days of food, we left the Berg Lake trail just above Emperor Falls and bushwhacked through forest that opened out to beautiful meadows of wild flowers with the Emperor ridge of Robson towering behind. Scree and snow slopes led to a comfortable bivouac on the right flank of the Phillips glacier.

We rose at 12.30am, anxious to become established on the route before the snow softened in the morning sun. A two-and-a-half-hour approach over the col east of the mountain saw us crossing the bergschrund at dawn, and we moved quickly up the lower spur on mixed snow and rock. Our pace slowed at two-thirds height where the spur abuts the steep headwall. I had hoped for a hidden ramp leading right to the west ridge. Instead we were forced into the 'jaws', a narrow ice gully that cut deeply into the headwall. It appeared to end in an impasse but fortunately a hidden icy gully led left to easier ground.

It was now midday and the sun was softening the snow at an alarming rate. Every time we dropped a rock it set off huge, surging wet-slide avalanches down the face below. The snow would accelerate below us like an express train and the roar would reverberate around the glacier cirque.

Mount Waddington from Mount Tiedemann in August 2000. The upper west ridge is the right crest. Welsted and Richardson traversed the skyline from right to left. The summit points from right to left are the Northwest Peak, the False Summit is hidden) Summit Tower and the Tooth. *(Simon Richardson)*

'Hey Ian, what's going on?'

'It's all part of the spring-thaw cycle in the Rockies, Simon. The snow has gone isothermic. It only lasts a couple of days. The avalanches will stop once the snowpack has had time to stabilise and adjust to the warming.'

It was all rather unnerving. I'd never seen snow behave like that before but we were perfectly safe and thankful for our alpine start. The next pitch across a snow band to reach the final part of the west ridge should have been a straightforward romp across a 45° slope, but instead Ian was forced to make a bold and demanding lead on dark hold-less limestone covered in wet snow. I marvelled at his skill placing knife blades. It all felt a world apart from my world of coastal ranges of predictable snow governed by freeze-thaw.

Then, suddenly, it was almost over. A broad ledge on the west ridge gave way to three exposed and intricate pitches up the sharp rock arête to the summit. It was 5pm, the weather was good and there was no need to hurry. Robson towered 700m above us and behind we could see down the Rockies chain to Mount Clemencau and beyond. To the north the view was even more intriguing. Steep and jagged peaks stretched all the way to the horizon holding countless possibilities for more adventures to come.

Mount Waddington

Over the winter, while discussing objectives for the Coast Mountains, I had came up with various options on attractive, rarely visited peaks deep in the range, but Ian was not convinced.

Mount Waddington's upper west ridge. The line of ascent took the hanging ramp on the right side of the jagged crest. *(Simon Richardson)*

Ian Welsted on the crest of the upper west ridge after exiting the Epaulette glacier on day three. *(Simon Richardson)*

'Hey Simon, I'd like to go somewhere big like Waddington rather than go rock climbing on obscure spires.'

'Well if it's Waddington you want, let's go for the complete west ridge,' I suggested. 'It's one of the biggest unclimbed features in the range.'

There it was, Mount Waddington's upper west ridge marching boldly across a double-page spread in Don Serl's guidebook: a sharp, 1,500m pinnacle crest rising up to a fine snow arête and the summit plateau. The central spine of the highest peak in the Coast Mountains should have been climbed years ago but somehow, in the chase for more technical objectives, it had been overlooked.

Don and Phyllis Munday's pioneering route up Waddington climbed the lower 3.5km of the west ridge to 3,300m and then followed the natural line of weakness up the Angel glacier to the north-west summit. It is a logical line and hugely committing for 1928. Unfortunately the Mundays did not have the firepower to continue to the main summit, which had to wait until 1936 when Bill House and Fritz Wiessner summited via the south-west face. This bold and committing undertaking was the most difficult alpine route in North America at the time and comparable with the advances being made in the European Alps on the Eiger and Grandes Jorasses.

Our plan was to traverse Waddington starting from Fury Gap at its western end. We would follow the Munday route to the foot of the unclimbed upper west ridge, climb this and continue on to bag False Summit (3980m), Northwest Peak (4000m) and Summit Tower (4019m) before descending the Bravo glacier route to complete our 12km journey at the eastern extremity of the mountain at Rainy Knob.

Two weeks after our ascent of Mount Phillips, the rain stopped, the clouds cleared and the weather was finally good enough for Waddington. Mike King dropped us off by helicopter at Fury Gap (2500m) on 3 August. We felt rather exposed to be in the deep heart of the Waddington range with just light alpine packs but with no further ado we set off up the snow slopes above towards Fireworks Peak, the first minor summit on the lower west ridge. The snow was knee-deep after days of storm and it was slow going. Ian's famous trail-breaking power saved the day and early that afternoon, a little after Herald Peak, I suggested we stop to bivouac.

'I'm not in the habit of stopping at 3pm when there is good weather in the mountains,' Ian countered.

Above: Waddington's Summit Tower (4018m) from the Northwest Peak on the third day. *(Simon Richardson)*

Left: Waddington's Summit Tower (4018m) from the Northwest Peak on the third day. *(Simon Richardson)*

It did feel ridiculously early but we were not going to make the start of the upper west ridge that evening so there was no point in pushing too hard.

'We aren't going to climb the upper ridge tomorrow, so why not let it clean off another day. And this is a perfect camp spot.'

Next day we traversed over the two Men-At-Arms summits and followed a spectacular corniced ridge over Bodyguard and Councillor peaks. The going continued to be tough in the deep snow but we were hopeful that the upper west ridge had been scoured and the sun would consolidate the snow and firm up the terrain. Once again we had a leisurely mid-afternoon bivouac, but this time we were perfectly positioned near the start of the ridge.

On day three we were up and away before dawn and sure enough, conditions on the upper west ridge were excellent, providing fast climbing on hard snow and easy ice along a ramp running below the south side of the crest. We moved together, with the occasional belayed pitch, until a hidden gully led up onto the previously un-trodden Epaulette glacier that sits astride the central section of the ridge.

We couldn't believe our luck that it had all gone so smoothly but we were soon confronted with the sting in the tail. As we left the glacier, the ensuing snow ridge narrowed to a knife-edge draped in delicate cornices. I traversed à cheval along the wafer-thin crest and belayed by excavating a deep hole in the snow on the east side of the ridge.

'If you fall, fall to the left!' I called across to Ian.

Ian was precise and sure-footed but our situation was precarious. There was no option other than continuing across the steep and heavily loaded slope on the north side of the crest to gain the upper ramp leading to Northwest Peak.

Ian made a long and committing traverse, manfully digging deep to find ice screw runners, but the snow on my pitch was too deep for screws. I ploughed a sideways trench for 30m until a blind three-metre jump into a bergschrund brought us back into contact with more reasonable terrain. That afternoon we tagged the False Summit and Northwest Peak before descending to the broad terrace below the main summit.

Day four was another beautiful day but we were nearly turned back on the Summit Tower due to falling rime ice. But as the sun moved behind the Tooth the onslaught abated and we enjoyed a succession of excellent mixed pitches up the icy central chimney. The weather was completely different to when I climbed Waddington in a storm with Dave Hesleden in 1997 but the climbing was similar, and reminded me of Scotland. On the summit we took in the 360° panorama, looking north to south along the spine of the Coast Mountains and west to the Pacific Ocean, before making a series of abseils back to our bivouac tent.

Before the trip, my friend Don Serl had warned me that descending the Bravo glacier might be the crux of the whole route. We woke at 3am and set off down steep névé slopes through the dawn to gain the Bravo headwall. How things had changed in the intervening 22 years. Instead of deep snow flutings it was now a broken rocky slope and we carefully abseiled down to the Bravo glacier icefall.

Soon we became lost in a maze of huge crevasses and serac walls and after an hour reached an impasse, trying three different routes without success. We were resigned to re-exploring the first option when Ian spotted some old footsteps in the distance on the lower glacier below. This gave us the incentive to force a way through and soon we were following a trail of wands planted by a US team several weeks before. Unfortunately they had been unable to find a way up to the Bravo headwall but their tracks saved our day.

We reached Rainy Knob (2120m) at 11am but were not ready to break the spell. We lounged on a huge flat slab of granite drinking coffee and taking in the magnificence of the surroundings and enjoying the deep glow that

Simon Richardson on day four above the icy chimney on the Summit Tower.
(Ian Welsted)

Waddington's spectacular upper west ridge. *(John Scurlock)*

comes when you achieve something that you have set out to do. Eventually we reached for the radio and within minutes we heard the throb of the helicopter. Our adventure was complete.

Summary

First ascent of Hyder Peak (7180ft) and four other summits, Stikine Icefield, south-east Alaska. (Mark Robson and Simon Richardson, May 2019)

First ascent of *North Spur*, Mount Phillips (3246m), Canadian Rockies. (Ian Welsted and Simon Richardson, 22 July 2019)

First ascent of *Complete West Ridge* of Mount Waddington via a 12km traverse from Fury Gap to Rainy Knob. (Ian Welsted and Simon Richardson, 3 to 7 August 2019)

'Other Annapurnas'

Plate 16. '*Village of the Shai*'

MICK FOWLER

Chombu Fever

The object of desire. Chombu (6362m) from the Sebu La. *(Mick Fowler)*

'**M**y hotel is broken.'

The hotel owner's tour of his premises left us in no doubt. He was not exaggerating. Like a fifth or so of the buildings in the small village of Thangu, his hotel was indeed very broken. Victor Saunders and I had arrived in Thangu to spend the night, on our way to attempt Chombu in Sikkim.

'Seven feet of snow in one storm,' announced a bystander.

'Heaviest winter snow since 1995,' added another.

We had been warned that the winter snows had been heavy but nothing had quite prepared us for avalanches across the road and the damage to property. Clearly we were facing unusually snowy conditions.

Sikkim was a new area for both of us. The deep, jungle-covered and winding valleys of the foothills made for a grand and varied approach to the mountains. Our approach was along the 'short route' followed by the Everest climbers of the 1920s, 'short' of course being a relative term. The 1921 Everest team took 36 days to walk from Darjeeling to their base camp. The perseverance and commitment of those pioneers in just getting to and from the mountain was remarkable. It was almost enough to make me feel guilty that the approach to our base camp involved flying to Bagdogra airport, 40km south of Darjeeling, two days driving to Thangu and two days of walking.

43

'My hotel is broken.' Winter snow damage at Thangu in Sikkim. *(Mick Fowler)*

Chombu is in a sensitive area and the expense and uncertainty involved in securing all the necessary permissions has played a large part in its climbing history, which is relatively short. Bad weather and soft snow stopped Cooke and McPherson in 1944. Doug Scott's team experienced much the same problem in 1996, as did Roger Payne and Julie-Ann Clyma in 2007. A widely discredited first ascent claim was made in 1961. The highest point thus far, still a long way from the summit, was reached by a Japanese team in 1992.

Noting the recurring mention of soft-snow problems, our plan was to attempt the west face. This we judged was steep enough not to hold snow and therefore give the sort of moving-one-at-a-time mixed climbing that Victor and I prefer. When we first started planning in 2016, we could never have dreamed that so many hurdles would arise.

After an initial refusal and much uncertainty, permits were promised for the post-monsoon season of 2017. But the promise was withdrawn as a result of a border skirmish with China. Then, out of the blue, I was diagnosed with cancer and rather than climbing in the Himalaya found myself experiencing the dubious joys of radiotherapy and chemotherapy. Pre-monsoon 2018 was spent recovering and preparing to go post-monsoon 2018. And then, that summer, a return of cancer resulted in an operation to remove my anus, which stymied any hope of Chombu that year. Argh! So it wasn't until in the pre-monsoon of 2019 that health and permit issues came together and we were finally ready to go.

Our team to walk in to base camp consisted of the two of us, four Sherpas, a cook, a kitchen boy and five porters. There was also a liaison officer who returned to Gangtok after ensuring we were underway. It felt an awful lot of people to support a lightweight two-man team.

Finding enough porters had been tricky. The local people were much more interested in searching for caterpillar fungus, the famous *yartsa gunbu* much in demand in China as an aphrodisiac and cure-all. The result was that our net had to be cast far and wide, the haul being five outrageously strong young men brought in from Darjeeling. Being as there were so few it was just as well that they were so strong.

The triple loads they shouldered must have weighed 70kg and matched the heaviest I have ever seen. Unfortunately this meant that as the day progressed and the snow softened they sunk in ever more deeply. The snow really was a problem and we were only able to make progress at all because the track was on the south-facing side of the valley where the winter snows were starting to thin. The north-facing side looked a lot like the Alps after a heavy winter snowfall.

The track was interesting. Those sections not completely covered with snow revealed rocks cemented into place with parallel sides. It was a tour de force. Later, when the snows had largely melted, we were to discover this amazing track did a loop of the valley, reaching a point only half an hour or so from our base camp. We never did get a clear explanation for its existence. Suggestions that it was built for military purposes or to take yaks up to a yak racing ground were dismissed in favour of it being some kind of tourist trail. Either way it would have been very useful had it not been largely buried.

It took two days and several ferries before we set up base camp by a clear stream 30 minutes short of the old Himalayan Club hut at the foot of the Sebu La. This pass connects the Lachen and Lachung valleys and back in the days of British rule it was a sufficiently popular crossing for the Himalayan Club to judge it worth building a substantial refuge either side. Nowadays the remains of the hut are crumbling quietly away in their summer yak-grazing grounds.

From the Himalayan hut, it could be seen, in sharp contrast to virtually everywhere else, that the mountain was surprisingly devoid of snow. It did though look exciting, with uncompromising steep slopes leading to an enticing, curling summit snow ridge. I almost felt emotional, finally seeing the object of my dreams for the last three years.

We climbed an easy 5,600m summit, spent a couple of days and nights lying at 5,500m sucking in thin air and returned to base camp in high spirits. We had chosen our line and the weather looked reasonable. All we had to do now was spend a day eating and then start climbing. Life was good.

By the next morning 10cm of snow had fallen, the temperature was hovering around freezing and base camp was in the cloud. Another day of eating was judged appropriate; we had a time cushion of about a week so could afford to be relaxed and wait out some bad weather. The next day dawned the same but, feeling the need to be in position at the foot of our intended line, we trudged up through the falling snow, pitched our little tent at the foot of the face and set the alarm for an early start. But the weather would not play ball. In the early hours it was still snowing and the temperature was clearly too warm for a good freeze. Days passed with little change. The boredom level grew. There is only so much time that can be spent in a two-man tent without going stir-crazy.

In between reading and brewing we stared at the tent fabric, righted the wrongs of the world and discussed the pros and cons of colostomy bags on constricted bivouacs. This was my first expedition with a bag and while a small tent was not the harshest of testing grounds, my experience thus far suggested that having control over when to empty the bag could be an advantage: no urgent exits into snow-blown nights for me. Victor, who had endured a nasty incident being caught short on our last Himalayan climb together, looked mildly envious without going so far as to wish he could have the operation. The trickiest problem for me was not being able to sit down properly. The operation had involved plastic surgery across both buttocks. While sitting in a well-cushioned environment is bearable, a sitting bivouac would require very careful planning. With endless hours to waste we whiled away the time discussing laughable possibilities interminably.

The weather still wasn't getting any better. Every day, come 3pm or so, it would start to snow and continue right through until about 6am. The avalanche risk was high and the underlying snow soft and exhausting. Despondency levels were rising. I had never experienced Himalayan weather quite like this. All in all it developed into the most frustrating wait that either of us had ever experienced. Eventually, all reading material had been read, all conversation topics exhausted, time was fast running out and conditions on the mountain remained awful. It became increasingly clear that we had failed without even crossing the bergschrund.

Ultimately the pre-monsoon 2019 British Chombu expedition accepted defeat and trudged forlornly back to base camp: a most disappointing outcome.

Victor and I must have very short memories, because back in the UK we somehow convinced ourselves that the weather and climbing conditions might be better in the post-monsoon season. Even so, I was almost surprised to find us back in Sikkim in September 2019.

Throughout the two days we spent in Gangtok it rained incessantly. During this time we were informed that a crucial bridge had been washed away and only locals were being allowed along a route through a sensitive army camp, which was now the only access into the Thangu valley. The expedition was dead in the water if we couldn't reach the village of Thangu and getting foreigners there when Indian tourists were banned seemed an almost insuperable problem to us.

That task was entrusted to Baichung, our liaison officer who was to drive us to Thangu in his Jeep and arranged to meet us at 8am next morning. At 9am he arrived explaining that his vehicle had been rendered un-driveable following a hit and run in the night. Being a devout Buddhist he was sufficiently concerned by the way things were going to suggest that we seek advice at Gangtok monastery to ensure he and the expedition were not to be plagued by bad karma. Fortunately a monk decreed that all would be well

Approaching the foot of the face was tiring. *(Mick Fowler)*

But at least the snow flutings proved enticing. *(Mick Fowler)*

Except the flutings proved to be an exhausting and insecure battle with unconsolidated snow. *(Mick Fowler)*

and we continued on our way. I'm not sure what would have happened if he had sensed less positive vibes.

Being as we were destined for a tourist free area it struck us as unfortunate that the vehicle secured to replace Baichung's Jeep had 'Tourist' embla-

Above: The vast quantities of snow at least made for easy tent placements. *(Mick Fowler)*

Right: Wonderful mountain, awful conditions. Day two. *(Mick Fowler)*

zoned on the side. I have no real idea what miracles occurred during our drive to Thangu. Approval from yet another senior official was secured, a special pass of some sort was granted, the guard at the army camp gate let us through and the villagers of Thangu couldn't believe it when we arrived. No Indian tourists were allowed and yet these two westerners had arrived in a vehicle with Tourist on the side. Maximum respect to Barap, our agent, and Baichung: I have no idea how they did it.

The weather looked reasonable, the snow line was high and with our porters only weighed down by 50kg loads this time we started the walk to base camp in high spirits. We hoped we had learned lessons from our April attempt and felt we were in with a good chance of success.

Fourteen days later Victor and I were sat in our tents at base camp listening to the rain. After much debate we agreed that in a combined 75 years of expeditioning, this was the longest spell of properly bad weather either of us had ever experienced. We had managed to acclimatise by spending a couple of nights at 5,600m but wading through soft snow to get there had been utterly exhausting and the frequent big avalanches coming down the west face had been enough to put us off our intended line. We had also managed to break a pole in our mountain tent and drop one of our walkie-talkie handsets into a lake. But we were ready to climb. Our reconnaissance had focused our minds on what might be done safely and all we needed now was a good enough window of weather to try and climb our newly preferred line on the north side of Chombu.

The rain continued. Days at base camp passed slowly. After bed tea at 6am the only reason to emerge from our sleeping bags was for breakfast at 8am, lunch at 1.30pm, afternoon tea at 3.30pm and dinner at 6pm. Each meal lasted perhaps 20 minutes. And so, much as we tried to force ourselves to stroll around occasionally, the total time outside our sleeping bags each day was often around 80 minutes.

On 10 October the weather suddenly improved. After three years and so many setbacks it seemed the time had finally come for us to try and climb Chombu. Two days of energy-sapping wading saw us camped below the face peering up at striking snow flutings and snow-cloaked buttresses.

'Have you ever tried to climb a face with this much snow on?'

'No,' said Victor. This would be a new experience for both of us.

The exhausting nature of deep powdery snow was such that we were reduced to moving one at a time from well below the bergschrund. As the ground steepened it became clear that everything, almost regardless of angle, was plastered with perhaps two feet of the stuff. Beneath it there was more snow that was only slightly firmer. Making upwards progress was painfully slow and insecure. Victor, being a very light chap at about 55kg, preferred an approach that stayed on the surface as much as possible. Whereas I, at a relatively porky 70kg, was reduced to clearing the top two feet away and trying to fashion steps from what lay below to support me. This meant I spent much of my time standing on 70° ground clearing away a snow overhang above my head before teetering up. My mittens froze like a couple of claws while the snow I swept away inevitably found its way down my neck.

Midway through the afternoon, Victor, who had been out of sight in the cloud, suddenly hurtled into view. He ended up dangling over a vertical cliff having fallen a good 60ft. There was quite a long silence and then:

'My first ever Himalayan fall.' He seemed rather sheepish about it but in 39 years of Himalayan climbing that struck me as rather a good record. It also said a lot about the terrain we were trying to climb. Grading it was impossible. It was like a powdery early season Cairngorms grade V route times 10. Even the easy-looking sections were exhausting and desperately insecure. We moved at a snail's pace.

After two full days of this kind of terrain we reached the base of smooth slopes leading to the north summit. At the foot of the face I had looked up at the flutings and wild snow mushrooms and felt our chances of success were slim. Now, though, we were above these obstacles. The weather was reasonable. The summit was only 250m above us and the open slopes ahead

Confidence began to rise as the team gained height. Gurudongmar on the left and Pauhunri on the right above morning clouds. *(Mick Fowler)*

looked likely to give easier and quicker climbing conditions. Much as the climbing itself had been a million miles away from the technical ground I love, we had reached 6,100m. I could sense enjoyment and confidence levels rising.

We shared a freeze-dried food pack that evening. Both of us commented that it didn't taste right. There was a nasty chemical smell and flavour to it. But tastebuds can be erratic at altitude, preparing food is a hassle and we were both tired and keen to get our heads down. Victor eats remarkably little and after just two or three spoonfuls he handed over to me. I persevered and ate the rest. It was grim but I think we just sort of assumed our bodies would cope and extract some energy from the awfulness.

It was about an hour later that it became clear that all was not well.

Victor was first to feel sick: a minor accident was followed by a rushed exit and a just-in-time explosion. Soon both of us were suffering repeated unpleasant chemical-flavoured burps. As Victor rushed to exit for a second time, I became aware that my colostomy bag was becoming uncomfortably full with liquid. No problem. I could simply change it without the hassle of getting outside the tent. It pleased me greatly to point this out to Victor.

I lay on my back in my cosy sleeping bag, removed the old bag and set about attaching a new one. Unfortunately those of us with a stoma find it impossible to tell when a discharge might occur. Having gloated over the inconvenience Victor was enduring the tables were suddenly turned when an unexpected fountain of poo erupted. A remarkable quantity of liquid

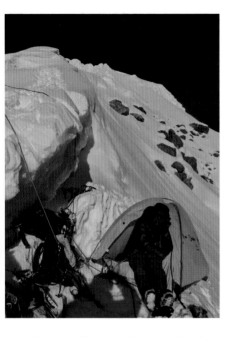

The morning after the night before.
(Mick Fowler)

poured forth. With both forearms containing the lake forming on my stomach I found myself unable to take any constructive action to resolve the growing problem.

'Help.'

It was the only thing I could think to say.

Poor Victor must have thought I had exploded. As the initial shock subsided emptying the poo pool became top priority. Toilet paper was in limited supply and soon ran out. Victor's book came next. The pages were not very absorbent but at least there were a lot of them. Spare clothing was the backstop. Remarkably the pool was emptied with minimum spillage but in my enthusiasm to apply a new bag, I quickly wasted several of my carefully calculated stock. The more serious on-going problem was increasingly severe nausea and frequent diarrhoea. The night developed into what felt like a non-stop session of bag emptying (me), rushing outside (Victor) and dry retching (both). By morning I was oozing transparent liquid, felt completely drained and had only two colostomy bags left. Victor too was suffering badly, albeit not so spectacularly.

I felt absolutely awful. What to do? After so many delays and so much heartache here we were within striking distance of the summit we had dreamed about so much and for so long. And yet this wasn't a little spot of the runs. We had clearly poisoned ourselves. Seldom had I felt more physically drained and nauseous. In eating something to give ourselves energy we had clearly had exactly the opposite effect. We discussed our predicament at length.

After all we had gone through to get to this point the temptation was to continue. But big mountains can be dangerous places. The wind could be seen to be whipping over the summit ridge and the temperature was well below freezing. Not only did I feel weak and exhausted, I would definitely run out of colostomy bags if we continued. But then little comes out in normal high mountain circumstances. And what's a little poo compared to achieving your goal of the last three years? We discussed various possibilities but in truth we didn't dither long. The decision came quickly, if painfully. I really did feel a sense of despair after all we had gone through to get to this point. Particularly after the health challenges of the last couple of years, I had wanted to prove to myself that I could still climb great Himalayan

Older and wiser? *(Mick Fowler)*

objectives. And, much as the reason we were going down had nothing to do with those health issues, they added to the sense of failure somehow. I was very aware of all the effort medical professionals had put into getting me back in good condition, not to mention the unfailing support of my family and Berghaus. We had overcome so much and I felt I had let everyone down because of one gone-off freeze-dried meal.

It was 48 hours before either of us was able to eat anything again. We abseiled slowly down the line we had come up, both of us surprised at how steep the ground was. By the time we arrived in base camp I could hardly put one foot in front of the other. I regarded that as confirmation, if confirmation was needed, that we had made the right decision. Another attempt was out of the question. The army would not allow us to extend our permit and bad weather had returned anyway. It was time to begin the long journey back home. Chombu had won.

Back in the UK, struggling with heavy bags, I managed to fall completely down the gap between the train and the platform at Cromford station. It somehow seemed a fitting end to the year's mountaineering efforts.

And so how do I feel now about Chombu? Well, in two trips not once did I crampon up any firm snow or swing my axe into any firm ice. The weather was rubbish, the climbing conditions were rubbish, the permit situation was rubbish. As we left base camp we both vowed that enough was enough and we would never go back to Chombu.

But time has passed. Bad memories fade. And, well, you never know.

Sugar Rush

Heavy traffic on the Eigerwand. Muskett and Gore's first attempt was turned back by the number of climbers ahead of them. *(Jerry Gore)*

'I'm freezing Jerry. We have to go down. I'm shaking already. We're too low and when this monster starts to wake up I don't want to be in the firing line.' Calum wasn't scared: just frustrated and impatient. He might only have been 21 years old but he had the wisdom of Gandalf and a similar level of magic when it came to floating up steep bits of rock or ice.

I stood balanced on a sliver of snow and ice clinging to the Eiger's rock shield looking up at the queue of climbers above me. There were at least five teams ahead of us on the Difficult Crack. We had been forced to hang around on the wall for more than three hours now, dressed in not much more than I would wear Christmas shopping in London. So much for a speed climb. Even though it was mid April, the temperature was -10°C and I was starting to shiver. My blood sugars had already gone from suicidally low to stupidly high and were now beginning to drop again as adrenaline seeped out of my body to be replaced by cold and despair. My head and shoulders dropped, as my familiar low self-esteem fermented inside me.

That sort of despair, I knew very well, was a consequence of my type-1 diabetes, a condition I've suffered from since 2001. Before going on the Eiger, I'd told everyone I was going to speed climb the north face and raise a ton of cash for diabetes charities. I was going to look so bloody stupid on Facebook. My body was full of pent-up frustration. I said nothing to Calum and continued with my mental calculations on the chances of reaching the summit that day. The line moved a metre as another team completed the technical section above us and I shuffled forward too. It's always so easy just to give in and bail out. I hate failure and I hate descending a mountain without the energy you get from the summit. But I was starting to accept that the lad was right. It was over.

The Eiger has an evil presence. A big sheet of black rock hanging vertically in the sky, like a canvas from the post-apocalypse film 'The Road' turned on its side. Imagine this painting as a room. It extends around the walls from floor to ceiling and when you walk in you feel totally enveloped in gloom. It's alive and breathing. Its surface moves and changes as it rots from the inside. It consumes the sun and the moon; it consumes your life as well, as thinking about the room occupies every waking hour for months before and then you creep tentatively inside.

When you step onto the north face, this black canvas of dirty rock-strewn snow, you feel sucked in, encased in a vertical vortex. And it's lethal. The Eigerwand is the biggest north wall in the Alps and arguably the most dangerous. Since it was first attempted in the early 1930s more than 70 climbers have died attempting the 'Mordwand', the 'murder wall'. Many good climbers aspire to climb it and many continue to fail. The Swiss mountain rescue helicopters whizzing around the face are a daily distraction to its more usual quiet emptiness.

Inspiration for our Eiger speed attempt had come in January from my friend Tony Whitehouse. Tony is a fell-running champion and climber who has spent much of his life in the mountains or else making climbing devices for his company Beta Designs. He and his wife Sarah were staying at one our apartments in Vallouise, as they do every year, cross-country skiing and climbing. Most afternoons Tony would put micro-crampons over his trainers and go for a run on the snowed-up trails. Despite being in his sixties, Tony is as passionate as ever about the climbing life and usually has a bone of contention to chew on. This year it was the Eiger and how armchair mountaineers on the Internet had been confidently discussing the challenge of the north face without going to the trouble of actually climbing it.

As Tony ranted on, I found myself becoming equally fired up. I hate it when people voice comments and opinions about things they know nothing about, even though I'm often guilty of that myself. People should get on the mountain before they opened their mouths about it and that, I decided, is exactly what I would do. I'd climb the Eiger and raise money for

Traversing up and left from the Second Icefield towards the Ramp. *(Jerry Gore)*

Action4Diabetics, the charity I co-founded after my diagnosis. The climb would make a difference to young children whose lives were far bleaker and harder than mine and at the same time prove to the world, or at least a few digital scribblers, that the Eiger is more than possible, even for a 54-year-old fossil with type-1 diabetes. But why stop there? The normal time to climb the north face is still two days, or even more, and consequently most climbers take bivy gear. Why not leave the bivy kit at home and do the climb in a day: a speed ascent.

The next challenge was to find a partner strong enough to keep up with me and yet patient enough to understand my diabetic condition. I spoke to a number of pro climbers and guides who all declined for various reasons. And then I asked Calum Muskett. Calum was just 21 at the time but already the youth ambassador for the British Mountaineering Council and one of the most talented, fit and mature mountaineers I've had the good fortune to share a rope with. The first time he picked up ice axes, aged just 15, was the same day he climbed the *Devil's Appendix,* the hard VI ice route in North Wales. His maturity must have something to do with the death of his younger brother, who had been killed in a car crash some years before. He isn't humble, but neither is he arrogant, just well balanced and unnervingly almost always correct.

At the end of January 2015, I asked Calum if he fancied having a go with me at a speed ascent of the north face of the Eiger that winter. I waited for him to say no. I waited for questions about fitness, route conditions and partner ability (i.e. me). Instead he simply answered: 'Yes, I would be really keen.'

Muskett leading in the Ramp.
(Jerry Gore)

The main issue for Calum was his schedule. The best time to climb the north face is in late winter or early spring, when the winter snows have cleared a bit but it's still cold on the face to reduce rock fall and there's still sufficient snow and ice to make the climbing easier.

'When were you thinking?' he asked me. 'Because my spring is already looking rammed. I have a really short period of spare time between 20 and 24 April.' We both knew that the end of April is right at the end of the cold season for the Eiger. By that stage the upper exit cracks leading to the summit ridge would almost definitely be melting out. Stone fall would also be an issue as the upper slopes would be in stronger sunlight. But it would have to do. I announced on social media at the beginning of February that my next insulin challenge would be a speed ascent of the Eiger's north face. I wasn't fit, conditions were uncertain and I still had to learn the technicalities of 'speed climbing' rather than just climbing – a totally different affair as I was soon to find out.

A part of almost every day from mid February until I left for Switzerland in April was spent looking at weather maps. It appeared that the Swiss Alps were in the middle of a high snowfall winter. That was good news. But would there be too much snow? Or would the temperatures have already started to soar by the time we arrived in early spring?

By mid February it was also high time I started my training schedule and learned how to prepare for a speed ascent. I contacted someone who ought to know best, someone I had communicated with before about various extreme mountain climbs in Switzerland. That man was Ueli Steck. His training and preparation techniques were innovative and hugely influential. His technique of 'active acclimatisation' involving repeated rotations from base camp rather than spending nights sleeping at high altitude is now used by the best high-altitude climbers operating today. He repeatedly opened minds and showed new approaches to long-established practices. I knew Ueli's advice would be golden and we spoke several times about what I needed and how to succeed in a fast time. He made a huge difference to our attempt and I still feel deeply honoured that he gave me so much of his valuable time in helping me. His death on Nuptse in 2017 was a real tragedy.

Ueli's speed record for the Eiger at that time was 2h 47m, climbing solo and recorded on 13 February 2008. On 23 February of the same year Swiss climbers Daniel Arnold and Stephan Ruoss created the fastest team record in just 6h 10m. I didn't think realistically that aged 54 I could beat a team of men in their early 30s with Swiss blood running through their veins. I also knew no British team had ever got close to such a time. But I was hopeful of a fast ascent with Calum and certainly in one day, not least because we wouldn't be carrying bivy gear. A night out could mean frostbite or worse.

So I started training under Ueli's guidance. He told me how he trained for his world-class ascents and from this I got into what I call vertical running. Simplistically it is about ascending steep hills involving vertical height gains of 800m or more but over short horizontal distances. From my house I would ski 15 minutes to the start of a very steep forest trail going up to an altitude of 3,000m in just 5km of horizontal distance. The trail starts at 1200m so height gains of 1,000m are easily accessible. You just need the puff to get up them. My fastest time for 1,000m vertical on this trail was 58 minutes. And as I got closer to my departure date, I started training with a 10kg rucksack full of plastic water bottles, so I could ditch the liquid and save my knees during the descent.

I did basic core workouts and upper body exercises like weighted pull-ups and tried to go ice climbing at least once or twice a week. Living in one of the premium icefall locations in France definitely helped. My long-suffering wife Jackie got on with the day-to-day business of running our company while dealing with my mood swings as my blood sugars began to oscillate. Exercise for insulin-dependent people is essential to help maintain stable blood sugar readings but extreme training requires a lot more input if the diabetic athlete in question wants to stay married.

Nighttime hypos are something I'm especially prone to because I'm often trigger-happy with my insulin. I tend to inject too much of the fast-acting kind, which metabolises with a three-hour profile, having forgotten to factor in the effect of intensive training. Usually I take five units of fast-acting insulin before each meal and 11 units of slow-acting insulin, with a 12-hour profile, before bed. When training I can drop these quantities by as much as 70%. Furthermore, the effect on my body after a big vertical run is greatest during the second night after the activity, not the first. So I am almost constantly in a state of forward planning with my insulin and if I get it wrong by just a few drops, I can find myself semi-conscious at 3am with the bed saturated in sweat and my wife Jackie patiently coaxing me to eat a honey sandwich, her day having already well and truly started. Too much insulin and my blood sugars go too low which at night can result in coma and death. Too high, and in less than five years I lose my eyesight or worse. It is a fine, hour-by-hour balance that last's a lifetime.

April arrived far too quickly. I had done fewer than 10 vertical runs and not nearly enough ice climbs. But it was time. My body was already complaining and injury is a real possibility for the over 50s. I loaded up my trusty Subaru and headed for Switzerland. Towards midnight and driving on fumes, I finally quit trying to reach a gas station. I had reached the crest of a col and thought that even if I ran out next morning I could free wheel down the other side to a garage. I parked up and went to sleep in a field in the middle of the Alps.

Six hours later I was woken by the sound of exaggerated mooing and loud cowbells in my ear. The car was surrounded and I was trapped. Newspaper headlines flashed through my mind: 'Himalayan climber dies in cow stampede in remote Alpine valley.' Looking into their eyes I saw malice and anger. I was going to miss my Eiger attempt because of a bunch of cows. Everything was going wrong and I hadn't yet started. And then, luckily, somewhere deep in my hypothalamus, a voice screamed: 'Stop! Test your blood sugars.'

When my blood-sugar level drops and I go into a hypoglycaemic attack, I can suffer black moments like this, when I feel that people, events, even cows are ganging up against me. I feel like I am under siege by whatever happens to be in my brain at the time and I start to sink into my own self-created pit of despair. I tested my blood and found that indeed I was low: exceptionally low. Carbs are to diabetics what chalk is to a rock climber. You don't need much, but when you do, you need it fast and in just the right quantities to bring your blood sugars up. Too many carbs and it clogs you up, too little and you fall down – literally. If I am not testing my blood sugars, I am measuring how many grams of carbs I am about to eat so I inject the appropriate amount of insulin. Because I needed carbs, I ate a couple of honey and nut cereal bars, put my shoes on and gave those cows a large bellyful of pent-up emotion.

I met Calum on the Chamonix road above Martigny. He dumped his gear in the car and we shot off to Grindelwald. It was so good to see him. His youthful confidence ran like a riptide of hope over my dark mood. I parked at the Eiger train station and headed for the nearest restaurant for a large plate of rösti. Little did we know it but this would be our last proper meal for three days. We looked up at the mountain. It was enveloped in a deep blue polar haze and actually looked inviting. The sombre canvas was sprinkled with white flecks: I started to feel positive for the first time in a long time. All the stresses of preparing for this challenge were melting away. I knew Calum was in a totally different headspace. For him this was little more than just another climb. Yes, he wanted to do it, and he wanted to help me raise a lot of money, but this was his office. And anyway, what could he be afraid of compared to a partner 30 years his senior?

The mood changed as we took the cable car to the base of the mountain and its presence started to weigh down on us. I realised that even Calum was susceptible to the fear it provoked. If I weren't careful, this monster would suck out our momentum before we had even started. We climbed quickly to the Eigergletscher train station and checked into the refuge. It was already early evening and we still had a lot of prep before we could sleep.

The alarm went at 5am. We brewed up, gulped down muesli and packed the last remaining items. I had one last task to check off: my insulin injections. I normally inject both the slow-acting type and the fast-acting at 7.30am during breakfast. Now I decided to inject 75% of my normal

Muskett in the White Spider. *(Jerry Gore)*

slow-acting dose and just 60% of my fast-acting. I should have spent more time researching and testing these doses because unfortunately for me I had guessed badly. We shut the door to the refuge quietly behind us and climbed towards the dark shape above us.

We moved quickly and unroped up the initial 45° snow slopes but within two hours of leaving the hut I knew I was low on blood sugar. I stumbled upwards but knew if I fought my hypoglycaemic state it would only end badly. Reluctantly I stopped and dug a snow ledge to test on. Calum immediately understood what I was doing.

'Low blood sugars Jerry?' Somewhat embarrassed, I mumbled agreement and then ate two cereal bars. Annoyed with myself for such a stupid mistake, I bashed on and within the hour we reached the Difficult Crack, the start of the technical difficulties. Here we discovered five teams lay in front of us and joined the queue, frustrated and annoyed at this inconvenient delay. It was late April. Conditions were good but this might be the last time this winter when they were good enough to climb the face. During the few hours at the refuge I had spoken to a helicopter pilot who had just brought down an exhausted climber. His English wasn't good, but I understood clearly enough when he said, 'snow is too warm. I think no more now, this time.'

Slowly the climbing teams in front of me inched forward, their large rucksacks rubbing against the rockface as the scratchy fabric of their sleeping mats produced grating sounds. There was little talk, just a line of men awaiting their fate. The sweat started to cool on my back and under my arms. I started to shiver. In the Alps speed is safety as you try to get up, and off a snow face before the sun hits it and certainly by midday. Now it was approaching that time and we all knew the sun would be hitting the upper snowfields releasing its deadly fusillade. I looked at the snow slopes around me and saw tell-tale black pockets littering the whiteness.

Experience told me that if you push on it usually works out okay and is invariably better than descending. Just going that extra mile can often result in victory. But in my heart, I knew I was kidding myself. Eventually, with a heavy heart and a feeling of exhausted failure, I climbed back to Calum and we started to rig the ropes for our descent. It was slow tedious work, like walking in quicksand: purgatory combined with zero motivation.

By the time we reached the refuge in the early afternoon I was covered in a cold sweat. I just felt exhausted. Calum went straight to sleep, but I collapsed in a chair and contemplated what had just happened. Was I still good enough to do this game? A lot of people had supported me on this challenge and now I was disappointing them. Mentally and emotionally I was destroyed. I had put a lot of time, energy, and determination into this challenge and now I was right back at square one. I sat with my head in my hands. I pondered and thought. Then I got up and started ambling around the refuge as my mind churned through a lifetime of challenges. Could I really be bothered? Could I really summon up the energy to have another go? How much did I really care? How much strength was there left in a rusty tank full of out-of-date gasoline?

Then I reflected on why I was here in the first place: raising money to help impoverished families with children who had type-1 diabetes. Graphic images of emaciated, struggling children came into my head. I saw their parent's faces, as awareness dawned on them about what was happening to their children. Right there in the middle of the gloomy refuge hostel a boy's name popped into my head: Nimuel. He was an eight-year-old boy I had met at a diabetes camp in the Philippines a year earlier. Nimuel had arrived on our first day, his eyes wide and full of fear. His mother was very poor and the two had been kicked out of the family home by the father. Insulin medication in many parts of south-east Asia is often beyond the reach of most households and without it a newly diagnosed type-1 child will die slowly and painfully within six months.

'Nims' as I called him, was one of those amazing children who just do not give up. He tried his best to learn and understand from the team of healthcare workers and supporters, but it wasn't easy. When he arrived at camp that first day he was dying, and he desperately needed help. His blood sugars were over 400mg/dL, or milligrams per decilitre: a death sentence given that the average for a non-diabetic person is just 100mg/dL. He knew that without help something bad would happen and he just tried and tried. By day four his sugars had dropped significantly and starting to stabilise. He had a long, difficult and dangerous road ahead but he now had hope. It was so obvious his childhood was returning, and it was really amazing to see. If Nims could do all that, then I had to be able to do as much. I had to match his courage with my own and have at least one more crack at that

On the Eiger's summit ridge.
(Jerry Gore)

bloody mountain. I wiped my eyes and woke Calum.

'What's up, what're you doing Jerry?'

'We are going back up. Set your clock for 1am. We are going for it.' I had given myself another chance. I had a huge barrier to overcome but I had a direction, and that was all I needed. Calum, of course, was fine with my decision. He dealt with it all logically. The weather forecast was fine for the next day. He knew we had the technical skills to tackle anything on the face. Calum had all the confidence you'd expect from an international fell runner and one of the best technical alpinists of his generation. Me, on the other hand, had much to think about: I hardly slept a wink.

The alarm rang seemingly before I had set it and we were soon up and running. At 1.22am my blood sugars were at 60mg/dL: that meant it was time to eat – a lot! I have seldom been first out of the tent or snow cave. I'm always frantically scrambling to get all my bits and pieces together to avoid embarrassment. This time was no different. I hurriedly tested my blood once more at 2.26am: 75mg/dL. This was still a little low but it was rising fast and I knew that my carb-rich breakfast would counter the effect of the intensive exercise coming up. I injected myself with two units, two tiny drops of fast-acting insulin, slammed the refuge door behind me and ran into the night after Calum, who was already ahead of me, striding across the frozen whiteness.

The black sky was a million tiny shards of light and I gulped it in as we raced across the base of the beast. It was cold, around -10°C, but already our hearts were beating quickly. The lower snow slopes seemed to pass in an instant. We arrived at the Difficult Crack to find it empty and inviting. Soon we were pulling ourselves across the legendary Hinterstoisser Traverse and I saw the sun for the first time: a smoky yellow ball hanging low on the horizon. Freed from the bubble of light of my headlamp, I no longer felt the unreality of moving through the dark wrapped in layers. I understood this was really happening. We were on the Eiger.

We climbed on, swapping leads, racing past Death Bivouac and soon we were into The Ramp. Unluckily for us its magic veneer of ice had gone and we were forced to take turns dry tooling technical sections of blank rock, pulling hard on ice axes hooked on millimetres of crumbly limestone. I loved this section the most since it reminded me of mixed climbs in Scotland. At the top of the Ramp I led the Ice Chimney. This overhanging slot rears up at you and was totally dry, devoid of all ice. The steep corner became a balancing act, each crampon claw scraping frantically against the smooth vertical sides. I had to take off my gloves so I could rock climb in places where I couldn't find purchase with my ice axes. Having always been more of a rock climber than an ice merchant, the smooth, slightly crumbly surface of the rock felt good underneath my fingers and I felt agile, loving the movement over cold stone.

I emerged panting in the dry air and suddenly felt a little weird. Normally that's the sign of an approaching hypoglycaemic attack. I tested my blood: 70mg/dL. My instinct was right. I immediately chomped down a Lion bar and then a small fruit bar. I had 12 cereal bars for the entire climb and hoped I wouldn't need more. I then swallowed a swig of water and carried on taking in the rope. Calum passed me with a grunt of acknowledgment.

'Good lead Jerry; Brittle Ledges now.' Why did he always make me feel like he was the adult and I was the kid? So annoying. We climbed together up easy snow slopes that lead to the flat plates of decomposing cat litter that make up this feature. Calum led this, running round to the Traverse of The Gods. Things were going well but I needed to maintain focus. We were already into mid morning and I could feel the temperature beginning to rise. I led round quickly into the bottom of the White Spider and suddenly felt immersed in a time-warp. So many climbers have written about this ragged white carpet, tilted at 65° and littered with small black grenades. We were climbing together now, with no protection between us. If either of us had been hit and fallen, we would have pulled the other off.

Calum was suddenly struggling and after shouting down I realised he had a nosebleed. I headed for a rock cleft at the side of the Spider and clipped a piton or nail hammered deep into a crack. He joined me and I asked if he was okay. Just that once, for a tiny instant, Calum acted his real age with a dismissive shrug, as if to say, 'It's only a nosebleed. What's the problem old man?' I asked him if it was okay if I led the Quartz Crack just above us.

This is the final barrier before the summit ridge, right at the top when it really is the last thing you want after all that precarious and mentally exhausting climbing. It's technical and smooth and your crampons are skittering on blank rock. I led round to a block and then had to wait with another team as a slow climber struggled above us. I could see the ice melting above me and knew each climber would take more of it away. When my turn eventually came the black crack was bare and I was forced to hook my way up, precariously fighting the cramp in my calves.

We were now above the technical difficulties. All that remained were a few hundred metres of steep ice that fell back in angle as we moved up it until we popped out onto the summit ridge. We were now in the sun and it was still only early afternoon. We knew we had time. At the summit Calum

Youth and experience on the summit. *(Jerry Gore)*

The diabetic kit Gore took with him to maintain his insulin levels. *(Jerry Gore)*

looked like he had just got out of bed. I looked like I had just done 15 rounds with Mike Tyson. But it didn't matter. We were a team. Our time up the face was 7h 56m. It wasn't a world record; it wasn't even close. That didn't matter either. We took a selfie and I tested my blood again: 132mg/dL. Perfect.

Calum took over as he was responsible for navigating the route off and soon we were bum sliding down the east side of the Eiger whooping with delight as we descended at speed. We were unroped, lying on our backs, legs held high so our crampon points didn't dig into the snow, using our ice axes like a rudder to keep us on course, sliding right under glacial seracs. It was like a scene from *The Chronicles of Narnia:* life felt very good indeed. We had climbed the north face in the fastest known time for a British team and had raised over $45,000 for Action4Diabetics.

On the walk down to Kleine Scheidegg the following morning we passed a reservoir just above the train station, a tranquil spot overlooking the Bernese Oberland. Walking along the shoreline, we both noticed that the boulders along the edge of the tarn each had a name chiselled into it. Each name was a climber who had died on the Eiger. The line of rocks was more than 100m in length on both sides of the rectangular pond. The first date was 1930 and the last was 2012. I ran back to the start of the line of rocks and picked out the name of Toni Kurz. A death of a climber is always tragic but what hit me was how many people would have been affected by these deaths: mothers, fathers, sisters, brothers, partners, sons and daughters. So many affected by so few. I looked across at the surrounding peaks now bathed in early morning light and sank to my knees.

Calum had gone, racing off down the hill, eager to be reunited with his car so he could get back to Chamonix in time for the last cable car. I dropped him in time above Martigny and went looking for a café and a big slice of cake. This time I wasn't worried about the carbs.

Alps

Plate 2. *'Country to the northward from Nowagurh Teeba'*

JON BRACEY

Beyond Reason

The north face of the Aiguille des Pélerins (3318m) in winter,
seamed with ice runnels.

Starting up the *Rébuffat-Terray*. (Jon Bracey)

'Only those who will risk going too far can possibly find out just how far one can go.'
T S Eliot

Darkness loomed. The temperature was falling, and the gusty frigid winds penetrated right through to the bone. Our numb fingers grappled with the fiddly shock cord securing headlamps to our helmets. Al Powell, that gnarly and incredibly understated British alpinist of the 1990s and 2000s, was dragging me up a winter ascent of the *Rébuffat-Terray* on the north face of the Aiguille des Pélerins.

I turned the bezel of my Petzl lamp anticlockwise but nothing happened. 'Damn,' I concluded, 'it must have accidently been switched on inside my rucksack pocket.' I must admit to a small voice inside my head at that moment suggesting that without a functioning light we would surely have to beat a hasty retreat from this miserable world of Alpine winter climbing.

Al quickly disabused me of that idea. If I wanted to get up any decent Alpine routes, he explained, then I had better quickly learn to suck it and suffer. Three difficult pitches later, completed in utter darkness, another lesson from the Alpine school of hard knocks was complete. Half an hour earlier, hanging in my harness from a belay made up of pitons most probably placed years before I was born, a pristine shield of grey granite across to the left had caught my eye. It looked so clean, so beautiful in form, almost

Helliker on the steeper new ground of *Beyond Reason*. *(Jon Bracey)*

inviting, but at the same time sheer and steep, like a ship's prow and apparently impenetrable. For some unknown reason this vision became etched on my mind.

Years pass by, life speeds up – work, family, expeditions – and people come and go. The climate changes, glaciers melt, recede and even disappear. Conditions for mixed climbing in the Alps have never been so

Bracey climbing thin slabs and blobs of ice. *(Matt Helliker)*

unreliable. Perhaps this game I love to play is coming to an end. But I don't despair; the optimist will always win I tell myself. A fleeting early autumn storm, then a September cold front hits and then another. Rain, then snow: the 0° isotherm shifts up and then down. My eyes squint again through binoculars at the Pélerins. Excitement builds and the psych returns. Finally, all the stars are starting to align.

My regular climbing partner Matt Helliker never needs persuading and we included in the party the Derbyshire lad Pete Whittaker, world-renowned master of crack climbing. His Alpine experience left a little to be desired, this being his first visit. With the three of us planning a big trip to the Himalaya in the autumn it would be a good opportunity to see whether the young 'wide-boy' was up to much.

Circumstances beyond our control meant we were short on time and instead of an appropriately early start from a bivouac at the Plan de l'Aiguille, we headed up on the first cable car: not ideal given the day's objective. Luckily, I had been up the day before to make a track through recent snow to the base, so we made good time to the bergschrund. We started up the *Rébuffat-Terray* for 200m with impeccable squeaky snow-ice. From here we continued directly up gradually thinning ice runnels towards the rather austere looking and featureless headwall. At this point I started to detect a little uneasiness in the team as we inched closer to the overhanging terrain with not the faintest indication of climbable features in view.

Unlike the others, I had spent hours of my life starring through binocular lenses at this wall of granite and was sure my eyes hadn't deceived me; somewhere there was a line of white dots. But even I was starting to ques-

Bracey climbs a blank section near the top of the route that almost ended their hopes. *(Matt Helliker)*

tion my own memory when suddenly the mythical line appeared seemingly out of nowhere: a diagonal ramp holding thin ice cutting back left and into the heart of the headwall. I breathed a sigh of relief that I'd not been deceived, and my motivation was bubbling again.

Next up was an awkward looking crack that would look at home amongst some of the nastier horrors of Curbar Edge. Matt and I took one look and without much hesitation passed the rack to the ever-chipper Pete. He danced up the pitch with minimal effort but then stopped above at some slippery snow, unsurprisingly as he was now wearing rock boots. The next section proved to be the crux of the route with thin, technical and slightly run-out mixed climbing, never desperate but taxing on the mind with having to commit to blank-looking terrain full of uncertainty.

Then, just as the jigsaw puzzle of the line seemed to be slotting into place, the way ahead seemed doomed. The snowy ramp we were following thinned to nothing except incredibly bold slab climbing out to the right. That didn't entice any of us. However, there was a slim chance up the rock slab on the left, although it was covered in 10cm or 15cm of powdery snow. I set off on a delicate voyage of shrouded hope and somehow reached the arête on the left, the final key to unlocking *Beyond Reason*.

Summary

First ascent of *Beyond Reason* (ED V, 5+/F5c, M6+, R, 550m) north face of Pointe des Pélerins, or Pointe Migot, 7 February 2020, Jon Bracey, Matt Helliker and Pete Whittaker.

A Ski Traverse of the Alps

Skiing the Col de Valpelline with the Matterhorn as a backdrop in 2016, the second portion of David Hamilton's ski traverse of the Alps. *(David Hamilton)*

This is an account of a 2,113km winter journey from Menton on the French Mediterranean coast to Vienna. Well over 90% of the route was completed on skis and the short sections below the snow line were completed on foot. No mechanised transport was used at any point. The trip comprised 102 stages and took 129 days to complete over four winters from 2015 to 2018. On 27 days no forward progress was possible, mostly due to poor weather or dangerous snow conditions. Logging the trip by GPS gave a total ascent of 115,060m. Without doubt this was the most physically and mentally draining mountain project I have ever undertaken, as well as being the most rewarding. My aim here is to share the lessons learnt from the planning and execution of this journey.

I consider myself a fairly experienced mountaineer and have been a professional expedition leader for over 30 years. I have led 20 expeditions to 8,000m peaks and climbed Everest 10 times. I have also led 12 expeditions to 7,000m peaks, and climbed each of the Seven Summits at least three times. I have worked as a guide in Antarctica for 15 seasons, climbing Mt Vinson 23 times. I have led ski-mountaineering expeditions in more than a dozen countries and made ski ascents of Muztag Ata, Denali, Damavand, Elbrus, and Ararat. I have decades of experience of multi-day ski tours in the Alps, almost all in the early season using winter rooms. All of this was essential in developing the necessary skills and preparing me for this project.

There is a significant history of parties making long ski traverses in the Alps. The 1956 journey of Walter Bonatti is commonly thought of as the first, and Alan Blackshaw led the first British group in 1972. Most of the early journeys used different start and end points and it was common to use vehicles to link adjoining mountain areas. In recent decades there have been traverses from east to west and from west to east, either in a single season or over multiple seasons. There is an attraction to completing this trip in a single winter but this was not an option for me as each year I work in Antarctica until the end of January and then in Nepal from the end of March. Instead my aim was to make the trip as 'pure' as possible, starting at the sea and finding a continuous route to Vienna by ski and foot that did not require any vehicle links.

The ski route from the Mediterranean coast to Chamonix is a great stand-alone project. It is probably one of the most interesting and varied four-week ski tours in the Alps. When Venetia Wingfield and I left Menton on 9 February 2015 the aim was 'just' to ski to Chamonix. Little did I realise that this would be the start of a project that would occupy the next four winter seasons. After the two-day hike from the coast to Col de Turini (43.4km, 3,470m climbed, three cols crossed), the only low-lying section that must be covered on foot is crossing the Maurienne valley from Val Fréjus ski station to Aussois. The entire route stays close to the France-Italy border passing through the Mercantour, Queyras, Vanoise and Gran Paradiso National Parks.

Accommodation is mostly in CAF refuges and small village hotels. Ironically the biggest problem was finding accommodation in large ski resorts where booking rooms for a single night can be difficult. Depending on the opening dates of the CAF refuges there may be as few as five nights in winter rooms (Merveillies, Nice, Vens, Rabuons, Mario Bezzi) although this could rise to seven if Dent Parachée and Col de la Vanoise are not yet open. The optimal route is fairly obvious with five sections starting from Menton, Isola 2000, Col de Larche, Montgenèvre, and Val d'Isère. Our average day length was seven to nine hours and we seldom saw other skiers or tracks once away from the ski resorts. This meant that we broke trail for most of the way. The most technical section was between Isola 2000 and Col de Larche. We were probably the first skiers of the season to cross the glaciers of the Vanoise from the Dent Parachée refuge to the Col de la Vanoise refuge. The longest stage was a 14-hour day from Bonne to La Thuile. Overall the 2015 leg of 26 stages covered 486km with 29,207m of ascent in 32 days.

In retrospect the Swiss leg of the journey, accomplished between 16 February and 17 March 2016, was less enjoyable than the French leg. This is probably due to the high proportion of bad weather days that made much of the travel and navigation difficult and stressful. Steve Kentish joined me for

Cross purposes. From top left clockwise: on the Rheinwaldhorn (3402m) in 2016; the Wilder Pfaff (3456m) in Austria in 2017; the Grosses Bärneck (2071m) in 2018; and the Hohe Veitsch (1981m), also in 2018. *(David Hamilton)*

the full 31 days, with John Kentish joining for days one to eight and Harvey Lyons for days nine to 31. Our start from Chamonix was delayed by a week due to bad weather and dangerous snow conditions. When we were able to start we were forced to take a low level route to Verbier via Col de le Forclaz and Orsières before continuing to Zermatt. Here John left the team and was replaced by Harvey. His introduction to the project was a 14-hour day, mostly in poor weather, crossing the Adler pass to the Britanniahütte. In the early morning the Zermatt avalanche cannons strafed us as we ascended the 'closed' pistes. Late in the day we navigated the gaping crevasses of the Adler glacier in the failing light, and spent several hours in total darkness searching for the closed hut. Harvey remarked that he had previously been on several ski tours that required starting in the dark, and also some that had required finishing in the dark, but never one that had done both on the same day.

The day from Saas Grund to Simplon pass was excellent, but we were then stuck for several days by poor weather. This dogged us for the next section on to Airolo and my memories of this eight-day stretch are mostly of long stressful days with difficult navigation in poor snow, punctuated by poorly equipped Italian huts. The weather improved for the five-day section on to Splugen, and we enjoyed good snow conditions and the excellent facilities of three SAC huts. This section ended with a traverse of the 3,402m Rheinwaldhorn and a descent through a Swiss army firing range (not shown on the map).

The fourth section of the Swiss journey had to be recalculated when we found that a key hotel was closed. The new route required long days linking villages and small ski resorts where the accommodation was comfortable if expensive. Time constraints led to the trip terminating at Bergun on 17 March. By then the snow was fast disappearing and onward progress would have been difficult. We had spent 18 nights in hotels and 12 nights in huts. The Mont-Fort hut was being used as cheap accommodation for Verbier skiers so should probably be reclassified as a hotel. Two huts (Castiglione and Margaroli) had wardens who were preparing for the season ahead but no other guests were present. The nine unstaffed huts were mostly excellent with cooking facilities and heating. Had we not lost a week at the start of the trip we would have completed the crossing of Switzerland, and reached the border with Austria. The 2016 leg of 25 stages covered 518km with 30,621m of ascent in 31 days.

Andy Helm joined Steve and myself for the first six days of the 2017 crossing of western and central Austria. We started from Bergun on 8 February and had an excellent trip to Klosters and on through the Silvretta. The weather was generally fine. The huts had not yet opened for the season and we saw very few other skiers. We completed the final seven Swiss stages and entered Austria at Ramosh north of the Reschenpass on 14 February. This was the first time that I had skied in Austria. Ahead of us the Ötztal, Stubai, Zillertal, Hohe Tauern and Niedere Tauern ranges promised classic ski-touring terrain.

As with the French and Swiss legs we rarely saw other skiers except when we passed close to ski resorts. The mountain scenery was spectacular and most of the days were acceptable in terms of risk and effort. Many days were six to 10 hours long, but six were between 10 and 12 and a half. Half a dozen times we found ourselves in seriously unpleasant situations due to avalanche and snow stability issues, or steep technical terrain. Fortunately we survived all of these without mishap. Looking back we had been too trusting of the ski routes shown on the OEV maps. These are not nearly as reliable as their French or Swiss counterparts. Ramosch to Solden would have been an excellent five-day section but for the difficult descent of Glockturmjoch and lack of accommodation that night. We endured our only bivouac of the entire journey in the Kaurnertal ski station after an 11h 40m day.

There seemed be an obvious three or four-day route from Solden to Steinach traversing the Stubai mountains. Only later did we learn that all ski tours in this area use the north-south valleys and few people attempt a west-east crossing. On the third day out of Solden, after traversing the summit of the Wilderpfaff (3456m), we completed the difficult ascent of

Approaching the Olpererhütte in the
Zillertal in 2017. *(David Hamilton)*

the Freigerscharte pass in the dark
and diverted to the Nürnberger hut
arriving after 11h 15m of effort. The
following day we covered 37.7km
in 12h 15m to reach Steinach. The
five-day section to Kasern held no
exceptional technical difficulty and
we reached the Berliner hut in three
days. However storm conditions
forced us to retreat to Mayrhofen
for supplies and this added three
days to the journey. After a heavy
snowfall we waited a day in Kasern
before continuing the three-day
section to Matreier Tauernhaus. We
should have waited longer and as a
consequence of our haste endured a
very fraught trip to the Warensdorfer
hut in extreme avalanche conditions.

We waited out a three-day period
of poor weather at Matreier before
managing five consecutive eight-
hour days passing north of the
Grossglockner and Heiligenblut to
Bockstein. The final descent from
Baumbachspitze to Sportgastein
being the worst example encountered
of a totally un-skiable cliff shown as
a ski route on the OEV map. Again
we were delayed for three days
by bad weather, fortunately in a
comfortable hotel. While it rained
in the valley we were unaware that
winter had ended and there was a
massive thaw happening at altitude.
For our final seven days into Schladming we faced a very different snowpack
made up of morning ice and afternoon slush. After the unpleasant climb to
the Hannoverhaus we resorted to very early starts in an attempt to avoid
the afternoon wet snow slides pouring from the hillsides. We pushed the
route onwards with five reasonable length days plus a 12h 20m day to
Albertbiwak (after a long fight with a drained hydro lake), and a 10h 20m
day into Obertauern. When we reached Schladming on 28 March the only
snow to be seen was of the artificial variety on pistes leading into the town.

We spent 22 nights in hotels, and 19 nights in 15 different DAV and OEV huts. All were winter rooms except the Hannoverhaus, where the warden initially suggested that we should not come, and then was reluctant to let us leave. The 2017 leg of 35 stages (seven in Switzerland plus 28 in Austria) took 49 days with 14 days lost to poor weather or dangerous snow conditions. We covered 746km with 39,800m of ascent.

Steve and I reconvened in Schladming on 19 February 2018 to complete the fourth and final leg of the journey to Vienna. Despite the lower altitudes this was to be a year with plenty of snow and very cold temperatures, but mostly dull and overcast weather. The trip divided naturally into three distinct sections. The first exited the Niedere Tauern and traveled through a predominantly forested landscape to the mining town of Eisenerz. This was a six-day journey with overnight stops in Donnersbachwald, Gulling, Rottenman, Johnsbach, and Radmer. These are similar days, each with some road walking, a mixture of forest trails and footpaths, and some good ski terrain.

The second section was more mountainous, traversing five high limestone massifs, each with multiple summits: Hochschwab (2277m), Veitchalpe (1981m), Schneealpe (1903m), Raxalpe (2007m), and Schneeberg (2076m). This would be considered a substantial tour anywhere in the Alps. Four out of the six travel days took nine hours or longer. We encountered quite a bit of poor weather including strong winds and temperatures below -25°C. We had two very cold overnight stops at the Sonnschienhütte and Schneealpenhaus.

The third section left the high mountains behind and traversed the undulating hills of the 'Vienna woods' gradually losing height until reaching the city limits. In four days we covered 95km and climbed 2,722m. On the final day we skied through woods to the Kammersteinerhütte (582m) and climbed the historic Josefwarte tower for our first view of the city below. A short ski descent led to vineyards on the edge of Vienna where we packed the skis and walked the final 15km to St Stephen's Cathedral in the city centre. We had travelled for 17 days (with a single rest day) covering 363km with 15,430m of ascent. We spent 15 nights in guesthouses and hotels, one night in a hut winter room, and a one-night bivouac in a tractor shed.

The Alpine mountains in winter can be a savage and dangerous place. It is easy to be fooled by 'accurate' maps showing red lines linking 'obvious' passes but in poor weather even map, compass and GPS are no guarantee of safe passage. Micro features a few metres high can easily cause a broken leg and the consequences of a night in the open without full camping equipment can be dire. Our pack weights (when not carrying skis) were around 12-18kg, depending how much food and fuel was carried. The extra weight of bivouac kit would have made the packs unacceptably heavy. Our climbing kit was restricted to 25m of 6mm static cord, one snow stake, one ice screw and a few karabiners. The key challenge of long distance ski touring is how to keep the pack weight reasonable without abandoning any 'essential' kit.

It takes considerable commitment to push on day after day into unknown terrain with no local knowledge and an awareness there are unlikely to be any other skiers or visible ski tracks. The only way to make this situation manageable is with detailed advanced planning. It may seem boring to spend hundreds of hours studying maps and programming routes into a GPS, but on a long tour through unfamiliar terrain this is essential to avoid navigational errors with potentially serious consequences. The main way of reducing risk is to have an in-depth understanding of the primary route and available accommodation plus all the possible alternate routes. Despite all my planning we were frequently the victims of inadequate maps, poor cartography and vague or wrongly marked ski routes.

The length of each stage was dictated by the available accommodation, but pacing is important too. It is possible to have a few long days of 10 to 14 hours if necessary, however it is important not to string too many of these together consecutively. It is good to have a few short stages of four to five to aid recovery, and this removes the need to have complete rest days. When the weather is good it is essential to make forward progress, and we never took a rest day unless this was forced by weather conditions, illness, injury or exhaustion.

These journeys were all completed between mid February and mid March. Some may regard this as early for Alpine ski touring but I have come to appreciate the advantages of the early season. The daylight hours are less and huts generally unstaffed, but neither of these are significant disadvantages. It is possible to have long days without having to make outrageously early starts to avoid the mid afternoon heat. Snow cover usually extends down to valley floors. This enables low altitude link sections to be skied, often on Nordic tracks, and reduces the need to walk. Lower temperatures also mean that slopes stay safer into the late afternoon and this can be important if forced to climb a south-facing slope at the end of a 10-hour day.

There is no getting away from the fact that making a long point-to-point ski trip has significantly greater hazards than other forms of ski touring. We travelled in weather conditions and crossed snow slopes that most sensible people would avoid. Had we not done so, we would not have completed the journey. We were not foolhardy but we set the threshold of acceptable risk much higher than most ski mountaineers would be comfortable with. Every day carried the risk of a serious skiing fall, an avalanche, a fall over a cliff, benightment or other mishap. This made each day stressful and this stress was cumulative, building day by day over the length of the trip. Despite more than 30 years experience of guiding and managing stress in mountain environments this surprised me. However this observation does not detract from the fact that this four-year project has been the most challenging and rewarding that I have been part of, and I would like to thank my companions named above for sharing it with me.

• A detailed day-by-day description of the trip can be seen at *https://highadventure.org.uk/introduction.html*.

Nature & Environment

Plate 1. '*Seran [Sarahan] Raja's Palace*'

ROB COLLISTER

The Cwm of Hats

How Botanical Prospecting on Snowdon
Led to a Litter Campaign

Cwm Hetiau, cwm of the hats, by the Anglesey painter and printmaker Kyffin
Williams (1918-2006). *(Llyfrgell Genedlaethol Cymru / The National Library
of Wales)*

Planning can be part of the fun of any mountain outing be it a day stroll
on the Downs or a Himalayan expedition; the importance of careful
planning is something we are constantly reminded of by pundits in the
interests of our health and safety. Nevertheless, sometimes it can be more
rewarding to set off without a plan, slave to no fixed purpose but free to
follow a whim or an enticing little path or whatever fate or fortune puts our
way. It was in just such a spirit of serendipitous enquiry that I drove up the
Llanberis Pass last summer.

Too vague to be called a plan, my intention was simply to renew acquaint-
ance with some of the arctic-alpine plants which still linger on in high, cold
places inaccessible to sheep, leftovers from the last ice age. Where better to
seek them than Cwm Glas on the north side of Snowdon? To be more precise, there is an upper and a lower Cwm Glas. The lower, known as Cwm
Glas Mawr is dominated by the steep rocks of Craig y Rhaeadr, best known

83

for its winter ice falls, and by Cyrn Las, vertiginous site of some of the finest rock climbs in Britain: routes like *Main Wall, The Grooves* and *The Skull.* The upper cwm is overlooked by the summit ridge connecting Crib Goch and Crib y Ddysgl and is split by the long spur of the Clogwyn y Person arête into two basins shown on the map as Cwm Uchaf and Cwm Glas. To complicate things even further, next to Cwm Glas Mawr to the north and separated from it by the Cwm Glas spur, is Cwm Glas Bach, at the very head of which is the tiny glacial hollow of Cwm Hetiau.

It was in the direction of Cwm Glas Mawr that I made my way initially, over disturbed ground where the pipeline for a thankfully discreet hydro scheme had been buried recently. Once into the cwm I bore away right to pick up a faint but helpful path, seemingly used more by sheep than people, which winds its way up the Cwm Glas spur. The ridge is never narrow but it becomes increasingly precipitous on the east side dropping down into Cwm Glas Mawr. Pausing at a little notch just before a steep step, I noticed that the rock of the walls to my left had changed character and was covered with specks of colour. Most prominent was the purple pink of wild thyme, not an arctic-alpine but an indication of less acid soils than usual hereabouts; and growing alongside were the white five-petalled stars of vernal sandwort, again not an alpine but in Britain found mostly in mountains or near lead mines. Carefully linking grass ledges I made my way leftwards, every step increasing the drop beneath my feet, lured on by the sight of dark rocks covered with bright orange spots. These I took to be lichens though I discovered later they were probably algae. The rock was seamed by cracks full of delicate ferns: brittle bladder fern, oak fern and green spleenwort, the latter easily identified by its green mid-rib and an indicator species of calcareous, or lime-rich, rocks. Clearly this was a band of the base-rich bedded pyroclastic rock that has made Cwm Glas famous for its plants. It wasn't long, however, before the ledges gave out into uncompromisingly vertical rock and I beat a careful retreat noting the tiny white specks of eyebright at my feet, prettily flecked with purple and yellow when I stooped to look closer.

Following the path rightwards to skirt the step, I continued up the spur with the odd section of steeper scrambling to arrive eventually at open grassy slopes below the summit of Crib y Ddysgl. Over to my right walkers could be seen on the Llanberis path up Snowdon and a train appeared from the direction of Clogwyn station, chuffing busily. In the other direction I was looking out across Cwm Glas and Cwm Uchaf, each with its own little lake, to the pinkish screes that give Crib Goch, 'red ridge', its name. Nearer at hand, to the right of the Parson's Nose Arête, were the clean, rhyolitic rocks so attractive to rock climbers and boasting classic routes like *Fallen Block Crack* and *Gambit Climb,* sitting on a plinth of darker, vegetated, horizontally bedded rock, an obvious target for botanists. That was familiar territory, however, so I chose to head down and to my left investigating another band of dark rock. In terms of interesting plants it proved disappointing but I found I could link grass ledges across an increasingly steep hillside until I suddenly found myself back on the Cwm Glas spur.

The Snowdon mountain railway opened on 6 April 1896 and suffered its first and only fatal accident when a descending train lost the rack and ran out of control. The driver William Pickles and his fireman leapt off the engine before it tipped over into Cwm Hetiau, its trajectory witnessed by hikers below. The carriages were luckily decoupled and gradually came to a halt but one passenger, Ellis Roberts of Llanberis, having witnessed Pickles' hasty dismount, ignored the guard's instruction to stay seated and jumped, fatally striking his head. *(Rob Collister)*

What now? At this point it occurred to me that it would be interesting to find a way down into neighbouring Cwm Hetiau, 'the cwm of hats'.

This little hollow at the very top corner of Cwm Glas Bach must have been formed in a final hiccup of the last ice age and has been well known as a repository for hats since Victorian times. It lies immediately beneath Clogwyn station on the Snowdon Railway at the point where the popular Llanberis path crosses under the line. It is the only point before the top at which the path comes right to the crest of Snowdon's long north ridge and it is a notoriously windy spot. In days gone by many a top hat went sailing out into the cwm below, caught by a sudden gust; nowadays it is more likely to be a baseball cap. In 1896, however, Cwm Hetiau became famous for a rather different reason.

On 6 April, Easter Monday, after two years under construction, the Snowdon Railway officially opened with two locomotives, each pulling two carriages filled with excited passengers, making their way to the summit of the mountain. However, when the first train set off on the way back down disaster struck. It later transpired that subsidence under the track in the cutting just below the top had caused the engine to jump the rack-and-pinion braking system so that it began to career downhill out of control. The engine driver and fireman in the cab quickly realised what was happening and were able to jump off without injury. The train itself stayed on the line going faster and faster until it reached the bend just before Clogwyn station where the engine left the rails and plunged straight over the edge down into Cwm Hetiau. Mercifully, the coaches were not coupled to the engine and somehow they stayed on the rails and eventually came to a halt where the line levels out at Clogwyn station. The guard had sensibly ordered the terrified passengers to remain seated and the only casualty was the unfortunate man who chose to jump out, struck his head on a rock

Looking into the little visited but much-abused Cwm Hetiau. *(Rob Collister)*

and was killed. Over the next year a public enquiry was held and modifi-
cations were made to ensure that the same thing could not happen again.
Exactly a year later the railway re-opened and has operated without major
incident ever since. Meanwhile, it was discovered that the main cylinder of
the locomotive was, to everyone's surprise, still intact so it was laboriously
hauled up some very steep ground to Clogwyn station and taken down to
Llanberis to be re-used. Nothing else was worth salvaging but anything that
could be removed very soon vanished as a souvenir.

I had traversed into the head of Cwm Glas Bach on a number of
occasions, mostly while walking or running the 14 3,000ers, without
seeing any evidence of the railway accident. But I realised that the easiest
line does not actually go into Cwm Hetiau itself but instead traverses in
above it. This was a perfect opportunity to investigate further. Descending
the spur as far as the point where I had first paused to look for flowers,
I followed a grassy rake cutting back left which took me under a line of
black, dripping cliffs bristling with interesting plants including several I
had not seen earlier: roseroot, golden rod, meadow rue, burnet saxifrage,

and the dead flower-heads of purple saxifrage. There were other plants that in Britain, curiously, are found in the mountains and on the coast but not usually in between, such as scurvy grass, bladder campion and thrift, or sea-pink.

Suddenly something made me look up and there, peering down on me intently in a slightly unnerving manner, was a hairy, yellow-eyed feral goat with long swept-back horns. Where there is one goat there are usually others but on this occasion I could not see any. Continuing down and across following the line of least resistance, I passed an old moss-grown sheepfold nestled against a huge boulder, crossed a little ridge and found myself in Cwm Hetiau proper. There is nothing of note here, just some clumps of rushes and a streamlet emerging from the hillside to quickly bend away northward. Yet it is a place of great charm and unspectacular natural beauty. Overlooking it are more flower-rich crags, the blue-green leaves of roseroot visible even from a distance and beneath them are scree slopes where parsley fern grows in profusion. Despite the noise of the train up above every half hour, it is out of sight of both railway line and path and feels secluded even in summertime.

Almost the first thing I spotted was a splash of orange in the scree. It proved to be a sheet of rusting metal much too heavy to have been blown down. It had to be a relic from the runaway locomotive and I soon discovered similar pieces scattered about the scree slope and embedded in the stream. But as well as these fragments of history there was also a vast amount of rubbish blown down from the path above along with detritus from the railway: plastic piping and sheeting, pieces of coal, a rucksack empty but for a can of Lynx deodorant. Within five minutes I had filled my rucksack with plastic bottles, aluminium cans and sweet wrappers. As I left I squeezed in a solitary black and pink ladies' mountaineering boot, scarcely used, wondering how on earth it came to be there and what had happened to the other boot and indeed to its owner. A brand new ski stick I had no compunction about purloining for my own use on the steep descent to the road.

As I walked down I encountered yet more debris, mostly accumulated in streambeds and runnels, and reflected gloomily on the profligate, thoughtless nature of our society. Yet it was not all bad. There were mossy and starry saxifrage and lady's mantle all in flower bordering the streams and, as I approached the mountain wall at the bottom of Cwm Glas Bach, the beautiful yellow breast of a grey wagtail acted like a ray of sunshine. It occurred to me that a gang of stalwart volunteers could clear up the whole area in a day and if helicopters could fly in stone for footpath repairs what was to stop them flying out bags of rubbish on the return journey? By the time I reached the road my spirits had lifted and there was a spring in my step once more.

Next day I contacted staff at the Snowdonia Society, a watchdog organisation of which I am a longstanding member, to outline my proposal. Before I knew it the Cwm Hetiau clear-up had been added to the programme for the 'Make A Difference' weekend of conservation activities being held at the end of September as part of the Society's 50th anniversary celebrations. Peter Rutherford, national park access officer, was supportive of the idea and could see no objection to using a helicopter to lift the stuff out on a return journey. His only concern was that the bags should be heavy enough to hang beneath the aircraft and not swing about. Remembering the weight of the metal plates I had seen in the cwm I had no worries on that score. Peter also rang the landowner to let him know and a few days later I picked up two of the heavy-duty bags used for airlifting stone from the warden's office at Pen y Pass.

Given we were working on a weekend, parking could have been a problem but through the good offices of David Medcalf we were able to leave our cars at Ynys Ettws, the Climbers' Club hut in the Llanberis Pass. Ten of us, including the Snowdonia Society's chairman, David Archer, set off well togged up against some unpromising weather and armed with litter-pickers and black bin-liners as well as the two big bags. Making our way through fields of dripping bracken and derelict walls, we traversed the hillside into Cwm Glas Bach. Right at the bottom, by the mountain wall, we filled our first bag with corrugated iron and other debris, from the remains of a small hut by the look of it. At first glance it all seemed impossibly buried and the sheets of tin too long to fit the bag but it is surprising what the combined efforts of 10 people all heaving, twisting and stamping can achieve.

Spreading out we made our way up steep slopes of grass and scree frequently losing sight of each other as the mist rolled in. Streambeds contained a fair amount of junk but on the open hillside there was less than expected and there was even some murmuring about the need for so many of us. That soon changed when we arrived in Cwm Hetiau about an hour after leaving the mountain wall: rubbish was everywhere for all to see. We paused for a rather soggy lunch in steady drizzle, glad to be sheltered from the strong south-westerly in this north-facing nook of the mountain, and then set to work. Over the next hour we retrieved numerous pieces of anonymous rusting metalwork, plastic piping of all shapes and sizes, not one but two wheelbarrows, the remains of two tents, a blanket, several tarpaulins, bottles, cans, batteries, various items of clothing including waterproof jackets, assorted sunglasses and goggles, gloves and, of course, hats: a lot of them, at least 20, mostly caps but also a trilby and a straw boater. There was too much to fit in our single lifting bag so we left the residue well weighed down for a later visit. Lest anyone be concerned that we were removing artefacts of important cultural significance, there was at least one sheet of metal, now part of the streambed, which resisted our best efforts to shift it. A large metal frame, nothing to do with the locomotive, had to be left for a park warden with an angle grinder to deal with at a later date. Tired and wet but satisfied with the day's work we headed down for a much-needed cup of tea at the ever-welcoming Siabod Cafe on the way home.

VICTOR SAUNDERS

Treppenwitz

On Avalanche Risk and the Human Factor

It was February. I had just suffered a major physical setback: a retinal detachment. It was the day after emergency surgery and I was feeling very sorry for myself. I decided to drown my sorrows in paper and ink, and write a note for my own interest: 'Risk Management and Avalanches'.

But first, and I could not (can never) help this, there was a bit of displacement activity. I watched my favourite chess column on YouTube. Black was doing well. White had tried to set up a defensive fortress but had run out of safe moves. It was unfortunate, but any move White made would end in loss. It was Zugzwang, the forced move.

As a climber, I find there is much to learn from chess. There are the chess-like problems to solve, moving body parts like chess pieces. But also, some of the Yiddish chess expressions describe climbing situations so much more precisely than climbing jargon does. Zugzwang is a good example: can't move up, can't move down but you can't hang on forever. The position is not lethal… until you're forced to move.

The thought brought back memories of an afternoon, decades ago on Holyhead Mountain. My eyesight was better then, even though I have been myopic since my schooldays and worn thick glasses. I had soloed into a slightly overhanging finger crack; the jams were in the wrong sequence, left-hand thumb up where it should have been right-hand thumb down. My feet were hidden from sight by a bulge at the level of my stomach. The ground had somehow withdrawn fifty feet lower than it had been a few seconds earlier and was now far too distant to invite a jump.

'What do you think?' I heard a concerned voice ask. There was something distinctly odd about the voice, but I was too preoccupied to boulder that one out. I answered as calmly as I could.

'I think… that we both think… that we should not be here.'

It was Zugzwang. And I still shudder at the thought of that moment.

There is more from chess. That day I climbed like a beginner, a blunderer, a bungler: a Patzer. And again, if you set up the board in public, often there is a bystander, the onlooker who offers unwanted advice. This is the Kibitzer.

'I will try to reverse the move and get my hands the right way round…' I said to myself.

'You can't climb down… you can't see your feet… you'll just have to pull and go up,' said the Kibitzer from far below.

'I can't pull… I can't reach… it's too far.'

A snow avalanche dropping more than a vertical mile off the east face of Shartse, with Chomolonzo in the distance: taken from Everest by Stephen Venables in 1988. *(Alpine Club Photo Library)*

'Pull hard, and then go off the edge of the crack on the way to the jug. A double movement. Zwischenzug. Just do it quickly.'

Zwischenzug: the in-between move. The unexpected move your opponent can't ignore. And so I pulled, knowing this was my only chance, and swiftly touching the edge of the crack the Zwischenzug allowed me to slide my fingers up again to reach and cling on to the bucket-sized thank-god life-saving jug that had previously been out of reach. Panting asthmatically, I flopped into the scratchy grass and thorns that occupy the cliff tops at Gogarth. Looking back over the edge of the cliff, holding tightly onto branches of gorse, I could see no one at the base of the cliff. There was nobody there to thank. The Kibitzer was gone. I still don't know how that happened. I don't think he had time to become bored and walk off. Perhaps he was there in spirit only. I was in north Wales and there is sorcery in that ancient land. Or maybe he was never there at all. Perhaps the Kibitzer was in my head. If I could hear the voice again I might recognise it in my mind's memory.

There was a loud knocking at the door. I closed the computer and let in Ben Tibbetts, accompanied by a flurry of snow. It had been snowing all night and all day, bringing the most dangerous avalanche conditions – Level 5 – to the Chamonix valley.

Two days earlier Ben had been injured in a large avalanche that enveloped two of his party of three. They were on the second lap of a route they knew well. (He knows it even better now.) In Level 3 conditions, he had been looking out for the usual signs of wind slab: that firm layer of snow the wind lays on a leeward slope onto a softer base. Triggered by a skier, wind

slab will slide like a magic carpet. Finding nothing conclusive, he stopped on a small shoulder to watch his two companions come down. They were all experts and yet two of the three were about to be taken for the big ride.

Watching from the shoulder he saw Lara trigger an avalanche and sink into the crumbling snow-slab. The cracks propagated widely and almost at once he realised that the avalanche included his part of the slope. Fear gripped him. There was no chance he would be able to ski away before the avalanche took him. Overpowered and helpless, he was carried down the slope and dumped, wrapped round a small stand of trees, buried upside down with one arm sticking out. His mouth and throat were packed wi' icy snow. You can't avoid inhaling snow-air while in the washing mach' (Don't believe people who insist you should shut your mouth. Yo' have to breathe, even if it is a snow-air mixture. Furthermore, as far as I know, there is no ethical way of testing the value of instructions to 'roll' or 'swim' once you are caught.)

Lara slid out of the bottom of the avalanche unharmed. Stuart, the third member of the party, reached Ben within a minute and dug the snow from Ben's mouth as he was passing out from lack of air. Had Stuart not done this so quickly, Ben would not have survived. He had dislocated his arm and torn ligaments in his knee but these were trivial in comparison to his near-suffocation. The thought was horrible. Ben wouldn't be able to ski or climb until his shoulder and knee recovered, so here he was for lunch. After lunch, we drank coffee as Ben told me his avalanche story. A question came into my head, a curiosity, an itch I just couldn't resist scratching.

'Ben.'

'Yes?'

'You observed the conditions. You covered almost the same ground twice. You dug a few pits. You knew the slope and its avalanche history. As a guide, you are an expert. You teach avalanche awareness. What lessons are we learning from your escape? What is the enemy here?'

'The enemy? I guess it's the avalanche because it doesn't know you are an expert.'

'But how do we know we really are experts? I mean, if we are experts, why are we caught in avalanches?'

'Victor... what are you saying?'

'I don't know, something I cannot put my finger on. We do avalanche awareness courses, we teach the stuff. And yet.'

'Eh?'

'I mean, if they don't stop us being avalanched...' There was something there: an idea hiding in his story. But I just couldn't get to it.

'Are you saying we should not do avalanche courses?'

'I'm not sure what I mean.' And I meant it. The itch was there, I just couldn't find the right place to scratch.

'I'm off to see the Nuptse guys lecture tonight. Be good to see someone else doing stupid dangerous things for once.'

'But how do we know? I mean, what...?'

'Bye,' Ben said firmly. I caught hints of boredom and frustration. He stepped out into the snowstorm. I climbed back up my steps, coffee in hand.

I felt defeated, irritated by my lack of clarity. It was like that after the retina operation. I couldn't see with my right eye. I bumped into things and my brain stumbled over the simplest ideas. It was all connected and it was maddening. And then, on the third step, my knotted thoughts began to unravel.

The steps. Of course, the steps! I had found the classic Treppenwitz response. You have family arguments. You give up in disgust. You stomp off upstairs, up the steps, Die Treppe, and then, suddenly, you find the precise, defining riposte just as it's too late. This is Treppenwitz. (The French call it l'esprit de l'escalier.) Not a chess word, but really it should be, given the number of times I would like to have taken back my calamitous last move.

Of course! I understand now. Avalanche courses are good for describing avalanches; they just don't help us to predict them. We know they occur in slopes of a certain angle and yet, these are the very slopes we want to ski. And the proof that you can't predict those slopes is that experts are forever coming unstuck on them. QED.

I was lecturing an empty house.

There are some things we can predict. For example, in 2009 it was clear that the seracs on the West Shoulder of Everest would collapse at least once during the expedition season. It was possible to estimate the track of the flow, and how much of the trail from Everest Base Camp to camp one the ice avalanche would take out. Inputting the time climbers would spend in that zone would give a percentage probability of being involved in the ice avalanche. The best assumptions gave the average climber a 0.83% chance of being caught in the avalanche for that year. In reality, the actual number of people caught in the avalanche of 2009 was 0.75%. On the other hand there are things we quite simply cannot predict, when we don't have the information to input even the most basic assumptions to calculate. And… avalanches are exactly that kind of thing. We can describe them but the information needed to predict them is hidden from us.

So. Thinking we are experts makes us our own worst… no… wait. Wait! Ben, it's like this… Ben, we already know the enemy, we know it really well. Look in the mirror. The enemy is us!

Only, Ben was not there to listen. I gave up on the coffee, poured the rest down the sink and pulled a beer from the fridge. I turned off my inner voice and enjoyed the silence, like a man who has finally stopped banging his head against a wall.

I wrote down a title on the blank paper, thought hard for a bit about things we can predict and things we cannot. Then I gave up. I put down the pencil and rested my head on the notepad. I thought about those nice Yiddish chess words. And then I fell asleep, and snored a little.

• Victor Saunders' new book *Structured Chaos* is published by Vertebrate Publishing in spring 2021.

Art

Plate 3. '*View of the Country from Urshulan Teeba*'

DAVID SEDDON

The Unseen Somervell

'Phari and Pauhunri 1922.'

It is difficult to be certain how many paintings T H Somervell completed during the 1922 and 1924 Everest expeditions. After almost 20 years of research, I estimate the combined total as between 140 and 180. Of these, perhaps a third survive, and there are others that he painted in later years. Some pictures have a story to tell and Somervell's paintings of Everest are no exception. The paper and canvas for these pictures would have been sent by sea to India, transported by train to Darjeeling, and from there carried by pony and yak into Tibet. In this article, I present 11 of Somervell's pictures of the two Everest expeditions. They are a selection of Somervell's unseen paintings of Everest, Tibet and Sikkim. All pictures are watercolour unless otherwise described. Three are undated.

'Phari and Pauhunri 1922'
Although considered by Tony Astill of *Les Alpes Livres* to be a watercolour by E F Norton, I think it more likely that this picture is by Somervell. The evidence for attribution to Norton is a similar sketch that was reproduced in *Everest Revealed* by Norton's grandson[1]. However, the sketch 'Chomolhari' referred to below is on an almost identically sized and shaped sheet of plain grey paper, suggesting that the two sheets had been detached from the same folio. In addition, a picture with this title was exhibited by Somervell at the Alpine Club in 1922 and 1923. There is no record of Norton exhibiting any of his pictures. I suspect that the resemblance of this watercolour to the sketch by Norton in *Everest Revealed* is likely to be coincidental.

1. C Norton, *Everest Revealed*, The History Press, Cheltenham, 2014.

'Everest and Lhotse from near Kampa Dzong'.

'Everest from Base Camp 1922'.

'Everest and Lhotse from near Kampa Dzong'

This small pastel bears the inscription, 'Everest and Lhotse from E [field glasses] first view of E [Everest] from Kampa Dzong'. Somervell probably sketched this undated work on 13 April 1922, as Norton also sketched Everest from Kampa Dzong on that date. Mallory had written these lines in 1921:

> *It was a perfect early morning as we plodded up the barren slopes above our camp (at Kampa Dzong) ... we had mounted perhaps a thousand feet when we stayed and turned, and saw what we came to see. There was no mistaking the two great peaks in the west: that to the left must be Makalu, grey, severe and yet distinctly graceful, and the other away to the right – who could doubt its identity? It was a prodigious white fang excrescent from the jaw of the world.'* [2]

'Everest from Base Camp 1922'

This image is of a small black and white postcard-sized reproduction of one of two paintings exhibited at the Redfern Gallery in 1926, in an exhibition arranged by Somervell's father. The majority of the pictures exhibited related to his two Everest expeditions. Both pictures were entitled 'Everest from Base Camp'. This one may be watercolour. The other, probably oil, was used to illustrate *The Fight for Everest: 1924* by E F Norton. This reproduction is held in the archives of the London Missionary Society at the School of Oriental and Asian Studies, London. The present whereabouts of both of these pictures is unknown.

'Peaks at the Head of the Goraphu Valley 1922'

At the end of the 1922 Everest expedition, Somervell and Crawford returned to Darjeeling independently of the rest of the expedition. They crossed from Tibet to Sikkim and, as Somervell was to write for the *Fell and Rock Climbing Club Journal.*

---

2. G L Mallory, in C K Howard-Bury, *Mount Everest: The Reconnaisance,* 1921, Arnold, London, 1922.

'Peaks at the Head of the Goraphu Valley 1922'.

> *...we journeyed into a small valley near the northern border of Sikkim called Goraphu. As far as we knew we were the only Europeans who had ever been in this valley ... July 16th [1922] dawned gloriously, and we saw in all their magnificence the fine peaks on the northern side of our valley; four or five of them, from 20,000-22,000 feet high with terrific precipices and hanging ice ...'* [3]

So this picture may have been painted on that date. It was exhibited at the Alpine Club in 1923 and was in Somervell's personal collection at the time of his death in 1975. His widow exhibited this watercolour as well as 'East Face of Everest 1924', referred to below, at Abbott Hall Gallery, Kendal in 1976.

'Valley in Sikkim 1922'

This watercolour was probably painted in late June or July 1922. Somervell used paper watermarked 'Michallet', which is different from the plain grey paper used for 'Chomolhari' and 'Phari and Pauhunri' described above. The scene is unknown but the monsoon is in progress. This picture was also one of 50 exhibited at the Redfern Gallery in 1926 and was acquired by one of Somervell's aunts, Dora Rachel Howard (1862-1947).

'East Face of Everest 1924'

This striking oil picture, dated 1924, and another similar one held by the Alpine Club, were inspired by the view of the east face of Everest from the

---

3. T H Somervell, 'Climbing North of Kangchenjunga', *Fell and Rock Climbing Club Journal* 1923, p272-6.

'Valley in Sikkim 1922'.

'Pumori'.

Raphu La. Somervell walked from camp three to the Raphu La alone on 12 May 1922. Two days later, he walked there again and was joined by Mallory who wrote:

> *[Somervell's] most important activity when we were not on the mountain was sketching. His vast supply of energy, the number of sketches he produced and oil paintings besides, was only less remarkable than the rapidity with which he worked. On May 14th he again walked over the uncrevassed snow-field by himself to the Rapiu La. Later on I joined him, and as far as I could judge, his talent and energy were no less at 21,000 feet than on the wind-swept plains of Tibet.* [4]

This picture and its companion were most probably painted at Neyyoor in south India in early or late 1924. Somervell's work as a surgeon had taken him there the previous year. Somervell did not visit the Raphu La in 1924 and it seems highly improbable that these pictures were painted during the 1924 expedition itself.

'East Face of Everest' may have been part of a consignment of some 50 paintings that Somervell sent to his father in November 1924, and may have been exhibited at the Royal Geographical Society in 1925 and the Redfern Gallery in 1926. It may well have been exhibited again at the Alpine Club in 1936 as 'Shoulder of Everest' and again at the Alpine Club in 1954 as 'South-east Face of Everest'. This picture was in Somervell's collection at the time of his death. In *After Everest* he wrote:

> *Whatever may be the route by which the world's highest mountain is eventually scaled, I am certain that it will not be by these south-east cliffs of grooved ice and pounding avalanche. A more terrible and remorseless mountain-side it would be hard to imagine.* [5]

'Pumori'

I am uncertain as to whether this watercolour dates from 1922 or 1924. Somervell painted at least one picture of Pumori in 1922 but may have only

4. G L Mallory, in C G Bruce, *The Assault on Mount Everest: 1922*, Arnold, London 1923.
5. T H Somervell, *After Everest*, Hodder, London, 1936.

'East Face of Everest 1924'.

used this size of paper in 1924 and not in 1922. The rounded bulk of Pumori is seen above the main Rongbuk glacier. On the moraine sit the ice pinnacles that remain a prominent feature of the East Rongbuk and Rongbuk glaciers, although diminished by climate change. This picture was part of an exhibition in 1978 at the Science Museum, London to mark the 25th anniversary of the first ascent of Everest. It is now held in their reserve collection.

'Kangchenjunga 1939'

Somervell would have seen Kangchenjunga in 1922 and 1924, and he visited Darjeeling again in 1928 and 1943. He wrote: 'March 31st [1924] Gnatong-Jelep La. 'What a glorious morning! A fine view of the complete Kangchenjunga range, clear and orange-white in the morning sun.'[6]

Somervell's mother died in October 1938 and it is likely that he returned to Britain at around that time, possibly staying until 1939. So this picture, oil on board, may have been painted in early 1939. At over one metre in length, it is more likely that this picture was painted in the United Kingdom than in India. The panorama includes, from left, Jannu, Kabru, Talung Peak, Kangchenjunga and Pandim. Of the six oil pictures of Kangchenjunga I have seen, it is easily the finest and is in the possession of a school in the West Midlands.

'From North Col of Everest 1924-47'

In *After Everest,* Somervell recorded his attempts to take a photograph from camp four on the morning of 2 June 1924. It was on this day that Somervell

6.   D J Seddon *T H Somervell,* published privately, 2016.

'Kangchenjunga 1939'.

and Norton with accompanying high-altitude porters set off for camp five. The photograph was included in *After Everest* and may have provided inspiration for this vast painting. At 122cm x 201cm it is by a long way the largest of Somervell's pictures.

Somervell was resident in the UK between April 1945 and early 1948, and for at least part of that time was living in Cambridge. His youngest son, Hugh, died there in 1947 and it is possible the tragedy may have impelled him to paint this picture. Somervell may also have been inspired to paint on this large scale by Nicholas Roerich who he had met in 1944. Roerich was known for his large landscape pictures of the Himalaya. This picture is in the possession of a school in the West Midlands but they have no record of the circumstances by which the painting was acquired. There is no record of it being exhibited. In 2018, it was consigned to Christie's with the title 'On the Way to Everest'. Once a more accurate identification was available, the school opted to retain the picture in its collection.

The view is north-west from the North Col. The peaks seen on the skyline include, I think, from extreme left, Menlungtse, and to the right, Cho Oyu and Gyachang Kang. Khumbutse, the next mountain west of Everest, is seen above the Lho La, and behind it, the bulk and rounded summit of Pumori. To the left is the western flank of Everest and to the right the slopes of Changtse. The main Rongbuk glacier is seen lower centre, and upper centre is the West Rongbuk glacier leading to the Nup La.

'Chomolhari 1922-74'

Somervell had first seen Chomolhari in 1922. Over 50 years later, this peak remained a source of inspiration for this picture and another completed in 1972. Most unusually, he has included a figure in the foreground with hat and

'From North Col of Everest 1924-47'.

'Chomolhari (Detail)'.

'Chomolhari 1922-74'.

Somervell occasionally gave his pictures two dates. There is no explanation for this given in any of his books or articles. I have interpreted these
'double dates' as indicating that the inspiration for the picture dates from
the first year given, and the picture itself was painted in the second year
given. Howard Somervell died in January 1975 and of his later pictures,
this is one of the best, with the form of the mountain clearly depicted and
flowing brushwork for windblown snow. There is a telling similarity to the
sketch of 1922.

'Chomolhari (detail)'
This undated and unfinished sketch of Chomolhari may be from the same
folio as 'Phari and Pauhunri'. This might date it to 7-8 April 1922. The geo-
metry and angles of the mountain would have appealed to Somervell. This
sketch although unsigned, was in the collection of his son Jim Somervell.
It seems unlikely that this was one of two paintings of Chomolhari exhibited at the Alpine Club in 1923.

'Matterhorn 1967'.   'Mount Fuji 1963'.

Conclusion

There are of course many pictures by Somervell that are unseen. He exhibited perhaps over 800 pictures in his lifetime. If he painted 50 pictures a year, his lifetime's output could have exceeded 3,000. I have traced some 500.

A fuller account of the life and work of T H Somervell, together with images of 200 or so of his pictures may be found in the Alpine Club Library or the Armitt Library near Ambleside. I would be pleased to have any information regarding paintings by Somervell that may be in the possession of readers of this article. djseddon@btinternet.com

BEN TIBBETTS

The Art of Confinement

Mountains in Lockdown

Les Drus. *(All drawings by Ben Tibbetts)*

As we flew up the glacier, through the helicopter's bulbous windows I could spot each solar panel emerging like seedlings from the winter snow. Just the tip of the four-metre aluminium stalks were protruding and a small disc-shaped GPS antenna atop every third pole. As the helicopter spun a loop around the uppermost site, I hurried to jam my camera back in its case. The pilot Pascal pressed the machine to the ground. Luc hung up his headset and slid out onto the sun-baked crispy snow. Valentine and I followed and ducked around the front to pull our skis and sacks out of the cage on the right-hand skid. Pascal watched us through the glass, his expression obscured by a respiratory protection mask. When we signalled clear, he accelerated the rotors, and the helicopter pulled away with a gasp of air.

As the vibrations disappeared down the valley, silence drew around us. It took a few minutes for the exhilaration of the ride to fade and for my mind to arrive 'in the moment'. When I pressed my eyes closed for a few seconds and reopened them it was like a corporeal shock, the sheer scale of

Matterhorn.

the forms around us stung my eyes. An alpine chough flew down to greet us; it felt like coming home to be up on a glacier after a period stuck in the valley. We gazed up at the massive walls of the Aiguille Verte and Les Droites: the last few weeks of perfect warm weather had stripped back any ephemeral ice that had built up at the end of winter.

Luc Moreau, our neighbour and a renowned glaciologist, has spiky grey hair and a sun-chiselled face. He's a veteran of scientific expeditions to Greenland and other remote regions but has centred his life's research on the Mont Blanc massif. Some of this work is for the Franco-Swiss hydroelectricity company Émosson, which gathers the sub-glacial water outflow of the Argentière glacier. Via a massive network of tunnels this feeds a reservoir and hydroelectric plant that straddles the border and is co-owned by Switzerland and France. During the Covid-19 lockdown in France only essential services were allowed to continue work, but this included Luc's role maintaining scientific equipment, as it was related to the hydroelectricity supply. To continue the work on the glacier – a study of the ice's seasonal flow pattern with an array of precision GPS installations – Luc had asked me, as a mountain guide, to help. Not wanting to miss out, my partner Valentine joined as team doctor and shovel monkey.

It was colder than I had expected. The sun hadn't reached the glacier floor and a gentle katabatic breeze flowed down from the head of the basin, cutting through my clothing. The silence was almost perceptible. Every few minutes a rock fell, loosened by the morning sun. With no other sounds we

Eiger.

could hear each one clatter down cliffs several kilometres away. This peace was broken as a serac collapsed above the Cordier couloir on the Aiguille Verte and roared down. Weeks spent indoors had honed my capacity for awe at the beauty of these masses of rock and ice, but I had a jumble of mixed emotions. Being up there didn't quite have the taste of freedom that I had anticipated, rather it felt like some illicit pleasure that I could only sip for fear of intoxication.

A few weeks earlier this glacier had been humming with ski tourers. As bizarre as it was to see images of the Champs-Élysées or Times Square devoid of humanity, it is equally odd to know you are the only people out in mountains. On such a clear day in April there is usually a steady caterpillar of ski tourers crawling across the glaciers and passes, many trying some variation of the Haute Route, planning to reach Zermatt in a week of high-altitude touring. As the Covid-19 pandemic advanced across Europe, confinement threw France off its feet and onto the sofa with strict instructions: 'Restez chez vous.' With police issuing fines with surprising abandon, Valentine and I had barely dared leave the house despite the warm, sunny weather.

*

A few weeks before lockdown, in those hazy rose-tinted days that now appear like a different epoch, I got an email from a climber based in New York. I work as a mountain guide based in Chamonix, and Jonathan had contacted me to enquire about my availability this summer. He asked if I might be interested in guiding him and his girlfriend, also an experienced climber, up the *Allain-Leininger route* on the north face of the Aiguille

Piz Badile.

du Dru (3754m). This was a relatively unusual request. The route was avant-garde when first climbed in 1935. An 800m-high granite pillar with pitches of 5c, it combines some mixed climbing, some loose rock and a complicated descent. All this ensures that it still a challenging and serious route today. Jonathan had already climbed the north faces of the Eiger, Matterhorn and Cima Grande di Lavaredo with guides and his long-term aspiration was to complete the six great north faces of the Alps, the list compiled and first climbed by Gaston Rébuffat back in the 1950s. Even for a mountaineer living in the heart of the Alps this is still an ambitious goal, and I know only a handful of climbers who have done all six. In addition to guiding, Jonathan had seen my photographs and drawings in my recent book, *Alpenglow,* describing my experiences climbing all of the 4,000m peaks in the Alps. He wondered whether I might be able to make drawings of each of the six peaks he was trying to climb. I tentatively agreed to have a go, but warned him that my tiny drawings usually took me upwards of a month each. Working with meticulously sharpened pencils while looking through a magnifying glass requires unusual concentration and is such hard work on the eyes that I usually only manage a few hours a day.

In the days that followed I hunted through my collection of photos for one from which I could base a drawing of the Drus. I made a few sketches, but most of the images I had were from the north side, where the Drus appears as a sideshow to the massive Aiguille Verte (4122m). At that point in mid March I was set to travel to Scandinavia for the following five weeks to work as a ski guide in the Arctic so I set the drawing project aside and began digging through the garage for cold-weather clothes, stoves, tents and pulks.

Grandes Jorasses.

The Covid-19 situation accelerated fast in France. Rumours of an imminent lockdown circulated on 13 March. On 14 March all non-essential shops,
restaurants and entertainment venues closed. On 15 March, a Sunday, ski
resorts ground to a halt and then on 17 March President Macron made a
solemn announcement of a countrywide lockdown. Immediately, anyone in
the tourist industry was out of work. Restrictions in France remained far from
the severity of Wuhan's confinement, but a few days after President Macron's
announcement that everyone except essential workers should stay at home,
many people were doing anything but the permitted 'brief, local exercise'.
One team of experienced Alpine climbers even thought it an opportune moment to make a hard mixed ascent on the Aiguille Verte.

While France is a country usually tolerant of minor digressions from the
letter of the law, the Covid-19 pandemic lockdown precipitated more draco-
nian measures than many French could ever have imagined. The country's
motto might be Liberté, Égalité, Fraternité but many had been taking the Liberté too far. Within a few days the authorities clamped down and clarified the
regulations. For exercise people could leave the house just once a day to walk
or jog for a maximum of one hour within a radius of 1km and within 100m
height-gain of their house. I envied friends across the Swiss border just 20km
away, who were still able to go bike riding, rock climbing and ski touring.

With lockdown in effect my work in the Arctic was cancelled and it became
apparent I would have little to distract me from getting down to an intensive
period of drawing. On the evening after lockdown, just before the 1km limit
on recreational movement came into force, I meandered up the valley on my
bike at sunset to take some images of the Aiguille du Dru from the west where

Tre Cime di Lavaredo.

it appears to dominate the skyline. Back at home I looked through the photos, made another sketch of the composition and then began to make the first marks on a clean sheet of thick paper.

*

Across the world, the short and long-term implications in many sectors of the economy have been dramatic, tourism being among the most devastated, in destinations in the developing world and here in rich industrialised societies. Like the theatres, restaurants and museums that cater for the tourists in cities, the refuges and lifts will likely remain closed for some time in the Alps. Having talked with many mountain professionals, the short and mid-term outlook is pretty bleak, especially in a town like Chamonix, which has based its economy almost exclusively on tourism.

Speaking with Philippe Collet, an instructor at ENSA, the national guides training centre, he confirmed 'if the activity does not restart very quickly, some guides will be obliged to look for work in another domain in order to ensure a basic income.' Although two-thirds of French mountain guides have another form of work, most of these other revenue sources are also indelibly linked to the tourist industry. Be it managing rental accommodation or working in a shop, with facilities closed and no tourists in the valley, almost everyone in these mountain communities is affected by the pandemic. Though many people are looking forward to a return to 'normal' as quickly as possible, there are hints that perhaps this will finally wake us up to how fragile and interdependent our economic activity actually is.

With a strong state healthcare system and governmental financial aid to soften the blow, the effects in this prosperous French valley will probably be much less dramatic than in developing countries. Nevertheless, I know mountain guides who are already on the ropes and may have to sell their houses due to loss of income. Some changes may be forced upon us, but others may be welcome. As Philippe suggests: 'Today we are 1,500 [French] guides. It is probable, and I think even desirable, that people can diversify if possible into various [employment] sectors ... In any case, given the power of the [economic] shock, I think it is now certain that the number of guides that can live from this job will significantly decrease. I have a feeling that our profession may be moving towards something more mellow, which can appeal to a broader public and where we learn to revisit the idea of having adventures closer to home ... Our relationship to travel – taking ourselves far away to quench our passion – is becoming a subject of serious reflection.'

*

Between hard sessions climbing in the garage bouldering gym, limited by a tweaky shoulder and the usual finger weakness, I had an unprecedented amount of time to work on drawings. The week after taking the helicopter to work up on the Argentière glacier we had to make another trip up to install a replacement electronic part that we hadn't anticipated the first time. We got permission from the PGHM and to save on aviation fuel skinned up the 1,200m from the valley floor. We also took a surreptitious path to avoid being seen by jealous eyes. Further on the only sensible way up was via the main piste, unfortunately in full view of the town of Argentière. I could almost sense the hundreds of skiers breakfasting on their balconies, looking up at us in disbelief. Despite having permission I felt a pervasive sense of guilt rather than any pleasure as we slid our way up the icy snow. Holes were appearing in the piste already. Patches of grass and gravel were spreading, the first flowers of spring unfurling. Once we were nearly a kilometre above the town I finally relaxed and began to savour the experience. As we turned the last corner and came within sight of the glacier Luc's phone rang. It was the PGHM checking that it was indeed us climbing the piste. They had received numerous calls from the public denouncing us to the police. So much for fraternité, I thought.

*

In Macron's speech of 17 March, his repeated declaration 'we are at war' against this 'enemy ... invisible, elusive', invited the comparison that some journalists made between the current confinement and that imposed by German occupation during the Second World War. Even a cursory understanding of history reveals this as a wild exaggeration: food isn't rationed, we can communicate with loved ones across the globe, but most importantly there are no bombs falling from the sky and we are unlikely to get

Ben Tibbetts at work on the north face of the Badile.

conscripted off to labour camps or shot for our ideology. However, perhaps it is only in moments like this when we are confined that we can truly appreciate the flavour of western liberty.

Friends that lived through the Soviet era in eastern Europe or Russia have told me that the lockdown gave them a taste of what their former lack of freedom felt like. Chancellor Merkel drew a similar comparison based on her experience of living half her life in East Germany. In a live broadcast she said:

Let me assure you. For someone like me, for whom the freedom to travel and move was a hard-fought right, such restrictions can only be justified if they are an absolute necessity … They should never be passed lightly and only ever temporarily – but they are indispensable at the moment to save lives.

The personal experience I drew on that most resembled our confinement was wintering in the Antarctic. A decade ago I lived on a British scientific base on the southern continent for 18 months. Between two summer fieldwork seasons I was part of a small overwintering team maintaining the buildings and equipment, and keeping the scientific experiments running. This was still far from the perfect analogy as we hadn't chosen this year's form of social isolation, whereas living in the Antarctic is a choice, rather like a monk or hermit that chooses to retire from society for a period of time. In Antarctica, as here, there is usually a plentiful supply of food and comfortable accommodation. We had stacks of films and books, and even when a storm raged outside for a week there were ways to get a workout. Where we worked the travel boundaries were strictly enforced: other than for specific training or scientific missions everyone had to remain just a short distance from the base.

Les Drus confined.

Everyone responded differently to the isolation but for most there were three strategies that kept us sane: maintaining a disciplined rhythm and routine in day to day work, setting personal creative projects or training goals to punctuate the period of isolation and keeping in touch with people back in what we referred to euphemistically as 'the real world'. As I lived through the most surreal period of life I have experienced in Chamonix, these same strategies helped me keep some sense of perspective.

Despite the suffering that is sweeping across the globe, perhaps the gravity of this pandemic could have a silver lining. Virologists have predicted for decades that something even more terrifying may wreak havoc upon humanity. This 'dress rehearsal' as some commentators a have dubbed it, has displayed with even greater clarity the weaknesses in our political narratives, and how health systems and supply chains rupture faced with such pressure.

As if I had ever taken it for granted, the period of confinement reinforced how much contact with friends and family matters. Moreover it recalibrated my appreciation of what mountains and wild places offer us. Hopefully, even if the lifts and refuges remain closed this summer, we can still get up high for adventures and sleep out under the stars. Despite weeks of rigorously structuring my days to keep anxiety at bay, trying to keep rhythm in my work and an optimistic spirit, I dream of nothing else but leaving the valley floor, of heading up to sleep in an exposed place, of climbing a ridge and catching the sunrise over some remote corner of the mountains. By the time this appears in print the world I am writing in will no longer exist. Lockdown may have eased in France and some people may have returned to work but no doubt the effects will be reverberating through our lives for a long time to come. Through all these challenging times my love for my friends and the mountains hold true as constants I can rely on.

DONALD M ORR

The Allure of Mountain Presence

'The Lake of Lucerne, Moonlight, the Rigi in the Distance'.
(Whitworth Art Gallery, Manchester)

Only very occasionally within the history of landscape painting has there occurred the image of the 'midnight mountain': mountains, usually single examples, in the darkness and under snow that project an enduring permanence, a fierce beauty which, if they are to be approached or climbed, can be linked to an idea of anticipated suffering or difficulties endured and through either, or both, the tempering of existence. The concept of the infinite runs parallel to this notion because within this visually simple image is often held an impression of limitless time, space unbounded and the unaccountable age of the landforms around us: a quality of the eternal, of an ageless austerity, whose minimalist modesty reflects an innocence that at once attracts and challenges us.

What aspects of scale, position, height or dominance in the landscape lend themselves to such qualities? What aspects of colour, light or distance add or create the suggestion of timeless permanence? Does the depiction of lofty isolation, deep snow and the night sky dominate the idea whereby only that which is big, bold and hardy will endure through the darkness of night? The perspective of the viewer becomes all-important; the blackness of night may reflect the darkness of our own nights. If a nighttime image of darkness, mystery and impenetrability can act as a metaphor, then a snowbound summit can be seen as the white, pure, enigmatic and virginal counterpoint. The unchanged and unchanging, remote and isolated yet physical and inviting, is placed before us. As mountaineers, we are especially aware of the nature and complexities of that challenge. There is a fine blend of honour, desire and status that operates internally and publicly. But we can also acknowledge the purity and presence of the image inherent in this encounter.

This idea of an image of apparent emptiness being pregnant with possibilities is not unique to winter mountain paintings under starry skies. Artists like Edward Hopper[1] or the Norwegian painter Vilhelm Hammershøi[2] depicted the resonance of empty rooms, images charged with latent events, suggesting half-memories or vague promises. A strange stillness pervades their work. While apparently empty, the rooms generate a degree of tension that makes them inscrutable, despite their seeming openness and accessibility. They are silent paintings; their stillness and emptiness are somehow also lonely. We are viewing connections and separations simultaneously. There's a sense of isolation and disorientation where the silence is not based on any notion of absence. What Hopper and Hammershøi are depicting in their internal spaces is not impersonal: the light they evoke is an active presence symbolising understanding as illumination. It is this quality that the mountain paintings discussed here share; the midnight light that dominates these scenes is a presence not limited in any way. These mountains offer an acute sense of the infinite, unending, boundless, an absence bathed in presence. In these midnight mountains loneliness and sadness are translated into a timeless quality: the language of infinity in a constructed silence.

To portray a mountain scene in all its vastness, colour and structure, to render this on canvas so as to convey the stark beauty of a massif may well be challenge enough for any artist but to imply presence, whether human or eternal, is a significant step beyond all this. This specific midnight mountain topic was never a popular choice of subject matter for artists and the three painters and their examples touched on here, from greatly differing periods and cultures, are merely a starting point for reflection and consideration.

'The Lake of Lucerne, Moonlight, the Rigi in the Distance'[3]

The world of J M W Turner (1775-1851) has been well documented in numerous volumes, documentaries and feature films that deal with his life as well as his work: his themes, travels, exhibitions and style. While some have seen him as an early influence on the French Impressionists, Turner was never solely concerned with the effects of light upon colour but as much with what may be termed atmospherics. His fondness for

---

1. 'Sun in an Empty Room', Whitney Museum of American Art, New York, 1963.
2. 'Study in Sunlight', The David Collection, Copenhagen, 1906.
3. 'The Lake of Lucerne, Moonlight, the Rigi in the Distance', 1841, watercolour, body colour on paper, some scratched out. 230mm x 307mm, Whitworth Art Gallery, Manchester.

cloud effects at differing times of the day, direct sunlight at dawn and dusk, and sheets of rain moving across the landscape all echoed his intense interest in colour and his desire to create a sense of movement in his canvases. Monet, while living in London from 1899 to 1904, may very well have been aware of his work and works like 'Charing Cross Bridge', of which there are seven versions throughout the world, certainly suggest that appreciation. Yet a greater influence may be found in the work of Whistler whose series of 'Nocturnes', for example 'Nocturne: Blue and Silver – Chelsea' from 1871 and now at Yale and 'Nocturne: Blue and Gold – Old Battersea Bridge' produced between 1872 and 1875 and now in Tate Britain, contribute much to the atmospheric theme.

Turner first visited Switzerland in 1802 and in 1819 spent time in Italy, and from then on 'his oil paintings tend more and more to the pale brilliance of colour.'[4] After this he seems to think in terms of coloured light: what Constable referred to as 'tinted steam'. Further trips to Italy, the last one in 1840, enhanced his work and allowed him to recreate almost magical effects of light on canvas.

Situated in central Switzerland at an elevation of 1,798m the Rigi massif is almost entirely surrounded by the waters of Lakes Lucerne, Zug and Lauerz. The main summit, Rigi Kulm, is technically not geologically part of the Alps but instead belongs to the Swiss Plateau. Over thirty paintings and sketches were produced of this view across the lake. The moonlit painting displays 'Turner's ever-changing rhetoric of sublime effects'[5] where the Rigi acts as a heart of darkness in the centre of this moonlit landscape. The central portion of this picture is thus dominated by those formless atmospherics where the movement of light is the central theme. Moonlight mirrored across the water is met by the same tone of smoke or mist held by the shadowed area of the massif whose upper section is caught in the moon's glow. The night sky is awash with lunar light held and reflected in the lake, thus generating a continuous circular movement of light flowing from top to bottom. The Rigi is not merely a backdrop but crucial to the composition, absorbing yet reflecting the moonlight in its elevated altitudes and creating the recessive core of the vision in the shadows beneath. The inclusion of the Rigi is not merely a useful background to a scene of Lake Lucerne but facilitates the constant movement of light in this delicate watercolour. Turner's mountain is intrinsically linked to atmospherics. Mist and moonlight are combined as part of the mystery of the scene and the allure of the mountain. The reflected moon-glow on the summit hints at the clarity that may be achieved by the mountaineer, but the journey is swathed in mist and uncertainty. The moonlight may endorse the calmness and serenity of the scene but inherent in the image is the dark verticality of the massif.

4.　P & L Murray, *A Dictionary of Art and Artists,* Penguin, Harmondsworth, 1964, p325.
5.　R Hughes, *Nothing If Not Critical,* Harvill, London, 1990, p78.

'Winter's Night in Rodane'. *(National Museum of Art, Architecture and Design, Oslo)*

'Winter's Night in Rodane'[6]

Harald Sohlberg was born on 30 September 1869 in Oslo and died there on 19 June 1935. As a youth he attended the Royal School of Art and Design of Christiania, modern-day Oslo, and later trained as a graphic artist under Johan Nordhagen and in the studios of several Norwegian painters. He also enrolled at the art school of Kristian Zahrtmann in Copenhagen where he became aware of Gauguin and the Symbolist movement while he, himself, maintained a strong interest in Naturalism and a Neo-Romantic outlook.

He gained recognition for his many depictions of the mountains of Rondane and the town of Røros. His theme of 'Winter's Night in Rondane' exists in several variations. The view across Lake Atnsjøen to the mountains of Rondane is now serviced by a viewing station named the Sohlberg Platform opened in 2005 to facilitate the many tourists wishing to view the range as the artist had. His first version of the mountains was painted in 1901. The second, now in the National Museum of Art, Architecture and Design, Oslo, was produced between 1911-1914, and has become the unofficial national painting of Norway. Dissatisfied with this effort he produced a chromolithograph of the subject in 1917 and went on to create a third painted version between 1918 and 1924. Alongside this he produced some 250 lithographic prints of the subject. He lived with his wife nearby in Røros from 1902 until 1905; a town situated on the high plains of central Norway surrounded by the landscape that became the principal inspiration in his career.

6. 'Winter's Night in Rodane', also known as 'Winter Night in the Mountains', 1914, oil on canvas, 160cm x 180.5cm, National Museum of Art, Architecture and Design, Oslo.

In his canvas the winter peaks around Rondane are condensed into a semi symmetrical composition and with the artist's reduction of actual space came a simplification in form and a dramatisation of their steepness. The seven major peaks compressed into the canvas stretch from Storsvulten at 1,871m to the far end of the range and Storronden (2138m). The viewer is framed on both sides by dark winter woodlands that part and drop away to reveal the vast snowy upland area around Rodane. Sohlberg compresses the physicality of the mountains to create a distant luminous realm, starlit and soft under its mantle of snow yet cold and distant. The mountains appear rounded, almost gentle, with a central valley leading off into the night where the higher peaks just catch a clearer moon-glow. Yet it is this very softness held by the areas of dark navy blue that is at once the allure and the warning: a beckoning and a threat to those who would venture there.

'Mount Adams, Washington'[7]

Albert Bierstadt was born on the 7 January 1830 in Solingen in what was then Prussia and died in New York on 18 February 1902. Emigrating with his family as a child Bierstadt returned to Germany for several years to study painting in Dusseldorf and on his arrival back in America was quickly linked to the Hudson River School in New York. (*Editor's note:* see also 'Thomas Moran and the American Mountain Vision', *Alpine Journal* 2019.) In 1859 he took part in one of the grand surveys of the American West organised by the American government. Much of the work developed from this explorative journey was completed in 1860 and saw him elected to the National Academy of Design. In 1863 he again visited the West, using the studies made to produce large-scale canvases in his studio in New York. Alongside Thomas Moran he became one of the pre-eminent painters of the western American landscape.

He visited London in 1867 and travelled through Europe for two years while still continuing to paint mountain scenes of the American West. His 'Among the Sierra Nevada, California' was painted in Rome and exhibited in Berlin and London before being shipped home. Bierstadt's drive for commercial success was directed and reflected by the grandiose quality of his subject matter and his capacity for self-promotion.

His involvement with a romantic treatment of his subject matter and overly dramatic lighting became heightened in his later years and was regarded as excessive by many critics. His inability to alter or moderate his style, or even temper his dramatisations, saw his work fall out of favour and attacked for its theatricality. In 1882 a fire destroyed his studio in New York and many of his paintings were lost. This, and the loss of his wife in 1893 to tuberculosis, must have greatly shaken his confidence and he narrowly avoided bankruptcy in 1895. By the time of his death in 1902 the desire for large landscapes of an epic nature had evaporated and his work was largely forgotten. The man himself is commemorated in Mount Bierstadt (4287m)

---

7. 'Mount Adams', 1875, oil on canvas, 213cm x 138cm, Princeton University Art Museum.

'Mount Adams, Washington', 1865. *(Princeton University Art Museum)*

and Bierstadt Lake in Colorado, and for the fact that he was probably the first European to visit, in 1863, the summit of Mount Evans (4350m) in the Front Range of the Rocky Mountains, some 70km south west of Denver.

Mount Adams, also known as Pahto or Klickitat, is a potentially active strato-volcano some 55km from Mount St Helens in the Cascades, which stretch from southern British Columbia through Washington and Oregon to northern California. At 3,743m it is the second highest in the range, behind Mt Rainier at 4,392m.

In Bierstadt's depiction the mountain emerges from low cloud drifting across lesser hills in the mid ground: a dazzling white ridge dominating the entire scene and seemingly controlling the cloud as some form of base material. The soaring verticality is balanced and enhanced by the flat grassy plain in the foreground where a group of Native Americans dwarfed by the mountain massif stand in awe of its majesty, thus granting a mystical, even sacred status to the landscape. (There are a number of indigenous legends that link Mount Adams with its volcano neighbours St Helens and Hood.) It is the mountain itself that highlights the scene since its overwhelming whiteness reflects light onto the plain below, where the scale of the figures and luminous quality of the mountain indicate its enigmatic character, beckoning yet unknowable, recognisable yet tremendous: hallmarks of this sub-genre.

What we become aware of in all these canvases is the idea of presence, of something greater than life, something indomitable, fearless, emblematic, something that endures through the ages. They set a scene that holds our attention as if something were about to happen, an action about to start. The only question is whether we are about to be witnesses or participants. Presence invites us to look but also to involve us in the image and in that psychological involvement to fire imagination and ambition. Presence is a declaration, an occurrence that we note but that defies easy articulation. It is presence that allows the experience of connectedness with the scene. 'Presence is the ephemeral apparition of the experience of oneness, wholeness and unity'[8] inserting itself into consciousness.

What is suggested to us is a distillate of the sublime and the physical. Midnight mountains combine the profound beauty of the mountain environment with the challenge and allure of adventure, a process that verges on the sublime as fascination offers the possibility of encounter. In that moment of recognition, the words of Robert Macfarlane come to mind: 'Time has flown over you and left its shadow behind.'[9] In the winter darkness there emerges a wildness and unpredictability that stretches beyond allure, that becomes part of the timeless magnetism of the high peaks and that continues to urge us to find out what the horizon has closed off.

What is intrinsic is the fact that the mountains do not care; we do, and we must search in, and for, that environment and the ambience it offers. The truth we discover is that 'mountains exert their greatest emotive power when they are lonely and unblemished.'[10] What this generates is essentially an uncomplicated love of the natural world that drives beyond the end of the known to where we sense a realm of mystery. It is the gift of these apparently simple images to shift the way we see ourselves; they allow us to focus and restore our wonder.

8. R Greene, *Searching for Presence*, Rodopi, Amsterdam & New York, 2004, p102.
9. From narration of 'Mountain', written by R Macfarlane & J Peedom, 2017.
10. M Moran, *Higher Ground*, Sandstone, Dingwall, 2014, p188.

ROBIN N CAMPBELL

'Views in the Himala Mountains'

The Drawings of James Baillie Fraser

James Baillie Fraser in 1833, drawn by William Brockedon (1787-1854), who crossed the Alps 58 times researching *Illustrations of the Passes of the Alps by which Italy communicates with France, Switzerland, and Germany.*

This year's frontispieces celebrate the bicentenary of the publication of James Baillie Fraser's *Views in the Himala Mountains* and of his book *Journal of a tour through part of the snowy range of the Himala mountains and to the sources of the rivers Jumna and Ganges.*[1]

Born in Edinburgh in 1783, Fraser was brought up at Reelig, the family estate near Moniack west of Inverness, and educated privately in Edinburgh, before going in 1799 to British Guiana, now Guyana, first as an apprentice merchant and later managing the family's plantation there. A collapse in sugar prices left the family in debt and the Frasers looked to India to restore their fortunes. In 1813 James travelled to Calcutta and early in 1815 joined his brother William, who was a political agent for the British forces engaged in the Nepal War, at Nahan in Himachal Pradesh, where a siege of the fort at Jaitak was in progress.[2] While the army was bogged down there, William was sent eastwards with a force of 600 irregulars to liaise with local rulers in the valleys of the Tons, Giri and Sutlej

---

1. The best online version of Fraser's *Journal* is at www.loc.gov/item/05006365. An excellent image of Fraser's map may be found on p25.
2. See Fraser's entry in the *Oxford Dictionary of National Biography* by Toby Falk for more details.

121

Rivers, and to investigate trade routes via the Sutlej to Tibet and James went with him. The Tons and Giri are tributaries of the Yamuna, while the Sutlej, farther west, drains to the Indus.

When Nepal settled for treaty in May 1815, the pair had reached Sarahan in the Sutlej and William was recalled to Dehra for new duties. James, with a smaller force of 60 soldiers and porters, parted from his brother in the lower Tons valley to explore the sources of the Yamuna and Bhagirathi rivers. The Bhagirathi is regarded by the Hindu faith as the source river of the Ganges, although modern geographers would prefer the longer Alaknanda.

While with the army at Black Hill near Nahan, James had become an enthusiastic sketcher. He wrote to his sister Jane Anne:

> *When at Jytock [Jaitak] with General Martindell's Army, I got seized with a desire to delineate some of the objects that there met our view and the first impulse was in an odd place, in our Batteries, when really it was not quite pleasant for the Enemies Shot were playing over our heads quite briskly ... When the Devil of Drawing broke loose there was no holding him.[3]*

James sketched throughout his Himalayan travels and kept a diary. His *Views in the Himala Mountains* exhibits 20 of the watercolour sketches he made, and his *Journal* records his travels, supplemented somewhat chaotically by an account of the War, and numerous lengthy anthropological, geographical and mineralogical observations. His sketches were elaborated in Calcutta with the help of regular instruction from the English artist William Havell, who was resident there between April 1817 and January 1819. Havell went out of his way to praise Fraser's work and Joseph Turner also praised some drawings sent home when he visited Edinburgh in 1819. So this was an extraordinary artistic development. 'The Devil of Drawing' had raised him to the top of his new avocation in the space of a very few years. The printmaking firm of Robert Havell & Son, perhaps acting on advice from William Havell, nephew of Robert, converted James's drawings to large hand-coloured aquatint plates and Rodwell & Martin published them in book form in 1820. Havell & Son's next project was to prepare the huge prints for John James Audubon's *Birds of America*. The AC Library owns a copy of the now rare *Views* and it may be of interest to members to know that copies change hands for upwards of £30,000.

I now offer a few comments on the thirteen plates selected for this year's frontispieces, in order of use, which follows Fraser's itinerary. **Plate 4** shows the siege of Jaitak. Elephants were used to carry or drag heavy guns up to Black Hill. **Plate 12** shows some of 'Fraser's Irregulars', so called because the force was assembled from defeated opponents bought into service: a common practice in the Presidency armies of the East India Company. So all were from the hill states. The Frasers' initial journey followed the Giri river and **Plate 16** shows the village of Shai on its east side, reached on 9 May.

---

3. National Register of Archives of Scotland, James Baillie Fraser Papers, B3.

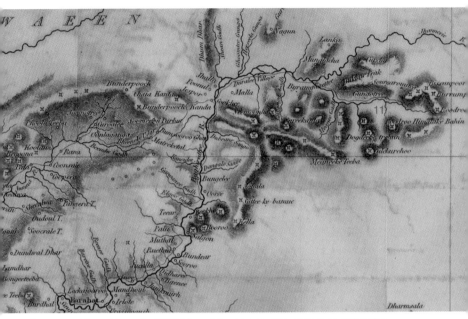

An excerpt from Fraser's 1820 *Map of the Himala Mountains,* showing the headwaters of the Jumna [Yamuna] and Bhagirathi rivers in Garhwal. The red numbers added indicate the locations for four of Fraser's plates from his *Views in the Himala Mountains.*

Fraser remarked that 'The village is poor and chiefly in ruins, but its situation is not unpleasant.' On 20 May the brothers reached Nowagarh Fort, situated on a high wooded peak at the head of the Giri valley. **Plate 2** presents the fine view of the Himalayan range obtained from there. They then crossed into the Sutlej valley, and after visiting Rampur moved north to Seran [Sarahan] on 16 June. The eight-year-old Rajah was in residence at his summer palace in Seran, shown in **Plate 1**. In the background there is a view possibly showing the north-west aspect of the Bandarpunch group of peaks.

Since William was then ordered to return, they set off for the upper Tons valley, once more crossing the head of the Giri. Near Urshalun, James climbed a nearby peak and sketched another fine view of the distant snowy ranges **(Plate 3)**. Descending to the Pabbar or Pabur river, the party made their way south passing the impregnable Fort of Raeengarh **(Plate 7)**. The road kept to the west side of the river, and where the Pabbar joined the Tons, a whole day was consumed in getting the company across the Tons to its east bank, one at a time. This perilous process is illustrated in **Plate 10**. Further south, near the village of Doongri, James and William parted company. William headed south to Dehra and James with his small company of 60 men crossed the watershed to the east where he sketched the upper Yamuna valley and Bandarpunch peaks, the subject of Plate 8 and then descended to the Yamuna.

The traverse of the Yamuna to its source was laborious and difficult, with frequent dangerous paths and bridges, but eventually James and a few companions reached the shrine of Yamunotri, where he made a magnificent sketch of the source with one of the Bandarpunch peaks in the background (**Plate 20**), probably Bandarpunch II known also as White Peak. After descending a little, he persuaded the party to make a high eastwards traverse across the lower slopes of the Bandarpunch group, in order to shorten the journey into the upper Bhagirathi valley. There were protests regarding 'poisoned air' from the men, but James insisted and they proceeded. The 'poisoned air' took its toll and progress was slow. They spent a night in a wet cave known as Bheem ke Udar, pictured in **Plate 7** but came down safely to Sookhi in the upper reaches of the Bhagirathi valley.

The party arrived at Byramghatee [Bhaironghati] on 19 July. James described the place:

> *A very singular and terrible place. The course of the river has continued foaming through its narrow rocky bed and the hills approach their heads, as though they could meet at a prodigious height above. At this point the Bhagiruttee is divided into two branches; that which preserves the name descends from the eastward, and the other, of a size fully equal, called the Jhannevie, joins it from the north-east. Both these rivers run in chasms, the depth, narrowness and rugged wildness of which it is impossible to describe.*

Fraser was able to do it justice, however, in a wonderful sketch that became **Plate 19**. A final short stage brought the party to Gangotri. James allowed himself a modest pat on the back:

> *We were now in the centre of the stupendous Himalas, the loftiest and perhaps the most rugged range of mountains in the world. We were at the source of that noble river, equally an object of veneration and a source of fertility, plenty and opulence to Hindustan; and we had now reached the holiest shrine of Hindoo worship which these holy hills contain.*

The final frontispiece, **Plate 11**, shows the small temple of Gangotri, built only a few years before by the Gorkhali general Amir Singh Thapa, a devout Hindu, with the mountains, which Fraser called 'Roodroo Himala' behind. That group of mountains around the Gangotri glacier constitute a modern Himalayan playground but to the Hindus they were the locks of Shiva from which the holy Ganges sprang.

Fraser's journeys were certainly remarkable for a European and it may be that he was the first such to reach the sources of the Yamuna and the Ganges. However, it should not be forgotten that these had been places of regular pilgrimage for Hindus for centuries beforehand. Fraser's main achievement was surely to bring European artistic sensibility and skill to bear on recording these beautiful valleys and peaks.

Until quite recently it was possible to wonder how much of the beauty of the plates in Fraser's *Views* was down to Fraser, and how much was down to the undoubted gifts of the printmakers Robert Havell & Son, since none of Fraser's original watercolour drawings from his Himalayan tour have survived. However, determined research by Mildred Archer and Toby Falk recently uncovered Fraser's original watercolours for a second publication of 24 plates: *Views of Calcutta and its Environs* (London, 1824-6).[4] These watercolours were discovered in the library at Longleat and were described in a long auction note by Christie's, which sold them for just under £250,000 on 13 June 2002.

It is plain that Fraser's Calcutta watercolours, painted around 1820, were superior to the published plates, and so there is no reason to suppose that his Himalayan watercolours were anything other than the authentic sources of Havell's plates in *Views*. His manner of painting is remarkably similar to some works of William Havell's and to many works of George Fennel Robson's. Discrete receding zones of lowered colour and tone are used to create strong perspective, accentuating impressions of distance and therefore height, and creating most attractive effects.

Fraser began his journey home in 1820, spending time in Persia and arriving in London in 1823, the year he married. In the mid 1830s he returned to Persia on behalf of the Foreign Office to report on Russian influence in the region. His last years were spent on improvements to his Scottish estate, where he died in 1856.

Fraser's life was an extraordinary succession of accomplishments, in India and in Persia, but none was more extraordinary than his achievement of mastery in watercolour painting, starting at the age of 31.

4. See M Archer and T Falk, *India Revealed: The Art and Adventures of James and William Fraser 1801-35* (Cassell, 1989), Archer & Falk, *The Passionate Quest: the Fraser Brothers in India* (Alfalak/Scorpion Publishing, 1989). T Falk, 'From Watercolour to Print. James Baillie Fraser and his Views of Calcutta', *Under the Indian Sun: British Landscape Artists,* eds P Rohatgi and P Godrej (Bombay, J J Bhabha for Marg Publications, 1995.)

History

Plate 9. *'Fort of Raeengurh'*

PETER FOSTER

Everest 1936

The Leadership Question Re-visited

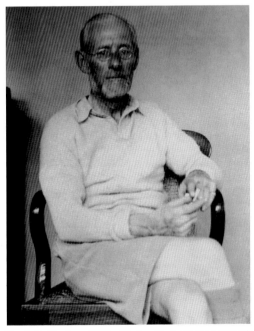

Hugh Ruttledge, 1936. *(Alpine Club Photo Library)*

The controversy surrounding who should lead the expedition to Everest in 1936 exposed deep divisions of opinion amongst those who cared and a bumbling Mount Everest Committee (MEC) responsible for the choice. Walt Unsworth, in his magisterial history of climbing on Everest, concluded that the re-appointment of Hugh Ruttledge as leader had been a 'sordid' business[1] and review of minute books and unpublished correspondence between some of the principal protagonists, on which this article is based, reveals new detail but does little to alter that view. The affair's significance was that it triggered an attempt to reform relations between the Alpine Club and the MEC and modernise the approach to climbing Everest. The disappointing outcome was that nothing really changed.

Ruttledge was 48 and recently retired from the Indian Civil Service when he led the 1933 expedition. A mountain traveller but with limited climbing experience, he had not been the first choice. The MEC's preference and

An expedition postcard of the 1922 Everest team including Colin Crawford, top left. *Back row from left to right:* C G Crawford, A W Wakefield, G L Mallory, T H Somervell, E F Norton, H T Morshead. Front row left to right: E L Strutt, C G Bruce, T G Longstaff, G I Finch. *(Alpine Club Photo Library)*

habit had been to despatch expeditions under military command but its favoured candidates, Brig Edward Norton and Maj Geoffrey Bruce, had been unavailable. But, despite the expedition's failure, the leadership of this unassuming and amiable man had, apparently, satisfied the committee which, in the expectation of another expedition in the following year, re-appointed him as leader:

> *Dr Longstaff's motion that Mr Hugh Ruttledge should be appointed Leader of the next expedition was seconded by Brigadier Norton and carried unanimously by the Committee.*[2]

Tom Longstaff was Ruttledge's friend – they had travelled together in the Himalaya – and his support was crucial, for he enjoyed considerable influence. His achievements as a mountain explorer – ranging across the Caucasus, the Himalaya, Tibet, the Canadian Rockies, Spitzbergen and Greenland, as well as accompanying the 1922 Everest expedition as medical officer – had gained him a deserved reputation and much respect. Small in stature, spare in frame, with a big red moustache and latterly a beard, he was never afraid to say what he thought. But Longstaff harboured misgivings concerning Ruttledge's leadership. He had heard mutterings of disquiet from members of the 1933 expedition: 'at least half-a-dozen of them said he had poor judgement.'[3] On learning that Ruttledge had been talking of dropping the likes of Jack Longland, Eric Shipton and Lawrence Wager, he grew indignant, for if there had been one success of the 1933 expedition

Tom Longstaff in 1947.
(Alpine Club Photo Library)

it was that there now existed a number of young men with experience
of climbing above the North Col
who could form the nucleus of any
future expedition, and he withdrew
his support.

In practice, the team for Everest in 1933 had been picked by the
MEC and Ruttledge left to manage
it. 'Very soon' he had realised 'the
party was not very well assorted'[4]
and set himself 'the task of trying to
run the party by persuasion rather
than ordinance.'[5] This experience of
expedition leadership led Ruttledge
to become 'absolutely convinced
that if you can get hold of a good
type of soldier who is a good mountaineer, you have the best material
for Everest,'[6] a telling but surprising conclusion given that the actions of two
soldiers, Capt E St J 'Bill' Birnie (Sam Browne's Cavalry) and Maj Hugh
Boustead (Sudan Camel Corps), had caused delay in establishing camp five
and arguably cost the success of the expedition. By contrast, 'the modern
British school of rock-climbers' did not 'provide the material we want for
Everest. Most of them are just gymnasts; bad travellers; a mutual admiration society, disliking outsiders and hating discipline'.[7] Longstaff, whose
instinct was to back youth and enterprise, was dismayed:

> *Things did not work out as I had hoped ... I told him frankly that I did not
> think he was playing the game, and I was sorry I was unable to support him
> any more on the MEC.*[8]

Ruttledge's letter tendering his resignation from the leadership was received and accepted by the MEC on 15 March 1934. According to the minutes of the meeting, 'the only reason' why the committee had accepted his
resignation was 'the doubt whether any expedition would be possible for
a number of years.' At the same meeting and at Longstaff's instigation,
the members of the committee[a] agreed to 'place themselves in the hands
of the bodies which had respectively nominated them and ... ask the RGS
and AC to reconstitute the committee by nominating three representatives
from each body.'[9] Longstaff, who had agitated consistently for the climbers

a. E H Bradby, Brig C G Bruce, Adm Sir W Goodenough and Sir F Younghusband.

Sir Percy Cox, c1930. *(RGS)*

having an increased say, wrote to Sir John Withers, president of the AC, expressing his view on the composition of the new MEC:

> *I think it is vital that AC committee should maintain control … As long as you put Crawford on the new committee the AC would be kept fully informed of the happenings – which is all I want to insure for the future.*[10]

Colin Crawford, 43, ex-Indian Civil Service, strongly built, enthusiastic and with a 'mischievous humour', had been a member of the expeditions to Everest in 1922 and 1933. On both occasions he had been slow to acclimatise but in 1933 had worked hard in support, making half a dozen trips to resupply camp four at 6,950m. Significantly, he was also one of the expedition's members whose criticisms of Ruttledge's leadership had reached Longstaff's ears.

The reconstituted MEC met on 23 May 1934. Representing the Royal Geographical Society were: Maj Gen Sir Percy Cox, soldier-diplomat and current president of the RGS, who was voted chairman, Lt Col Kenneth Mason, soldier, surveyor and recently appointed to the chair of geography at Oxford, and Lawrence Wager who, with Percy-Wyn Harris, had reached 8,595m on Everest the year before. The AC appointed: Lt Col Edward Strutt, who would assume the presidency of the Club at the end of the year, Ruttledge and Crawford. The first item on the agenda was to approve the minutes of the previous meeting, which none of the new committee had attended, and if they were read out rather than nodded through, some members were not paying attention: Cox would later complain to Longstaff that he had been unaware of Ruttledge's resignation from the leadership.[b]

Six months later, at the beginning of 1935, the MEC received news that the Tibetan government was likely to grant permission for an expedition in 1935 or 1936. A meeting was called at short notice and Crawford was unable to attend. Ruttledge spoke authoritatively and 'proposed that application should be made for both years; that a small expedition should go out in June … main expedition in 1936' and undertook to 'do his utmost in the next few days to make an estimate for an advance party in 1935.'[11]

b. Beneath Cox's signature approving the minutes, there is an exculpatory, pencilled addendum, initialled by him, which states: 'Sir PZC was not present at the meeting of 15/3/34 but signed at next meeting.'

Go fish. Colin Crawford, strongly built, enthusiastic and with a 'mischievous humour', with friend in India during the 1933 expedition. He would bear the brunt of the Mount Everest Committee's fury at moves against Ruttledge. (RGS)

There was no discussion about who would lead the expeditions and there appears to have been a tacit assumption it would be Ruttledge, his earlier resignation forgotten or ignored. Yet when the committee met on 31 January 1935 the issue of leadership dominated proceedings. Ruttledge, who must have had an inkling of what was afoot, absented himself.

Tom Brocklebank and Raymond Greene, both members of the 1933 expedition, had been invited to attend in order 'to assist the Committee in its deliberations on how the experience of 1933 and previous expeditions should suggest improvement in the organization of future expeditions'.[12] Brocklebank's selection for the expedition had resulted from a chance meeting with Longstaff at the Athenaeum, not the Alpine Club where such meetings might have been expected to occur, and exemplifies Longstaff's influence and the importance of the old-boy network. As Brocklebank later admitted, 'I was a complete amateur and chosen quite wrongly in every possible way.'[13] Greene, who had reached the summit of Kamet in 1931, had been selected as a climber and principal medical officer. Both men spoke with the same voice, Greene summing up the views of the younger members of the expedition:

> [Ruttledge] is too nice a man to be a good leader ... In the opinion of many members his leadership was weak.[14]

Longstaff, 'who had been expressing strong views on the question of the leadership of the expedition,' was also asked to attend the meeting because Cox considered it was 'only fair to the Committee that Dr Longstaff put these views before them, seeing that they differed materially from those which he had previously expressed as a member of the MEC.'[15] Longstaff reminded the committee that Ruttledge had relinquished the leadership nine months earlier and advised that his replacement should be chosen after consultation with the climbers: 'These are the people whose opinion ought to be known to this Committee if the ideal of a really homogenous party is to be attained.'[16] Nonplussed, the committee decided that: 'in view of the statements made that afternoon impugning the leadership of Mr Ruttledge it would be necessary for the Committee to give the matter urgent and anxious consideration [and] it was resolved that Mr Ruttledge should be informed of this without delay.'[17] Ruttledge withdrew from the leadership for a second time, observing resignedly to Sydney Spencer, honorary secretary of the MEC:

> *the young men … are the products of their time and, as you know, the young men of today are primarily critical. It is in his blood to criticize anyone of the War or pre-War period. I don't believe there is an atom of personal ill will in all this. But unfortunately since we came home there has been a lot of wild talking and that always breeds trouble.*[18]

Predictably, the MEC looked to the military for an alternative leader but Norton, Bruce and Maj Gen Roger Wilson were unavailable. Strutt and Mason turned to each other and neither was prepared to go. Longstaff was asked: 'what an astounding message I got on the phone – suggesting I [underlined] should lead the Everest show,' and responded by throwing his weight behind Crawford: 'that's who the climbers want. Not a military outsider.'[19] Although Crawford would later claim: 'I do not consider I should make a good leader of an Everest expedition,'[20] his view that neither would Ruttledge was not entirely disinterested. Remarkably, Ruttledge allowed himself to be persuaded to reconsider accepting the leadership and the scene was set for a contest between the two. The voting members of the committee split evenly: Strutt and Wager for Crawford; Cox and Mason for Ruttledge, who was appointed on Cox's casting vote. Unsurprisingly, Ruttledge wasted no time in informing Crawford that he should not expect an invitation to join the expedition.

Crawford reacted intemperately, accusing Ruttledge of 'personal ambition'[21] and disingenuousness: 'you snatched at the opportunity of slurring over your resignation,'[22] and his supporters waded in. 'Smythe showed me a letter from Longland, a most bitter one [and] I've had a horrid letter from Brocklebank too,' Ruttledge informed his ally, Mason, and 'Strutt tells me that TGL [Longstaff] continues his dementia, but it's not confined to TGL.' Furthermore, Ruttledge had 'evidence that Crawford is continuing his malignant activities'[23] and suspected that he had 'corrupted' Longstaff and poisoned their friendship. The usually equable Ruttledge had had enough:

> *I will not have my honour impeached by Crawford … Nothing can excuse his continued abuse and intrigue after the question of the leadership was decided. I will have nothing more to do with him.*[24]

He wrote to Cox 'asking that the Committee should tackle Crawford in the open' and to Strutt to 'change the representation of the Club', meaning

The 1933 Everest Expedition at Phari, Tibet. *Back row (L to R):* Smyth-Windham, Greene, Wood-Johnson, Brocklebank, British trade agent at Gyantse Capt A Russell, Shipton, McLean, Smythe, Thompson, Wyn-Harris. *Middle row:* Ruttledge, Shebbeare. *Front row:* Longland, Birnie, Wager, Crawford, Boustead. *(RGS)*

to replace Crawford.[25] Cox responded by politely inviting Crawford to resign from the MEC:

> *Having regard to the views which you hold as to the leadership and the personality of that leader, it seems to me as Chairman that you should not continue to be a Member of the Committee … I feel bound now to ask you to consider the propriety of resigning.[26]*

Crawford, unwilling to roll over sought support from the AC Committee and Strutt, now president of the Club, asked Cox to come before the committee to present his case.

Sir Percy Zachariah Cox, GCMG, GCIE & c, had spent almost 25 years as a resident or chief political officer in the Gulf region, his career culminating in his appointment, in 1920, as high commissioner to the newly formed state of Iraq, where he had played a principal role in forming the government and installing Feisal as king. Patient, courteous, inscrutable – it was said he could remain silent in a dozen languages – and with a 'Wellingtonian' presence, he had proved a formidable negotiator and administrator. An amateur ornithologist and keen horseman – he would die on the hunting field – he knew nothing of mountaineering. Mason considered him 'a good judge of men'; Longland described him as 'a deeply deceitful diplomatic old soldier.'[27]

Running on empty: Percy Wyn-Harris tests closed-circuit oxygen apparatus at Thangu (3692m) in Sikkim on the way to Everest in 1936. *(Alpine Club Photo Library)*

'Cox took rather a "pro-consular" attitude and was pretty direct,' recalled Mason, and 'would brook no interruption.'[28] After giving his version of the events leading to Ruttledge's appointment as leader, Cox addressed the issue of Crawford's resignation. Ignoring a protest concerning the propriety of reading extracts from private letters, he quoted from Crawford's letters to Ruttledge and concluded:

In my view, Gentlemen, no Chairman of any Committee with a policy to carry out and work to do could possibly tolerate the presence on his Committee of an individual who comported himself in this way.[29]

The AC Committee deliberated. Charles Meade, who had been a member of the original MEC in 1921 and was now vice-president of the Club, proposed the motion that Crawford resign his membership of the MEC with the significant proviso, 'on the understanding that the whole question of the relationship between the MEC and the AC Committee be reconsidered before any expedition subsequent to 1936 sets out.'[30] Tom Graham Brown seconded the motion, which was duly passed.

Almost immediately, Meade had second thoughts. Cox's account of Ruttledge's appointment had glossed over the disquiet expressed by members of the 1933 expedition. His use of extracts and unwillingness to produce full letters hinted there had been something to hide. Meade suspected that the AC Committee, some of whom were 'still breathless from the glamour of his [Cox's] visitation,'[31] had been duped. With Graham Brown's agreement, he advised Crawford to defer his resignation but a week later Cox sacked Crawford, turning disquiet and suspicion into a furore. 'It is an incredible gangster melodrama. As far as I can make out the plot is to save the face of the Mt. Everest committee by blackening Crawford's,'[32] wrote Longstaff. Meade, now convinced that Cox had 'behaved like a shit,'[33] sought the AC Committee's endorsement of his action in advising Crawford not to resign, arguing that Cox had treated Crawford with 'discourtesy and unfairness', and that reading extracts from private letters in support of a charge was 'a dubious expedient'.[34] Defeated in a vote, Meade resigned from the Committee, together with Graham Brown, Crawford and Longland. Crawford who felt he had been hung out to dry made a final and pathetic statement:

> I have been impugned ... When a man is attacked by powerful and unscrupulous forces if those in a position to protest do not do so, they cannot avoid responsibility. It seems then, I can in no circumstances have any redress. Can you therefore criticize me, gentlemen, because as a last protest, I have resigned this Committee? [35]

But it did not quite end there. Graham Brown with characteristic tenacity requested a legal opinion of Cox's action from the master of the rolls, Lord Wright,[c] who declined to comment: one trusts he had more important matters to consider. Longstaff continued his plotting by recruiting to the cause George Finch, who had had his own disputes with the MEC.[d] At the Club's AGM on 9 December 1935 Longstaff drew Finch aside, showed him the list of likely candidates for the planned expedition, and asked for his opinion. Finch responded:

> I told Longstaff that I considered the relative climbing strength too low, that I was fed up with such evident mismanagement and that I would give notice of a motion of no confidence in the Everest Committee.[36]

But it was too late to change the team for Everest. On 1 February 1936, Ruttledge and the advance party set sail for India. However, the goal of enhancing the Alpine Club's role in the conduct of any future attempts on Everest, should they be required, remained.

Finch put down a motion, which, if approved, would have transferred influence from the Club's Committee to the membership. Strutt tried to dissuade him but, as Finch recalled, 'if anything had been wanting to spur me on, Strutt's implied challenge "there's no chance of your motion being adopted" was irresistible.'[37] Introducing the motion, he pointed out that the ascent of Everest was now predominantly a matter for mountaineers and argued that the responsibility for organising future expeditions should lie with a committee of experts in mountaineering, as opposed to explorers and scientists. And 'since mountain climbing is peculiarly the business of the Club these experts should be representatives chosen by this Club.'[38] Scott Russell, who was present, explained what happened next.

> Colonel Strutt, the president, was in the chair. Giving no opportunity for anyone else to speak, he said that George's motion would have the useful effect he had

---

c. Robert Wright (1869-1964). Elected in 1910, he was also a member of the Alpine Club. In 1945 he was appointed chairman of the United Nations War Crimes Commission which collected the material for the charges at the Nuremberg trials.

d. Excluded at the last minute from the 1921 expedition on the basis of a sloppy and possibly tendentious medical report, Finch reached 8320m on Everest the following year but was not invited on the 1924 expedition.

suggested, and then went further. He assured the Club that its committee would examine the organization of future expeditions and report back to the Club. That was exactly what the critics of the old Everest Committee had wished for years ... the discussion ended with speed and apparent harmony.[39]

Longstaff, who must have thought he had finally won the argument, wrote delightedly to Finch:

> *I must write a line of congratulation to you for the magnificent way in which you carried through a very difficult part on Tuesday ... it will not be possible with impunity to bluff the Club again.'*[40]

A lull followed, but once news of the failure of the 1936 expedition reached England the campaign to change the MEC's approach went public. Meade attacked first, writing to *The Times* on 19 June to argue in favour of a smaller expedition: 'the perfect model for Everest expeditions is not far to seek, for it is to be found in Mr Shipton's reconnaissance expedition of 1935.' Longstaff followed up with a letter making the same points. In October, commenting on the attempts on Everest in an interview to the *Morning Post,* Finch famously said, 'we are beginning to look ridiculous.' A few weeks later, Graham Brown, fresh from the comparatively small and successful expedition to Nanda Devi, added his criticism in an article for *The Times:*

> *These extravagant and formal affairs, with their publicity, their cohorts of trained porters, their armies of coolies, their squadrons of yaks, and their small achievement have caused most of us to wonder what mountaineering is coming to and whether failure may not be inherent in the method.*[41]

As he had promised, Strutt convened a special committee to advise how the AC should bring its influence to bear on the MEC. The great and good were represented by: Sir Claud Schuster, a quintessential civil servant[e], who would succeed Strutt in the presidency; Sir Leonard Pearce, eminent electrical engineer who had designed and overseen the construction of Battersea power station; and Brig Edward Norton. Longstaff and Meade spoke for the modernisers and were 'surprised' by their co-members' 'friendly' response to their views. Meade reported to Graham Brown with satisfaction:

> *Findings were unanimous ... AC representatives to be elected to the Everest Committee in similar fashion to the members of the AC Committee and to be representatives not mere nominees ... It is suggested with the consent of the RGS, the Chairman of the Everest Committee should be an experienced mountaineer. Small expedition was also recommended.'*[42]

---

e. The title of Schuster's biography, 'Yes, Chancellor', is a nod to the popular 1980s television series, 'Yes, Minister,' in which the cynical permanent secretary, Sir Humphrey Appleby, ran rings around his political master.

The revamped MEC retained a familiar look, however, comprising the stalwarts, the brigadiers Bruce and Norton, Longstaff, who had been re-called, Mason and James Wordie, more an Arctic explorer than moun-taineer who had joined the committee *vice* Wager, and Wager himself, now returned from his year-long expedition to Greenland. Greene was the only newcomer. All were members of the AC. This committee oversaw the or-ganisation of the 1938 expedition under Tilman's leadership, undeniably smaller and cheaper – to the point of frugality, some said – than its prede-cessors and also unsuccessful.

After the Second World War, the MEC was reconstituted as the Joint Himalayan Committee and reverted to its old structure: the presidents and secretaries of the AC and RGS, *ex officio,* two members each from the AC and RGS, plus a representative of the Himalayan Club, with the result that the committee was populated by men of distinction but whose man man-agement skills would be found wanting. In 1952 the committee comprised: Claude Elliott, chairman, president of the AC and provost of Eton, whose climbing days were long past; Wordie, now president of the RGS; Law-rence Kirwan, director and secretary of the RGS, who was not a moun-taineer, his main interest being the archaeology of the Sudan; Sir Clare-mont Skrine, also a non-mountaineer, ex-British consul in Kashgar who had travelled widely in Central Asia; George Lowndes, a former colonel in the Garhwal Rifles and more a plant-hunter than a mountaineer; Harry Tobin, 'elder statesmen' of Himalayan travel and at 73 the oldest member; Wager, now professor of geology at Oxford; Peter Lloyd, who in 1938 had reached 8,230m on Everest using supplementary oxygen; and Basil Goodfellow, sen-ior executive of ICI, a competent alpinist and honorary secretary of the AC. It was, as Unsworth observed, 'the final flowering of the Old Guard.'[43] When the committee was faced with sacking Eric Shipton as leader of the 1953 expedition and replacing him with John Hunt, unseemly wrangling and vacillation characterised its actions, as Kirwan recalled: 'if ever there was a case of the right thing done in the wrong way it was this.'[44]

Plus ça change.

Acknowledgements
I thank the National Library of Scotland and the Royal Geographical So-ciety (with IBG) for permission to reproduce quotations from unpublished material in their possession.

Endnotes
1. W Unsworth, *Everest: The Mountaineering History,* London, 2000, p191.
2. Minute book 1923-35, Royal Geographical Society/EE/98/3.
3. RGS, EE/44/7/2.
4. Ruttledge to Spencer 27 Feb 1935, British Library, Add ms 63120
5. Ruttledge to Crawford 5 Mar 1935 (copy); National Library of Scotland acc 4338/5.
6. Ruttledge to Mason 26 Aug 1935, RGS/EE/45.
7. Ruttledge to Mason, 12 Aug 1935, RGS/EE/45
8. RGS/EE/47/7/2.
9. Minute book 1923-35, RGS/EE/98/3.
10. Longstaff to Withers 22 Mar 1934, BL/Add ms 63120.
11. Minute book 1923-35; RGS/EE/98/3.
12. Minute book 1935-39 RGS: EE/99/1.

13. Quoted in P Steele, *Eric Shipton: Everest and Beyond,* London, 1998, p43.
14. RGS/EE/44/7/2.
15. Minute book 1935-39 RGS/EE/99/1
16. RGS/EE/44/7/2
17. Minute book 1935-39 RGS/EE/99/1.
18. Ruttledge to Spencer 27 Feb 1935; BL/Add ms 63120.
19. Longstaff to Spencer 28 Mar 1935; BL/Add ms 63120.
20. Crawford to Graham Brown 18 Oct 1935; NLS acc 4338/5.
21. Crawford to Ruttledge 2 May 1935 (copy); NLS acc 4338/5.
22. Crawford to Ruttledge 21 May 1935 (copy); NLS acc 4338/5.
23. Ruttledge to Mason 19 Aug 1935 & 14 Sep 1935; RGS/EE/45.
24. Ruttledge to Spencer 28 May 1935, BL/Add ms 63120.
25. Ibid.
26. Cox to Crawford 29 Sep 1935 (copy); NLS acc 4338/5.
27. P Steele, *op cit,* p63.
28. Mason to Tyndale 5 Feb 1945, NLS acc 4338/215.
29. NLS acc 4338/204.
30. AC archives 1922/E4.
31. Meade to Graham Brown 30 Oct 1935; NLS acc 4338/5.
32. Longstaff to Graham Brown 3 Nov 1935; NLS acc 4338/5.
33. Meade to Graham Brown 29 Oct 1935; NLS acc 4338/5.
34. NLS acc 4338/5.
35. BL/Add ms 63120.
36. Finch to Meade 8 Jan 1936 (copy); NLS acc 4338/6.
37. Ibid.
38. Quoted in S Russell, *George Ingle Finch, The Mountaineer: A Memoir,* London, 1988, p89.
39. Ibid.
40. Ibid p90.
41. *The Times* 27 Nov 1936
42. Meade to Graham Brown 8 Feb 1937; NLS acc 4338/7.
43. W Unsworth, op cit, p296.
44. P Steele, *op cit,* p199.

DENNIS GRAY

Marco Pallis and
the Round of Existence

Marco Pallis on the 1933 Gangotri Expedition. *(Alpine Club Photo Library)*

'Poor is the pupil who does not surpass his master.' Leonardo Da Vinci

Recently I re-read two books from my earliest climbing days, *Helvellyn to Himalaya* (1940) and *Let's Go Climbing* (1941), the first by Freddy Spencer Chapman and the second by Colin Kirkus. Within their pages is the story of how both made it to the Himalaya through the inspiration and organising abilities of Marco Pallis: Kirkus in 1933, and Chapman in 1936. The climbs they made on these expeditions were amongst the most important ascents by British climbers in that decade. Intrigued, I began researching Marco Pallis and then contacting a wide range of individuals with specialist knowledge about his life.

Marco Pallis was born in Toxteth Park, Liverpool on 19 June 1895 into a wealthy Anglo-Greek family. His father Alexander was at that time head of the city's Ralli Brothers trading house, whose operations stretched from American cotton to Indian spices and jute, as well as banking. Alexander had married Julia-Eliza Ralli, daughter of one of the principals, on New Year's Eve 1881. Alexander was also one of the foremost Greek scholars

Marco Pallis in his Grenadier Guards uniform. He was wounded at Cambrai in 1918. *(Family of Marco Pallis)*

of his era, editing *Antigone* and translating *The Iliad:* he was a strong advocate for ordinary Greeks having access to their great literature. Pallis also translated *The New Testament* into Modern Greek for the Oxford University Press, which caused deadly riots in Athens in 1901 when the Greek Orthodox Church banned it.

I suppose it's rare for such a scholar to be a successful businessman, but Alexander eventually became one of the richest men in Liverpool; these were impressive achievements for someone who abandoned his studies in Athens in 1869 to travel to England and seek his fortune. In Manchester he got a job with Ralli Brothers, always supportive of the Greek diaspora, and from there he moved to Bombay in 1875 before finally settling in Liverpool in 1894 to become a British subject. Whilst in Bombay he wrote a book of poetry, *Little Songs for Children,* which was popular in the Victorian era.

Marco was the youngest of five children, three boys and two girls, and after schools in Liverpool he spent two years at Harrow, where he sought extra religious instruction from the chaplain. Back in Liverpool a growing interest in Roman Catholicism was soon curtailed by his mother, who made Greek Orthodox attitudes to apostasy quite plain to the local priest: 'If my son becomes a Roman Catholic there will be no money.' At 16 years of age he journeyed to British Guyana to study insects and flora, and the following year joined the Greek campaign against the invading Ottoman armies. During the siege of Ioannina, ancestral home of the Pallis family, he worked at a field hospital in Arta, all part of the First Balkan War. Returning to the UK he enrolled at Liverpool University to study zoology, but after the first year switched to entomology. Having reached physical maturity, he was 5ft 8in with dark hair, rugged features and a lithe physique.

The First World War then intervened and he volunteered with the Red Cross to work in Serbia, then becoming a translator for the British army in Macedonia. This ended badly, with Pallis developing malaria and a serious eye infection and he was evacuated to a hospital on Malta. At Christmas 1916 he was sent home and worked for a short while for the government censors. But the work frustrated him and having made friends in the Grenadier Guards he applied for a commission, specialising as a machine gunner. He endured some terrible experiences in the trenches before his war

Marco Pallis with his viola da gamba.
(Family of Marco Pallis)

ended at Cambrai in 1918. During an assault on enemy lines, both his captain and lieutenant were killed and he found himself in charge as the senior surviving officer until he was also shot, and badly, through a knee. Returning to England for convalescence and rehabilitation, he was warned not to try anything too physically challenging. One doctor warned him he might never walk properly again. Any anxiety must have been allayed somewhat by the £50,000 he inherited on his 21st birthday.

Free to do as he pleased, this period marked the start of his climbing life, sparked by the deepening of another lifelong passion as musician and composer. Pallis had studied music as a boy and by 1920 was at Haslemere studying under Dr Arnold Dolmetsch. Thanks to his influence, Pallis discovered a love of early chamber music from the 16th and 17th centuries and for playing the viola da gamba. Dolmetsch was French and besides being a major influence in re-awakening interest in early music, was also a skilled craftsman making replicas of viols, recorders and harpsichords. Pallis was so impressed by this ability, that he provided money in 1921 to build Dolmetsch a new workshop.

Two other events at Haslemere had a major influence on Marco. One was meeting his life partner, a brilliant harpsichordist and composer Richard Nicholson, ten years his junior and son of C E Nicholson, the celebrated yacht designer. Pallis also had a chance meeting with the brother of one of the other students who was a climber. He persuaded both Pallis and Nicholson to go climbing with him and they both became hooked on the sport.

He arrived back in Liverpool as the climbing scene there moved into a golden age. Just as at the end of the 1940s, the recovery of the sport from the losses of the First World War led in the late 1920s to new leaders bolstered by advances in technique and equipment. Pallis joined Liverpool's Wayfarers' Club in 1925 and over the next few years shared a rope with some of the most outstanding climbers of that era: Menlove Edwards, Ted Hicks, Jake Cooke, A B Hargreaves, Ivan Waller and Colin Kirkus.

In 1929, with A B Hargreaves, he and Nicholson made the third ascent of *Longland's* on Clogwyn du'r Arddu, and he seconded Kirkus on the first ascent of *Birthday Crack* on that same cliff. He and Ivan Waller also supported Colin in pioneering the first ascent of *Mickledore Grooves* on Scafell's east buttress in 1931. Bill Stallybrass and Marco seconded Menlove Edwards on the first free ascent of the *Central Buttress* on Scafell. These were hyperactive years for Pallis and Nicholson, attending Wayfarers' meets in the Lake District, the Peak, Snowdonia, and the Scottish Highlands. They also made trips to the Arctic, the Dolomites and the Alps, one of their first visits being to Saas Fee in 1926, when the highlight was a traverse of the Mischabel. Kirkus' first Alpine season was with Pallis and Bob Frost, whose immense potential, accepted by all who knew him, ended in his tragically early death in a motorcycle accident.

The Alps summoned them every year but wherever Pallis and Nicholson travelled to there was always music. Ted Hicks was a fine singer and others from the Wayfarers' would join in. Pallis was also a keen innovator of equipment and liked testing his ideas in extreme conditions. In the winter of 1929 he and Kirkus bivvied on the summit of Snowdon in -16°C to test his new sleeping bag design. Marco reported that, 'Colin slept so soundly, I feared he must be dead.' A short while later he and Nicholson repeated the exercise on the summit of Ben Nevis but Pallis found this outing far less comfortable than the Snowdonia adventure. He put down his ideas about equipment development in an article for the 1933 *Wayfarers' Journal* entitled 'Bivouacs', suggesting ways to improve lightweight gear for camping: tents, sleeping bags, and the design of mountaineering boots. He even suggested a collapsible pee bottle for personal emergencies. He was obviously thinking of the Himalaya and an expedition he was shortly to lead.

Pallis was elected a vice president of the Wayfarers' in 1931 and two years later its president. There is an amusing published note by one of his fellow club officers about meetings at Pallis' parents' house Tatoi. They lived in grand style and by order of Marco's mother his 'scruffy' climbing friends could only meet in their basement, where Marco had set himself up after the war. (His mother would complain: *'Pierre et Paul,* my dear,' meaning 'Every Tom, Dick and Harry.') Yet Marco still showed his progressive side, suggesting that the climbing clubs should meet together and produce a scheme to help poorer young climbers visit the Alps. He also noted, unlike some other well-known mountaineering commentators of the 1930s, his admiration for leading Continental alpinists and the way they trained physically and mentally for major climbs.

In 1932 he had a successful Alpine season in the Valais with Ted Hicks and Nicholson, climbing amongst other peaks the Alphubel, the Dom and the Täschorn. Some alpinists of that era remarked how Pallis' times on his ascents were slow but for a man who a decade earlier was told he might never walk again, his climbs were remarkable, and he would prove so again in the coming years in the Himalaya. Freddy Spencer Chapman, among the most decorated soldiers in the Second World War, noted how 'Pallis hides a good deal of determination behind his mild manner.' And despite being a 'steady as you go mountaineer', he was elected to the Alpine Club shortly afterwards.

The 1933 Gangotri expedition on the SS Custodian in Liverpool, at the start of the expedition. From left to right: Richard Nicholson, Marco Pallis, Ted Hicks, Charles Warren, and Colin Kirkus. *(Alpine Club Photo Library)*

Pallis organised and led the 1933 Wayfarers' Gangotri Expedition, comprising Colin Kirkus, Dr Charles Warren, Richard Nicholson and Ted Hicks, one of the happiest and most successful of its time, enlivened by Pallis and Nicholson playing their viols in the evenings to the amazement and delight of villagers and porters as they progressed to base camp on the Gangotri glacier. Different partnerships climbed several peaks but the standout climb was the first ascent of Bhagirathi III (6454m) via its south ridge by Kirkus and Warren. This entailed some high-altitude rock climbing, led by Kirkus, at a standard hardly achieved in the Himalaya before then.

With the first half of the expedition completed, Hicks and Kirkus returned to work and with the arrival of the monsoon Nicholson, Warren and Pallis trekked north towards the Tibetan border to avoid its affects. There they settled on a peak Pallis called Riwo Pargyul North (6791m), successfully climbed by Warren and Pallis. *(Editor's note:* this massif, comprising three peaks, including the highest in Himachal Pradesh at 6,816m is most commonly referred to as Reo Purgyil, sometimes Leo Pargial, and many variations of those names. See *Himalayan Journal* 48 for more detail on its confusing nomenclature, a consequence of colonial surveying.) It was this journey to the border and meeting with Tibetans that awakened Marco's interest in that country, its peoples and Tibetan Buddhism. It should be noted that all the climbs on the 1933 Expedition were achieved without porter support, a source of pride to all those who took part.

The Wayfarers' held a meet each Easter in Fort William, with winter climbing on Ben Nevis its raison d'être. Many 'irregulars' joined in, including Jack Longland, Graham MacPhee, compiler of the first climbing guide to the mountain, and in 1934 Maurice Linnell. Climbing with Colin Kirkus, the pair set off up The Castle on Carn Dearg, which I know from an ascent I made in 1953 as a teenager is a notorious avalanche trap, especially after heavy snowfall. Maurice and Colin were victims of such conditions, resulting in a serious accident in which Linnell was killed and Kirkus badly injured. One can never know what might have been, but both men were amongst the most outstanding climbers of their era and though Kirkus survived, the accident marked the end of his bold pioneering. After a long period of recovery he returned to climbing but his desire for new routing was sated. It must have been traumatic for Pallis as the Wayfarers' president but his kindly and caring nature was much to the fore and appreciated.

In 1936 Pallis organised another Himalayan expedition, this time to Sikkim and the Kangchenjunga area with Simvu (6811m) as the main objective but other nearby mountains as possibilities. The party included Jake Cooke, of *Main Wall* on Cyrn Las fame, Freddy Spencer Chapman, Dr Robert Roaf, later one of the world's leading spinal surgeons, and Richard Nicholson. *(Editor's note:* See Roaf's article 'Sikkim, 1936', *Alpine Journal* 2001.) Simvu turned out to be a much harder mountain than expected and they were challenged high on the peak by a difficult pitch. Chapman described it as a vertical corner, which once negotiated was blocked by a 20ft section of extremely steep ice. Pallis led this with a lot of difficulty, cutting handholds and footholds in the ice. Chapman confessed, 'I would not have liked it much without the support of a rope!' With that climbed, and having gained an easy ridge, Nicholson, Cooke, Pallis and Chapman were convinced they had the main difficulties behind them and the summit in view. But they were stopped on easy ground by a huge crevasse and as they searched for a way to cross this, it started to snow and then blizzard. Descending through this was a trial and with no let up in the adverse conditions they had to abandon Simvu.

Pallis had expected to visit Tibet on this expedition but Frederick Williamson, the political officer who had granted permission, had died unexpectedly and his replacement Basil Gould was negotiating his own access to Lhasa. Pallis had his application rejected and so he, Nicholson and Roaf travelled west and then trekked north over high passes into Ladakh. Cooke, Chapman and Jock Harrison, who had by good fortune joined up with the other two when his own companion had retreated out of the mountains due to illness, made ascents of the technically straightforward Sphinx Peak (6970m) before finishing with the more difficult Fluted Peak (6085m). When Chapman returned from the mountains, he was invited by Basil Gould to join his mission to Lhasa as his secretary.

Ladakh was everything that Pallis had dreamed of, with its monasteries, its lamas, and its ethnically Tibetan peoples. Both he and Nicholson converted to Buddhism. Pallis explained this spiritual journey in a book that has become a classic of its genre, *Peaks and Lamas,* first published in 1939. It influenced people far beyond the mountain world, everyone from Gary Snyder, Philip Glass and

Colin Kirkus at camp two on Bhagirathi III, looking towards Kedarnath summit, 1933 Gangotri Expedition. *(Alpine Club Photo Library)*

Allen Ginsberg. While it tells the story of the two climbing expeditions, and contains some lucid and sensitive travel writing, underpinning this narrative is an explanation of Tibetan Buddhism's history, precepts and practice. It can be a difficult read, with abstract doctrines that for many are difficult to grasp, but the American writer Wendell Berry wrote after reading it that 'I find no other writer on Buddhism surpassing him.' I counted ten editions published so far of *Peaks and Lamas,* and Pallis is certainly among those who introduced Tibetan Buddhism to many in the West.

In 1938 Pallis visited the Alps again, climbing a host of peaks with Jake Cooke including the Obergabelhorn, Wellenkuppe and the Breithorn. But the darkening storm of war caught up with such idyllic outings. Cooke would perish a short while later at Dunkirk. Pallis retreated to Liverpool and at the start of the war worked at the Citizen's Advice Bureau by day and in the evenings took on the duties of a special constable, working during the massive air raids on the city. After his mother's death in 1940, he sold Tatoi, which had been in the family for 46 years, and bought a house in Knightsbridge on Egerton Terrace. Although he was older than the age of conscription, he was nevertheless called to appear before a tribunal for conscientious objectors in Liverpool's St George's Hall on 1 October 1943. His objection to military service was upheld on the basis of his Buddhist beliefs.

Charles Warren's photograph of two climbers, unidentified, crossing a glacier in the Garhwal in 1933. *(Alpine Club Photo Library)*

In 1947 he and Nicholson were at last able to visit Tibet where they travelled widely around the Tsang region. At Shigatse they were 'ordained' in a ceremony at the Tashilhunpo monastery, the seat of the Panchen Lama and one of the major sites of the Geluk sect (there being three others, all older: Nyingma, Kagyu and Sakya). Both he and Nicholson liked their Tibetan names, Pallis being known as Thubden Tendzin. By that date he was fluent in the language, writing a short book in Tibetan to warn of the dangers as well as the opportunities of modern 'civilisation' and how it posed a threat to a society he found spiritual, traditional and serene. He and Nicholson then retreated to Kalimpong where they lived for nearly four years. Marco would astonish visitors to their bungalow by playing on the harpsichord he'd acquired. The town was a centre of literary and cultural activities and later a refuge for many of those forced to leave Tibet after China's occupation. Pallis would later become active in the Tibet Society, the first support group to aid the Tibetan people, created in 1959, the year the Dalai Lama fled into exile.

Returning to Britain in 1951, Pallis picked up his previous life as a musician, re-establishing his ensemble, the English Consort of Viols, that he'd first formed in the 1930s. They toured widely in the UK and USA: the *New York Times* described a sell-out concert in the city as 'a solid musical delight'. The English Consort released three records, of which *Music of the English Home* is accepted as a classic of early music. By the mid 1950s he was teaching at the Royal Academy of Music and was given an honorary fellowship in recognition of his work. He also developed as a composer. His 'String Quartet in F#' was performed by the Salomon Quartet at the Queen Elizabeth Hall in London.

Pallis kept to his Buddhist beliefs, writing two further books around that subject: *The Way and the Mountain* was published in 1960; *Buddhist Spectrum* appeared in 1980. He was acknowledged as a major contributor to perennial philosophy, which believed that all religions shared core truths. He became a frequent contributor to the academic journal *Studies in Comparative Religion,* which carried articles from prominent perennialists like Frithjof Schuon and Aldous Huxley. Pallis also translated several works by fellow perennial writers from French into English.

As he moved deep into old age he continued to write and compose. At the age of 89 his 'Nocturne de l'Ephémère', the Mayfly's Evensong, was performed at the Queen Elizabeth Hall. The audience insisted the composer should appear at the end of the concert on stage, and he received a rousing reception, which he accepted with the same affable modesty that characterised his life. For many years he also worked on an opera based on the life of Milarepa, the celebrated Tibetan poet and saint, composing music, writing the libretti and designing the costumes. It remains almost finished and only requires a talented composer to complete the task and do it justice. Perhaps someone will take this on.

Pallis died in 1989 aged 93. Among those paying tribute was Charles Warren, doctor on the 1936 and 1938 Everest expeditions and a member of Marco's 1933 Gangotri trip. It read: 'Marco Pallis! A household name amongst most mountaineers of my generation, a very gentle, gifted and most lovable man.' To those readers who have never been on a climbing expedition, particularly one like the 1933 Gangotri trip that lasted for half a year, you would be hard pressed to find anyone as willing to pay such a heartfelt tribute to his leader.

ERIC VOLA

'Vote Livanos'

The Life and Times of a Marseille Legend

Georges 'Le Grec' Livanos, after a cold, wet bivouac in the Dolomites.

I was 18 years old when I met Georges 'Le Grec' Livanos in the Calanques. In many ways he became my master and my mentor. I was absolutely a fan, and not just of Le Grec but also of Sonia, his wife and climbing partner. He honoured me with his friendship and we remained close until his death in 2004. Every time I had the chance to go back to the Calanques, I would climb with him and his group of friends, sometimes participating in one of his many first ascents. He was a happy man who shared his joie de vivre with everyone who came near him. But I hesitated for a long time, almost three years, before accepting this invitation to write about him in English. How could I do him justice? How could I make a British climbing audience appreciate his unique appeal when almost all are unaware of Le Grec and his deeds? Then I thought of Don Whillans and something Doug Scott said at the funeral of Jean Afanassieff, or 'Afa' as he was known.

Climbing with his parents in Chamonix.

In the course of climbing with English climbers such as Roger Baxter-Jones, Brian Hall, Alan Rouse and Andy Parkin, [Afa] did a lot for the entente cordiale. He joined our Karakoram expedition of 1983 of which he was a very popular member, even with Don Whillans who wasn't that keen on foreigners and affectionately called Jean 'Have-a-sniff'. Jean called Don 'un rosbif'.

In defence of Afa, it was I who taught him *rosbif,* when he was 17 and living in Paris. He knew both Don and Le Grec, and so I imagined him introducing Le Grec to Don. Just as they both liked Afa, I know that Don and Georges would have enjoyed each other's company. Both men were larger than life. Le Grec liked to quote Sir Francis Younghusband on the schoolmaster Bentley Beetham, from *The Epic of Mount Everest:* 'The kind of man that nothing less than a ton of bricks could keep down: nineteen hundredweight would have been of no use.' Both of them were like that. Both had an instinct for quick repartee. Le Grec had a knack for aphorisms: 'Big adventures make short careers,' he suggested, and 'There's no such thing as bad rock, just bad climbers.'

When he first met Lucien Devies, that titan of the French mountaineering establishment, someone introduced Le Grec as 'the best Calanques climber'. Le Grec stepped forward, hand outstretched: 'The best,' he said, 'and the most modest.' Such humour might have been wasted on Devies. As he used to say himself: 'If you want to make it funny, talk to someone else.' On the other hand, they became good friends, sharing a correspondence for over 40 years. In 1972 Le Grec was writing to Devies about his attempt, in his fiftieth year, on a new route on the west face of the Moiazza, close to the Civetta, with a gang of young Italians, 'fans' he called them, from Agordo. He told Devies:

Three long days of preparation and the attempt was stopped by two of my three companions' tiredness. The last one, the young guide Gianni Costantini, was up for it, but we could not abandon the two others. Seven 40m abseils … and basta. We had climbed ten pitches. After that? Bad weather, bad weather, a female friend killed in a car crash, my holiday finished, I went back home. We will climb the pillar next year. On 21 August Gianni Costantini was killed in the mountains. So what next? What next? [It's my] target for 1973! I will avenge Gianni. This 'old bloke' will return to battle (I had an immense liking of Gianni) to avenge his young friend, to avenge himself, for he is the Greek …

He was as good as his word. The following year he was writing again to Devies, then in his last year editing *La Montagne et Alpinisme,* house magazine of the GHM and the French Alpine Club. Le Grec told Devies that he had completed the line, 'a beautiful, unbelievably beautiful route and even more, it is one of the "moments" of my life.' It was, he told Devies, his 53rd new route in the Alps. 'What a present for my 50th birthday!' The summit they reached had never been climbed before. 'Now it is the *Punta Constantini:* 650m, ED, 90 pegs, two bivouacs and 12 abseils to come down.' He had almost burst with joy, he told Devies, but

> ... *a deep joy which brought peace to me, which I offered to Gianni and to Germana, his wonderful spouse; this route, she wanted it as much as I did. She came to Vazzoler, the day before, with her little Michele (15 months old), she wanted to be there, to participate, encourage me maybe. Encourage me? An SS division would not have stopped me! I lived one full year solely waiting for that moment, that summit day.*

Both Le Grec and Don Whillans were true greats with respect for other climbers from new as well as older generations. If there is a climbers' paradise it may well be that they are having a battle of wits to the benefit of all present, because as everyone knows there is no language barrier in heaven. There will be others gathered round. Many of the great names of alpinism tied onto a rope with Le Grec, particularly when they came to the Calanques: Jean Franco, Maurice Herzog, Lionel Terray, Gaston Rébuffat, Jean Couzy, Michel Vaucher, Claudio Barbier, not to mention his Italian friends, Gino Soldà, Armando da Roit, Beppi de Franchesch, Marcello Bonafede, Ménégus, Stenico and many others. Not that he was overawed by another's reputation. Far from it. In a freewheeling interview from 1984 with Bernard Amy and Pascal Sombardier for *Montagnes* magazine, Le Grec was asked about that other great alpinist from Marseille, Gaston Rébuffat.

> *Ah, him, he did well. He never did anything exceptional, but he was a very complete chap: not brilliant, but safe. I liked climbing with him for that reason. With him, we were 100% sure to get to the top. As the guys climbing with me knew ... well, a 98% chance. There were more brilliant guys with whom I'd never have teamed up.*

Where did he get this confidence? Maybe it was the city that nurtured him. Born in 1923 to a Greek father and a Greek grandfather, Le Grec was one hundred per cent Marseille, a city like no other in France, full of swagger and historically diverse. A third of its inhabitants are of Italian descent, alongside Corsicans, Greeks, Armenians and more recent arrivals from the Maghreb. Le Grec loved to play his own part in the city's legend, one of colour and humour at its best.

He was the only child of loving parents. His father, Ulysse, a coffee broker, regularly took his wife, Marguerite, and their son Georges to the mountains,

Demonstrating the *Grande Arête*
at Les Gaillands for Armand Charlet
during the Fête des Guides in 1938.

staying in hotels in Chamonix, in Ailefroide or in La Chapelle-en-Val-gaudemar. So Le Grec did not start climbing in the Calanques but in the Alps and specifically the Mont Blanc range. At age 13, Georges climbed his first summit, the Aiguille du Tour, with his parents and the guide Alfred Burnet. In the following two summers, his father hired Ulysse Simond to guide Georges on classic easy routes. Georges was talented enough as a rock climber to be selected by Armand Charlet during the Fête des Guides in 1938 to demonstrate how to climb the *Grande Arête* on the Gaillands crag. He was then 15 years old.

Back in Marseille, climbing now obsessed him. His parents made sure Georges joined the CAF in 1939. If the boy were determined to climb, it would be in the company of known personalities and alpinists they had met and climbed with in Chamonix: the Marquise d'Albertas and Jean Save de Beaureceuil, both members of the GHM. His parents asked them not to let him take the lead but it wasn't long before Le Grec would disobey his father, as he wrote in his memoir *Au-delà de la Verticale:*

> … *one day, our leader failed on a pitch because of a bruised wrist; he came down and asked me to go and fetch the peg he had left. Reaching the peg, I saw above me beautiful grey slabs… too tempting. Madame d'Albertas saw what I was up to only as I finished the pitch. She was a little worried, not that much though, as in the 'gang' everyone was more or less leading and my father's fears made them smile. It was one of the great joys of my life.*

Soon Georges was adding new routes and the legend was born: in 1941 he put up 24 of which *La Centrale* was the longest grade six in the Calanques and the *Yellow Wall,* climbed with Gaston Rébuffat, was the toughest aided climb for quite some time. In 1942, he climbed 28 new routes, of which the highlight was the second ascent of *Pilier de Bertagne,* dubbed the Walker Spur of the Marseillais and only just climbed by Robert and Suzanne Tanner. (Le Grec considered Robert as the best climber he had known, but unfortunately Robert stopped soon afterwards.) Georges then added his own new route to its left, *La Plaque.*

In April 1943, he joined the Camps de Jeunesse et Montagne, as Le Grec put it 'an ersatz military service in an ersatz time'. Already that year he had done another 15 new routes and become the best climber in the Calanques, by far. Georges was lucky in his new role. His parents had needed to work hard to keep him from being one of the six hundred thousand French workers recruited to work for the Nazis in Germany under the Service du Travail Obligatoire. As Le Grec put it:

> *Winter having arrived, I had just done my first ski descents when I was appealed to in the most pressing manner by the Nazi regime to participate in some work in Germany. It was indeed flattering to think that my modest assistance was thought essential to the triumph of Hitler's war effort but though deeply honoured by this invitation, I thought it better to decline.*

The Calanques remained close to his heart, but as a young man in post-war Marseille climbing wasn't so easy. In contrast to today's 'professionals' and young athletes, he could only climb at the weekend, which in his heyday started on Saturday afternoons, or else during his summer holidays, which were a maximum of four weeks. In the 1950s, there was no 35-hour working week or five-week allowance, plus public holidays. Le Grec called himself a 'Sunday' climber, not a sportsman, not compared to those who in his old age were climbing the eighth grade. He also relied on public transport. He never learned to drive just as he never learned how to swim (for a Marseille man that really was taking the biscuit). So to climb on the Bertagne peak, 30km and an hour's drive away, he and his friends would take the tramway to Aubagne, then the bus to Gémenos before walking to the foot of the wall. To go to Chamonix, he took the train. For places like the Vercors, he used his Vespa, the same vehicle he relied on for his work as a sales rep for a printing materials company. Using the moped he travelled up and down the Bouches du Rhône, the Var and Vaucluse. When his pal Robert Gabriel stopped climbing in 1956, he started climbing with Marc Vaucher who had a Citroën DS. Only then did he discover the comfort and convenience of a car.

Altogether Le Grec climbed 500 new routes in the Calanques of Marseille but his home crags were always a springboard to go further: to big walls, to the mountains. At the end of the war, in September 1945, his mother managed to get him a place on a mountain camp in Ailefroide. (As he wrote, 'contrary to most mothers, mine always encouraged my passion for mountaineering, which allowed her to be my mother a second time.') This gave him a season in the Oisans, climbing the south face of La Meije with Albert 'Pépé' Ouannon, his first serious mountain route, as well as the west ridge of the Pic Sans Nom and the third ascent of the south pillar of Barre des Écrins, the latter with Jean Franco and Gudérian at a blistering pace: four hours from the bergschrund to the summit. The following year he was back in Chamonix, making the second ascent of the Grand Dru's south face and the fifth of the north face of the Grand Charmoz, both with Charles Magol, and an attempt on the west face of the Dru that was ended by stonefall. In 1947, he was part of a four-man team that made the first

On the key traverse of the *Cassin* on the Cima Ovest, shortly after encountering Hans Lobenhoffer. Livanos made the tenth ascent, announcing his arrival. *(Robert Gabriel)*

ascent of the Grépon's west face, as well as the second ascent of the Requin's north face.

That summer was the first season he climbed with Robert Gabriel, who would become his regular partner for the next few years as he and Le Grec switched focus from the western Alps to the Dolomites. Gabriel wrote a foreword for Le Grec's climbing memoir *Au-delà de la Verticale,* 'Beyond the Vertical', published in 1958 after they stopped climbing together, that gives some idea of the power of their friendship.

> *I gained a great deal from knowing him. Without Le Grec I would never have gone so far. There is no doubt about it: Georges Livanos was a leader. I had a confidence in him that was almost blind. So much so that if I was climbing with someone else, I felt somehow embarrassed. Climbing together, each move one of us made followed the other with perfect synchronisation; we never needed to exchange words, the rope was tight or slack just at the right moment. ... Always very cheerful, totally a southern man, it was a pleasure to listen to his jokes and his tales. Even during our darkest bivouacs, he was ready for a laugh, and his sheer presence generated optimism.*

Having made the second ascent of the north-east face of the Aiguille de Leschaux in 1949, the pair switched the following year to the Dolomites, the start of a love affair that would last the rest of Le Grec's career. That first summer they started with a masterpiece, making the tenth ascent of the *Cassin* route on the Cima Ovest. Following behind them was Hans Lobenhoffer, who had been on the German expedition to Nanga Parbat in 1939 with Heinrich Harrer and was afterwards imprisoned by the British. Seeing the crucial traverse pitch, Lobenhoffer, by then in his mid 30s, asked to tie into the French team. They were happy to oblige but then Gabriel handed Lobenhoffer the rucksack, making him their porter, before delicately picking his way across the traverse like a ballet dancer. You have to keep an eye on climbers from Marseille.

In 1951, the pair really made their mark on Dolomite climbing with the first ascent of the direct on Cima Su Alto, a route of 'sesto superior' standard

Left: Sonia in Les Calanques during the 1930s. Her climbing shoes were homemade from sneakers with bike and truck inner tubes stuck to them. *(Robert Gabriel)*

Middle: 'My Sistine chapel', Le Grec called called his first ascent of the Su Alto, pictured here with an inscription from Riccardo Cassin: 'To Georges Livanos, who 20 years ago climbed this marvellous new route.'

Right: *From left to right:* Fortunato Dalpiano, Le Grec, Sonia and Robert Gabriel, outside the refuge following the first ascent of the Spigolo Ouest of Monte Cavallo in 1953.

done without any preparation and two bivouacs. It was, Le Grec said later, 'my Sistine chapel.' For the next quarter of a century, Le Grec continued to climb hard new routes in the Dolomites. In 1953 for example, he and Robert Gabriel did the first ascent of the west pillar on Monte Cavallo, also known as Heiligkreuzkofel that dominates Val Badia. Reinhold Messner repeated it 15 years later and said it was still one of the most difficult routes in the Dolomites. As the years passed, Le Grec's haul of new routes increased: the northwest faces of Terranova and Torre del Lago; the west face of Torre Venezia; the first ascent of Castello de la Busazza; the west faces of Sciora di Fuori and the Crozzon di Brenta; the first ascent of the Torre Gilberti on the Cima Tosa.

Even today his list of first ascents is extraordinary. Above all, they were of high quality. Oh, the Livanos routes! They really were a must. Repeating them was enough to convince yourself that you were among the special ones. And they weren't just confined to the Dolomites. He continued to climb in the Oisans and on the big limestone cliffs further west, like the Vercors. Bruno Fara, for example, one of the stars of the 1970s, wrote how the ability to do the Livanos pillar on the Archiane without a bivouac was a qualification for trying big north faces in the Alps. But his most significant contribution was in Italy. Le Grec kept track of his ascents in small notebooks and in larger ones stuck photos of big routes that he had climbed in the Alps and the Dolomites. When he finally retired in 1978 he tallied up the score. (This was a typical piece of self-mockery, by the way.) Of the 60 new routes he had climbed in the Alps, 40 were in the Dolomites. Of the 242km

When Gabriel gave up climbing,
Le Grec's partners, apart from Sonia,
included Roger 'Baffo' Lepage, here
belaying.

he climbed, more than half were in the Calanques, with 500 new routes along the way, but 64km were in the Dolomites. Next, by some distance, came Chamonix, with 8.9km.

His affection for Italy was understandable. Apart from the appeal of big limestone walls, they appreciated his interest in the Dolomites and Le Grec's sense of humour. Early in his career, journalists from the Marseille press became his fans and followed his career closely but that wasn't repeated elsewhere in France. Yet in Italy there were a number of articles in the press and he became better known there than in his home country. And as he told Bernard Amy and Pascal Sombardier in 1984:

> *I had my habits. In the refuges, I had 'my' room. Once, I arrived, it was occupied. So, the guardian, she went to see the guy and told him: 'You're in room 10, but that's Livanos'. He's just arrived so you have to go.' The guy said, 'No sweat…'*

> *Without a question? [Amy asked.]*

> *No, none at all. There was no question to ask. 'If he's here, it's final. How do you want the key for Room 10? With Provençal herbs or mayonnaise?' [Laughter] It was great. The guy was in fact delighted to have slept in my room.*

> *You liked the Dolomites for that also, no?*

> *Ah, it's not unpleasant. Because in France, to be sent to bed like a dog with kicks in the ass…*

He was an expert aid climber, that being the big-wall technique before the free-climbing boom took hold. In his compendium of statistics, he calculated he had placed 25,000 pegs. One of his favourite aphorisms ran like this: 'Better one more peg than one man less. Especially if that man is me.' Free climbing, for Le Grec, meant being 'free to do whatever one likes: put an etrier on if one feels like it, climb a grade III if one feels like it, or go pick strawberries.' His ethical position was pragmatic, but humorously so. 'For me, the ideal is to start from the bottom, reach the top and come back down. And not too fast.' But as Robert Gabriel pointed out: 'from being the champion of aid climbing, he became the champion of free climbing. Some of our routes, opened in the 1950s, are still quoted grade VI by today's climbers.' Le Grec himself acknowledged this transition in his frank conversation with Bernard Amy and Pascal Sombardier. The loss of prestige in aid climbing was 'logical', Le Grec said. How else would climbing progress? His inquisitors were unconvinced. Hadn't he placed 25,000 pegs? That must have represented something.

> *Yes, it represented effort, but I never thought that aid climbing was superior to free climbing. It was a means to progress when there was nothing else. Still, with guys such as Vinatzer and Comici, you had nothing to teach them. There are some moves still graded VII- put by Papi Vinatzer in 1933. And you should see what he had on his feet.*

Until he got married and quit, Robert Gabriel was his rope-mate in a great number of first ascents on the breath-taking walls of northern Italy. 'Gabriel was not a brilliant climber,' Le Grec said, 'but he was for me always a marvellous partner. I only have one regret, that he stopped in 1955, which undoubtedly deprived me of some nice first ascents. Afterwards, I only occasionally met another Robert Gabriel. In terms of spirit, energy, impermeability to adversity, Gabriel was the man.' Le Grec climbed with all sorts of people, 'around 300 guys' according to his notebooks, and as he put it: *'E basta!'* Regular partners after Gabriel included Marc Vaucher and Roger Lepage, who climbed with him until he stopped. But it was his wife Sonia who would be his ideal partner, always ready to follow him up the north face of the Civetta or the *grand dièdre* of the Cima Su Alto.

Georges met Sonia at a CAF camp in the late 1940s. Her real name was Geneviève Brès but like his hero Tartarin de Tarascon Georges was in the habit of calling all girls Sonia. Geneviève was the best of the girls climbing as well as the prettiest. Georges was the best male climber. Soon they started climbing together and from then on there was only one Sonia for Le Grec. As there were then not many women climbers at the time, Sonia accumulated the largest number of first female ascents in the Dolomites for her era. For example, in 1951 during his second season in the Dolomites, Le Grec did the fourth ascent of the north-east face of the Torre di Valgrande, which was a female first for Sonia. Many routes Le Grec repeated in the Dolomites were first female ascents for Sonia. This aspect of her climbing career went mainly unnoticed in France; Le Grec being the leader was taking all the glory. But in Italy the Dolomites climbers were astounded by this French lady who was so natural, simple and joyful and so good on the rock, even more astounded than they were by Le Grec.

Le Grec characterised his marriage with the same wry self-deprecation he applied to most things.

Le Grec in the Brenta, pictured here with the great Bruno Detassis, left and seated, hut guardian, philosopher, leader of the first expedition to Cerro Torre with 200 new routes in the Dolomites to his name. Roger Lepage is resting his foot.

Some of my friends have envied me a companion always ready to follow me on the most overhanging adventures. Poor chaps, if only they knew! If only they understood what it is to climb day after day with a feeble woman of 4ft 11in who ignores difficulty, fatigue, cold, hunger and thirst, while HE is much sensitive to all those inconveniences! If they knew what it is, after a tough pitch of grade VI, to see HER arriving, smiling, calm, detailing the tones of a floweret on the overhang, while HE, on that same overhang… Well, forget it.

In my climbing life, I knew two exceptional female alpinists: Denise Escande, with whom I climbed; and Sonia with whom I never shared a rope because Le Grec was her leader. Even the great Gino Soldà tried to take her up a climb but in vain; Sonia only ever had one climbing partner. Those two great ladies of alpinism had this in common: they had no fear of anything and certainly not of dying. This allowed them to live their passions fully and for Sonia there were two: Le Grec and climbing, which melded so well. Le Grec showed his love in his inimitable fashion. 'If she was a spud,' he said, 'I would say it… or rather I would not as I would not have married her.' But his respect was never far away. He liked to remind his male climbing friends that when they climbed an overhang with a 10kg rucksack, that was only an eighth of their bodyweight. For Sonia, it was a quarter.

A galaxy of climbing stars at the Trento film festival in 1961. Le Grec is dressed in a black suit, standing to Gaston Rébuffat's right. *Front row left to right:* Claudio Barbier, Gaston Rébuffat, Otto Herzog, Mario Stenico, Michel Vaucher. Second row left to right: Cesare Maestri, Georges Livanos, Toni Kinshofer, Riccardo Cassin, Walter Bonatti, Toni Hiebeler, Pierre Mazeaud. *Third and last row together left to right:* Gigi Alippi, Aleš Kunaver, Pierliugi Airoldi, Annibale Zucchi, Giancarlo Frigeri, unknown, Yvette Vaucher, Sepp Inwyler, Pierre Marchard, René Dittert, Bepi de Francesch, Aldo Klaus, Maria Teresa De Riso, Dino De Riso, Toni Serafini, Toni Masé, John Harlin, Luciano Ghigo, Romano Merendi.

In 2002, Georges and Sonia were in Auronzo di Cadore to receive the Pelmo d'Oro Prize in recognition of their extraordinary shared career in the 1950s and 1960s. First awarded in 1997, the Pelmo d'Oro was founded to recognise the true greats who contributed to the Belluno Dolomites. The citation praised a 'golden couple on the rocks and in life': it was given to them equally. They were the only non-Italians to win it. Even Claudio Barbier, who besides his staggering solos put up so many new routes in the Dolomites, didn't get it. Perhaps it was because he didn't have Le Grec's *tchatche,* his gift of the gab. Italians in the Dolomites have a soft spot for comedians and considered Le Grec one of their greatest. As for Sonia, they were bowled over by a climber with so much talent, cheek, mastered calm and kindness. You didn't meet many like that on big walls in the Dolomites in those days.

Happily for us, the humour his Italian friends appreciated is preserved between the covers of his book *Au-delà de la Verticale,* 'Beyond the Vertical', first published in 1958 and still in print, although sadly not translated into English. 'Every community has its bible,' the publisher Guerin said in its blurb when it reissued *Au-delà de la Verticale.* 'This book, obviously, is one for all alpinists and climbers. Restorative, funny, cunning: it is a landmark.' In his review for *La Montagne,* Jacques Teissier du Cros claimed three books as the greatest of that era: Rébuffat's *Starlight and Storm,* Bonatti's *My Mountains* – and Georges Livanos' *Beyond the Vertical.*

The book is suffused with the twang of the Marseille accent, the smell of pastis and Le Grec's very specific sense of humour. He's a great alpinist, and he isn't going to hide that fact but he will have a lot of fun not taking himself at all seriously. 'As far as advertising is concerned,' he would say, 'one is never better served but by oneself.' It's naïve to imagine that success doesn't come without a little self-regard. His inspirations are Sancho Panza, the down-to-earth and sceptical sidekick of Don Qixote, and even more so Tartarin, from Alphonse Daudet's novel *Tartarin of Tarascon,* the self-deluded hunter whose bravado lands him in an adventure he can't handle. Honesty with oneself lies at the heart of Le Grec's book, of his alpinism too, and his life, but it's all masked with some preposterous clowning.

I first climbed with him in 1961, the *Voie de la Écaille* at La Tête de la Mounine, outside Marseille. Le Grec had done the first ascent ten years before with Robert Gabriel. He wrote our day up for an article, casting me as one of the 'new wave' of young climbers. The story is full of his teasing humour: he noted that with a name like 'Vola', or 'flew', he needed to keep an eye on me. 'During the walk-in,' he wrote, 'I realised Eric was a swell guy. Indeed, he seemed to know one of the masterpieces of mountain literature inside out.' Meaning of course his own book *Au-delà de la Verticale.* We had a grand day out on baking hot rock, during which I climbed a new pitch of aid, tapping in the pegs lightly so the great man wouldn't have to work hard to get them out. ('What a guy!' Le Grec wrote. 'He does an A3 up an A1 pitch! But poor chap, what you're supposed to do is the exact opposite.') After that we retreated to a bar to drink. Or rather, in my case, to eat, since, as Le Grec observed, 'He swallows a camembert as others swallow an aspirin.' His article concluded:

> Our first outing went well. There will be others, because if Eric still ignores many things, I am starting to forget many. From him, I learn once more that one must take a risk; Eric for his part will learn that it is sometimes good to hesitate. In other words, if we climb together, I will improve and he will get worse.

Two years later, in 1963, I joined him in the Dolomites and saw for myself how much Le Grec and Sonia were loved there. It was during one of the climbing camps Le Grec organised with the benevolence of Lucien Devies, his sponsor, admirer and friend. As soon as we arrived in Belluno, we – and by 'we' I mean 'him' – were given a star's reception. Among the Italian climbers present was Armando da Roit, guardian of the Vazzoler refuge and the soul of the Civetta, just as Bruno Detassis was the soul of Brenta. Nicknamed 'Tama', Armando was a great man, later a senator in the regional government at Belluno. He smoked black Tuscans, as hard as wood and so bloody strong I couldn't stand more than one puff without getting sick.

I started the meet climbing with the youngest of us, Henri Paul Plathey, who had just been accepted at the École Polytechnique in Paris. We did several climbs together, one with Armando, Le Grec and Sonia, the fourth ascent of Armando's route on the Busazza. I wasn't in great shape;

Livanos and friends at the climbing camp he led at Vazzoler in 1963. *Front row left to right:* Jérôme Brunet, a friend of Armando da Roit, Marcello Bonafede, Beppi de Francesch, Claude Deck. *Back row left to right:* Carla da Roit, Eric Vola, Ottilia da Roit, Jacques Martin, Sonia, Le Grec, Maurice Negri.

I'd spent too long under grey Welsh skies for that. Plathey wanted to climb Le Grec's route on the Cima Su Alto and since I wasn't prepared for a climb like that, he convinced Marcello Bonafede to go with him, much against his will. The worst storm Armando had ever seen from his Vazzoler refuge hit them soon after they crossed the Su Alto roof. They had only 180m to go but it snowed continuously for 36 hours. There was a metre of snow at the hut.

Beppi de Franchesch, Le Grec and Armando were confident in Marcello Bonafede's ability to survive the worst conditions and after two days of storm the weather was glorious again. I woke up early and coming out of the refuge I saw Marcello returning alone with a look of despair on his face, hollow cheeked and haggard. The dump of snow had blocked their progress one pitch above the roof. They bivouacked. The following day was worse than ever, snow everywhere. Only retreat could save them. Above the roof, Plathey made the first abseil, reached the wall only with the greatest difficulty and then collapsed. He'd suffered a fatal heart attack. Imagine Bonafede's situation, in this horrendous storm, hearing nothing from his companion and with the rope blocked. In the end, after several hours, he made it down the rope using prusik knots to reach Plathey's body, made a pendulum with him under the roof and clipped him to a peg.

collection Altitudes
dirigée par Michel Schulman

Both Le Grec's books are highly regarded, neither are available in English: the Italian edition of *Beyond the Vertical* and *Cassin: Once upon a Time in the Sixth Grade*. Le Grec signed Vola's copy of the latter with the following dedication: 'To Eric Vola. Friend (for a long time and loyal, which is rare). Climber (Brilliant). Roisterer (Ditto). Smoker (Average). Boozer (Excellent). Muncher (Not bad. Hide your glasses and ties!). [Vola's party trick was to eat wine glasses.] Bullshitter (Honourable mention).'

Then he could get the rope down but had to bivouac a second time. On the third day, at last, he reached Vazzoler.

For Beppi and Armando, it was out of the question to do as they would in Cortina, abseil down and throw the body off the wall. With Le Grec's help, they organised a rescue to return Plathey to his family intact. Beppi asked 10 of his friends, mountain soldiers from Canazei to join us. With their help, Le Grec and Armando organised zip-lines on the lower 400m section of the wall. Meanwhile, Bonafede, who wanted to be first to reach his companion's body, climbed with Beppi towards the roof. Meanwhile Bonafede's best friend, Natalino Ménégus and I paid out a specially long rope from the foot of the corner as they made progress towards the body, some 190m above our heads.

By the end of that day, everything was ready to get Plathey's body down. We had to heave on 30m of slack before we felt his body on the rope and 100m down it stuck in the middle of the wall on a small ledge. We had no choice but to go down to the Tissi hut for the night and come back next morning. This time four of us pulled more than 40m of slack before the body came free. At least the final part went smoothly. The zip-lines Le Grec had organised with Beppi's friends were professional work. Then we carried Plathey's body from the Tissi hut to Vazzoler, before going on down to Agordo where Plathey's elder brother was waiting. We came across a priest with his flock who raised his camera to take a picture. Furious, Armando, without removing the Tuscan from his mouth, tore the camera from the priest's hands and crushed it on a rock. You can see why local people asked him to become their senator.

Thanks to Armando, Le Grec and the others, Paul Plathey's parents were able to see their son for the last time in a presentable state. It was not much, but at least we had managed something. Compared to how rescue worked in Chamonix in those days, I felt proud to have been part of this group of benevolent alpinists who did not hesitate to give a full week of their time to take down a dead body and without asking any compensation. So, I started to smoke Tuscans to imitate Armando, but the green ones, which weren't as strong, and in Belluno I bought a red pullover with a black V, like the one Le Grec wore.

I was always broke in those days because my mother couldn't stand me running off to the Alps. Sonia reminded me that I borrowed money from Bonafede and that Le Grec had to telephone my mother to be reimbursed, since this 'loan' was a big amount for a young guide like Marcello on a modest income. I also borrowed money from Le Grec at the railway station to buy some comics for the journey home. When he saw me coming back, he said to Sonia: 'Look what this nit has done with my money!' We didn't share the same literary interests. I must confess Preuss was not my cup of tea, in contrast to Le Grec who had an encyclopaedic knowledge of mountain literature, having read Sir Francis Younghusband's *The Epic of Mount Everest* as a student.

In 1978, aged 55, Le Grec stopped climbing altogether. He liked to quote one of Tartarin's companions: 'The eagle doesn't hunt flies.' As he wrote in a new edition of *Au-delà de la Verticale:* 'One day, I wrote to Robert Paragot: 'When you have hunted lions, rabbits look meagre.' And I must also quote Robert Gabriel: 'If I killed myself in the Calanques or on easy ground, I wouldn't dare go out again.' When Bernard Amy and Pascal Sombardier asked him about his retirement, he was a little more serious but no less sanguine. 'It was tiring me more. So, I preferred to stop with good memories, rather than memories of grade IV, then III. When one climbs, one must climb well, or not at all. Brasillach has said "youth adorns everything it does. Wanting to prolong it, one risks ending as a parody."' They wondered why the climbing world no longer heard from him. 'It's not modesty,' he told them, with a smile. 'It's a matter of pride. The ass on Olympus. You're lucky, you can put me in your autograph book.' As for getting involved in one of French climbing's institutions, he almost choked with laughter. 'As [the French comedian] Coluche said, "The last man to see me work, he's old."' No, the climbing was over and his long retirement beckoned.

The world had not heard the last from Le Grec though. In 1994, Jean Afanassieff made a film about him that was aired as part of the series 'Sunday in France'. As it happened, Yvan Audouard, a well-known humourist and television critic for *Le Canard Enchaîné,* was watching. Audouard was a man from the south, like Le Grec, who had coined the aphorism: 'Heureux les fêlés... car ils laisseront passer la lumière.' ('Blessed are the cracked, for they let in the light.') Although Le Grec was the subject of a number of articles in the national press, Audouard's article was the best tribute a journalist paid to my hero, not least because he didn't know him. He simply went by what he saw.

Le Grec met Geneviève Brès at a climbing camp in the late 1940s and in honour of his literary hero Tartarin de Tarascon dubbed her Sonia. They were inseparable until his death in 2004. Sonia Livanos is credited with more first female ascents in the Dolomites than any other woman of her generation. *(Vinicio Stefanello)*

The article came out in late 1994, as the following spring's presidential elections that would see Jacques Chirac become president got underway. It carried the headline: 'Vote Livanos'. Audouard was not a climber and admitted that he was irritated by some 'conquerors of the useless' who sometimes take advantage of their lofty position to look down on those condemned to live the humdrum life of *'métro-boulot-dodo'*, or 'Tube-work-sleep'. And for those millions facing the challenge of unemployment, the challenge of the mountains must seem irrelevant. Their 'dodo', he wrote, is filled with nightmares and distress. But still, Audouard goes on, they must have enjoyed seeing Le Grec. 'In his eyes there is all the irony and humour of someone who climbed his whole life without treading on anyone else, who never looked to amaze anyone, certainly not himself. When asked who is the best alpinist, he answers with hesitation: "The oldest."' For Audouard, Le Grec offered a sharp contrast to politicians offering voters the world:

The sight of a happy man who did not achieve his happiness at the expense of others ... that sort of happiness even the unfortunate are able to share. He offers an uplifting message during this election season. Right now the political spiders are in a frenzy to get into power, distributing kicks with their feet in the teeth and gums of their opponents. It seemed to me essential to talk to you about a man who did not become a star but instead became a master. He never ceased to be himself and never had any other ambition than to find happiness on earth: for himself and for others.

Le Grec died in 2004 aged 81. Fourteen years later, Sonia left us as well. She was 94 years old and had decided it was time to catch up with him.

Sonia and Le Grec were happiness itself, to all those met them and to those who became their friends. One might have feared that after Le Grec's departure, Sonia would not be the same. This did not seem the case, and if it was, she never let it show. Her joie de vivre remained intact, as did her pleasure in the company of friends, particularly when she could speak of her Grec. During her last few years she was in a care home where, as her nephew Jean-François said nicely at her funeral, 'her memory slipped away.' Our meetings were always joyful and cheerful. For her, Le Grec was by then alive and always near. Many times, when we went to see her, she asked if we had seen Georges who had just gone to get the newspapers.

Sonia would not have allowed sadness at her passing. Jean-François told me that during one of his last visits, she asked him to lend him his walking stick. Astonished, because she never had any need for one, he asked her why: 'To hit those nurses who continually bother me!' Until the moment she left us, she remained the free soul she always had been.

External Links

Eric Vola has a website about the life of Georges Livanos at *https://sites. google.com/site/georgeslivanos/Accueil.* Jean Afanassieff's film on Le Grec is on YouTube. There is also a good French entry on Wikipédia. For more information on Le Pelmo d'Oro: *https://sites.google.com/site/georgeslivanos/ lepelmod%27oro.*

J G R HARDING

The Other Gertrude Bell

Gertrude Bell.

Gertrude Lowthian Bell, granddaughter of Sir Isaac Lowthian Bell, the greatest metallurgist of his day, was a phenomenon. Her courage and character held men of her generation in awe. Her achievements as a linguist fluent in six languages, as a traveller, archaeologist, Orientalist, author, poet, photographer, diplomat and nation-builder are unsurpassed. Less well recognised has been her prowess as an outstanding woman mountaineer. At the close of the First World War, Gertrude Bell's contribution to the cause of Arab independence had made her world famous. Yet few recognise her name today, notwithstanding Werner Herzog's 2015 film *Queen of the Desert,* with Nicole Kidman sadly miscast as the heroine.

The foundations of Gertrude's early reputation rested on the half-dozen journeys of archaeological exploration she undertook throughout Lebanon, Syria, Turkey and Mesopotamia between 1900 and 1913. Funding these herself and travelling with no other European companion, she covered some 20,000 miles in the saddle, often through hostile, little-known desert country, surviving brigandage and capture, risking death at a time when Arab provinces in the Ottoman Empire were mostly lawless and in revolutionary ferment. These experiences, compounded by her boundless self-confidence and mastery of Arabic, Turkish and Farsi gave her so profound a knowledge of the tribes and geography of the Middle East that,

Above: Nicole Kidman as Gertrude Bell and Damian Lewis as Charles Doughty-Wylie in Werner Herzog's biopic *Queen of the Desert. (Benaroya Pictures)*

Left: Gertrude Bell painted c1890 by Flora Russell (1869-1967).

at the outbreak of the First World War, the British government enlisted her support in mobilising the Arab revolution that overthrew Ottoman rule.

During the war, her daring political and military missions behind enemy lines liaising with and influencing tribal chiefs led to her appointment as the first female political officer in the British army. She became oriental secretary in Baghdad, an important British representative at the 1921 Cairo Conference and, having played a key role in creating the free and united post-war Iraq that secured the succession of Feisal I to the throne, was appointed by him as director of Iraq's antiquities in 1922. The following year, she established the Iraq Museum. In his obituary tribute, Feisal described her as ' the greatest woman of her time ... to whom no danger or exploit was too great for her to face.'

Almost everything Bell attempted was crowned with success. Her pre-war archaeological journeys earned her the Royal Geographical Society's Gill Memorial Prize (the first awarded to a woman) and both its Gold and Founder's Medal. At her memorial service at St Margaret's, Westminster, King George V and the British Parliament paid her fulsome tributes. Yet her last years were embittered by disappointment and remorse. Why should so brilliant a star have faded thus? Her autocratic and confrontational character did not endear her to everyone. Throughout her life, she had challenged authority and espoused a policy towards Arab independence that ultimately ran counter to official British policy. HMG's miserly official recognition of her exceptional wartime and post-war service was the CBE in 1917, the very year in which the rank of dame was initiated. By the early 1920s her reputation was being eclipsed by that of T E Lawrence, whose role as the champion of the Arab revolution was vigorously promoted by the American journalist Lowell Thomas.

MITTELSPITZE. URBACH ENGELHORN. ULRICHSPITZE. GERTRUDSPITZE.

Photo. P. Montandon.
ENGELHÖRNER, East side, from saddle between HOHJAGIBURG and VORDERSPITZE.

The limestone spires of the Engelhörner in the northern Bernese Oberland from the east with the Gertrudspitze marked.

The Engelhörner from the foot of the Simelistock ridge above the Engelhörn hut. From left to right: Vorderspitze, Gertrudspitze, Ulrichspitze and Mittelspitze. *(Paul Rudkin)*

Monika Romang on the last few metres of the first ascent of *Queen of the Desert*, named in Bell's honour, an eight-pitch 7a+ on the Gertrudspitze. *(Daniel Anker)*

These were grave disappointments, but the fundamental source of her disenchantment was that despite a passionate nature, circumstance and her moral code prevented her from having a full relationship with any of the three men in her life. First was the romantic young diplomat Henry Cadogan whose proposal of marriage she accepted when staying in Tehran aged 24 as the guest of her uncle Sir Frank Lascelles, the British minister. But Cadogan was a gambler and Gertrude's father disapproved of the match and the following year he died of pneumonia. Next was the dashing but unhappily married soldier-scholar Capt Dick Doughty-Wylie. Gertrude wanted him to leave his wife but she threatened suicide if he did so. The matter was solved when he died a hero's death at Gallipoli in 1915. After that Gertrude focussed on work. Finally, towards the end of her life in 1925, came the dazzling Kinahan Cornwallis, Britain's intelligence chief in Cairo. Fifteen years her junior, his brusque rejection of her marriage proposal shattered her self-esteem. With her world crumbling around her and her health undermined, she took a fatal dose of barbiturates on 11 July 1926, two days before her 58th birthday. She was buried in the British Military Cemetery, Baghdad. Arab leaders and tribesmen throughout Iraq and Syria still mourn her passing.

Gertrude Bell's prowess as a mountaineer is the least known of her achievements. Much credit for what recognition they received must go to

Col Edward Lisle Strutt, First World War hero and the deputy (if unpopular) leader of the 1922 Everest Expedition. Strutt, for ten years editor of the *Alpine Journal* and president of the Club has an unenviable reputation as a die-hard Alpine traditionalist and controversialist whose wartime experiences left him virulently opposed to the nationalist philosophy of German and Italian Alpine climbs of the inter-war 'Iron Age'. But he was never a misogynist, a direct consequence of his boyhood mountaineering apprenticeship under the tutelage of his governess Beatrice Tomasson (1859-1947), an outstanding woman mountaineer whose first ascents included half a dozen Dolomite peaks and most memorably the south face of the Marmolada in 1901, then reckoned to be 'the longest and most difficult climb in the Alps'. Their relationship was rumoured to have been more than platonic but whatever the truth, Strutt understood how strong women climbers could be and became a fervent admirer of Gertrude Bell. On becoming editor of the *Alpine Journal* in 1927, the year after her death, he published the insouciant accounts of the climbs she recorded in the private letters she wrote to her family. Some of these were compiled by her stepmother Frances and posthumously published in *The Letters of Gertrude Bell*. Strutt himself echoed the judgement of King Feisal in his obituary (*Alpine Journal* 38, Nov 1926) that Bell was 'one of the greatest women of all time'.

Curiously, George Band's *Summit* (2006), recording 150 years of the Alpine Club, makes no reference to Gertrude Bell. Her reluctance to publicise her climbs, with the exception of an article, 'Concerning Mountains: Die Engelhorner', for the *National Review* (1901) reflected an innate modesty and that mountaineering was simply a diversion in her multi-faceted life, covering no more than five Alpine seasons from 1899 to 1904 The achievements of such distinguished British women mountaineers as Lucy Walker, Elizabeth Jackson, Katherine Richardson, Beatrice Tomasson, Mrs Aubrey Le Blond and Emily Bristow were more numerous and better known. Yet it was not so much the quantity of Gertrude's climbs, but rather their quality and style that earned her the admiration of her guides and accolades from such luminaries as W A B Coolidge, another *Alpine Journal* editor, who ranked her as the 'best of all lady mountaineers'.

Gertrude's upbringing, natural gifts and character forged the mountaineer she became. From childhood, she had exhibited an exceptional intellectual and physical vitality. Slim, slight even, but immensely strong, her early years were privileged but disciplined and rigorous. Assertive and self-opinionated, she went up to Lady Margaret Hall, Oxford in 1886 aged 18 to follow a strict academic regime of seven hours daily study leavened by rowing, hockey, acting, and dancing. Unflinching when challenging her tutors in debate, she became the first woman to get a first in modern history at Oxford.

She spent four years loosely anchored to the family home Rounton Grange, a masterpiece of high-Victoriana built by her grandfather in 1870, designed by Philip Webb and decorated and furnished by William Morris and Edward Burne-Jones. Then she travelled to Tehran in 1892 to fall in love

A big day out. From Gertrude Bell's entry in the Hotel Rosenlaui's climbing book. 'Sep. 3. [1901] Leaving the shoulder of the Simili Stock at 8.30 we ascended the peak to the South of the saddle and reached the top at 9.15. We christened this peak the Vorderspitz. We descended the south side to the west saddle & ascended the west peak by some smooth rocks on the N W side reaching the top at 9.55. We named the peak Gertrude's Peak. We descended the rocks onto the same saddle & then followed down a smooth couloir for about 5 minutes & kept to the S W along the foot of the peak taking the next couloir for about 5 minutes & kept to the S W along the foot of the peak taking the next couloir onto the saddle to the south of the peak. The rock in this couloir is much more solid than that of which the rest of the arête is composed. When we were on the southern saddle we saw a good chimney on the S E side of Gertrude's Peak by which it could be ascended on this face. We followed along the arête & reached the top of the vert peak at 12.45. We named it Ulrich's Peak. We descended this peak by the southern face & continued along the arête past a gendarme until we reached the top of the fourth peak (1 of 5) which we named the Mittelspitz, it being the centre of the chain between the Vorderspitz & the Engelhorn.'
(Daniel H Anker/Hotel Rosenlaui)

not only with the ill-fated Henry Cadogan but the whole Islamic world. To assuage her grief after losing Henry, she embarked on an exhaustive travel programme that included four family holidays to Switzerland between 1893 and 1896. On first visiting the Dauphiné in 1897, she was held spellbound by La Meije (3983m) and, after hiring a couple of local guides, scrambled as far as its Promontoire ridge before turning back, vowing that she would return ere long to complete the climb.

Two years later, after a social visit to the Wagner family in Bayreuth, she returned to fulfil her vow, though still without proper rock-climbing experi-

Bell in Iraq, where she founded the Baghdad Museum. *(San Diego Air and Space Museum Archive)*

ence and yet to put on a rope. Engaging the same guides, the trio warmed up on the Grand Galibier – three hours up and two down – before moving on to La Bérarde. Here, she ran into the formidable German lady mountaineer Helene Kuntze who had just climbed La Meije's summit peak herself: 'Very nice,' was Gertrude's surprised comment about the woman who was soon to be her rival.

Then as now, La Meije is a serious climb and its first ascent in 1877, after 28 unsuccessful attempts, was hailed by Arnold Lunn in his *Century of Mountaineering* (1965) as 'the greatest achievement of the Silver Age'. Gertrude had already decided to outdo Fraulein Kuntze by attempting the mountain's complete traverse: a feat only accomplished eight years before and still regarded as one of the great expeditions of the Alps. After a sleepless night at the Refuge de l'Alpe de Villar d'Arène, they left at 1am on 29 August 1899 and nine hours later, after 'hanging by my eyelids over an abyss,' reached La Meije's main summit. The challenge of the Cheval Rouge was overcome by straddling it *à cheval*. After summiting the Pic Central, they followed La Meije's teetering crest over 'endless dents' before reaching La Bérarde at 6.30pm that evening to complete their triumphal 17 and a half-hour expedition.

Gertrude allowed herself a two-day break before attempting the Barre des Écrins (4101m), the highest peak in the Dauphiné, inspired by Whymper's account of his harrowing first ascent in 1864 with Moore and Walker and guides Almer and Croz. Bitter weather, a profusion of ice couloirs and rotten rock made this 19-hour traverse far less enjoyable than La Meije. Gertrude had swapped her heavy skirt for a pair of men's trousers, which kept her nether regions warm, but the intense cold cost her three badly frostbitten fingers.

Undeterred, she completed this 1899 season with a lightening seven-hour ascent and descent of the Pelvoux before investigating the mysterious Aiguille Meridoniale d'Arves: an 'inhuman and forbidding needle … one of the most singular views I have ever seen.' Unbeknown to Gertrude, she had already been forestalled as the aiguille's first female summiteer nine years earlier by Katherine Richardson, another exceptional British woman climber who had made the first ascent of the Aiguille de Bionnassay's knife-edge south ridge in 1885. Nonetheless, the Aiguille Meridoniale retained a notorious reputation due to a 50ft overhanging pitch known as the Mauvais Pas which had previously defeated many parties and which, 29 years later, merited a future Club president Claude Wilson's 10-page article in the *Alpine Journal* (AJ 40, May 1928) about its difficulties. Gertrude tossed off her own four-hour ascent as 'amusing climbing ... better than anything I have done,' and dismissed the dreaded Mauvais Pas as 'most enjoyable'.

Now bitten by the climbing bug, Gertrude based her 1900 season on Chamonix, and after fitting herself out with a bespoke blue climbing suit, engaged Ulrich Fuhrer and Ernest Simond as her guides. They climbed Mont Blanc, the Grépon and then romped up the Grand Dru, 'a heavenly rock climb', in record time as a prelude to attempting the complete Drus traverse. However, the passage to the Petit Dru, involving several abseils and a dangerous *pendule,* proved 'extremely difficult' and although their overall time of 24 hours was exceptional, Gertrude again found Katherine Richardson had pipped her, having done the traverse in the marginally more difficult opposite direction eight years earlier.

In 1901, Gertrude established herself at Grindelwald and engaged Ulrich Fuhrer and his younger brother Heinrich as guides. Their first objective was the south-east ridge of the Schreckhorn (4078m), a mountain described by Leslie Stephen as 'the most savage and thrilling' in the Oberland. Initially, Gertrude was unimpressed with the mountain's 'absurd reputation', but after a final hour of 'capital rock climbing' up-graded it into the 'first class of mountains ... though somewhat low in its class'. When the weather broke, she de-camped to Rosenlaui for a fortnight's climbing in the 'fascinating' and then virtually unknown Engelhörner. With Ulrich and a journeyman local guide, she came away with 10 new or first ascents including the first traverse of the Unbachthaler Engelhorn, a demanding two-day expedition involving one bivouac, several long stretches of seriously hard climbing with one pitch that necessitated a do-or-die boots-on-shoulder move and the temporary abandonment of the assistant guide who was unable to follow. Afterwards, Ulrich admitted that they would never have completed the traverse without her climbing skills ('as good as any man'), drive and determination.

It was now that Gertrude first conceived her audacious plan to climb within a single week the Finsteraarhorn's virgin north-east arête before attempting the hitherto uncompleted traverse of the Lauteraarhorn and Schreckhorn. However, after recceing the route on 12 September in heavy snow and rain, she sensibly called it off. The following year, after several months of archaeological research in Greece, Turkey and the Lebanon, Gertrude returned to Rosenlaui in July to discover that Helene Kuntze, guided by her very own Ulrich, had already made several Engelhörner first ascents the previous month. Gertrude graciously acknowledged these as 'very good indeed', but not to be outdone put up another new route there herself before switching operations to the neighbouring Wellhorn group. Here, on 14 July, she and the Fuhrers made the first complete traverse of the Wellhorn and Klein Wellhorn from the Lastsattel to the Unter Wellhornsattel, a climb involving 10,000ft of ascent previously reckoned 'impossible' and described by Jeremy Talbot in the West Col *Engelhorner* guide (Collomb, 1968) as 'one of the finest ridge climbs in the Bernese Oberland'.

Six days later, their attempt on the Wetterhorn by a new route was frustrated by seracs, but after regrouping Gertrude and the Fuhrers decided to launch their first assault on the Lauteraarhorn-Schreckhorn traverse which had so far rebuffed all-comers. Starting from Grimsel with three days of provisions and 500ft of rope, an assortment of guides and several other hopefuls, including Prince Luís of Orléans-Braganza, crammed into the Pavillon Dolfuss that night. A tremendous thunderstorm boded ill for the morrow and when the braver hearts eventually got under way, progress up the Lauteraarhorn's seemingly endless, gendarme-studded ridge in bad visibility, unremitting rain and snow gave Gertrude 'the nastiest day of my life'. On reaching the summit in a blizzard, they called it a day and then hazarded a risky, unsighted descent to the glacier. Gertrude vowed never to attempt the climb from Grimsel again, but four days later, on 24 July, she made her second and this time successful attempt on the traverse from Grindelwald, spurred by the news that Helene Kuntze was bent on doing it in the opposite direction. There appears to be no detailed description of this achievement, but Strutt regarded it as Gertrude's most important climb.

With that behind her, she again set her sights on the north-east arête of the Finsteraarhorn (4274m), the 'Monarch of the Oberland'. This huge, isolated chunk of rock is notorious for bad weather and when she disclosed her plan to the Fuhrers, they reckoned the climb so difficult and dangerous that they kept it secret from the valley. On 31 July 1902, the trio left the hut at 1.35am in uncertain weather. As the day progressed, it steadily deteriorated with persistent snow and mist before developing into a raging storm with thunder and lightning that sent their ice axes humming. At 8pm, high up on the shark's fin north-east rib, they were forced to bivouac. Huddled together on a tiny ledge Gertrude surveyed the scene with sublime detachment 'to enjoy the extraordinary magnificence of the storm and the lightning bolts which made the rocks crackle.'

At dawn, with the storm unabated, they began a desperate retreat involving several near-fatal falls on the ice-coated rocks, and eventually reached the glacier in blinding mist. The weather never relented and as the day wore on, a second bivouac on the glacier in sodden clothes became inevitable. Dawn on the third morning saw them staggering into Meiringen dehydrated, hypothermic, frostbitten and utterly exhausted after spending 57 hours on the mountain mostly roped together. Later described as 'one of the greatest expedition's in Alpine history', Ulrich Fuhrer's tribute was that 'few surpassed her in technical skill and none equalled her coolness, bravery and judgement ... had she not been full of courage and determination, we must have perished.' Twenty-eight years elapsed before the ambitious

'The Dôme de Neige des Ecrins', by Charles Henri Contencin (1898-1955).

Miriam Underhill climbed the rib with the Swiss guides Adolf and Fritz Rubi. Underhill rated its objective dangers as 'unjustifiable'.

Gertrude's Finsteraarhorn epic was not the end of her mountaineering career. During a six-month world tour in 1903 taking in Afghanistan, the Himalaya, Burma, Singapore, Hong Kong, China, Korea and Japan, she stopped off in Vancouver for a few days climbing in the Rockies. That same July she based herself on Zermatt where she met Geoffrey Winthrop Young 'a very nice creature, charming to look at.' After asking herself the question 'Why do people climb?', she traversed the Matterhorn with the Fuhrers from its more difficult Italian side: 'a much better climb than I expected.' The rope ladder normally placed as an aid above the Tyndallgrat was broken that year and Heinrich Fuhrer found free-climbing the 40ft pitch 'immensely difficult'. Gertrude thought it 'beautiful' and described the descent down the Hörnli as 'more like sliding down bannisters than climbing'.

Gertrude's penultimate climb that season was an ascent of the Lyskamm (4527m) by its east ridge. This was a very different proposition to the Matterhorn traverse due to the immense double cornices, which, in those days, could make the ridge impossible. From the Betemps hut, their route to the summit involved 1,742m of climbing, much of it on pure ice which, at times, could only be done by traversing the sheer face of the ridge underneath the cornices. For once, Gertrude 'went through ten minutes of unmixed fear.' Reversing the ridge in descent was even more perilous, but they reached the safety of the Marguerita hut that night, at 4,556m the highest in the Alps, and the following day completed the circuit of Monte Rosa's highest summits. It was Gertrude's last climb.

Gertrude's mountaineering years were amongst the happiest of her life: halcyon days before the post-war years brought disappointment and embitterment. Her stepmother Frances described her life revealingly as one in which 'great joys came with great sorrows', but she was spared the demolition of her beloved Rounton Grange in 1950. She was also spared the madness of the Second Gulf War and the devastation of Iraq when the Anglo-American invasion resulted in the looting of 10,000 of the Iraq Museum's artefacts and its closure. In 2019 English Heritage erected a blue plaque outside Gertrude's London home to honour an almost forgotten British heroine whose star still illuminates the wasted lands of Iraq and Syria.

Gertrude Bell was incomparable. However, like her, a visit to Persia altered the course of my own life. My attempt to climb the Finsteraarhorn on ski only got as far as the 4,089m Hugi Sattel, but in 1968 Nick Allen and I did two of the great Engelhörner rock climbs and our traverse of the Schreckhorn ended in drama when we rescued a badly injured German guided party who had fallen down its south-east face. The fearsome Lyskamm double-cornices were not in evidence in 1971 when Michael Baker and I did the traverse but I shall never forget our negotiating the nightmarish crevasses of the Zwillings glacier.

One Hundred Years Ago

The early months of 1920 were notable for a number of major winter expeditions by the Swiss topographer Marcel Kurz. Accompanied by the guide Josef Knubel and with the aid of ski he completed the first winter ascents of the Obergabelhorn, Schalihorn and Täschhorn. Kurz and Knubel also climbed the north-east, Hörnli ridge of the Matterhorn intending to descend the north-west, Zmutt ridge to complete a winter traverse of the peak. On reaching the summit a violent wind forced a retreat to the Solvay hut where they were thankful to shelter before continuing the descent. In May Arnold Lunn and Knubel climbed the Weisshorn using ski to the foot of the rocks below the east ridge.

Conditions during the climbing season were unsettled with severe storms experienced in all the principal regions. Following a week of heavy rain in September a section of the Mer de Glace collapsed causing serious damage and flooding in the Chamonix valley. Several guideless Alpine Club parties were in action during intermittent spells of fine weather: Raymond Bicknell, Harold Porter and Leslie Shadbolt completed a number of successful expeditions including traverses of the Meije and the Col des Grandes Jorasses; and a group with Noel Odell climbed the Aiguille du Grépon and other peaks while based at the Montenvers hotel.

In the Zermatt district O K Williamson with Heinrich and Albert Fux traversed the Täschhorn by way of the south-east and north ridges intending to continue to the Dom. This plan was abandoned in deteriorating weather and the party descended the very steep west slopes of the Domjoch to reach the Kin glacier and Randa late in the day. To the east in the Dolomites the guideless climbers Gunther Langes and Erwin Merlet opened two fine routes: the north-west ridge of Cima della Madonna and the south-west pillar – the *Gran Pilastro* – of Pala di San Martino.

During the summer Alexander Kellas returned to Garhwal to resume his scientific work in connection with the use of oxygen at high altitude and to continue his exploration of Kamet (7756m). Accompanied on this occasion by Henry Morshead, an army officer attached to the Survey of India, Kellas established a series of camps on the East Kamet glacier reaching a height of some 7,190m before being forced to retreat.

In South Africa members of the Mountain Club continued to pioneer new routes on Table Mountain (1087m). George Londt and other leading climbers completed *Ascension Buttress Direct, Connaught Face* and *Silverstream Corner,* all very severe routes for the period.

In the Southern Alps of New Zealand Samuel Turner paid a second visit to the Fiordland region where he hoped to make the first ascent of Mount

Serenity Mountain, Canadian Rockies. *(Allen Carpe, Alpine Club Photo Library)*

Tutoko (2746m), the highest peak in the Darran range. Accompanied by Alfred Cowling, a guide at the Hermitage hotel, and Jack Cowan as porter Turner continued to explore the approaches to the peak before being obliged to retreat due to lack of provisions and the rugged nature of the terrain.

In the Canadian Rockies a party led by W W Foster made the first ascent of Mount Sturdee (3155m) in the Assiniboine district. Further north Allen Carpe and Howard Palmer reached the summit of the unclimbed Serenity Mountain (3223m), one of the major peaks in the Whirlpool group.

At home the revival of mountaineering after the war was continued by outstanding climbers in the Lake District including G S Bower and H M Kelly. *North Wall Climb* on Dow Crag, *Upper Deep Ghyll Buttress* on Scafell and numerous other severe or very severe routes were completed during the year.

In November a note in the *Alpine Journal* referred to the Groupe de Haute Montagne, which had been formed by Jacques de Lépiney and other active members of the French Alpine Club. Many famous climbers including Lucien Devies and Maurice Herzog have belonged to the ranks of the GHM.

An event of considerable interest in October was the publication of *Mountain Craft,* edited by Geoffrey Winthrop Young. The work was reviewed in the *Alpine Journal* where it was described as a 'great storehouse of accumulated wisdom.' Other books published during the year included *The Life of Horace-Bénédict de Saussure* by D W Freshfield with the collaboration of H F Montagnier and *Mountain Memories* by Sir Martin Conway.

In February the death occurred of Hermann Woolley, a former president of the Alpine Club who had made numerous ascents in the Alps, Norway, the Caucasus and the Canadian Rockies during a long and successful climbing career.

This account is concluded with a recollection of Alexander Seiler, the head of the Seiler hotels in the Zermatt valley, whose death was announced in March and who is remembered for his generous offer of hospitality to Alpine Club members during the war. Writing in the *Alpine Journal* Capt Percy Farrar paid tribute to a great personality, adding that Zermatt would not be quite the same without Alexander Seiler, the friend of every English mountaineer.

Area Notes

Plate 10. *'Crossing the Touse [Tons]'*

LINDSAY GRIFFIN

Alps & Dolomites 2019

It seems clear that we are witnessing a decreasing number of major new lines climbed in the Alps. Climate change has produced a damaging effect on the mountains, rather limiting the periods in which one can climb safely in appropriate conditions. Climbing exploration now appears to be playing second fiddle to speed and steep skiing.

Steep skiing has produced the most 'exploration' in recent years, even if many new descents rely on old routes. Steep skiing has really boomed in the last two decades due to the evolution of both skis and ski-touring websites. Social media has played a huge part in destroying myths and breaking down barriers. Extreme descents can be found all over the Alps and across to Slovenia, but they appear to predominate in France and Italy. Some of the old classics, such as the Glacier Rond from the Aiguille du Midi, have in recent times become dangerous when too many people try to descend at the same time without consulting each other.

Amongst the many notable descents in 2019, perhaps the most outstanding were made by the French guide Paul Bonhomme. With Stéphane Rouget he completed an impressive descent of the 550m east face of Étale (2484m) in the Aravis range. The pair first climbed their proposed descent route, which turned out to be TD with one section of M5. Finding exceptional snow conditions, they were able to ski this with just one short rappel. A little later Bonhomme, unable to convince anyone of the feasibility of his proposed project on the Dent Blanche (4357m), had to go it alone on the east face. This is the face left of the Arête des Quatre Anes and Bonhomme climbed it by a new 1,100m line named *Nico,* coming in from the left and then rising directly to the summit. The descent involved an initial narrow ridge, then 50° snow through complex rocky terrain. Other notable descents include a previously untravelled line on the south face of the Aiguille du Rochefort (4,001m), with an initial section of 55°, by Philippe Batoux, Christophe Jacquemoud, and Alexandre Pittin, and the Plan-Blaitière link-up by Batoux, Michel Fauquet, and Fred Gentet. These three skied the north face of the Aiguille du Plan, climbed the south-south-west couloir of the Aiguille de Blaitière and then slid back down it.

Following the development and increased popularity of sky and ultra trail running (as famously practised by, for example, Kilian Jornet) and fast solo ascents of technical routes (e.g. Steck) we are seeing more speed ascents. These comprise not only the lowering of record times on iconic routes, generally by climbers who have the route wired after many practice attempts, but also incredibly quick times on long classics or fast link-ups. A few examples from 2019 follow.

The new British route *Beyond Reason* on the north face of the Aiguille des Pélerins. *(Matt Helliker)*

In the Mont Blanc range, François Cazzanelli and Andreas Steindl made a rapid ascent of the classic *Peuterey Integral.* Starting at La Sorgente campsite in the Val Veni early one morning in July, and having previously cached their sacks at the foot of the south ridge of the Aiguille Noire, they reached the summit of Mont Blanc in 12h 12m. The pair then descended the normal Italian route and Miage glacier, and were back at the campsite just under 16 hours after leaving, a round-trip of 45km with nearly 4,300m of ascent. It is hardly surprising that just two months later Cazzanelli was able to make a record speed ascent of Manaslu (8163m), climbing from base camp to the top and back in 17h 43m, a total distance of 44km with 3,280m of ascent.

Previously, on 19 February, two parties arrived at the foot of the Grandes Jorasses for a winter ascent of the classic *Walker Spur* (1200m, ED1). Caroline 'Caro' North (Switzerland) and Carlos Molina (Argentina) had never climbed the route before and graciously allowed the 'home' team of French guides Léo Billon, Sébastien Ratel and Benjamin Védrines to go first. Twelve hours later these three stood on the 4,208m summit. North and Molina arrived a few hours later. It is suggested this is the first time the Walker has been climbed in a day by parties in winter. The French report that the granite was so dry they were able to climb some of the hard pitches in rock shoes.

Over in the Pyrenees, Rémi Thivel made a solo ascent of the classic *Barrio-Bellocq* route (800m, D+, 5b) on the north face of Vignemale (3258m) in just 57m 30s from rimaye to summit. Although not sustained, the rock on this route still demands respect, and for an on-sight attempt (not applicable to Thivel, a highly experienced *pyréniste* who has guided the route many times) finding the correct line is difficult. With over 1,100m of climbing to the summit, Thivel's speed was around three seconds per metre.

In the Valais the same Paul Bonhomme mentioned above made a rapid crossing of eight 4,000m peaks. In a round trip of just 11h 6m from Randa (1400m) he climbed the Alphubel (4206m), continued over the Täschhorn

(4480m), Dom (4545m), Lenspitze (4294m), Nadelhorn (4327m), Steck-nadelhorn (4241m). This 36km outing had 4,200m of ascent with difficulties up to D+.

Over in the Dolomites, in September the Swiss Dani Arnold set a speed record for the famous *Comici-Dimai-Dimai* route (550m, 6b) on the north face of the Cima Grande di Lavaredo (2999m). The previous record of 48 minutes achieved in 2014 by Christoph Hainz was only to the Ring Band. Arnold climbed from ground to summit in 46m 30s. When he arrived at the base of the route there were already three parties on the face and he had to wait until 2.30pm, when they were high enough that he wasn't forced to overtake on the difficult lower pitches. Impressive though this is, let's not forget that in September 1937 Emilio Comici returned to solo his route in just 3h 45m, an ascent still considered one of the most remarkable in the annals of mountaineering.

With hard ice and mixed routes generally climbed in winter and spring, there were a number of important winter ascents and new routes, not least of some ephemeral ice lines in the Dolomites. However, one of the most significant ascents throughout the entire Alps took place on rock during a single day in February, when Léo Billon, Julien Ravanello and Benjamin Védrines made the much coveted and long awaited first winter ascent of any route on the north side on the north-west spur of the Pointe Orientale de l'Épéna (3348m) in the Vanoise. The team climbed the *Rod-Schneider* (765m, TD, 5c), first climbed by Jean Rod and Marcel Schneider in two days in September 1966 and perhaps the most travelled route on this infrequently climbed wall. Over the last couple of decades strong teams, largely from the Groupe Militaire de Haute Montagne (GMHM), have made a number of unsuccessful winter attempts on the *Rod-Schneider,* one team that included Manu Pellissier retreating just 130m below the top.

The Pointes et Aiguille de l'Épéna were among the last 'big peaks' in the Alps to be climbed (1900) and the north face is revered by the French mountaineering community due to its relative isolation, tranquillity and being arguably the highest limestone wall in the French Alps (as opposed to their Préalpes). The descent is long and complex and the rock on the route is both compact and often friable, with characteristically small downward-sloping holds and poor protection, even if using pegs. Even today sound belays are considered so difficult to arrange that on some of the easier sections (IV to V) climbers will need to move together with little or no intermediate gear. The great French guide and alpinist Pierre Chapoutet, who wrote a monograph on this mountain, considered it one of the finest in all the French Alps. In 2000-01 the late Patrick Berhault made a celebrated on-foot traverse of the Alps with a difference: he linked ascents of historic climbs that to him truly represented the evolution of alpinism. Bérhault had included an ascent of the north-west spur in his itinerary but conditions at the time did not allow it.

Moving east to the Écrins, on the 3,769m west summit of the Rateau, Mathieu Détrie and Octave Garbolino added *Bonne Pioche* (500m, ED, M6,

6a, A1) during one day in February. The second ascent was not long in coming: during one day the following month Sébastien Ratel and Benjamin Védrines repeated the line free at M7, 6a, and added a direct finish.

On the remote east face of the Aiguille de l'Amône (3584m) the Swiss Simon Chatelan and Silvan Schüpbach put up the sustained *L'Accidentelle et l'Accidenté* (850m, M7) over two days in February. The pair climbed the wall between the *Drouot-Girard-Gréloz* (1942, IV) on the east pillar and the *Gréloz-Roch* (1935, D) on the north-north-east face, noting that it is possible to escape right onto the latter at various points. After topping out the wall but below the summit, the two immediately descended the north-north-east face, which gave straightforward down climbing on good névé.

Sadly, one of the most notable events in the Mont Blanc range was the tragic deaths in November of two of France's finest alpinists: Max Bonniot and Pierre Labbre. It appears they were most likely moving together up the approach couloir to the Pilier Septentrionale on the west face of the Plan when they slipped and fell around 300m. As noted in *AJ* 2015 Chris Bonington climbed three major new routes in the massif during 1965, the second, with American Lito Tejada-Flores, following the obvious 700m left-hand pillar on the west face of the Plan at V+ and A3. Although they noted that in good conditions the route would give enjoyable climbing of high-order difficulty, it appears that for more or less half a century no one was enticed by this pronouncement. It's likely there was no repeat of this line until 2014, when Jeff Mercier and Korra Pesce took a modern approach to the ascent, climbing it free at M7. Over the years the spur leading to the crux headwall has suffered much rock fall, leaving it loose and unpleasant, so Mercier and Pesce climbed the couloir alongside it. It seems this was the tactic adopted by Bonniot and Labbre until their fatal fall. Both were guides, Bonniot with the GMHM, and both had climbed outstanding lines in the Alps as well as major new routes in South America and the Himalaya.

The Italian guide and noted ice climber Enzo Marlier has been developing the accessible Grand Flambeau (3566m) close to the Torino hut. In crisp snow the north ridge is a little classic at PD but the faces of the Flambeau have been generally left alone due to a reputation for very poor rock. However, in low temperatures and after blizzards have plastered the mountain to provide exemplary 'Scottish conditions', Marlier has been able to establish around half a dozen relatively short mixed climbs of good quality, four to five pitches maximum and with difficulties from around M6 to M8.

In the Bregaglia climbers were also taking the opportunity to explore the massif for ephemeral winter lines. In December Marcel Schenk and Natascha Knecht climbed the short but worthwhile *Un Poco Mondo* (200m, WI4 M6+) on Al Balzet, a subsidiary formation below Piz Balzet in a side branch of the Albigna valley.

In the Dolomites, it seems for the local climber able to grab fleeting conditions when they occur, the world can be your oyster. In January, on the Brenta's Cima Tosa (3173m), Fabian Buhl and Luka Lindič climbed

The ephemeral ice and mixed route *Pandora* on the west face of Sass Pordoi climbed by Simon Gietl and Vittorio Messini.

Sau Hladno! on the 500m west face at AI6 M5. The line runs to the right of the 2013 Tomas Franchini and Allesandro Lucchi route, *Selvaggia Sorte* (WI5+, M5+) and had been spotted by Lindič while making the second ascent of *Selvaggia Sorte* with Ines Papert on New Year's Day 2019. Also in January, Daniele and Enrico Geremina, and Fabrizio della Rossa spent two days climbing *Pelmoon* (800m, 18 pitches, M7 WI5) on the north face of Monte Pelmo (3,168m). The route was rappelled, with one bolt placed at each anchor. The following month Gabriele Colomba and Giuseppe Vidoni climbed *Via degli Allievi* on the 700m north face of the Cimon della Pala (3184m) at AI5 M4.

Towards the end of the year Simon Gietl and Vittorio Messini found that bizarre autumn conditions had led to a huge ice curtain forming on the west face of the Sass Pordoi (2952m). Prompted by a message from a generous friend informing them the ephemeral ice line left of *Ghost Dog* (750m, WI6, X, M5, 6a), climbed in 2013 by Jeff Mercier and Korra Pesce, appeared to be extraordinarily fat, the two duly reached and then dispatched this ice formation over two days in December, finishing on the huge terrace below the summit. The route follows existing summer lines in the lower part of the face, beginning with the initial section of the 1953 *Abram-Oslo-Perti* route.

Simon Messner and Manuel Baumgartner climbed the ephemeral ice route *Rapunzel* on the north-west face of the Sass dla Crusc in December. *(Simon Messner)*

A good snow-covered ledge enabled the pair to use a small tent for their overnight bivouac. The route has been named *Pandora* (600m, V, WI6, M5, A0). The aid is a committing diagonal rappel at around half height before reaching the bivouac ledge and the main ice section above. As the two left all their bivouac gear at half height, they were unable to make the easy walk-off from the top and had to rappel the face.

The west face of the Sass dla Crusc (2907m) carries a weight of history. It was here in 1968 that a certain Reinhold Messner, while making the first ascent of the central pillar, committed to an off-vertical wall of friable rock above an ankle-snapping ledge to create the first alpine VII in Europe. Even today opinions of this pitch vary from VII through to VIII-. In 1979, during the first ascent of *Mephisto*, well left of the central pillar, Reinhard Schiestl led (on natural gear) what is now considered the first confirmed alpine VIII- or VIII in Europe. In one day during December, Messner's son Simon added

The north side of the Piz Badile in winter. The *Via Nardella* on the east-north-east face was freed at 7b+ in September 2019.

an ephemeral line, well to the left on the north-west face, when with Manuel Baumgartner he climbed *Rapunzel.* This is a long snow face followed by four steep pitches (120m) with difficulties up to WI6+ M8. On the very thin ice forming the crux pitch Baumgartner rested twice on his axes whilst placing two pitons, then had to run out the last 20m above a poor ice screw. Messner, following, climbed with no rests. The pair stopped at the end of the difficulties, just below the top of the wall, and made a rappel descent. This line has been a well-known objective amongst local alpinists for many years and had seen several attempts. However, the ice builds only rarely and lasts but a short time, quickly becoming very brittle. Local ethics dictate no bolts on the Sass dla Crusc. This was one of several difficult ice and mixed lines put up by Simon Messner and partners in the Dolomites during the year in addition to his fine first ascents of Geshot and Muztagh Tower's Black Tooth in Pakistan.

Finally, in the Austrian Ötztal, one of the final, long new routes recorded by Hansjörg Auer before his untimely death on Howse Peak in the Canadian Rockies was a solo first ascent on the north-west face of the Rofele Wand (3345m). Climbing on 27 February during the last days of an amazing spell of fine weather in the Alps, Auer found ideal conditions. Although he carried gear for an expected bivouac, he was able to complete the 500m face in one day at VI A1.

On summer Alpine rock one of the most outstanding achievements of the year was the (more or less) first free ascent of the *Via Nardella* on the east-north-east face of the Piz Badile (3305m). Climbed over five days in September 1973 by Daniele Chiappa, Giulio Martinelli, Tiziano Nardella, and Elio Scarabelli, this route up the very steep slabs right of the *Isherwood-Kosterlitz* and between this and the *Brothers' Route,* features sustained aid climbing up to A3 and the use of bolts for almost the entire 350m middle section. It was repeated the following year in a single day by well-known Swiss activists Toni Holdener and Rudi Homberger, and then again over six days during the winter of 1983-4. It's not clear whether there have been any subsequent ascents. David Hefti and Marcel Schenk waited all summer for the right conditions but it wasn't until mid September they set foot on the wall (like all routes attempted outside winter on this part of the Badile's east-north-east face, the pair approached from the south and the Colle de Cengalo, rappelling the couloir to the foot of the route). The pair climbed around 11 pitches that day, reaching the top of the main difficulties and spending the night in a portaledge. They found the granite to be perfect but the central section a huge psyc gical challenge. Many of the existing bolts and pegs could be removed by hand, but the pair only replaced a couple of bolts on main belays. They on-sighted every pitch except for seven and 10 (6c+ and 7a+), which were climbed free by the second. The serious run-out nature of the climbing meant that only two or three pitches could be led at a time before the man on the sharp end became mentally drained and had to hand over the lead. On the second day, half a dozen long pitches, less difficult but with more snow, led to the summit. *Via Nardella* is now 7b+, 7a obl R, and likely the most demanding free route on the Badile. At the end of the same month they completed the first continuous redpoint of a project on the Cattedrale Val da l'Abigna, a very steep rock wall visible during the ride up the Albigna cable car. The pitch grades of 260m *Sotsura* are 8a, 7b+, 6c+, 7a+, 7a, 7c and 8a.

Prior to this, on 5 July, Hefti and Schenk had concentrated their energies on free climbing an old problem on the Cima dal Largh (3188m). This triple-topped summit, first climbed by Christian Klucker, was once a celebrated ascent. Nowadays, a very long approach (at least four hours from the Albigna cable car via the Forcella dal Bacun) is largely considered too much for what amounts to a few pitches of good climbing. In 1974 Fleuri Koch and Paul Muggli climbed the striking *South Pillar,* 200m of excellent red granite largely overcome with pegs and wooden wedges (V A2). It is a testament to the remote setting of this pillar that it still awaited a free ascent. With spring snow covering a long approach over boulders, Hefti and Schenk were able to make a fast approach (three hours) and climb all five pitches to the summit fairly swiftly, but without free climbing the crux third pitch. Hefti took several falls on lead and Schenk cleaned the holds and practiced the moves on top rope. The pair rappelled from the summit to the start of the third pitch, which Schenk in the lead, then Hefti, were able to climb free at 7b/7b+ 6c obl, using small cams and clipping pegs.

In the Bernese Oberland on the north face of the Eiger, Roger Schaeli achieved a long-held ambition when with Sean Villanueva he made the first one-day free ascent of *La Vida es Silbar* (900m, 27 pitches, 7c+). *La Vida es Silbar* was put up by Daniel Anker and Stephan Siegrist during 1988-9, and free climbed by Siegrist and Ueli Steck over two days in 2003, the same year that Schaeli (with Simon Anthamatten) first climbed it. At that time Siegrist estimated the difficulties at 'around 7c', making it the most continuously difficult free climb on the Eiger. In 2016, with Mayan Smith-Gobat, Schaeli managed to redpoint the route over three days, only the second free ascent, with two bivouacs on the face. However, he dreamt about making a one-day redpoint and worked the route for three years before July 2019, when on his first attempt he found rock fall had altered one of the key pitches, making it harder. On the ascent with Villanueva, he was kept awake most of the night on the bivouac below the route by shoulder pain. Despite this misery, both climbers managed all pitches free, with Schaeli leading the harder ones. From the summit they rappelled the south face in the dark, with a bivouac part way down. That summer Schaeli had already made his 50th ascent of the Eiger, his first via the Mittellegi when he was 18. Most have been via difficult routes on the north face.

Villanueva noted the climbing on *La Vida es Silbar* to be very complex, making the possibility of an on-sight a 'very different story'. However, that's exactly what the Swiss Nina Caprez would have liked to have done a short time later, when with Aymeric Clouet she completed the route in a 20-hour push. It was the first time on the route for both climbers. Caprez climbed all pitches free, while Clouet failed on only two pitches. The crux and another pitch of 7b required multiple attempts and the two stopped at 10pm two pitches (6b, 6a) below the top and rappelled to a bivouac. Not long before this Caprez had joined another woman, Martina Cufer from Slovenia, to make a fast repeat of *Voie Petit* on the east face of the Grand Capucin (3838m). This 450m (12 pitches) route was first climbed by Arnaud Petit and friends in 1997 and subsequently freed in 2005 by Alex Huber at 8b. Caprez almost climbed it with Villanueva but bad weather forced them down. On the second, successful attempt she needed just 11 hours to lead every pitch free. Around the same time that Caprez and Clouet were charging up *La Vida,* over on the right side of the face Robert Jasper rope soloed the first ascent of *Meltdown* (11 pitches, 7a+). He worked ground up for five days, protecting his new line with trad gear, pegs and the occasional bolt.

In July, Schaeli joined old friend Siegrist on the Jungfrau to redpoint *Silberrücken* (350m, 8a+), a route they had created but not freed in 2018. The new route climbs the steepest central section of the west face of the Rotbrätt ridge, close to the Silberhorn hut, leading to the summit of the Silberhorn (3695m). The only other route, closer to the ridge crest, is *Fätze und Bitze* (7a). The new line is protected by both bolts and trad gear but the crux pitch is still somewhat run out. The Swiss pair climbed the nine-pitch route, continuously vertical or overhanging, over two days, with pitches four to seven thought to be 7c+, 8a, 8a+ and 8a respectively.

Back west to a quiet corner of the Mont Blanc range, where Tony Penning revisited old haunts on the Italian side of the Grandes Jorasses. In 2006, with Gavin Cytlau, Nick Gillett, Nic Mullin and Ali Taylor, Penning climbed a 2,862m granite tower in the Pra Sec basin below the south side

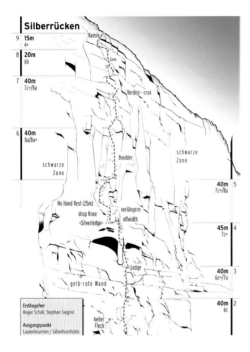

Topo of *Silberrücken* on the Silberhorn, now free at 8a+.

of the Grandes Jorasses. It was later named Punta Giancarlo Grassi after the sorely missed but arguably most productive exploratory alpinist ever to come out of Italy. Penning returned in 2012 to create *The Climb that Time Forgot* (eight pitches, E4 6a) up a fine groove system on the upper face of Punta Grassi. In August 2019 he returned to solo a four-pitch line starting down to the left of the 2012 route. He self-belayed using a Silent Partner and named the route *The Long Goodbye* (E2 5b).

In the Dolomites there are still strong teams willing to tackle big unclimbed lines without taking a drill. On the vast north face of the Sassolungo, Aaron Moroder, Titus Prinoth and Matteo Vinatzer put up *Parole Sante* (1050m, VIII and A1) on natural gear with very few pegs (650m of new ground). The climb follows a logical line and is described as a fine example of a route dictated by natural features that can be climbed very well without recourse to bolts.

Over three years from 2009, three of the most active modern pioneers in the Dolomites, Alexandro Bau, Alexandro Beber and Nicola Tondini, noted for their bold ascents of hard new routes on big walls without recourse to bolts, put up *Colonne d'Ercole* on the north-west face of Punta Tissi (2992m), home to famous lines such as the *Philipp-Flamm*. The route has 29 pitches up to 7c or 7c+, with obligatory moves of around 7a+, and is protected with trad gear and in-situ pegs. It climbs the 1,200m wall between the *Philipp-Flamm* diedre and *Kein Rest von Sehnsucht* to the left. The three climbers eventually made a one-day free ascent in September 2012. Over three days in August 2019, with comfortable bivouacs at the top of pitches 10 and 23, Antonin Cechini, Aurélien Vaissière and Symon Welfringer made the first on-sight free ascent. Welfringer led the most difficult pitches and managed to on-sight every pitch of the route. Not surprisingly, the three French found a number of long run-outs and a scary crux pitch that involves a hard boulder problem some distance above a cluster of dubious pitons.

A little to the right, climbing the narrow pillar to the right of the classic 1954 *Aste-Sussati* (700m, 18 pitches, VI+) on the north-west face, Davide Cassol and Luca Vallata put up *Capitani di Ventura* (700m, 15 pitches, VIII-, A1). The

Tony Penning's new four-pitch route *The Long Goodbye* on the Punta Giancarlo Grassi. *(Tony Penning)*

climb was completed over four separate days without a drill: not bivouacking on the wall was not so much a question of choice but more a result of short weekends and bad weather. Most of the route climbs solid grey limestone, but the crux section – four pitches through a yellow rock band – involved friable rock. The pair resorted to aid on two of the pitches but feel if more time can be spent cleaning, then these should go free.

There are still moderate lines being discovered on well-known, well-climbed, even 'iconic' peaks, proving that the Dolomites still hold vast potential for new routing. One such example is the famous Cima Grande di Lavaredo, where two South Tyrol guides, Dietmar Niederbrunner and Hannes Pfeifhofer, climbed a new route, *Zeitsprung,* up the east face. The route begins 20m right of the normal *Grohmann* route, the rock is good, the belays bolted and the grade never more than V+ for its 14 pitches.

Outside of the main Alpine regions but notable for the progression of exceptionally difficult Alpine sport routes is the Rätikon, straddling the Swiss-Austrian border. Well-known in this range is the seven-summited Kirchlispitzen (2552m) with its 2km wide south face up to 500m high and of excellent steep limestone. In November, on the seventh Kirchlispitze, the talented German Fabian Buhl completed a longstanding problem when he made the first continuous free ascent of *Déjà.* This line was first bolted in 1992 by Andres Leitha and Michi Wyser and has been attempted over the years by many climbers. Four years ago Buhl started work and finally, be-layed by Leitha and in just five hours, achieved the coveted continuous red-point. The 400m route has 12 pitches up to 8c+. Apart from the crux fifth pitch there is one of 8a+, two of 7c+ and one of 7c. *Déjà* lies just left of the legendary 1990 Beat Kammerlander route, *Unendlicht Geschichte* (8b), which in its day was considered one of the hardest long multi-pitch free climbs in the world. This is now a mantle that *Déjà* can clearly assume.

SIMON RICHARDSON

Scottish Winter 2019-20

Roger Webb making the first winter ascent of *Nethy Crack* (V,6) on Cnap Coire
na Spreidhe on Cairn Gorm. *(Simon Richardson)*

The Scottish International Winter Meet has long been recognised as a key event on the world mountaineering calendar. It had been held on a two-year basis by the BMC since 1997, but had not run since 2016. Partnerships formed on previous meets have resulted in dozens of new routes across the globe such as *Light Traveller* on Denali, and the first winter conditions ascent of the north face of North Twin in the Canadian Rockies. The most recent example is the first ascent of the north face of Latok I in the Karakoram climbed by Tom Livingstone, Aleš Česen and Luka Stražar (Slovenia) who met on the meet two years earlier.

After an AC lecture in Keswick, John Porter and I sat down over a few whiskies and talked late into the night. If the Alpine Club contributed some funding and the Scottish Mountaineering Club provided accommodation perhaps we could resurrect the winter meet? The idea quickly gained traction: the BMC filled the shortfall in funding, Salewa kitted out the hosts, and Mountaineering Scotland took on the crucial event host role. Previous events were based at Glenmore Lodge but this time, climbers would rotate between Mill Cottage, Raeburn, Lagangarbh and the CIC huts. The meet was held at the end of February and was the undoubted highlight of the season with ascents of over 150 different climbs and seven new routes. The timing was something of a miracle, squeezed in between poor mid-season conditions and the onset of Covid-19 international travel restrictions.

Overall, the 2020 season will be remembered as a challenging and frustrating one. It started reasonably enough, with good early season climbing on the high cliffs, but a devastating Christmas thaw stripped the mountains bare and it was not until the end of January that significant snow cover returned. February was a story of gales and never-ending storms, although this did have a significant upside of plastering north-west-facing cliffs with snow-ice.

Finally, in the third week of March, a long-awaited high-pressure system arrived and winter climbing conditions were outstanding. Unfortunately this coincided with the rapidly escalating pandemic and eventual lockdown on 23 March. Scottish winter climbers were left frustrated, staring at long-distance webcam shots of the Ben in perfect condition wondering what might have been.

Early Season
Winter arrived in late October when a cold north-westerly deposited a layer of snow over the high tops. The best climbing was found in the colder and less snowy Cairngorms with routes climbed in the Northern Corries, Creagan Cha-no and Braeriach. Jamie Skelton and Dave Almond had two excellent days climbing in the middle of November that resulted in an early repeat of *The Snowpimp* (VIII,9) in Coire and Lochain and *Berserker* (VI,8), an excellent new addition to Lurcher's Crag. The Almond-Skelton team maintained an excellent run of routes early in December with the second ascent of *Dark Angel* (VII,8) in Glen Coe, and an early repeat of *Brass Monkey* (VII,8) on Ben Nevis.

Rene Lisac from Croatia climbing *Gully of the Gods* (VI,6) on Beinn Bhan during the International Winter Meet. Lisac said afterwards that this was the finest route (of any description) that he had ever done. *(Scott Grosdanoff)*

The big early season event took place in mid November when Greg Boswell and Guy Robertson climbed *Local Hero* (VIII,9) on An Teallach. This spectacular route lies on the *Hayfork Gully* wall and was named in memory of Martin Moran. Roger Webb, Neil Wilson and I took advantage of the same cold weather window to climb *Dundonnell Face* (IV,4) on Benn Alligin. This is the first route to tackle the 200m triangular face between *Backfire Ridge* and *Diamond Fire*.

Mid Season
January and the first half of February were characterised by deep thaws and generally thin conditions. Roger Webb, Gary Kinsey and I took advantage

All go on the South Wall of Garbh Bheinn. The final day of the International Winter Meet reached a climax with first winter ascents of *Gralloch* (IX,10) and *Scimitar* (VII,8) doubling the previous number of winter routes on the wall. *(Neil Adams)*

of an early January snowfall to make the first winter ascent of *Nethy Crack* (V,6) on Cnap Coire na Spreidhe on Cairn Gorm. Conditions were lean in the west and a well timed early repeat of *Archangel* (VII,7) on Ben Nevis by Malcolm Bass and Nick Clement was possibly the finest technical winter climb in January.

Things began to pick up mid February with more snow and cooler temperatures. On Skye, Mike Lates and Lucy Spark made the first ascent of *Christmas Comes but Once a Year* (IV,4) on Sgurr nan Gillean, a beautiful icy groove on the left side of High Crag. The same day Callum Johnson and Andy MacKinnon made the first repeat of *Crack of Dawn* (VII,8) on Sgurr Mhic Choinnich. The following week, Tim Miller and Jamie Skelton made the first ascent of the serious *Sapiens* (VIII,9) on Lost Valley Buttress in Glen Coe, which climbs the upper *Neanderthal* corner with a new start. Two days later, the same team made the first winter ascent of *Butterknife* (VI,6) on the South Wall of Garbh Bheinn.

Winter Meet

On the evening of Saturday 22 February, 28 guest climbers from 22 countries and 28 British hosts met up in Aviemore, and the following morning dispersed to the huts before hitting the cliffs. In Coire an t-Sneachda ascents were made of *Fingers Ridge, Fluted Ridge Direct, Doctor's Choice, The Lamp, Vortex, Original Summer Route, Yukon Jack, The Slant Direct* and *Aladdin's Mirror Direct*. Jamie Skelton and Damian Granowski from Poland had an impressive day with *No Blue Skies, The Message* and *Pot of Gold*.

A couple of pairs ventured north to Torridon and found excellent conditions on Beinn Eighe. On the Far East Wall, Neil Adams and Peter Hoang (Canada) made an ascent of the modern classic *Sundance* (VIII,8), and on the Eastern Ramparts, Callum Johnson and Lukas Klingora (Czech Republic) came away with the fourth ascent of *Boggle* (VIII,8). In Glen Coe, Paul Ramsden and Wadim Jablonski (Poland) climbed the superlative *Central Grooves* (VII,7) in Stob Coire nan Lochan.

Greg Boswell powering up the first pitch of *The Israelite* (VIII,8) during the first winter ascent. This highly prized objective on the awe inspiring Central Gully Wall on Creag an Dubh Loch was climbed on the fourth attempt. *(Guy Robertson)*

On Ben Nevis, ascents were made of *Waterfall Gully, The Curtain, 1931 Route, Italian Climb, Route II/Route I Combination* and *Orion Direct.* Dave Almond and Trym Saeland (Norway) climbed *Darth Vader* (VII,7) and Rich Bentley and Seokju Woo (South Korea) made an ascent of *Tower Face of The Comb* (VI,6).

The weather forecast predicted Scotland would be in the eye of a storm on day two providing a break in the wind, but the exact timing of the anticipated heavy snowfall varied from forecast to forecast. Unfortunately, after a calm start it soon started to snow and blizzards persisted all day.

In Glen Coe, four teams made the long haul up to Church Door Buttress. Willis Morris and Steve Towne (USA) were particularly impressive making a possible second ascent of Greg Boswell and Uisdean Hawthorn's 2016 route *Hoargasm* (VII,8), followed by *Crypt Route* (IV,6). Paul Ramsden and Wadim Jablonski chose a lower level option and made a rare ascent of *Antichrist* (VI,7) on Creag an Socach above Bridge of Orchy.

Big news from Ben Nevis was a new route on Minus Two Buttress by Maarten Van Haeren (Canada) and Andy Inglis. *Calculus* (VIII,8) takes a line directly through the overhangs that girdle the buttress at one-third height. Inglis led the grade VI entry pitch up icy grooves and Van Haaren pulled out the stops with a superb lead up a stepped corner through the overhang on tenuous hooks.

On day three, excellent ice conditions focused the climbing on Ben Nevis. *Minus One Gully* (VI,6) had three ascents, and Callum Johnson and Lukas Klingora climbed the route so quickly that they also had time for *Minus Two Gully* (V,5). Fresh from his success on *Minus Two Buttress* the day before, Van Haeren soloed *Orion Direct* in a two-hour round trip from the hut. Other ice routes climbed include *Left-Hand Route, Waterfall Gully, Vanishing Gully, Thompson's Route* and *Tower Ridge,* which was plated in ice from bottom to top.

The mixed routes in Coire na Ciste were very icy and in challenging condition. Dave Almond and Trym Saeland (Norway) made an ascent of *Sioux Wall* (VIII,8), and Rich Bentley and Seokju Woo climbed a very bold and icy *Gargoyle Wall* (VI,6), finding only seven pieces of protection in five pitches. Mixed conditions were more amenable lower down the mountain and Neil Adams and Peter Hoang made an ascent of the rarely climbed Kellett's *North Wall Route* (VII,7).

The wind finally dropped on day four, and all eyes turned to Ben Nevis with close to 40 climbers from the meet active on the mountain. The standout performance came from Peter Hoang and Neil Adams who made an ascent of *The Shroud* (VI,6) followed by *Mega Route X* (VI,6). *The Shroud* had not touched down and was climbed as a hanging ice fang. Hoang used his extensive Canadian icefall experience to judge that this potentially very risky ascent was in safe condition. Even so, he rated the climb at WI6/WI6+ on the Canadian scale and commented that he had never climbed an icicle that did not hang vertically before: it had been blown sideways by the wind.

Mike Lates on the first ascent of *Christmas Comes but Once a Year* (IV,4) on Sgurr nan Gillean on Skye. This superb-looking route was climbed in mid February immediately following Storm Ciara. *(Lucy Spark)*

Mega Route X was also climbed by Murray Cutforth and Tom Phillips, and *Gemini* (VI,6), another highly sought after Ben Nevis classic, was climbed by Alex Mathie and Franz Friebel (Switzerland). Other routes climbed on the Ben included *Boomer's Requiem, Minus Two Gully, Minus Three Gully, The Curtain, Orion Direct, Platforms Rib* and *Route II/Route I* combination. CIC hut host Robin Clothier made a rare ascent of *Right-Hand Route* (VI,6) on Minus Two Buttress with Nicholas Wylie. This route also saw an ascent from Masa Sakano and Frano Udovic (Croatia).

Further north, Scott Grosdanoff and Rene Lisac (Croatia) climbed *Gully of the Gods* (VI,6) on Beinn Bhan and Dave Almond and Trym Saeland (Norway) made the third ascent of *Feast of the East* (VIII,9) on the Eastern Ramparts of Beinn Eighe. Saelend, who is best known for the first ascent of *The Corkscrew Route* on Cerro Torre, was absolutely buzzing after the ascent. In Glen Coe, meet volunteer John Higham took a break from resupplying the huts with food to make the first ascent of the 350m *Ephemeron Buttress* (IV,4) to the right of *Ephemeron Gully,* with John Hutchinson.

Heavy snowfall overnight on strong westerly winds resulted in dangerous wind-slab conditions on the fifth day of the meet. On Ben Nevis this confined teams to wind-scoured cliffs such as the Minus Face, where the three Minus gullies saw multiple ascents. I took time out of my meet coordinator role to team up with volunteers Stuart MacFarlane and Ian Dempster to make the first ascent of *Superwoman* (V,6), a line of icy grooves up the lower east flank of Tower Ridge. The route was named after Carole Hawthorn who kept everyone superbly fed and watered in the CIC hut throughout the meet.

In Glen Coe, Andy Inglis and Maarten Van Haeren made an ascent of *Central Grooves* (VII,7) in Stob Coire nan Lochan, and Luca Celano, Carl Nystedt (Sweden), Nicolas Dieu and Michael Poulsen ploughed through deep snow along the Aonach Eagach traverse. Other Glen Coe based teams headed to Creag an Socach above Bridge of Orchy in search of less snowy conditions. *Messiah* (VI,7) had ascents from at least three teams but the most notable climb was the third ascent of *Defenders of the Faith* (IX,9) by Peter Hoang and Neil Adams. This very steep mixed route was first climbed by Dave MacLeod and Fiona Murray in 2006, and was the first Scottish grade IX to receive an on-sight first ascent. Also of note was the first ascent of *A Very Naughty Boy* (VII,8/9) by Tim Miller and Damian Granowski from Poland. The route takes a left-trending line across the steep wall to the right of *False Rumour Gully* finishing up *The Enemy Within.*

Two new routes on Garbh Bheinn were the big news from the last day of the meet. The South Wall is very rarely in winter condition, but continuous storms had plastered it in snow making it a very wintry proposition. Tim Miller, Callum Johnson and Damian Granowski made the first winter ascent of *Scimitar* (VII,8) and Neil Adams, Peter Hoang and Lukas Klingora made the first winter ascent of *Gralloch* (IX,10). Damian led the crux of *Scimitar* and Peter made an outstanding lead of *Gralloch,* which is E2 in summer.

The weather deteriorated quickly through the day and the avalanche danger was very high. Teams on Ben Nevis wisely restricted themselves to the Douglas Boulder and Vanishing Gully areas. The weather was wild in the Northern Corries, but ascents were made of *Honeypot* and *Wachacha* on the Mess of Pottage, and Jamie Skelton and Trym Saeland climbed *Big Daddy* (VII,7) in Coire an Lochain. Everyone was back in good time for the final celebration event in Aviemore.

The 2020 Scottish International Winter Meet was a major success. Great routes had been climbed, ideas shared, friendships made and new partnerships formed. Our international guests had been given a magnificent taste of Scottish winter climbing and left with huge smiles on their faces.

Late Season
Guy Robertson and Greg Boswell pulled off a long sought after first ascent on 4 March when they made the first winter ascent of *The Israelite* (VIII,8) on Creag an Dubh Loch. This summer E4 provides superlative rock climbing but is often wet, so it was a logical winter target. The same day, the first ascent of *Hindmost Ridge* (IV,4) on The Devil's Point, demonstrated that there are still major unclimbed features even in well-known parts of the Highlands. Iain Young, John Higham and Kenny Brookman's ascent of the 400m ridge bounding the right side of *Geusachan Gully* on the south side of the mountain was a significant coup and one of the finest exploratory ascents of the season.

Good conditions extended to the Northern Highlands. Dave Almond and Jamie Skelton visited the Eastern Ramparts on Beinn Eighe and climbed a more direct version of the summer line of *Claustrophobic Corner.* They called their route *The Irony* and after some careful pondering graded it IX,9. The following day they returned to add *Scotophobia* (VII,8), which is based on the summer E1 *Fear of the Dark* on the Eastern Ramparts. Mark Robson and I had a fine adventure on *End of Days* (VI,6) on An Ruadh-Stac. This takes an unlikely six-pitch line taking in all three tiers to the left of Patey-Bonington summer line *North Face.* Finally, just before lockdown, Tim Miller and Jamie Skelton made the first winter ascent of *The Modern Idiot* (VIII,8) on Beinn Eighe's Eastern Ramparts.

In the days leading up to the enforced close of play on 23 March, many teams enjoyed superb conditions on Ben Nevis and multiple ascents were made of the Minus gullies and Orion Direct. The most significant took place on Skye however, when Will Rowland completed the Greater Cuillin Traverse followed by the Red Cuillin. This is thought to be the first time this link-up has been achieved in winter, and Rowland follows in his father Clive's footsteps, who was first to complete the feat in the summer of 1982.

TIMOTHY ELSON

India 2019

Climbing on the granite shield of the west face of Bhagirathi IV.
(Matteo Della Bordella)

The 2019 Indian climbing season was much quieter than normal with 74 Indian expeditions and 41 foreign expeditions registered with the Indian Mountaineering Foundation, a decrease of around 25% from 2018. The major event was the dissolution of the state of Jammu and Kashmir by the Indian parliament in August 2019; this led to the effective curtailment of all expeditions to all parts of Kashmir from then on. It is understood that former Kashmir is now re-open for climbing expeditions notwithstanding the current nationwide shutdown due to the Covid-19 outbreak. There appears to have been no expeditions to the Indian East Karakoram.

The major climbing event in the Indian Himalaya in 2019 was the first ascent of the west face of Bhagirathi IV (6193m) in the Garhwal by an Italian team led by Matteo Della Bordella at an impressive 7b A0. Another major ascent was the six-day first ascent of the south ridge of Menthosa (6443m)

The topo of the Italian route on the west face of Bhagirathi IV. *(Matteo Della Bordella)*

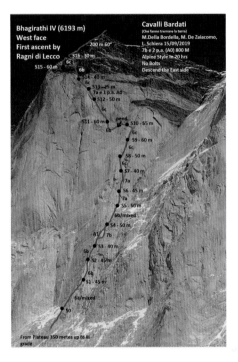

and traverse of the mountain by the US team of Spencer Grey and Rushad Nanavatty.

In May 2019 there was the very sad news of the passing of well known British guide Martin Moran and seven clients in an avalanche on the unclimbed peak 6477m southeast of Nanda Devi. This led to an extensive and well-publicised search-and-rescue effort by the Indian Disaster Relief Force.

The Indian government 'opened' 123 new peaks in 2019; previously one had to apply to the home ministry and ministry of defence for permission for these peaks, whereas now a permit can be obtained from the Indian Mountaineering Foundation directly. Peaks fees for the 123 newly opened mountains had a 50% discount in 2019. The list includes 51 peaks in Uttarakhand, 10 peaks in Sikkim, 15 peaks in the former state of Jammu and Kashmir, and 47 peaks located in Himachal Pradesh, ranging from above 7,000m to trekking peaks. See the IMF website (www.indmount.org) for more details. For peaks lower than 6,000m only trekking permits are required, an example being the Kullu Eiger (5646m).

In other news the Atal, or Rohtang tunnel was still on course to open in September 2020. The 8.8km tunnel will give all-year access to Keylong (Kyelang), the administrative headquarters of Lahaul and Spiti, from Manali, and significantly reduce travel times on the Leh-Manali highway. First conceived in 1983, current prime minister Narendra Modi announced in late 2019 that the tunnel would be named in honour of the former BJP prime minister Atal Bihari Vajpayee, who initiated the project in 2000. The tunnel is somewhat west of the Rohtang pass and had been plagued with contractual difficulties as well as engineering ones. Forty-two labourers were killed in a flash flood during construction of an access road in 2003.

Bhagirathi IV

The major ascent of the 2019 season in India was the first ascent of the west face of Bhagirathi IV (6193m) by the Italian Ragni de Lecco team of Matteo Della Bordella, Luca Schiera and Matteo De Zaiacomo. The team had attempted the face in 2015 and reached the shale band at 5,900m but could

Approaching Kishtwar Shivling during the hastily rearranged Swiss-French expedition. *(Caro North)*

not find a way through and retreated. Slovenians Matjaž Jamnik and Silvo Karo first attempted the wall in 1995, reaching 5,500m before retreating and again in 1996 by a Spanish team. The face is characterised by 400m of easier angled rock to a 700m shield of vertical to overhanging granite with a 100m high shale band at the top. Mixed-ice routes either side of the face had been climbed by Slovenians Rok Blagus, Luka Lindič and Marko Prezelj in 2009 and French climbers Thomas Arfi and Simon Duverney in 2010.

The Italians first acclimatised on the normal route on Bhagirathi II (6512m), then set to work on the west face of Bhagirathi IV. They intended to climb the low part of the same route they tried in 2015 but traverse left below the shale band. However, on 3 September while at their ABC they saw two large rock-falls down their proposed route and changed plans for a

Nanda Devi East with Nanda Devi sunlit behind and left. Longstaff's Col is on the bottom left of the picture, with the south-east ridge to Nanda Devi East dividing sun and shade coming up from the col. *(John Crook)*

The team of Caro North, Maud Vanpoulle and Lise Billon on Kishtwar Shivling. *(Caro North)*

more direct steeper route. Yet after three days of fixing ropes they retreated having been blanked out. They removed their equipment from the wall and headed down to base camp but once regrouped decided to have a single-push attempt at their original line, reasoning that the temperatures were now much lower and they would not spend too much time on the climbing. They set off at 3am on 15 September, finding the cracks clogged with dust and debris from rock-falls where in 2015 they found clean 6c/7a cracks. They reached the summit at 11pm having climbed the last couple of pitches in the dark and then descended the east face (normal route). They named the route *Cavalli Bardati* and graded it 7b A0.

The south pillar of Ali Ratni Tibba. *(DAV/Expedkader)*

Menthosa

The US-based team of Spencer Grey and Rushad Nanavatty made the first ascent of the 8km long south ridge of Menthosa (6443m), located on the west side of the Miyar valley in Himachal Pradesh. Menthosa was first climbed by a British military team in 1970 via the east ridge and this is now a very popular route, and the only route on the mountain until last year. The US team arrived in India to find that they could not travel to Ladakh where they had originally planned to climb due to the dissolution of the state of Jammu and Kashmir. So they changed objectives to Menthosa's impressive south pillar, based on a single photo and that it seemed to be made from granite. On arriving at base camp in August they had a heavy monsoon storm that deposited a metre of snow and took some time to thaw. On viewing the south pillar, they realised that it had several hundred metres of loose rock threatened by overhanging guillotine flakes to overcome and then gain the main pillar, which appeared to be granite. So they changed plans for the south ridge. Grey and Nanavatty set off up the ridge on 22 August, climbing up a jumbled icefall to a col at 5,600m. The next three days were spent climbing mixed pitches, first on the east side of the ridge and then on the west with a hanging bivy at 6,220m at the end of day four. The next day they climbed perfect névé to a bivy just below the summit topping out on 26 August. They descended the east ridge.

Kishtwar

The Swiss Caro North and the French climbers Maud Vanpoulle and Lise Billon headed to Kishtwar in the spring climbing season to travel up the Kijai Nala to attempt Arjuna (6220m). However, reaching Gulabgarh they were told they could not visit the valley, as officials thought there may be

The DAV women's expedition from left to right: Veronika Hofmann, Jana Möhrer, Raphaela Haug, Laura Tiefenthaler, with Ali Ratni Tibba behind them. *(DAV/Expedkader)*

terrorists in the valley. It is unclear how much this had to do with this being an all-female team, a prelude to the dissolution of the state of Kashmir in August 2019 or genuine safety concerns. Whatever the reason, the team had to come up with a new objective. North had made the first ascent of Monte Iñaki next to the Kishtwar Shivling in 2016, so with this in mind they changed plans to attempt Kishtwar Shivling (c6000m). They travelled from Gulabgarh to the Sumchan valley and set up base camp. Having lost a lot of time with logistical challenges, on their summit attempt they reached 5,700m having climbed lovely compact granite only to be turned around by a snowstorm that signalled the start of the monsoon and the effective end of their trip.

Himachal Pradesh

The German Alpine Club (DAV) female cadre team of Dörte Pietron (team coach), Franziska Dünßer (expedition doctor), Raphaela Haug, Jana Möhrer, Veronika Hofmann and Laura Tiefenthaler visited the Manala valley, south east of Manali in October 2019. Their original aim had been a trip to Zanskar but the dissolution of Jammu and Kashmir and tensions with Pakistan stopped them visiting this area. Haug, Möhrer and Tiefenthaler made the first ascent of the south-west pillar of Ali Ratni Tibba (5490m) at F6a in a long day from their advance base camp on the same day Pietron and Hofmann climbed an unnamed 5,000m peak via a glacial route. A few days later, Haug, Möhrer, Hofmann and Tiefenthaler climbed a peak to the south of Ali Ratni Tibba, via a prominent pillar at 6b+ in a day from their advance base camp. They had hoped to attempt the north-west pillar of Ali Ratni Tibba but did not get another weather window.

Bapsa Valley

Iker Pou, Eneko Pou, Jacopo Larcher, Sieve Vanhee, Matty Hong, Matteo Mocellin and Alex Faedda visited the Bapsa valley in October 2019 and established three new multi-pitch rock climbs on 4,000m peaks. The first was F7c+ on 4670m, which they dubbed Midi d'Ossau; they called their route *The Latin Brother* (560m) in memory of Hansjörg Auer who was meant to be on the trip with them. They then climbed a 4,900m peak by a F6c route

Miguelink (600m) named in memory of Miquel Riera, who kicked off deep water soloing in Mallorca. Finally, they climbed a route they called *Beti Alavés* on Peak 4560m at 6b+.

Uttarakhand

In Uttarakhand the main news of the season, other than Bhagirathi IV (see above), was concentrated on Nanda Devi East (7424m). There were three expeditions to this peak in 2019, the 80th anniversary of its first ascent, but in May there was the tragedy on Peak 6477m when eight climbers died. In June a Polish team summited and in September an Indian team also summited. All teams were attempting the south-east ridge, which rises from Longstaff's Col and was the first ascent route.

On 26 May, the well-known British guide Martin Moran was leading a group of seven up 6477m to the south of Longstaff's Col. At some point on that day an avalanche broke away on the face they were climbing, sweeping them all off the mountain. The deceased climbers were Martin Moran (UK), Ronald Beimel (USA), Anthony Sudekum (USA), John McLaren (UK), Richard Payne (UK), Rupert Whewell (UK), Ruth McCance (AUS) and Chetan Pandey (India). On 29 May the rest of the team, who had been pre-paring the route on the south-east ridge o f Nanda Devi East, returned to base camp where they were expecting the other team. Unable to contact them via radio, Mark Thomas, the co-leader, went up to the 6477m team's high camp and found evidence of the avalanche and from there a rescue was summoned. Following this, the Indian Air Force conducted a helicopter search and on 23 June an Indo-Tibetan Border Police search party located seven of the bodies, which were recovered by helicopter on 3 July. Martin Moran had led over 40 treks and expeditions in India, often climbing new routes and unclimbed peaks with clients, was highly respected and will be greatly missed.

Nanda Devi East was first climbed in 1939 by Jakub Bujak and Janusz Klarner, members of the first Polish Himalayan expedition. It is considered one of the most technically difficult pre-war Himalayan climbs. To mark the 80th anniversary of the first ascent a Polish team aimed to repeat the their route, the south-east ridge. The team consisted of 10 members: Rafal Fro-nia, Dariusz Zaluski, Wojtek Flaczylski, Bartlomiej Szeliga, Jan Lenczowski, Marcin Galus, Stanislaw Pisarek, Filip Babicz, Oswald Rodrigo Perira and Jaroslaw Gawrysiak. Gawrysiak and Flaczylski summited on 27 June during a 21-hour summit push.

On 26 August a four-member Indian team from South Calcutta Trekkers Association of Kolkata arrived at Nanda Devi East base camp with five support Sherpas. On 15 September Pradip Bar, along with Phurba Sherpa, Lopsang Sherpa, Chongwa Dawa and Palchen Sherpa summited, the first civilian Indian ascent of Nanda Devi East.

Sikkim

Mick Fowler and Victor Saunders attempted Chombu (6362m) the 'Mat-terhorn' of Sikkim both before and after the monsoon in 2019. Chombu

Chombu with the north face on the left and the west face on the right. The line attempted by Mick Fowler and Victor Saunders climbs the gully bottom left of the picture then up the north face. *(Mick Fowler)*

is unclimbed and had been attempted four times prior to 2019. The pair overcame various issues even to get to the mountain. They first planned an attempt in the post-monsoon season of 2017 but their permits were withdrawn. Then in 2018 Mick was diagnosed with cancer and had radiotherapy and then surgery. So it was only in pre-monsoon 2019 that they were able to visit. On arrival at the start of April it transpired the winter had been the heaviest seen 1995, snowing seven feet in a day at one point, leaving the approaches and mountains covered in snow. After an initial acclimatisation period when they climbed a 5,500m peak near the Sebu La, they turned their attention to Chombu itself. However, from this point on in their trip it snowed every night around 10cm and did not freeze, leaving an old wet snowpack covered in more and more fresh snow. After a week of these conditions they realised Chombu was not on, so climbed Chungukang North (5322m) via the moderate south ridge.

Mick and Victor returned post monsoon for a second attempt on Chombu, intending to climb a line on the west face. They acclimatised on the col below the south-west ridge, observing that their intended route was not safely climbable. So they switched objectives to the north face and ridge. During their acclimatisation they encountered 14 days of solid bad weather with precipitation each day. On 10 October the weather improved, and they set out for Chombu, via a couloir and glacier plateau below the north face. On 13 October they set off up a face buried in deep snow, burrowing upwards for two days with Saunders taking his first Himalayan fall when the snow gave way beneath him. They had 250m of easier ground to go to gain they summit when they bivouacked. However, that night their dehydrated meal was off and they soon had diarrhoea and were vomiting. By morning both felt weak and were unable to eat for the next two days. They made the decision to descend and abseiled down the line of ascent. They have not ruled out trying the mountain again.

Correction

In the *Alpine Journal* 2019, it was reported in the Sikkim notes that a British team went to try the first ascent of Brumkhangshe (5635m). However, this peak was first climbed in 2006 by Roger Payne and Julie-Ann Clyma via the north ridge and again in 2018 by an expedition run by Martin Moran. This team was attempting to repeat the north ridge.

IAN WALL

Nepal 2019-20

During the first ascent of the west face Tengi Ragi Tau (6938m), for which Tino
Villanueva and Alan Rousseau were awarded a Piolet d'Or.

A s I sit down to complete my contribution to the *Alpine Journal* 2020,
the Nepali government has just announced it has closed its borders
to foreigners and ex-pat Nepalis alike 'from 20 March midnight and will
remain in place until 15 April.' This is of course in response to fears raised
over Covid-19 and the devastating effect it could have if and when it got
into Nepal, a country with limited infrastructure capable of containing the
pandemic. *[Editor's note:* Kathmandu was back in lockdown in mid August,
despite the government announcing the country would be open for the post-
monsoon tourist season.]

It is 70 years since Nepal first opened borders previously closed because
of fear about the intentions of the East India Company and then the British
Raj. In April 1950 Ang Tharkay, the Annapurna expedition's highly experienced sirdar, led French team-members into Nepal from India, continuing
by truck through the jungle and terai to Butwal where the road at that time
ended. From Butwal, the approach march began, in essence the start of
mountain tourism in Nepal. How things have changed since.

From the mountaineering expeditions of the 1950s, the hippies in the
1960s, the Himalayan big-wall ascents of the 1970s, the development of

alpine-style ascents in the 1980s and the boom in trekking, and then commercial expeditions in the 1990s, tourism has flourished. Even through the difficult times of the insurgency, the royal massacre and the earthquake travellers continued to arrive in Nepal, with international tourists making a significant contribution to its GDP Tourism provided a certain amount of financial stability to thousands of middle-hill families. Now, sadly, all that came to a standstill.

I have just returned from the remote region in east Nepal where communities in the lower Hongu valley provide over 30,000 workers to the mountain tourism industry in the Khumbu region alone: trekking porters, commercial porters, guides, lodge managers, cooks and other staff plus the people employed in the service industries, airport staff and the like. On the same day as Nepal closed its borders, Khumbu closed lodges and trails into the upper Khumbu valley. This essential lock-down policy will have had a crippling effect on many thousands of citizens living a hand-to-mouth existence.

Winter 2018-19
A late report surfaced just after last year's *Alpine Journal* deadline reporting the successful first ascent of **Choppa Bamare** (6109m) in the Rowaling. John Kelley (USA) and Benjamin Billet (France) named their route *Seto Hi'um,* 'white snow' in Nepali, and graded it TD (1150m, M4, WI4) with many pitches of WI3/3+. February and March 2019 were among the snowiest winter months in 25 years. Conditions made the approach to base camp hard going and added several days to the trek in. The team left base camp at 2am on 22 February, initially climbing a spur followed by a snow-filled gully and mixed climbing at M4. The bottom of the south face was reached at 6.30am and there followed a long stretch of WI3. At 5.30pm they cut a small ledge and endured a standing bivy subjected to numerous spindrift avalanches. The following day the weather prevented much progress and a second bivy was arranged on a slightly larger ledge. Day three, and a long pitch of M3/3+ took the team to the top of the south face where they again bivouacked approximately 150m below the summit. Thinking they would summit the following day, they woke to appalling conditions that kept them pinned down for a further three nights at approximately 6,000m. The summit was eventually reached on 28 February, the last official day of the Himalayan winter season. The descent was via 18 rappels down the south face to the team's high camp where they dug out their reserve supplies. Continuing down to base camp, they realised avalanches had scoured the whole valley; base camp and all their equipment had been swept away. They report there are still a lot of amazing lines that could be done on the south face as long as conditions are conducive.

Post-monsoon 2019
American alpinists Tino Villanueva and Alan Rousseau climbed the main peak of **Tengi Ragi Tau** (6938m), establishing a new route up the hitherto unclimbed west face. The pair had attempted the west face before and in

The west face of Tengi Ragi Tau, with Villaneuva and Rousseau's line marked.

2014 they were forced to retreat just 400m short of the summit. Drawing on their previous experience, they finally topped out on 16 October at 9.30am after 'eight years of planning, effort and three expeditions'. The pair made their ascent in an eight-day push from Thame, taking three days to get to the base of the route and then another five up the face (1600m, WI5, M5+), which was consistently difficult with snow flutings below a summit that is almost 7,000m. They called their route *Release the Kraken,* which won them a Piolet d'Or (see Alpine Notes, p370). Rousseau and Villanueva have formed a formidable climbing partnership, choosing technical 7,000ers rather than 8,000m giants. They claimed the first ascent in 2018 of the Zanskar peak **Rungofarka** (6495m). Tengi Ragi Tau was added to the permitted list in 2012 and was climbed that autumn by a Japanese team led by Koichi Ezaki.

Having been pipped to the post for the west face of Tengi Ragi Tau, French-Swiss pair Symon Welfringer and Silvan Schüpbach instead made the first ascent of **Tengi Ragi Tau North** (6820m) later in October 2019. (The summit is located on the Finnish map not to the north of Lanmuche Kol (6552m) but to the south-east.) Another teammate Charles Noirot had to withdraw from the expedition due to illness. Their first attempt in mid October was curtailed by wind-slab risk at 6,100m. The team finally got back to work on 25 October, reaching their ABC at 5400m. On 26 October, they started up the wall with two pitches of steep ice, followed by moderate snow and ice slopes up to 60°. Wind and spindrift accompanied the pair all day. Welfringer and Schüpbach established camp on a small ledge at 6100m.

Symon Welfringer and Sylvan Schüpbach on the summit of Tengi Ragi Tau North (6820m) following the first ascent via the west face.

Bivouac on Tengi Ragi Tau North.

Steepening ground high on Tengi Ragi Tau North.

On day two the weather got better, but the steepening wall, technical pitches and thin air slowed progress. The pair struggled to find a bivy spot but having overcome a pitch of M6, eventually found a spot to pitch their tent at dusk at 6,450m. Next morning, they set out on a summit bid, leaving their bivy gear behind. Here they encountered the hardest but best pitches on the route, with a variety of steep ice, technical mixed terrain up to M6 and ice flutings of 70° to exit the face. They reached the north summit that day, the altitude of which was 6,820m according to their altimeter. Welfringer and Schüpbach rappelled back to their bivy using headlamps and spent one more night on the west face. The next day they rapped 1,000m, arriving back in base camp the day before the end of the expedition. They dubbed their new route *Trinité* (1500m, M6, AI5). It was noted in the expedition report that while the team was at Na they met a big group preparing to install a shelter near the Tashi Lapcha in memory of David Lama.

Also in the Rolwaling, a Spanish expedition climbed the south pillar of **Tengi Ragi Tau East** (6660m) between 2 and 19 October. This was the second ascent, following the first by a French team in 2005. Roger Cararach Soler, Alberto Fernandez Santiago and Marc Toralles established ABC at 5,100m below the start of difficulties on the pillar. Starting on 14 October, their approach was from below the west face consisting of snow and mixed climbing at approximately 60° to reach their first bivy site at 6,000m. The following day the team climbed

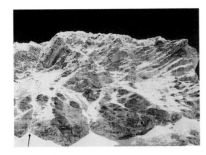

Left: The entry point on the face for the Swiss-French team of Welfringer and Schüpbach

Below: The line taken by Pemba Sherpa and Hiroki Nakayama on the north-east face of Hongu (6764m), following a long approach via the Hinku valley.

several pitches of 6a/b on solid granite followed by mixed climbing to reach the second bivy at 6,250m. On 16 October they started up slopes of poor snow before reaching rock and one M6 pitch before the final snow ridge at 6,400m. They bivouacked at 6,550m. On 17 October they continued to follow the snowy ridge, but with the late 2019 monsoon there was a lot of unconsolidated snow on the ridge resulting in this section being the crux of the whole route. The team summited at 8am and then abseiled and down-climbed to ABC, which was reached at 6pm on the 18 October.

An all-female team comprising Kanchhi Maya Tamang (Nepal), Margaritta Lucia Silvestre (Peru), Yin Hung Tsang (China) and Ma Soledad Castro Serrano (Mexico) made the first ascent of **Linku Chuli II** (6659m) in the Rolwaling, reaching the summit from the north at 10am on 28 October. Three support climbers, Nima Gyalzen Sherpa, Mingma Nuru Sherpa and Lhakpa Nuru Sherpa also summited.

The north-east face of **Hongu** (Hongku, Sura, 6764m) got its first recorded ascent on 25 October from Pemba Sherpa and Hiroki Nakayama (Japan), who approached via the Hinku and Hongu valleys. Their base camp and camp one shared the same location as camps used to climb Baruntse. The pair crossed the west col, south of Baruntse, descended the top section of the west Barun glacier, the lower Barun glacier and then entered the glacier bay

The Georgian team below Pangpoche I before the first ascent.

to establish a final camp at around 6,360m immediately below the north-east face of Hongu. The final 350m section was steep snow and ice with serac barriers. The pair left the top camp on 25 October with minimal gear and alternating leads climbed nine pitches. Some of the ground was steep and the snow was often poor. They reached the top at 3.15pm in a strong wind and snowstorm and after only 10 minutes began their rappel descent, using snow stakes and, when these ran out, an ice screw and Nakayama's Nomic axe. They reach camp at 8.30pm. The history of climbing on Hongu is not completely clear; most ascents have been made by parties either without permits or on permits for other summits. The easiest and logical way to climb the mountain in good conditions would be the north-east face. The first known ascent was in October 1983 by Sepp Egarter and Volker Klammer, who climbed the south-west ridge.

Dawa Yangzum Sherpa a 27-year-old woman from the Rolwaling valley has become the first Nepali woman to stand on the summit of **Makalu** which she achieved on 29 May 2019. Dawa is the only Nepali female IFMGA guide.

To the east of Samagoan in the Manaslu region is the Pangboche Himal. A Georgian expedition lead by Archil Badriashvi with Bakari Gelashvili and Giorgi Tepnadze made the first ascent of **Pangpoche II** (6504m). Base camp was established on 18 September at 3,900m two hours walk from Samagaon. During 20 and 21 September the team followed the south-west ridge from

The summit ridge proved serious and committing.

BC to a suitable bivy location. Leaving their bivy on 22 September at 5.30am they reached the summit at 5pm. The weather throughout the expedition was bad resulting in quite dangerous climbing conditions; the summit ridge comprised loose rocks with few options for belays. Although the ridge is not vertical it is very steep with minimal protection. From the bivy they traversed onto the south-west face, which was then climbed to the summit via a steep 80° snow face. From the summit, a six-hour descent was made to a bivy site. The descent was on a slightly different line on the south side, down a couloir with bad snow and steep sections. The majority of the route was soloed due to the lack of solid protection and belays.

After a few days rest in Samagoan the same team turned their attention to **Pangpoche I** (6620m). The first bivy was established at 5,600m, the second at 5,850m and the third at 6,380m. Leaving the top bivy at 5am, the team reached the summit at 2pm following the north ridge but then turning to traverse a wide plateau just east of the ridge. Tough snow conditions resulted in quite dangerous avalanche risks. The summit ridge was narrow and dangerous with sharp cornices and no possibility to place protection. Due to the poor snow conditions it took about fourth hours to reach the summit. They descended the same route back to their third bivy. The descent line was a reversing of the whole route to BC.

The route taken on the first ascent of Ardang, starting up a glaciated section then through the rock-band as shown.

Located in the northern section of the Annapurna Conservation Area, **Lugula** (6889m) stands between Bhrikuti Sail (6361m) on the left and Chako (6704m). Paulo Grobel (France) climbed a new snow route on this peak at PD, describing the route as pleasant with the concentration of the difficulties at the start of the route.

A Sherpa climber, Sanu Sherpa from Sankhuwasabha district Nepal, scaled **Dhaulagiri** in autumn 2019 thus becoming the third Nepali mountaineer to complete all 14 mountains above 8,000m after a two-member team of rope-fixing Sherpa climbers opened a route to the summit on 3 October 2019.

Canadians Sunny Twelker and Bryce Brown made the first ascent of **Ardang** (Chyoro Ri, 6034m) via the north-west shoulder from the Limi valley in north-west Humla. Their route followed a major moraine-drainage outlet via an obvious glacier feature to a col. A rocky ridge was then followed to the summit snowcap. Camp one was established on 11 November in a protected spot below the right side of the glacier tongue at 5,200m. The glacial snow ramp was difficult: trail breaking in unconsolidated facets and waist to chest deep in some areas restricting height gain to only 450m above camp one the following day. Avalanche risk on the lee-loaded 35° slopes was too great so they took a route to the right-hand side, trying to stay close to the safety of the lower-angled edges and rock walls. Camp two was established on 12 November at 5,650m just below the right edge of the col. An early start was made on 13 November for the summit, now only 450m above the climbers. A loose, rocky cliff-band to reach the upper snowcap provided some exhausting climbing in unconsolidated snow conditions. The rock-band was mostly lower angled at c40° with only one steeper mixed section requiring a few pieces of protection (50m, 60°, M4, AI3). The upper snowfield, in poor condition, led to a final steep snow ridge and then a loose rocky summit block that required delicate mixed climbing for 10m to reach the top at 2pm.

Project Possible

One of the big mountain stories here in Nepal in 2019 was the ascent of all 14 of the world's 8,000m peaks in six months by Nepali mountaineer Nirmal

In the rock-band of Ardang, high above the sacred Limi valley.

'Nims' Purja, dubbed 'Project Possible'. A former British special forces soldier, he completed the project in just six months and six days: 189 days. He climbed them in the following order, with the summit date in brackets: Annapurna (23 April), Dhaulagiri (12 May), Kangchenjunga (15 May), Lhotse (22 May), Everest (22 May), Makalu (24 May), Nanga Parbat (3 July), Gasherbrum I (15 July), Gasherbrum II (18 July), K2 (24 July), Broad Peak (26 July), Cho Oyu (23 September), Manaslu (27 September) and Shishapangma (29 October). He would have done it sooner had visa issues with China not required resolution.

Not surprisingly, a project of this kind raised interesting debates in the international mountaineering community. Issues regarding the use of helicopters, bottled oxygen, established routes, fixed ropes and of course a large support team have all been discussed, scrutinised and even criticised by world-class and well-known mountaineers. The general feeling seems to be that although this was a record-breaking feat of stamina and logistical planning it was not historically, in the true context of the term 'mountaineering', that important. Purja's style was so completely different to the ideals of established alpinism that it failed to impress the present-day elite. But it can be argued that Project Possible was set against completely different criteria. Nirmal Purja was completely open from the outset and never claimed he wouldn't take advantage of existing technology to help him achieve his

High on Ardang in the western Nepali district of Humla.

goal, a speed completion of all the 8000ers. The bar has now been set if others want to take on the challenge in a more lightweight or ethically clean way, for example without oxygen. However, in Nepal Nirmal Purja is regarded as a mountaineering legend and on return to Kathmandu received a public ovation during his motorcade through the capital's streets.

Robert Anderson 'soloing' towards the
summit of Everest in 1988 having
climbed the Kangshung face.
(Ed Webster)

Everest

As usual, the world's highest mountain hit the headlines in May when
several climbers posted Purja's images of a traffic jam of climbers
heading towards the summit. On 22
May it was reported that over 200
climbers and clients were heading
towards the summit after a second
weather window opened up. The
first two-day weather window that
allowed 150 climbers to reach the
summit closed on 16 May and the backlog began to build up. Three Indian climbers made false summit claims for Everest while a Kashmiri woman, Sharad Kulkarni, produced a doctored image of herself on the top to
claim her summit certificate. Mountaineers have suggested difficult weather conditions, a lack of experience and the growing commercialisation of
expeditions as contributing factors to the backlog. Kami Rita Sherpa, 24
times a summiteer, added that one of the main considerations for the 'jam'
was that the 'cheap expeditions' only provide inexperienced guides and that
they were not always capable of dealing with 'difficult clients' at altitude
as opposed to 'difficult conditions' and that they are the main cause of the
problems.

'Climbers can turn stubborn and uncooperative, insisting on climbing
even when they are likely to not make it,' Kami Rita said. 'At times like
these, Sherpa guides are well within their rights to scold, harangue, yell and
berate their clients – and in case the clients are especially obstinate, even
slap them. We [should] ask them [clients] to sign a document at Base Camp,
agreeing that they will not sue us if we yell at them or slap them. At high altitudes, we can't afford to spend a lot of time dealing with stubborn clients.'
Sadly, by the end of the season 20 mountaineers had perished on the slopes
of Nepal's 8,000m peaks.

The Nepal government, through the media, stated that overcrowding was
not to be blamed for the deaths on Everest. That is true to an extent: other
concerns include clients feeling over confident with the support systems installed on the mountain, the safety net of Sherpa support and fixed ropes,
the lack of personal accountability on the part of the clients, their lack of
experience, ego and greed – the list goes on. However, we are also told again
and again that Everest belongs to the nation and that the government 'man-
ages' the mountain on behalf of the nation, so ultimately whose responsibility is it to sort out problems on Everest?

In late July an article appeared in the Nepali newspaper *Republica* stating that a powerful group of liaison officers (LOs) pocketed millions of rupees and helped award summit certificates to climbers through a complicated collusion between LOs and expedition agencies. The newspaper exposed the ghastly story behind the scam. Politicians and those in powerful positions vouch for individuals to be LOs, who often have little mountaineering experience. The majority of those selected never stay at Everest Base Camp during the climbing season. Some readers may have seen Nepal's prime minister K P Oli discomforted during a live BBC interview during his UK visit in May when journalist Matthew Amroliwala asked tough questions on anomalies in Nepal's mountaineering sector.

The National Geographic Society announced on 13 June 2019 that they had successfully installed the world's highest operating weather station on Everest to provide researchers, climbers and the public with near real-time information about mountain conditions.

The autumn season saw a return of expeditions attempting **Everest** at this time of year, but on 23 September Mountain Hardwear Everest expedition members Joe Vernachio and Tim Emmett called off their bid after witnessing the lethal 300ft serac overhanging the Icefall; an unsettled weather forecast added additional risk. In a similar development, Polish climber Rafal Maciej Fronia also abandoned his bid to climb Everest as did another Polish team, Andrzej Leszek Bargiel, Andrzej's brother Grzegorz Bargiel and Jakub Poburka, along with their five base camp staff and filming crew. All 10 members of the **Lhotse** expedition led by Marcin Piotr Kaczkan also decided to return due to freak bad weather conditions in the Everest region.

After the spring season's issues of overcrowding on Everest, which resulted in 11 deaths the Nepal government introduced new rules for the 2020 season. However, the government later stated these new rules would not be imposed for the coming climbing season, which should have begun in April 2020. Despite international scrutiny and intense pressure from climbing groups around the world to tighten operations on Everest, officials say the rules need further review before they can be put in place.

The local administration in the Everest region introduced a new law that came into operation in January 2020 banning all single-use plastic containers less than 30 microns.

Winter 2019-20

Jost Kobusch set himself the extremely ambitious goal of climbing Everest solo and without supplementary oxygen via the infrequently climbed west ridge and Hornbein couloir on the north face. He ended his expedition after two months on the mountain; conditions did not allow him to climb to the summit but he reached a highpoint on the west ridge at 7,300 m.

Due to a heavy amount of deep unconsolidated snow, Alex Txikon's Everest winter expedition called an end to his winter project at 6,479m, stating that the imminent expiry of his permit would not provide sufficient time for conditions to improve for another attempt. Although no one succeeded in these purist approaches in winter, their efforts did recall a time, not so long ago, when Everest was a true expedition of exploration and not just conga lines and controversy.

Tashi Lakpa Sherpa was also on Everest attempting to complete a five-day winter speed ascent. His team wanted to reach the summit by 29 February without bottled oxygen. The Sherpas had pre-acclimatised while on expeditions in the Argentine Andes, however conditions on Everest were not conducive for their attempt.

On 13 March the Mountaineering Sports Administration of Tibet and Mountaineering Association of Tibet issued a joint statement restricting foreign mountaineering expeditions on Everest in the 2020 spring season. However, there is confusion as China has just announced that, as a contradiction to previous 'closure' reports, it has now opened Everest up to allow its nationals to attempt the summit from Tibet. This will allow the Yarla Shampo expedition with at least 26 members, including six female climbers onto the mountain, the confusion being: nationals resident in China or more widely, Chinese nationals?

On 13 March Nepal also suspended all permits for mountaineering expeditions that have already been issued and has put a restriction on new permits for the spring season 2020.

Sadly, as I draw to a close, Nepal has just registered its first case of Covid-19. None of us know for how long this situation will last. It is reported that over 1.5 million Nepali citizens left Kathmandu to return to their villages. Looking on the positive side, city pollution has been reduced and hopefully the mountains, and the Everest deity in particular, will have time to breathe. I'll leave you with an image of what it was to climb Everest in 1988 and the thought that the mountain people of Nepal need your continuing support.

Pakistan 2019

The line of the first ascent of Link Sar (7041m) and high on the peak during the climb. See p258 for an account of this Piolet d'Or-winning climb.
(Graham Zimmerman)

Teams from around the world continued to capitalise on improved access in the Pakistani Karakoram, with expeditions to the rarely-visited Hindu Raj and the Yarkhun valley as well as to more popular destinations like the Charakusa and Baltoro Muztagh, and of course perennial attempts on 8,000m peaks in both summer and winter. Particular highlights of the 2019 season included a new route on Gasherbrum II, the first ascent of Link Sar via the south-east face, and the first ascent of Koyo Zom's west face.

In May, a French team visited the Yarkhun valley, where they made the first ascent of **Risht Peak** (5960m). They found good quality rock with excellent protection, and noted the number of unclimbed peaks in the area and the potential for new routes.

The team comprised Symon Welfringer, Aurélien Vaissière, Pierrick Fine and Antoine Rolle. Risht Peak sits right at the end of the Risht glacier and has hardly been visited since the 1980s and an increase in regional conflicts. Starting from a base camp at 3,000m, the team ski toured up the glacier for six days finishing at 5,600 before skiing down. They then found an excellent bouldering venue before returning back up the glacier, this time in two days,

High on Link Sar during the first ascent *(Graham Zimmerman)*

taking advantage of a short, three-day weather window to make two new routes climbing in two pairs. While Rolle and Vassière made the first ascent of *Sueurs chaudes* (150m 6c+ max) Fine and Welfringer discovered an incredibly beautiful and committing line. 'After the first part up easy snow slopes,' Welfringer reported, 'we encountered more difficult terrain with a pitch of ice up to 90° that we graded 5. The following pitch was the crux of the route, I managed to lead this and we estimate M6 with some tricky section past poor pro. Then followed amazing ice pitches were a bit easier but still really sustained up to the final ridge.' See Nepal notes for Welfringer's success on Tengi Ragi Tau.

In late June, Simon Messner made the first ascent of **Geshot Peak** (6200m), also known as Toshe III, solo, climbing from an advance base camp at 4,600m to the summit in just five and a half hours, in spite of having to break trail alone in knee-deep snow. The 29-year-old South Tyrolean mountaineer travelled to Pakistan with Günther Göberl, Robert Neumeyer and his father, Reinhold Messner, with the initial plan of climbing the mountain together, but due to difficult snow conditions the others chose not to continue. Messner said the weather was poor in June, with rain or snow almost every afternoon. 'What a beautiful mountain,' he said afterwards. 'The great thing was how happy the locals of Bunar valley were that their mountain had been climbed. On the way back I received wreaths of flowers in every village, that really made me happy!'

In July, Simon Messner joined Martin Sieberer, Philipp Brugger in the Baltoro Muztagh, where they aimed to make the first ascent of Muztagh Tower's

Three view of Messner Junior. Simon Messner, right, with Martin Sieberer before their ascent of Black Tooth, the same pair on the summit, and Messner on the summit of Geshot Peak following his solo ascent. *(Simon Messner)*

Black Tooth (6719m) via the south-east ridge. They found the rock quality low on the ridge to be extremely poor, and instead reconnoitred a way to gain the upper south-east ridge via the south face of the Black Tooth. Brugger did not feel sufficiently acclimatised to attempt the route, so after resting in base camp, Sieberer and Messner climbed their chosen line in a five-day roundtrip, encountering difficulties up to M5. At the final bivouac before the summit, it became apparent that the route they had climbed could not be descended by means of abalakovs. Instead, they chose to traverse the summit and descend the French route, abandoning their tent and other equipment at the bivouac.

The line of Messner's route on Geshot Peak (6200m). *(Simon Messner)*

In September, a British team comprising Tom Livingstone, Will Sim, Uisdean Hawthorn, Ally Swinton and John Crook visited the Hindu Raj, with the aim of climbing new routes on **Koyo Zom** (6877m). Sim, Hawthorn and Crook spent five days attempting a new line on the north-east buttress, but were repelled by poor conditions. Livingstone and Swinton made the first ascent of Koyo Zom's west face over five days, overcoming extremely technical mixed terrain to forge a path through the headwall. The pair then descended Koyo Zom's eastern flank where, on their sixth day out from base camp, Swinton took a large fall into a hidden crevasse at 5,900m on the Pechus glacier, necessitating an emergency rescue by the Pakistani air force. Fortunately, both climbers were fine. They called their line *The Great Game* and graded it ED+ 1500m.

Arguably the most impressive feat of the 2019 season, however, was the first ascent of **Link Sar** (7041m) by a strong international team made up of two Himalayan veterans, Americans Steve Swenson and Mark Richey, and two young guns, Graham Zimmerman and Chris Wright. This was Swenson's third attempt on Link Sar, having tried it once in 2001 with George Lowe, Joe Terravecchia, Steve Larson, Andy Tuthill and Eric Winkleman, and again in 2017 with Zimmerman and Wright, when atrocious weather turned them around at 5,900m on the south-west face. This time, armed with a greater understanding of the mountain, the team opted for a line on the south-east Face, which Swenson and Zimmerman had spotted

The line of the first ascent of Black Tooth (6719m). *(Simon Messner)*

in 2015 while making the first ascent of nearby Changi Tower (6500m) with Scott Bennett. The south-east face weighs in at M6+, WI4, 90° and 2,300m. Swenson calls it 'one of the most complex and difficult routes I have ever climbed,' which is something coming from someone with Swenson's resumé.

Link Sar has been a sought-after prize for many talented alpinists over the years, being the target of some nine expeditions ranging back to 1979. Jonathan Griffith (who himself undertook three expeditions to Link Sar) reached the west summit (6938m) with Andy Houseman in 2015.

Perhaps the most impressive ascent on a Karakoram 8,000er this summer was Denis Urubko's new route on **Gasherbrum II** (8035m) in July, completed in an extremely minimalist style: largely solo, without supplemental oxygen

The British team under the impressive Koyo Zom (6877m). See page 3 for Tom Livingstone's account. *(Tom Livingstone)*

and in a 24-hour push from 6,350m to the summit. Urubko, now in his mid 40s, hit several obstacles that threatened to foil his plans, including a successful rescue on nearby Gasherbrum VII. Following that effort, Urubko participated in not one, but two further rescues, bringing his rescue total for the season to three and raising question marks about whether he had sufficient reserves to attempt a new route. To complicate matters further, Urubko's partner, María Cardel, injured her back earlier in the expedition. She was unable to join him.

Nonetheless, Urubko decided to go for it. He was certainly well acclimatised, having already summited once on 18 July. On 30 July, his birthday, Urubko made his way to camp one, accompanied through this dangerous and unstable section by Canadian Don Bowie, the Finnish climber Lotta Hintsa and American Matthew James. During the evening of 31 July, Urubko continued up alone taking took no satellite phone or radio.

July also saw the second phase of Nirmal Purja's astonishing ascent of all fourteen 8000ers in a single season. Across just 20 days, Purja made lightning-fast ascents of **Nanga Parbat** (July 6), **Gasherbrum I** (July 15), **Gasherbrum II** (July 18), **K2** (July 24) and **Broad Peak** (July 26) in a slightly less minimalist style than Urubko, using supplemental oxygen above 7,500m and helicopters to fly between base camps. See Nepal notes for further details.

The winter season was markedly less successful on the Karakoram 8,000ers. Simone Moro and Tamara Lunger abandoned their winter attempt on Gasherbrums I and II after Moro took a major fall into a crevasse, and Don Bowie and Lotta Nakyva were rescued from 6,600m on **Broad Peak** by the Pakistani air force. Denis Urubko, also on Broad Peak as part of the same expedition, abandoned his attempt at 7,400m after encountering high winds. A Polish team, attempting to make the first winter ascent of **Batura Sar** (7795m), turned around at 6,600m due to heavy snowfall and high winds.

JIM GREGSON

Greenland 2019

Motoring in Uummannaq Fjord. *(Gabriel Clarke)*

There was a noticeable fall-off in expedition numbers to Greenland in 2019, at least in terms of grant applications from British climbing teams to the Arctic Club, the Mount Everest Foundation, the Gino Watkins Memorial Fund and the British Mountaineering Council. However those who did apply were successful in obtaining grant aid and some were also part funded by the Austrian Alpine Club (Sektion Britannia). Grants are also available from the Scottish Arctic Club for Scotland-based groups, although a number of trips with support from that source were cancelled or postponed. The Montane Alpine Climbing Fund has for reasons harder to understand decided not to award grant aid for groups heading to Greenland, potential expedition leaders should take note. *[Editor's note:* The current position for the Montane ACF is as follows: 'Grants will now not typically be given for the more well-travelled mountain areas in Central Alaska, Patagonia, or Greenland (unless the applicants are young members who are new to expeditionary climbing).' This suggests remoter parts of these regions would qualify.]

Tom Harding's team of four journeyed to Renland from the end of June until the end of July, and after being delayed by masses of sea ice inside Scoresby Sund were taken by boat to a landing on the south-east shore, together with all of their kit transported by air, as opposed to it being shipped

Topo of an unfinished line and *Arctic Heatstroke* (200m, E4) on Ukalilik, with Henry Francis on the crux. *(Gabriel Clarke)*

in advance. They then had quite a tough time over eight days relaying everything inland to establish camps on the unnamed glacier previously visited by Geoff Hornby's group in 2016. Eventually they made a high camp at 1,290m and over 13 days made first ascents of five peaks and also climbed three long rock routes. Their best ascent was **Northern Sun Spire,** climbed from the west, although they also noted the more impressive 700m east face, a virgin big wall for an ambitious group in the future. No less interesting was their decision to 'repatriate' to the UK all their garbage at the end of the trip, and also the creation of a superb detailed map of the expedition area that is far better than others currently available: see full expedition report via the MEF website.

The trend for sailing-to-climb trips continued as Gabriel Clarke used his own 32ft fibreglass sailing boat *Safe Arrival* to make the long journey from Cornwall to the west coast of Greenland. His crew of six experienced some rough north Atlantic weather en route with some sail damage along the way but eventually visited several landings in Nuuk Fjord, Storø island, Manitsoq, Uummannaq, Drygalskis Halvø, and then on to Disko Sound and Ilulissat. From these landings a number of quite demanding rock routes were made up to E4 standard. On Ikerasak Island two of Clarke's group also repeated the Ditto-Favresse E3 line *Married Men's Way,* climbed during Bob Shepton's Wild Bunch voyage. Clarke reported that as owner-skipper of the boat he found the expedition had greater stresses than anticipated. A successful return voyage back to the UK rounded out a trip that started in early May and ended in early September.

The instant classic *Married Men's Way,* climbed on Bob Shepton's Wild Bunch tour. *(Gabriel Clarke)*

Simon Baker led a team that visited the head of Permdal in northern Jameson Land, lying west of Carlsberg Fjord. This was largely an exploratory trip into an area not known for overly technical climbing but his group made a number of ascents in fairly impressive terrain. He also reported that there were periods of heavy rain – during July – which at one time would have been most unusual for east Greenland in the summer time. Baker had his team lifted into and out from their base area by helicopter from Constable Pynt airstrip.

Two groups awarded grants made kite-skiing icecap crossings, one of them a really long-distance journey, and the other the two-woman team of

Climbing on Uummannaq Peak. *(Gabriel Clarke)*

Celine Jaccard and Katie Crafts, who made their first kite-ski crossing of Greenland as 'Sisterhood of Adventure': quite a steep learning curve for the 515km route from near Tasiilaq over to Kangerlussuaq on the west side.

Dave Gladwin made a solo trip to a location a short way north-east from Kulsuk to put up a new 620m rock route at 6a on a free-standing summit on an island at the opposite side of the fjord from the abandoned Second World War airbase at Ikateq. (This large area is covered in rusted derelict buildings, machinery and thousands of fuel drums). Gladwin reports that his new route took six hours to climb but his descent in rock shoes over scree, boulders and slippery grass took more than seven hours to reach the shoreline.

In August, Brian Jackson, Dave Head and IFMGA guide John Lyall went by boat from Kulusuk to a landing point near to the tongue of the Kaarale glacier. From a camp there they made six ascents of nearby peaks. It is not clear if any of these were first ascents as this area has had numerous

The line of *La Cura,* on Nalumasortoq's Middle Pillar.

visitors over the years, including one by the writer of these notes in 1991 (the glacier tongues in this area have retreated considerably since that time) and a particularly active Scottish group in 1966.

Apart from teams originating in Britain, three other groups made some new climbs in Greenland in 2019. Another sailboat expedition started out of Nuuk and went to a number of locations, including Torsukkatak Fjord where Canadian Charlie Long, Swede Andreas Widlund and Norwegian Rune Harejo Jensen climbed three routes of 600m, 1,000m and 450m with difficulties up to 5.11.

Italians Federica Mingolla and Edoardo Saccaro were active in Tasermiut Fjord where they made a new big-wall route *La Cura* (525m, 7b+, A2) climbed over three days on the previously unclimbed south face of **Nalumasortoq's** Middle Pillar.

Much further north, on the south coast of Renland stands the prominent peak of **Grundtvigskirken** (1977m), which has had a number of ascents. Stefan Glowacz and four fellow Germans travelled first by train to Scotland where they joined a steel-hulled yacht to sail via the Hebrides in stormy weather to reach Scoresby Sund on 30 July. They were aiming to climb a new route on the peak's 1,300m north face. This attempt was brought to an abrupt end when Glowacz and Philipp Hans suffered a severe rock-fall issue as a table-sized block fell from 100m above them to hit a ledge after 50m showering the climbers with debris. Glowacz suffered injuries to his right thigh and forearm, Hans was unscathed. After this shock the team decided to switch objectives to an ascent of the peak's safer south ridge, previously attempted by a British army team in 1978. The Germans climbed 1,500m to a bivouac before moving onto the front of the huge summit tower where they climbed 15 pitches on the front face of the tower to the summit. They regained their bivouac 24 hours after leaving it and next day descended to their base camp on the shore. A 20-day journey by boat and rail got them back home to Germany. Glowacz and his team called their new route *Suffer and Smile: Boys Don't Cry* and claimed it was a 'by fair means ascent', although in their photographs a large power-drill is on show. Perhaps this was used to fix bolted belay stations.

At the time of writing, the Covid-19 pandemic is still at large across the world. Among its many impacts is the likelihood that expeditions planned

Just three of the large number of unclimbed peaks in Greenland to attract mountain explorers back when conditions allow. *(Jim Gregson)*

for 2020 may well be cancelled, and as many airlines will find it difficult to stay in operation in the future the prospects for already costly expeditions to Greenland may be in some doubt for a number of years. Nevertheless, Greenland still holds vast reserves of unclimbed peaks in areas already visited and some that have not yet been trodden by exploratory mountaineers. There are many prizes waiting out there, and wonderful experiences for those harbouring an ambition to go to this fantastic Arctic realm. As a means of whetting the appetite I have selected for these notes a number of images of still unclimbed peaks visible in or close to areas where my own expeditions have made numerous first ascents. There are many more fine peaks just like these waiting for adventurous climbers to get to them. No doubt there are also hidden reservoirs of impressive rock walls for those who may not wish to be based on icecap or glacier.

MARCELO SCANU
Argentina 2019-20

Passing a high-altitude lagoon on the windswept Veladero-Baboso traverse.
(Griselda Moreno)

Argentina formed a new government on 10 December 2019, a Peronist alliance politically in the centre with Alberto Fernández as president. There is interest in tourism, with new flights and connectivity with mountain regions. Hard currencies are much appreciated since the Argentine peso has been significantly devalued. The country is in the process of concluding an agreement with bondholders.

The mountain season was a good one despite the lack of snowfall. Most problems came with the global pandemic. Although we are a population of 45 million, there have been only 23,620 infections and 693 dead (figures for 8 June 2020). Brazil, Chile and Peru have been much more affected. Argentina was in strict quarantine following the first cases and at the time of writing most of the country is returning to normal, except Buenos Aires and the region around it as well as other few provinces.

The economy has been hit. Mountain climbing came to an abrupt halt with the quarantine but is beginning slowly to resume activity. Heavy snowfall in the dry Andes augurs a good season. Like so many, we are waiting for a return to normality to revisit the summits.

Pissis
Pissis (6882m) is the second-highest volcano on Earth and the highest extinct one. Located in the provinces of Catamarca and La Rioja, its official height of 6,882m looks to be a little on the high side and the real figure is nearer 6,800m. Argentine Ulises Kusnezov and Arkaitz Ibarra, a Basque living in Argentina, began a winter traverse of the peak on 3 August 2019, departing from the Pircas Negras road and heading north past the mighty Bonete Chico, another huge volcano. They also passed the huge Cráter Corona del Inca. The pair endured strong winds and low temperatures throughout the traverse, camping at altitudes usually above 5,000m and being prevented from moving on some days because of the wind. On 9 August, after descending a depression and gaining height once more, they camped at 5,550 and next day the pair climbed the south face of Pissis, once more in strong winds, reaching the summit at 6.30pm with the last light. They entered the province of Catamarca descending swiftly to base camp (4600m) on the normal route at 11.30pm. In the next two days, the followed a system of ridges to finish the traverse on the Paso de San Francisco road.

Cumbre Lucía
During June 2019 an Argentine team of Andrés Zapata and Marcelo Scanu climbed the last virgin peak in the Bayo ridge (see last year's *AJ*), in the province of Catamarca. The group started up the Río Pillahuasi and camped by an unoccupied hut. They took the east ridge reaching the summit (4190m) calling it Pico Lucía.

Veladero-Baboso
From 3 to 10 February, a team of three Argentines from Salta in the mountainous north of Argentina, Griselda Moreno, Mariela del Valle Flores and Gustavo Soto Nedir, completed the first traverse from south to north of the volcanoes Veladero (6436m) and Baboso (6079m), in the province of La Rioja. Veladero is a sacred mountain and has on top an Inca temple, one of the highest human constructions in the world. Their traverse began with the first section of the Sierra de Veladero at 4,300m, with a new route up the south face of Veladero. The unsupported team camped seven times in 60km before finally ascending Baboso to reach its summit during the night with a spectacular view. They descended to the road and were picked up.

La Ramada
Austrian Christian Stangl climbed a new route on Cerro de la Ramada (c6400m), on the ridge of the same name in the province of San Juan. This interesting mountain is 10km south-east of Mercedario. During March 2019 he approached from the Valle de las Leñas close to the historic Portezuelo del Espinacito. This pass, with its attractive view of Aconcagua, was used by Gen José de San Martín during his famous crossing of the Andes, a pivotal moment in the Chilean War of Independence and one of the most difficult in the history of warfare. Stangl erected a camp at 4,350m at the base

Cerro de los Diablos in the Cordón del Potrero Escondido and the line of ascent.
(Glauco Muratti)

Ask not for whom the bell tolls. Cerro Campanario (4049m) in Mendoza province and the difficult and rubbly aid climbing on the summit tower, where Tomás Pellizzari and Carlos Bravo celebrate. *(Tomás Pellizzari)*

The line of the new 450m 6c on the Aguja Ectelion, one of many granite needles in the El Sosneado region. *(Lucas Alzamora)*

Aguja "Ectelion"
450 mts. 6c

of La Ramada, another at 5,200m and then summited on 25 March by the south-south-east ridge. He found snow, ice and rotten rock.

Cerro de los Diablos
From 21 to 27 October, Argentines Glauco Muratti and Ezequiel Dassie climbed this interesting mountain in the Cordón del Potrero Escondido, Mendoza province. They began the expedition in Penitentes at 2,400m on the road that connects Argentina and Chile. Then heading southwards by the Quebrada de Vargas they camped at 3,800m in the Portezuelo Serrata. Next day they descended to the valley of Río Blanco at 3,300m and then ascended the untrodden Cajón Norte del Potrero Escondido, an eroded zone that hasn't even evidence of guanaco marks that can be seen elsewhere. They camped at 3,800m and next day at 4,100m in a place they called La Cancha. They had good weather during the mornings and snowfall on the afternoons. It was not possible to climb the mountain by its north face because of rotten rock, so during the fourth day they ascended easy snow slopes, some grade III rock sections and rock scree to a col (4790m). The ridge has great rock towers so they traversed the east face and then climbed directly to the summit up 40° slopes with recent snow and some easy but exposed mixed passages on rotten and exposed rock. There were no traces on the summit of any previous visit. The official height is 5,007m but the climbers had a 5,090m reading on their GPS. They rated their route as PD. The name chosen for the summit refers to the curious rock towers on its south ridge, which the climbers said looked like dancing devils. The return took two days in heavy snowfall.

El Sosneado
During 2019 three different expeditions visited this interesting climbing zone near El Sosneado in Mendoza province. It's becoming a classic spot for climbing in Argentina. There are some 20 granitic needles with routes up to 500m with much potential in a range that averages 2,500m. During March, Juan Girolamo and Lucas Alzamora opened a new route on a needle called Pilar Roja: *Perro Chivato* (150m, 6c). Later, in April, Alzamora joined Matías Korten and Andrés Tula in climbing a new route on Aguja Preñada (145m, 6c+). Also during April, Alzamora teamed with Diego Nakamura and Carloncho Guerra to finish a route (450m, 6c) on the Aguja Ectelion they had tried twice before in preceding years.

Campanario

Campanario means 'bell tower' in Spanish and this appealing mountain in the province of Mendoza, lying between Chile and Argentina, has a legend. It's said that the peak makes a sound like the tolling of a bell before a storm hits the region. It was known as a place to avoid because of these old myths. On 14 February 2020, 61 years after the first attempt, the summit of Cerro Campanario (4049m) was finally ascended by a Chilean group. Since 2011, there had been five attempts on this eroded volcanic skeleton, two of them led by climbers from the successful team.

On 9 February Tomás Pellizzari, Carlos Bravo and Erasmo Gonzaléz arrived in Argentina and on 10 February camped at 3,842m. Their ascent was made via the south ridge before switch to the west ridge, all on rotten rock. The climbers found ancient nails which were drafted in to help with the climbing. The route was 10 pitches, with pitches seven, with the worst rock, and eight the hardest and most serious, with climbing up to 5.10 and A6 on pitch seven, a commentary on the state of the rock, while pitch eight was 5.9 and A4. Bravo and Pellizzari reached the summit before reuniting with Gonzaléz and descending to the Real del Pehuenche hut, which they reached at 11pm.

ED DOUGLAS

Peru 2019

The impressive limestone wall of *Cabeza Clava* (470m, 6c+), on the south-west face of the Huanka Punta (4,670m) during the first ascent. *(Iker Pou)*

Cordillera Blanca

Marek Holeček and Radek Groh (Czech) climbed a new route on the east face of Huandoy Norte (6360m), mostly to the right of but sharing a little of its ground with a line soloed by Adam Kovacs in 2003. After watching their line for several days, they started on 7 August from the Pisco hut (4664m) and camped at the foot of the face below a crevassed section. Leaving at dawn, the angle increased and snow turned to ice and then mixed sections interspersed with rock steps. After two hours simul-climbing, they reached a 150m rock step that offered some protection from the rock fall that threatened them. Above the rock step they were committed, traversing an icefield to some more mixed climbing and a section of loose ice where, as Holeček put it, the rope was 'more of a fashion statement'. Above this they found two ledges for a bivouac 300m from the summit ridge. Starting at first light next day they were on the summit at noon and six hours of rappelling brought them to the foot of the face and the hut after 55 hours. They called their route *BOYS 1970* (1200m, ED+, WI6, M6) in honour of the 14 Czech climbers who died in the 1970 earthquake and avalanche below Huascarán, which killed 70,000 Peruvians soon after.

Huanka Punta and Cerro Tornillo (right), showing the Pou routes.

The line of *BOYS 1970* (1200, ED+) on the east face of Huandoy Norte (6360m).

Mixed ground on the east face of Huandoy Norte.

A team comprising Italians Alessandro Fracchetti and Andrea Spezialli and the Chilean guide Renato Rodriguez climbed the north-east face of **Huandoy Este** (5950m), also from the Pisco hut, arriving on 17 July, waiting out a day of bad weather, and leaving at 1am on 19 July. The team had made a previous attempt on their line in 2017 but were shut down some 200m from the summit ridge by poor snow conditions. This time they followed a line 30m to the right of their previous attempt because of drier conditions, following a spur with a lot of mixed sections. At dawn they saw bad weather developing and it arrived as they moved left on the face some 200m from the summit ridge. Opting to continue, they reached the ridge 100m below the summit and immediately descended, first the north ridge and then the east face with two rappels. They were back at their camp by 4pm. Their route is called *Come Moco Spur* (650m, MD+, 75°, M4/5, V+). This face has been climbed before several times and some of the ground covered has likely been climbed before also, but conditions have changed dramatically and are variable.

The Spanish brothers Iker and Eneko Pou climbed a number of long mountain rock routes south and east of the main Cordillera Blanca in the underexplored region east of San Marcos. They made the first ascent of the north-west face of **Cerro Tornillo** (4900m), *Burrito Chin de los Andes* (700m, 6b) and in the same area climbed *Cabeza Clava* (470m, 6c+) on the south-west and therefore cold face of **Huanka Punta** (4670m). These routes were on high-quality limestone, a rare commodity in the Cordillera Blanca. The team then returned to Huaraz before travelling to **Cashan West** (5686m) south of the Quebrada Rajucolta. Here they climbed *Animal Kingdom*

The east face of Huandoy Este (5950m) and the line of *Come Moco Spur.*

(800m, 7a+) in two days, with a cold bivy, and then a day of descent. They rated this as one of their best ever routes. They also climbed a hard route on a wall close to the road in the Quebrada Llaca, taking time off when Eneko was struck on the leg by a stone and they had to return to Huaraz for stitches. Two days later they were back to finish the job: *Aupa Gastgeiz* (160m, 7c+).

On 27 August, Felipe Proaño and Simón Bustamente from Ecuador climbed what they described as **Putacaraju Oeste,** due to its orientation to Nevado Putaca, a peak name that exists and which, they were later told later, had been previously climbed decades ago. However, they may have been right in their initial assessment that the peak they were on was un-climbed. They spotted their peak (5380m) from the top of Cerro Parón, which they climbed in double quick time, leaving them with a couple of days for another objective. Their 11-pitch route up the east spur was *Justo en las Ganas* (6a+).

Cordillera Central

In May, Malu Espinoza and Beto Pinto Toledo from Peru and the Belgian Guy Fonck climbed the south-west face of **Antachaire III** (c5670m). The mountain was first climbed in 1966 from the north side by a German team. It was Fonck and Toledo's third attempt, having been turned back previously by dry conditions in 2015 and from the halfway mark in 2018. On 8 May the team reached Laguna Rinconada (4600m), the usual base camp in this area, and next day they approached the face, camping at 4,900m on the glacial plateau beneath the mountain in bad afternoon weather. High temperatures persuaded them to stay put for a day to watch the face and they started their summit attempt on 10 May at 11.30pm to traverse under a serac-fall zone at night. The first pitch was the crux, a vertical and unconsolidated snow runnel followed by 200m of 70° snow and ice before the angle eventually eased. They were on the summit at 8am, naming the route *Waiting for Axelle* (630m, D+) after Fonck's expected daughter.

Few have reached the main summit of **Nevado Tunsho** (5730m) but in May, Peruvian guides Octavio Salazar Obregón and Eloy Salazar with Erick Llantoy climbed the south-east face, believing it to be unclimbed, although it is likely that a team in 2005 had previously climbed this face albeit by a different line. They set up a tent on the shore of Suitucancha, from where they could watch the face and then moved up to a moraine bivy from where they started their ascent at 11pm on 28 May. The first part of the face was 400m of névé up to 80° that they simul-climbed. The last part was even

Above: The south-east face of Salkantay (6279m) in the Cordillera Vilcanota with the line taken by Baró et al.

Left: The line of *Via Adrenaline* (ED+) on the south face of Jatunhuma (6127m), the most technical of six new routes done by Oriol Baró and his Spanish team in 2019.

steeper and the ridge above proved in terrible condition. They reach the summit at 11.30am (600m, TD, 60-90°) and took another eight hours for the descent, opting to descend the north side.

Spanish guides Sergi Ricard Ibars and Pablo Rosagro were also in the area, climbing the south-west face of **Tukumach'ay** (5357m) in 12 hours for the round-trip and calling their route *Open Arms* (300m, AD-, 55°), a reference to the continuing migrant crisis in the Mediterranean. Having warmed up on that, they climbed a new route on the south-west face of **Tunsho Central** (c5650m) via a goulotte to the right of *Chinita* (Pinto-Morales, 2011) and the easier-angled ridge above to give *Nómadas del Kangia* (500m, MD+, 90°, A1), descending more or less the way they had come, down-climbing and rappelling for a 24-hour round-trip. They believed this to be the fourth ascent of the peak.

Cordillera Huayhuash

Following a tip from Sergio Ramirez Carrascal, long-time Peru resident Nate Heald climbed a new route on the unfrequented south side of Siulá Grande (c6344m), whose access is made difficult by the icefall to the cirque beneath this aspect of the mountain. Carrascal told Heald there was 'a beautiful unclimbed ramp' that offered an elegant route to the south-east ridge. Heald was able to get photos of the line in May from French climbing partner Benjamin Billet who was trekking in the area, and these two with Finn Arttu Pylkkanen formed a team to attempt the line, going with a second rope comprising Peruvians Luis Crispin and Thomas Schilter, both 16 years old. On 24 June they entered the icefall hoping to get through it in

Pumasillo (5991m), left, and Nevado Sacsarayoc (5918m), with its south face in shadow on the right. Baró and Jordi Mamolejo climbed straight up the middle of this face to make the mountain's second ascent. *(Maurice Chédel)*

a day, but it was early next morning that they reached the glacial plateau beneath the face, having bivouacked in the glacier. At midnight on 26 June they started the climb, the ramp proving to be snow and ice up to 70°, giving straightforward access for 800m to the ridge, which they reached in late morning. A crevasse across the ridge slowed progress to the summit and a final 100m section of WI3 meant they reached the top late in the day at 4.30pm, where they remained for half an hour. It took 17 rappels to reverse the ramp and they reached their high camp at 3.30am after more than 27 hours on the go. They called the route *Peruana Supreme* (1000m, TD, AI4), Crispin and Schilter making the first Peruvian ascent of the peak, a remarkable effort for two so young. For Heald, it was another step along the way of becoming the first person to climb the 10 highest peaks in Peru, a feat he accomplished in October.

Cusco Region
The well-known guide Oriol Baró, from Vall de Boí in the Pyrenees, starting with teammates Ferran Rodriguez and Guillem Sancho, enjoyed one of the more spectacular seasons in Peruvian alpinism, climbing six new routes around Cusco. Having acclimatised in the sport-climbing venue of Chacco Huayllasca, they moved round to the north side of the **Cordillera**

Vilcanota, basing themselves at the Jampa pass (4900m). From here they climbed two new routes, a direct line on the south face of **Concha da Caracol** (5640m) called *Via Pirenaica* (TD+) and then a much harder route on the south face of **Nevado Jatunhuma** (6127m) to the lowest of its three summits. They called this route *Via Adrenaline* (ED+, WI6, M6 R, A2) and with a mixed icy roof at M6 and A2 as the crux at 5,900m, it is the range's most difficult climb. They were still only getting started though. After rest in Cusco, they established a camp at the base of the south-east ridge of **Salkantay** (6279m) to observe the mountain's south face and pick out a possible new line, which they did, up the south-east face in a 25-hour round-trip.

After Salkantay, Rodriguez went home, to be replaced by Jordi Marmolejo and the new trio travelled round to the north side of the **Cordillera Urubamba** north of Cusco to try Nevado Terijuay (5330m) but a refusal of access by the local village headman sent them elsewhere, not the first time this has happened. Instead they climbed a new route (400m, TD) on the south face of **Chicon** (5530m). Back in the Vilcanota, and with Sancho now returned home, Baró and Marmolejo teamed up with local climber Jorge Sirvas to climb a new route (400m, TD) on the south face of **Surimani** (5420m) on 2 July. Baró and Marmolejo managed one more climb, this time in the **Cordillera Vilcabamba.** Just south of **Pumasillo** (5991m) along a dramatic crenelated ridge, **Nevado Sacsarayoc** (5918m) had had only one ascent from a New Zealand team in 1962. Starting in darkness on 10 July, Baró and Marmolejo climbed the peak's stunning south face, reaching the summit in mid morning, naming their route *Pisco Sour* (800m, TD+). They deserved them.

Mount Everest Foundation Expedition Reports

SUMMARISED BY JONNY DRY

The Mount Everest Foundation was established as a registered charity following the successful ascent of Everest in 1953. It was financed initially using surplus funds and subsequent royalties from that expedition. It provides financial support for expeditions of an exploratory nature in mountain areas, and is administered by trustees appointed by the Alpine Club and the Royal Geographical Society.

The exploration is mainly of a geographical nature, but may also cover disciplines such as geology, botany, zoology, glaciology and medical research. In return for the funding the MEF requires only a comprehensive report, and copies of these reports are lodged with the AC and the RGS. The reports can be consulted at these establishments, or alternatively online.

The MEF has made total grants of well over £1m to more than 1,600 expeditions with members from the UK and New Zealand. Donations to allow us to continue with this work are always welcome. We particularly encourage donations from former beneficiaries of MEF grants.

In 2019 we supported 31 expeditions with grants totalling £68,000. The following notes summarise the 2019 expedition reports; full reports are now available on the Alpine Club Library website.

NORTH AMERICA

Cardiopulmonary and Cerebrovascular Acclimatisation in Children – Mike Stembridge, Joseph Donnelly, Ali McManus and Philip Ainslie
The expedition team, drawn from several universities, spent 11 days at the White Mountain Research Station in order to further understand acclimatisation to high altitude in children. Currently, there is no scientific data to support safe ascents in children; current advice given by the Union Internationale des Associations d'Alpinisme for children > 14 weeks old is drawn from advice for adult trekkers. It is hoped data gathered from this expedition will begin to fill that knowledge gap. Arriving in August the team collected their baseline data at the University of California before travelling onwards to Crooked Creek Station (3050m) and the Barcroft Laboratory. Once here they established their field laboratory to collect the last of their data.

MEF ref 19-03.

North Face of Thunder Mountain – Tim Blakemore and Mike 'Twid' Turner
Travel to the north face of Thunder Mountain was hindered for several days due to poor weather before the team was dropped by aircraft. Once established they found their objective covered in recent snowfall but noted three

potential lines on the face: a line with high avalanche risk to the right of the original line climbed by Jack Tackle and Jim Donini; a right-slanting ramp giving access to the main wall which was capped by a large snow mushroom; and a line on the right-hand side of the face that looked possible but was found to be at high risk of serac collapse. With all three options considered too dangerous in the current conditions, they moved to Mount Hunter where they again found poor conditions and further poor weather that covered their intended route in large amounts of snow. They moved again to a third objective further east on the West Fork of Ruth but were shut down again by heavy snowfall that saw them unable to climb and repeatedly digging out the tent. From here they decided any potential weather and condition window was unlikely and were picked up by plane. They note that their experience is indicative of a shift in the Alaskan climbing season; winters are colder with less potential for snow and therefore ice, equally storms seem to now be coming later in the year in May rather than April as was often historically the case. They suggest that the ideal conditions normally found in May have now shifted to June and climbers may likely find better success going later in the year.   MEF ref 19-07.

Baffin Paddle Climb – Bronwyn Hodgins, Jacob Cook, Thor Stewart, Zack Goldberg-Poch

Flying first into Pangnirtung, the team paddled 30km up the Pangnirtung Fjord over eight hours before hiking another 30km further up the valley to their base camp at Summit Lake. They established an advanced base camp at the confluence of Parade and Caribou glaciers where they split to make varying ascents. Bronwyn and Jacob made a new route they called *Never Laugh at Live Dragons* on the South Tower of Mount Asgard, whilst Thor and Jack made a likely second free ascent of *Polar Thievery* on the North Tower. After a few days rest, Bronwyn and Jacob made a three pitch variation to the Scott-Henneck route which they graded at 5.11+, and Thor and Zack made a first ascent of a 5.10+ route on Mount Midgard. The team linked back together and paddled onwards to Mount Thor where they made a full team ascent via the south ridge. Bronwyn and Jacob then went on to make a further first ascent of a 5.13- line they named *The Niv Mizzet Line,* climbing the line over two days. Thor and Zack rounded the trip off with a possible first recorded ascent of Ulu Peak by a 5.10+ line they named *The Beached Whale*. They evacuated the same way they approached, arriving back in Pangnirtung after eight hours of paddling.   MEF ref 19-10.

Oasis Peak Expedition – Simon Richardson and Mark Robson

From research in advance of the expedition, the pair believe they were likely the first documented expedition to North Baird glacier in over 40 years. They set themselves two objectives: to make the first ascent of the west face of Oasis Peak and explore further unclimbed mountains north and west of it. They reached the glacier from the village of Petersburg by helicopter but found conditions were extremely unfavourable, with heavy snow lying everywhere forming large cornices and snow mushrooms. The temperature was also warmer than expected and with little overnight freezing, they moved instead to the North Arm of the North Baird glacier. Here they noted a large number of unclimbed peaks, the largest of which was 7180m. With a 24-hour gap in the weather they made a successful ascent up a 1,200m route via the south-east face and north-east ridge and went on to successfully climb a further four peaks of around 5,800m before flying out.

MEF ref 19-14.

Mount Crillon Expedition – Paul Knott and Jacob Downie
After almost a week of delay due to insufficient visibility for the glacier landing, the team reached base camp on the Brady glacier close to the east ridge of Mount Crillon. Deep soft snow meant difficulty for the aircraft but after landing safely and establishing camp they began making an access route towards the start of the route on the 11 April. However the team got no further after a series of fronts carrying significant snowfall and poor freezes prevented further safe activity. Following a forecast update projecting a continuation of the same pattern until at least 23 April, they decided they would have insufficient time to climb Mt Crillon, or any other significant objective, even if conditions subsequently improved. With this decision made they requested a pick up and flew out during a brief clearance of weather. Once back they saw that the unsettled and at times stormy low-pressure weather continued in the area, and any high pressure that might have allowed for climbing did not commence until 27 April which would have been too close to their originally planned departure date. The ridge remains a substantial unclimbed line in Alaska, having only seen two other recorded expeditions by Loren Adkins and Paul Barnes in 1988, and Paul Knott and Kieran Parsons in 2014.

MEF ref 19-25.

SOUTH AMERICA

Novel Remote Sensing of Glacial Change – Liam Taylor, Duncan Quincey, Mark Smith, Lee Brown, Joshua Chambers, Joshua Wolstenholme and Michael Grimes
The expedition from the University of Leeds travelled to Peru to test a novel remote-sensing system providing real-time assessment of glacial change. When published, the data should help inform how glaciers in the Cordillera Vilcanota are responding to climate change. After experiencing problems getting their equipment through Peruvian customs, the team conducted a limited survey of the Quelccaya ice cap using the equipment they had. However the bulk of their research was conducted two months later after they returned to the area following confirmation of further funding and the arrival of the rest of the equipment. Despite now working in the midst of the rainy season, they deployed 16 of the 30 planned cameras which produced accurate 3D models and managed to capture a major calving event which raised the level of the outflow lake by approximately 1cm. With this data

they hope to be able to model the glacier in more detail and predict with greater accuracy when it is leaning before calving. The team plan to return again in 2020 to place the rest of the equipment and build a more complete picture of the glacier.   MEF ref 19-13.

Jorge Montt Glacier Ski Expedition – Marian Krogh and Stephanie Jones
This team of two had the joint objectives in Chile of exploring both the Jorge Montt glacier and Chico glacier on skis and kayak to make the expedition entirely human powered. After kayaking for four days in to the Jorge Montt glacier from Tortel, the team hiked further up the glacier to set a base camp where they could begin to identify potential routes onto the icefield. They tried a number of routes but were forced to retreat in the face of often heavily vegetated conditions. They instead changed tack and relocated to Villa O'Higgins where they assessed their options to access the southern icefield by the Chico glacier. After crossing Lago O'Higgins they began their approach from Lago Chico and reached the glacier three days later. They continued up the glacier for a further day, reaching the upper section before they received reports of approaching storms and decided to retreat.
                                                        MEF ref 19-30.

GREENLAND & ICELAND

Scoresby Sund, Renland – Tom Harding, Niall Newport, Cameron Ree and Neil Cox
After overcoming initial delays due to excessive sea ice the team arrived at their desired objective on Renland. They established successive mid and high camps further up the valley over eight days. Once there they spent 10 days making six ascents up to AD+, one of which was a second ascent of The Bastion and the remainder of which were first ascents. Most routes were between 300m and 400m in length and involved mixed conditions on both snow and rock. They experienced good conditions for the majority of the trip with temperatures often above freezing and only two short periods of bad weather. Whilst most of the remaining unclimbed summits are easy snow peaks, there is extensive potential for further climbing, including an impressive 700m big wall facing eastwards that saw attention in 2016 but is yet to see an ascent.   MEF ref 19-08.

UAV Glaciological Analysis – Nathaniel Baurley and Chris Tomsett
The original objective was to carry out UAV surveys of the Breiðamerkurjökull and Fjallsjökull glaciers. However, due to time and logistical constraints, the expedition decided to focus solely on surveying the Fjallsjökull, and spent spent five days gathering data. On the first day they set their control points and marked out various locations with DGPS before taking the first initial UAV surveys. The second day they were unable to undertake work due to adverse weather conditions and continued instead on the third day where they gather a full set of UAV surveys. Then the weather closed

in again and after being kept inside for the fourth day they collected their control points on the fifth day and returned to Reykjavik. There is substantial potential for future research into glacier dynamics and hydrology, and the team hope to return in 2020 for a longer period in order to expand the data set further with a more advanced UAV, capable of undertaking longer and more remote surveys of the glacier. This data will ultimately provide more insight on velocity, hydrology and calving activity that can inform the understanding of how glaciers will develop into the future. MEF ref 19-15.

Greenland West Coast – Gabriel Clarke, James Steevenson, Sam Nunn, Henry Francis, Mark Harris and Oscar Van Simina
After three years of planning, the expedition set sail from the UK to Greenland, aiming to explore north of Nuuk as far as Uummannaq Fjord and establish new routes along the coast as they went. After purchasing and refitting a 1973 32ft Rival the initial team members set sail from Mallaig on 28 May and negotiated gale force winds up to force nine, arriving in Nuuk on 13 June. After repairing the vessel and resting in Nuuk they set out for Storo Island and made their first ascent up a 250m route they graded HVS 5a. From here they continued to Manitsoq where they made further ascents including an aborted attempt on a route on the Shark's Fin Wall. Henry joined the team in Sisimuit and they continued to Uummannaq, stopping at Disko Fjord on the way and finally Ukalilik Island where they made an ascent of *Arctic Heat Stroke,* an E4 line on the island's southern spit. They attempted a further route on Uummannaq Peak but retreated and moved on to Drygalskis Halvo for further exploring but the weather turned which prevented any climbing. On their return they stopped again in the Uummannaq area where they made a repeat ascent of Ben Ditto and Olivier Favresse's route *Married Mens' Way* (E3) and another line in Drygalskis' south-west bay. After returning to Mantisoq for repairs to the boat, they continued on to Nuuk where they met a new crewmember, who accompanied them on their journey back to the UK.   MEF ref 19-26.

CryoCarbon Expedition – Dr Emily Stevenson and Dr Mel Murphy
In the summer of 2019, Stevenson and Murphy undertook three weeks of fieldwork in the Zackenberg river catchment to determine the impact increased physical erosion has on carbon dioxide removal and release to the atmosphere. Glacial lake outburst flood (GLOF) stems from the A P Olsen glacier, flows downstream into the Zackenberg river and causes massive river bank erosion, vast sediment deposition and the delivery of up to 90% of the catchment's annual sediment budget in 32 hours. Unexpected injury on the expedition prevented the full planned research at the foot of the glacier, however the team were able to capture a GLOF event and take other water and sediment samples as planned. The work has so far generated over 500 data points which are still being analysed, however initial data shows that concentrations of sulphate in the water increased dramatically relative to alkalinity during the GLOF which was as the team hypothesised. Further

data on isotopic measurements taken and the impact this means for CO_2 release into the atmosphere is due to be analysed and published.

MEF ref 19-35.

PAKISTAN

Kondus Valley – Graham Zimmerman, Chris Wright, Steven Swenson and Mark Richey
This international team from New Zealand, the UK and USA travelled to the Kondus valley with the objective of making the first ascent of the east face of Link Sar. The team opted to fly initially from Islamabad to Skardu before taking vehicles to their base camp in the Kaberi valley. From here they established a further advance base camp at the top of the valley's steep slopes. Conditions were favourable and the team began acclimatising. They began the route on 31 July, climbing the first section early in the morning to reach a camp at 5,100m and making further ground in the early evening. They continued throughout the night due to the temperature drop and made a bivy spot at 5,900m the next morning. From here they encountered a serious serac barrier that had not been present when the team were last in the area in 2017. They negotiated this round its right-hand side on good ice and found a higher bivy at 6,200m. After enduring a period of poor weather they made an attempt to continue in less favourable conditions but were forced to dig in to wait for further improvement. After the weather cleared they made good progress on the upper section of the route that gave way to challenging snow, ice and mixed climbing at the top. The final pitches gave difficult climbing on unconsolidated snow, which was negotiated to gain the summit at sunset. From here the team descended over three days and arrived back at advanced basecamp nine days after first heading out.

MEF ref 19-16.

Sani Pakush Expedition – Peter Thompson and Philip de-Beger
With prior experience climbing the north-east spur of Sani Pakush in 1998, Peter Thompson returned with Philip de-Beger to attempt a new alpine route on the north-east spur and east ridge in what would be a second ascent of the peak. Returning in July however, they found that the route contained far more seracs than last time and evidence of substantial avalanche fall. They nonetheless began acclimatising and began to carry equipment to the base of the route but found the glacier approach very difficult with no obvious routes around. They decided instead to switch to an alternative unclimbed 5,920m peak near the Khunjerab pass. They reached the bivy site without the aid of porters and reached a height of 5,800m but were forced to turn back after encountering a heavily corniced final ridge covered with poorly consolidated snow. With the expedition over, they arranged transport to collect them from the Karakoram Highway to return them to Karimabad.

MEF ref 19-28.

SOUTH-EAST ASIA

Mulu Caves – A Team of 20 Members
Following continued exploration of the Mulu Caves over many years, the primary aim for the Mulu 2019 expedition was further exploration of the system to connect a number of caves in the southern peninsula of Gunung Api. This focused on trying to join Cave of the Winds, Racer Cave, Easter Cave and Lagangs to significantly lengthen the Clearwater System. A sump from Cave of the Winds was proven to connect to Racer so all that remains is for a diver to pass through. Lagangs and Easter were not connected but significant extensions were found. Additional exploration was completed in the northern end of Clearwater towards the Blackrock connection. This has opened up interesting leads to be examined by future expeditions and alongside this exploration the team undertook further scientific work that examined microbiological features found in the cave. This work had originally aimed to examine four types of secondary deposits but also found unusual moonmilk deposits and an interaction between bird guano with host rock, which leads to highly aggressive dissolution. These early field observations suggest that there is a significant, but little understood microbial ecosystem within the caves, driven by temperatures, humidity and the uniquely high levels of trogloxene organic carbon input into the system. MEF ref 19-42.

EUROPE

Izvor Licanke Cave Diving – Christine Grosart, Richard Walker, Rick Van Dijk, Ash Hiscock, Mark Burkey, Roberto Varesko, Rita Mallinson Cookson and Jessica Burkey
Successive expeditions have expanded the mapping for the Izvor Licanke cave network since the first expedition travelled to the cave in 1992. This expedition, which is in its fifth year of exploration of these caves, looked to build on this work by exploring new cave passages both above and below water. The expedition went to plan, with three exploratory dives conducted and 601m of new cave passages discovered. This brought the total length of the cave to 1.5km, of which 1,125m has been discovered by this 2019 team. Four sumps were explored in total, with new lengths found in each of them and evidence that the cave is still trending north and heading straight into the mountains north of the lake, appearing to pass beneath a mountainous, perched lake. Following this expedition, the team have been asked to gather water samples when they return in 2020 on behalf of the local water board.
MEF ref 19-40.

INDIA

British Chombu Expedition – Mick Fowler and Victor Saunders
The objective was the first ascent of Chombu (6362m) in north Sikkim. Despite closely controlled access to Sikkim, the two climbers obtained permis-

sion to make an attempt in April. Arriving on 1 April they made base camp by 6 April and spent a further 18 days scouting the route and acclimatising in poor weather before making an attempt. After two days resting, they moved up to the base of the route in heavy snow. Poor weather continued with heavy snowfall that refused to freeze. Each day a further fresh fall of snow would arrive and cover the unfrozen snow from the day before. With progress proving slow and a high risk of avalanche, they retreated and instead opted for a secondary objective on a peak they named Chungukang North. The weather continued in the same pattern but they were successful in ascending its south ridge. Following this they broke camp and walked out to Tanggu on 26 April. They concluded, as have a number of other previous expeditions, that better conditions would be more likely after the monsoon season.   MEF ref 19-01.

NEPAL

Himalchuli Glacier – Anne Stefaniak, Benjamin Robson and Asha Rai
This scientifically focused expedition planned to test a number of theories on the formation of supraglacial ponds on the Himalchuli glacier. During September the expedition departed for Manaslu from Kathmandu, trekking up to the glacier on 4 September before spending six days collecting data. The three hypotheses they planned to test were: supraglacial ponds expand via deepening if area expansion is impeded; slope angles are less important than hydrological networks in supraglacial pond formation; and valley topography represents a key control on pond locations in combination with suitable conditions of down-wasting and stagnation. The expedition had originally planned to access the Himalchuli glacier on foot yet had to change to the Hinang glacier further north after they found their intended footpaths to the Himalchuli glacier overgrown. After completing their research they returned to Kathmandu on 14 September via the Manaslu circuit.
                                                            MEF ref 19-02.

British Rolwaling Expedition – Ken Hopper, Simon Teitjen, Connor Holdsworth, Rich Lade and Will Rowland
During November 2019 this British expedition travelled to the Rolwaling where they established base camp on the Ripimoshar glacier. Their primary intention was a new route on Drangnag Ri. Following a heavy monsoon season the party found difficult snow conditions on the mountain and despite finding a route up the glacier and reaching the col between Drangnag Ri and Khang Kharpo they were forced to abandon their original plan after climbing to a high point of 6,100m. They switched instead to a smaller secondary objective: an unclimbed mountain (5981m) close to their base camp. Leaving at 3am they set out with the aim of first reaching the col. However the rock quality was found to be poor, and despite persevering a detached block caused Connor to fall and break his leg. Rescue was requested and they began lowering from the route, eventually meeting the rest of the party

who were coming up from base camp. The helicopter arrived the following day to take Connor to the Norvic Hospital and the rest of the team returned separately to Kathmandu. MEF ref 19-37.

British Ardang Expedition – Emily Ward and Mark Bielby
After waiting out a few days storm near their first planned objective on peaks south of Nying Khola, the team ultimately decided to move on rather than wait for more settled weather. They trekked over to Ardang (6034m) looking to make an attempt on the mountain's north face and north-east ridge. After setting their high camp at 4,650m, they twice tried to make an approach but both times were forced to turn back. The first time, after slow progress in waist-deep snow, they retreated but were able to drop equipment at 5,100m in preparation for their next attempt. This saw them make a further 300m on the route to where a rocky rib began ahead. However, here they found a number of layers of wind slab sandwiched between heavy powder on top of a 10cm layer of very faceted depth-hoar about 50cm down. Discovering this they were forced to turn back and trekked over to Nyalu La, getting in a couple of days ice climbing in Salli Khola before returning to Simikot.
MEF ref 19-38.

British Kangchung Expedition – Paul Ramsden and Jim Hall
The team had two objectives on the north faces of Kangchung Shar and Kangchung Nup, both of which have seen previous ascents from their south faces. Flying first from Kathmandu to Lukla, they then hiked up to Namche Bazaar and on to Gokyo, setting base camp at the foot of the Gyubanare glacier. After Jim began experiencing chest pains with a suspected pulmonary edema, they descended back to Gokyo and were recommended to drop back lower to Machhermo for Jim to recover. They then returned to base camp where they first attempted a direct line of ice on Kangchung Nup, but were only able to make 300m of height, after which the ice turned very thin. They changed instead to Kangchung Shar deciding to try the line first attempted by Simon Yates in 2016. After making a smooth ascent of the north face to Kangchung La they proceeded along the north-west ridge on soft snow to the upper rocky section below the summit. Here they found an impassable section of blank granite slab covered in powder snow, and with no way to bypass this they were forced to retreat. MEF ref 19-11.

Lachama Khola Expedition – Derek Buckle, Drew Cook, Lorna Earl, Mike Fletcher, Steve Humphries and Nick King
Between September and October, six Alpine Club members travelled to Lachama valley in the Changla Himal, trekkingg from Simikot. They made their first base camp at the confluence of the Lachama Khola's north and south branches and an advanced base camp south of the Lachama glacier. They approached what they believed to be their intended objective of 5822m but on closer inspection found that the photo they had been given was in actual fact a lower peak of 5590m. They decided to

switch to this new true objective and negotiated a difficult boulder field to take a closer look but decided ultimately that an attempt would likely take longer than the time they had. Instead they switched to their original lower objective and established a second camp close by. They made the pass at 5120m where they set their high camp but could not see a clear route up the west face and opted instead for a rocky outcrop on the ridge. However once on the ridge they found a steep snow-covered wall they were unable to pass and turned back 20m below the summit. Returning to base camp the weather began to indicate a change for the worse and they decided to return to Simikot.   MEF ref 19-12.

Glacial Drainage Systems on the Langtang Glacier – Catriona Fyffe, Evan Miles, Marin Kneib, Simone Jola, Mike McCarthy, Alban Planchat and Reeju Shrestha
The team trekked initially from Syabrubesi to their Morimoto base camp over six days and set about undertaking their research. Their objectives were twofold: firstly to determine the structure and efficiency of the glacier's drainage system, and secondly to understand how the drainage system and resulting runoff is influenced by thickness and topography. Once at base camp they took discharge and water chemistry measurements and injected dye traces higher up in order to track the drainage systems that were then subsequently caught by the gauging station they installed. Over three days a total of eight dye gaugings were conducted and the data they gathered will allow the relationship between stream level and discharge to be understood, and ultimately give a more complete picture of the glacier's discharge. After 11 days in the field they trekked back out to Syabrubesi and onwards to Kathmandu. The team plans to return post-monsoon 2019 to complete further dye traces and take water chemistry samples.
                                                MEF ref 19-24.

TIBET

Topographic Catchment Assessment – Rebecca Stewart
The original objective of this expedition in the Bomi region of Tibet was to create a catchment wide topographic survey of Glacier 24K that could assess the sediment cascade through the system. Following an initial field campaign in June 2019, where initial scans were obtained of the catchment, the October expedition spent seven days surveying the glacier employing dye tracing, thickness measurements, time-lapse photography and scanning of the main headwall. The expedition also noted obvious visual changes between June and October including changes to the proglacial flow and movement of the stream. The final data analysis is continuing.
                                                MEF ref 19-36.

CENTRAL ASIA

Pamir Ski Expedition – Ryan Taylor, Elliot Smith, Peter Biskind and William Saunders
The objective of the expedition was to make a number of ski descents close to the village of Jilandi. After gaining permits locally, the team travelled by 4WD to Jilandi and arranged assistance to help take them further up the valley. They made their first camp on foot with the help of a number of locals, arriving on the 2nd May. From here they made four descents on Peak 4518, Peak 5150, Peak 5105 and Peak 5574. These culminated in a challenging final descent on Peak 5574 which saw the team climb for 8 hours and sit out a number of days of poor weather before skiing the planned line. During the expedition they noted a number of potential ski lines and climbing routes in the area, including a mixed line on Peak 5468 that they identified on the day of their second descent.   MEF ref 19-05.

Western Torugart Too Expedition – Derek Billings, Robin Ohlssen, Dave Ryan, Rob Hughes-Games, Jenna Hughes-Games
Following information from Pat Littlejohn about unclimbed peaks in the Altai, Pamir and Tien Shan ranges, the team opted to look in more detail at the western area of the Torugart Too range. The area they chose had seen a number of expeditions in 2008 and 2010 but held a number of c4600m peaks still unclimbed. They made basecamp on the 28 August and acclimatised by ascending a number of smaller peaks close by. Once acclimatised they climbed four routes in very good weather and turned back on an additional fifth route at 4,300m after encountering unstable rock and climbers experiencing altitude sickness. Few issues were encountered aside from an impact to the head after one member paraglided during a descent that saw him treated for wounds to his nose and left eye. The team broke camp after heavy snowfall arrived and retreated to Naryn a day earlier than planned. They note that there is still additional potential for further first ascents in the area.   MEF ref 19-09.

KMC Western Zaalaisky Expedition – Andy Stratford, Steve Graham, Emily Thompson, Andy Vine, Jared Kitchen and Stuart Hurworth
Six members of the Karabiner Mountaineering Club travelled to the little explored western Zaalaisky region with the aim to attempt unclimbed peaks and gain greater insight for future expeditions. After arriving in the Altyn Daria valley via the city of Osh the team established their base camp at 3,170m before the first ascent was made of Ak Chukur (4958m) from the Bel Uluu valley. The other valleys of Kaska Suu and Min Terke proved difficult to access due to dangerous river crossings, and instead further objectives were identified as Pik a Boo (5122m) and Broken Peak (5122m) which were ascended within two days of each other. The fourth peak was made a further two days later on Ak Kalpak (5112m) via a challenging route through crevassed terrain that saw Graham and Kitchen negotiate various sections

of steep ice. On the same day Stratford, Vine and Hurworth attempted a route up the north face of the glacier on 5084m but were slower than expected on the complicated glaciated terrain and were forced to turn back after running out of time. The team note the extensive potential still remaining in the area for unclimbed summits, particularly in the Min Terke group, but note that changing climate could cause further glacial retreat and instability which should be factored in.   MEF ref 19-18.

High-altitude Cryosphere Processes – Dr Joel Fiddes, Dr Simon Allen and Mark Witcomb
This research project aimed to fill a vital knowledge gap concerning permafrost in high mountain environments, a topic of growing importance in light of climate change. The expedition was based in the Fann mountains near Iskanderkul in Tajikistan and set out to establish an elevation profile of ground temperature readings between 2000m and 5000m on Peak 4820m. Their aim was to establish a pilot project, which could serve as a reference for further expeditions planned in 2020 looking to establish a full metrological station in central Pamir. Alongside this data they noted areas of retreat and down-wasting on the glacier they were studying and a host of climbing potential. They encourage any future expeditions that come here to make contact with them to help gather more data from the region.
                                                                                              MEF ref 19-19.

Sayan Mountains – James English, Megan Picken, Harry Williams, David Warnes, Dr Alexander Shchetnikov and Dr Ivan Filinov
The expedition to the Sayan range in southern Siberia aimed to provide data to better understand past climatic conditions in the region using chironomids, diatoms and spheroidal carbonaceous particles, and also to extract two cores from four lakes in the range. After arriving at their designated field site from Khoito-Gol, the team set about sampling Lakes Kascadnoe and Khikushka over three days. They were unable to sample further lakes after the weather closed in and one team member fell ill. Conditions on the approach to another intended site, Lake Shas-Nur, meant circumnavigating large areas of bog that added five hours to the journey and with the daylight left there was not enough time to sample the lake. The data gathered from this expedition will be processed and studied at Newcastle University.
                                                                                              MEF ref 19-31.

Reviews

Plate 8. *'The Valley of the Jumna [Yamuna] with two grand peaks of Bunderpooch'*

Reviews

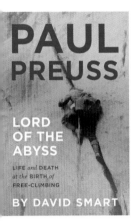

Paul Preuss: Lord of the Abyss
Life and Death at the Birth of Free-Climbing
David Smart
Rocky Mountain Books, 2019, pp247, £24.80

'No one will ever equal Preuss,' said George Mallory. But who was Preuss? As David Smart observes at the opening of this absorbing biography, most modern climbers have never heard of Paul Preuss and fewer still English-speaking climbers are sure how to pronounce his name. It's *'Proyce'*.

Yet it is to this fin de siècle Viennese gentleman we must look for the root of the set of ethics we use to this day in the definition and practice of free climbing and, more pertinently, solo climbing. Preuss regarded the use of pitons and ropes as a sin against the truth and practised what he preached with a succession of breathtaking solo ascents in the Dolomites and Austrian Alps.

But there is an almost inevitable trajectory to the Preuss story and a parable, perhaps, for our times. Celebrity as a climber is further fuelled by success as a writer and lecturer, a craving for attention leads to more daring climbs, and the necessity to complete each route clouds the mind. When the search party found Preuss' broken body at the base of the north face of the Mandlkogel on 14 October 1913, in his jacket pocket was an appointment book with his lecture dates, a reminder, Smart notes, of the relationship between Preuss' goals as a climber and his reputation.

Preuss laid down a marker aged 21 with a first solo ascent of the northwest face of the Planspitze in the Gesäuse range. A mix of loose rock, steep cruxes and long traverses, the 1,200m route had been pioneered by Viennese climbers Eduard Pichl and Friedrich Panzer. It was regarded as one of the more serious propositions in the Gesäuse.

What really grabbed the attention of Austrian and German climbers was his solo of the west face of the Totenkirchl in the Kaisergebirge: a 660m route as forbidding as the peak's name, 'Chapel of the Dead'. The first ascent in 1908 was by a team of three led by the Dolomites ace Tita Piaz, Paul's inspiration, friend and rival, and the man who coined the appellation 'Lord of the Abyss'. Preuss earned the accolade when, nearing the top of the wall, he turned up a difficult unclimbed crack to a higher finish.

Less than a week later he made the solo first ascent of the east face of the Campanile Basso in the Brenta Dolomites, a face so steep, smooth and relentless that even Piaz thought it impossible. No one had even attempted it. (Incidentally, Smart seems to expect a certain cultural sensibility of his readers, likening the Campanile Basso to Giotto's 14th century bell tower in Florence.)

On 28 July 1911 Preuss set out up the Campanile by its *Via Normale* with his sister Mina – Preuss was unusual for his day in often climbing with women – and close friend Paul Relly. As they rested 200m up, Preuss asked Relly for a belay while he traversed around a corner to look at the east face, rising a further 110m to the summit. It appeared smooth, without ledges and the rock hard to predict. 'What do you see?' Mina asked. 'Not much,' her brother replied. A few minutes later he set out to solo the 'impossible' pitting, in Smart's words, 'his skill and bravery against his mortality'.

Nima and Relly must have wondered if they would see him alive again. They soon did. Preuss reached the summit in just two hours, then down-climbed the *Via Normale* and climbed back to the top with his sister and Relly. Two days later he and Relly returned to the Campanile and climbed the Fehrmann Dihedral after which Preuss down-climbed the east face: an emphatic underlining of his maxim that if you cannot climb down a route you shouldn't climb up it.

The audacity of Preuss's ascents on the Totenkirchl and Campanile Basso left climbers of the German and Italian-speaking worlds in awe. The young Austrian soloed many more bold routes but these two have the merit of being both exemplars of Preuss' climbing ethic and are in ranges familiar to many British climbers. For Preuss was essentially a man of the eastern Alps, not just the well-known Kaisergebirge but ranges such as Gesäuse, Totes Gebirge and Gosaukamm, little visited by Brits a century ago or now.

Only towards the end of his all too brief life – he was dead at 27 – did Preuss visit the western Alps, and generally the weather wasn't kind. His standout climb in the Mont Blanc range was a solo first ascent of the south face of the Dent du Géant. As Smart relates, soloing the Burgener Slabs, even in dry conditions, would have taxed Preuss's abilities, climbing the same rock covered in snow, as it was, he would have been at his very limits. At the summit the storm became yet more intense and he had still to down-climb the Géant's south-east face, at the time one of the hardest routes in the Alps.

Lord of the Abyss was rightly shortlisted for the 2019 Boardman Tasker Award. Had I been a judge I might well have rooted for it as a winner. However, I gather not everyone is as enthusiastic about the book as myself. The downside, it seems, is that unfamiliarity with the eastern Alps. How many British climbers could even point to the Mandlkogel, the peak where Preuss met his end, on the map? (It's in the Gosaukamm.) Or to the nearby resort of Altausee where the Preuss family had a country home and where young Paul was captivated by mountain flowers and had his first solo adventures?

For myself, having lived long ago in Vienna for three years, sojourned in the Totes Gebirge and Dachstein, and spent long summer evenings on the limestone crags beyond the city's furthest tram stops, *Lord of the Abyss* was something of a trip down memory lane.

What distinguishes this biography from the stories of more contemporary climbers, is Smart's exploration of Preuss' inner conflicts and their very

Left: Paul Preuss, 1912.
(Albert Asels)

Below: Paul Preuss on the north face of the Hochtor in the Gesäuse in September, 1911. *(Walter Schmidkunz)*

Viennese origin. A Jew who converted at age 22 to Protestant Christianity, who dressed as a *senner* (Styrian farmer or woodsman) in the mountains and a bourgeois gentleman in the city, who loved flowers and the company of friends yet preached a merciless doctrine, Preuss climbed as if both to prove his superiority and to fuse his contradictions into a single identity.

When Preuss donned his *senner's* garb of lederhosen shorts, waistcoat and jacket with deer horn buttons, he 'subverted the circumstances of his birth,' says Smart. As the book's grainy photographs illustrate, Pruess remained 'almost ritualistically fastidious' about his clothes. A climb might reduce his suit to tatters but his tie would still be neatly in place.

Smart's portrayal of the currents that shaped Preuss in imperial Vienna, capital of the Austro-Hungarian empire, and the decidedly unsentimental code of its rock climbers is fascinating. He reminds us of the old saying: 'Death is a Viennese.' Yet Preuss was no gloomy, angst-ridden fellow. Nor was he solely a rock athlete. He was also an avid ski mountaineer: indeed, his ski tours may sound more familiar to AC members than most of his rock routes.

In 1910, with Relly and another Viennese friend Alexander Hartwich, he made a nine-day ski traverse of the Silvretta, including climbs of Piz Buin (3312m), highest summit in the range, and six more 3,000ers. Next the trio headed for the Ötztal and a 60km trek, skiing over five 3,000m passes. This was pioneering stuff, barely 20 years after Fridtjof Nansen's celebrated crossing of Greenland that effectively launched ski touring. (Preuss shared something of Nansen's spiritual aesthetic in his reverence for nature and isolation in a frozen, mountain world.) Relly and Hartwich returned exhausted to Vienna but Preuss journeyed on alone: a double ski traverse of glaciated Grossvenediger (3666m), a first ski ascent of the Grosser Geiger (3360m) and three other 3,000ers in the range.

Remember, those of you who may, like me, have skied those same mountains, that we did it on modern ski-mountaineering gear: widish skis and safe, heel-locking bindings. Preuss and his friends were on primitive wooden Nordics: freeing the heel and freeing the mind! Also, without the *apfelstrudel* comforts of wardened 'huts' that are today more like inns, ski tourers had to be entirely self-sufficient. One of Preuss' regular companions, Martin Freud, wrote that 'each of us carried a hundredweight of food and equipment. We lived largely on dried food like Arctic explorers.'

Martin's father was the pyschoanalyst Sigmund Freud. The Freuds were one of several Viennese Jewish families who regularly vacationed in Altausee. Preuss rock climbed with Martin's sister Anna and would have known the family both as holiday friends and part of his intellectual circle in the city. However most of his friends and social contacts were Protestants, part of the 'Away from Rome' religious revival that took firm hold in the early 20th century, not least in the German and Austrian Alpine Club.

Smart writes of a 'fiery ascetic' side of Preuss, one that 'resonated with the Christian theology of sacrifice.' The mountains were to be accepted as they were. Better to risk death by staying on the right route than to stray into error for the purpose of safety.

In August 1911 Preuss set out his uncompromising philosophy in a short article in the *German Alpine Times* entitled 'Artificial Aids on Alpine Routes'. It was published by Walter Schmidkunz, a friend with whom he'd been at university with in Vienna. Both men were by then living in Munich: the city of climbers. Smart describes the article as 'one of the most explosive, idiosyncratic, anachronistic and yet perennially relevant documents in the history of climbing'. The so-called 'Great Debate' about rock-climbing style would rage for decades. Does it ever really end?

Preuss ended the piece with the famous words of Martin Luther, founder of his adopted Protestant evangelism: *Hier stehe Ich, ich kann nicht anders.* ('Here I stand, I cannot do otherwise.') For Tita Piaz, seven years older than Preuss and with a wife and two daughters, his friend had gone too far. Piaz proclaimed an Alpine freedom: 'I do not understand at all how a person can be so cruel as to want to constrain rock climbing within limits; after all, we go into the mountains to be free of limits.'

The most personal attack came from Austrian rock-climbing authority Franz Nieberl, nicknamed the *Kaiserpapst* (Pope of the Kaisergebirge), who labelled Preuss the 'newly arisen Puritan of rock climbing' and accused him of spreading false doctrines. Uglier still, Nieberl tapped into Austria's vein of anti-Semitism, calling Preuss a 'terrible Moloch'.

Stung by the responses of Piaz and Nieberl, Preuss moderated his stance somewhat and in a further statement acknowledged the use of pitons as an emergency reserve and the rope as 'relief-bringing means', but one that ought never to be one true means for making an ascent possible. He believed that if climbers followed this free-climbing style they would no longer be waging war against the mountains but would 'learn once more to fear and love them.'

Smart raises the interesting question of whether modern free climbing was defined in response to an anti-Semitic slur. Whatever the answer, the reader is left wondering how carefully Preuss had weighed up that balance between fear and love before he set out on his fateful attempt on the Mandelkogel's north face. Was he over-determined to finish his 1913 season with one more headline ascent: fodder for his next lecture series? He was alone on the mountain and the cause of his fall will almost certainly never be known. A big factor was likely the sheer difficulty of the climb, with loose rock and cold, poor weather closing in.

Piaz, bold 'Devil of the Dolomites' though he himself was, had warned against making a feast for the ravens in the dark abyss. But Preuss had nailed himself to his true cross. Some things seem inevitable. Smart suggests we look upon Preuss as a 'necessary saint called to a way that few can follow, rather than a climber like others are climbers.'

Stephen Goodwin

Alpenglow
The Finest Climbs on the 4000m Peaks of the Alps
Ben Tibbetts
Ben Tibbetts, 2019, pp320, £50

It seems almost impossible that you could be reading this and not already have at least heard of *Alpenglow*. Ben Tibbetts and his work have been spread across the Alpine Club and its publications and even its very shopfront like an unstoppable mountain sunrise that now dazzles passers-by at our headquarters in Shoreditch thanks to an arresting, large-format image of climbers on the Innominata ridge moving steadily towards the viewer on Charlotte Road with the Matterhorn and Monte Rosa aligned distantly between their helmets and a perfect sunburst overhead.

In another bright beam of recognition, one of the highlights of last year's *Alpine Journal* was (more or less) a chapter from *Alpenglow:* an account of Tibbetts' and Colin Haley's sensational Ultra Royal Traverse of the Mont Blanc massif in April 2018. Even the Club's newsletter has yielded to the phenomenon; in November 2019, several parochial matters and meet reports lost their place to five pages of promotion for Ben and the book. And yet the work is so fine and the achievement so colossal that anyone familiar with it would call all this coverage fully deserved.

If you agree with that sentiment, you won't help wondering where it figured in the considerations of the Boardman Tasker jury, who didn't even shortlist it. Perhaps they didn't read it. At first glance you might assume you're looking at an expensive coffee table photographic book. On closer inspection it becomes clear this is a substantial contribution to the tradition of mountain photography originating with Vittorio Sella, even with pre-photographic artists like Gustave Loppé, and continuing today in work

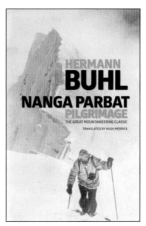

Vertebrate have reissued three classic works from the 1950s, including Geoffrey Sutton's translation of Lionel Terray's seminal *Conquistadors of the Useless*. Born in 1921, Terray, who made the second ascent of the north face of the Eiger and was a major force on the ascent of Annapurna in 1950, typified the optimism of post-war alpinism in France. Also republished is *Nanga Parbat Pilgrimage,* Hermann Buhl's account of his inexorable rise from a frail childhood to becoming one of the best rock climbers in Austria, his career interrupted by the war and his capture by Allied troops. On his first Himalayan expedition in 1953 he climbed Nanga Parbat in bravura style and against the instructions of his martinet leader. Finally, Vertebrate has also reissued the haunting epic *The Last Blue Mountain* telling the story of the tragic 1956 expedition to Haramosh and the heroic efforts by leader Tony Streather and Rae Culbert to rescue teammates Bernard Jillott and John Emery after they are swept away in an avalanche, merely the start of an agonising sequence of events with a twist at every turn.

by peers of Tibbetts like Jon Griffith. But when you sit down for a steady read of what he's written (maybe lean it on something, it weighs nearly five pounds), a work of real literary merit emerges from between the images vying for your attention. What's more, although it is by no means a conventional guidebook, *Alpenglow* is an immense practical resource and a guiding inspiration for active climbers.

It joins a list of books immersed in the cult of the 4,000m mountain. But Tibbetts is careful to delineate his 50 chapters as the 'Finest Climbs on the 4000m Peaks of the Alps' rather than as an inventory of the mountains themselves in the style of Goedeke, or Moran, or Dumler and Burkhardt. Nevertheless, the 50 routes described would if completed take a climber over all 82 tops in the modern UIAA list. Each chapter heading highlights the route itself in bold, foregrounding the ridge, face, feature or traverse and not the name of the peak. 'For me, the summit is like a punctuation mark in the story, so the 4,000m contour and the goal of producing this book served as a framework for gathering experiences rather than peaks,' he asserts. There's a reminder too that this metric benchmark counted for nothing amongst our imperial-measuring forebears of the Golden and Silver Ages.

The efforts of those forebears and those that came after them, their first ascents and their technical advances, are woven into the narrative of each chapter: there are AC giants from Whymper's and Walker's time through the age of Mummery and onwards past Mallory through Bonington to MacIntyre. But superhuman mountain guides like Christian Klucker are named with equal recognition whenever historical ascents are referenced. Route by route there's a gradual accretion of Alpine climbing history. The shift into guideless climbing imperceptibly shifts back to a style where the unguided climbers are guides themselves. Tibbetts of course is a guide, as are many of the partners he collaborates with on the featured routes. And as his fine prose moves from the past to the present day the reader finds Tibbetts tying on with living legends like Liv Sansoz, Victor Saunders and Mick Fowler.

Which brings me to Valentine Fabre, speaking of super-humans, 'doctor, lieutenant-colonel and world champion skier', climbing partner to Tibbetts and partner in life. As he unfolds his 50 routes, Fabre (whose name I for one didn't know before) emerges not only as a consummate and elite mountaineer but also as a patient saint of his photographic project intruding on her climbing. We are all accustomed to early starts but Fabre must have lost count of the times it was necessary that 'we left hours before any other alpinist,' or that she was required 'to repeat a couple of passages to milk the opportunity.' Again and again she features, moving steadily through sensational terrain against breath-taking backdrops, seemingly invincible.

Almost always her head is down or her cheek is turned away from the camera. The same is true of all the featured climbers, a clear photographic and editorial choice allowing us sight of human figures in ferocious landscapes and yet veiling their faces, safeguarding the grain of their individuality that elsewhere, in his writing, is so warmly and keenly mediated. Susan Sontag said that to photograph people is 'to violate them, by seeing them as they never see themselves, by having knowledge of them that they can never have; it turns people into objects that can be symbolically possessed.' Tibbetts understands this, and his instinct is to protect and respect his subjects almost fastidiously, exposing their exposure to risk with sacrosanct care.

Risk, 'the central and persistent mystery of mountaineering', is explored and questioned with depth and lived experience throughout the book. It has its share of shocks and near misses. A long shadow is thrown by the avalanche that nearly killed Tibbetts while powder skiing in deteriorating weather across the valley from Mont Blanc. The first page of the Ultra Royal Traverse chapter almost makes you snap the book shut as you read first of Stéphane Brosse's death on a previous attempt and then of Ally Swinton's extraordinary survival after falling 600m through a cornice warming up on a mere Royal Traverse. In the signature photo of the Innominata ridge that adorns the Charlotte Road premises the reader unbelievably learns that Bertrand Gentou, pictured leading strongly over precipitous ground, has minutes earlier been hanging unconscious and upside down after being hit by a block inadvertently dislodged by one of Tibbetts' partners. And in all the coverage of the extraordinary and admirable Valentine Fabre it's impossible to forget what we learn about her in the very first chapter, that she lost her equally impressive former partner Laurent in an accident when he was guiding above Chamonix. In a much later chapter, on an exhausting ascent of the *Cecchinel-Nominé* with her on the Grand Pilier d'Angle, the pair are gripped by thoughts of 'friends and family that have died in the mountains ... When I looked upwards towards the Peuterey Ridge,' he concludes, 'I had the feeling that if I continued I was going to die.'

But Tibbetts' writing moves as deftly towards the light as it dwells on darkness. Sometimes his descriptive prose approaches the gracefulness of Robert Macfarlane. At times he gives vent to a political awareness not commonly expressed in climbing circles, questioning for instance how his own 'insidious gendered preoccupations' affect his approach to the mountains and to his collaborators, noting how male domination in the Victorian world of the pioneers is still perpetuated in a significant imbalance of power, wealth and expression in modern society. There's a straightforward awareness of the impact of climate change on the fabric of what we climb; he confidently forecasts that 'May and June (which now resemble July and August 50 years ago) could become the safest and most productive period for alpine climbing.' And there are passages that just make you laugh, like his affectionate portrait of Victor Saunders getting soaked in icy melt-water during a traverse of the Fiescherhorn with a couple of clients. This evolves into a whole new episode of *Les Tribulations de Vic et Mick* when he and Saunders join Fowler on the *Lauper* route of the Mönch and the north-east ridge of the Jungfrau. All this richness is available in a French edition too, translated of course by Valentine Fabre.

There's an extraordinary spectrum of Alpine experience contained in these pages. The book is a masterpiece. It will double your appetite and sharpen your wisdom. If what I called impossible is true and you really haven't laid eyes on it yet then you need to get hold of a copy as soon as possible.

Nick Fletcher

• *Alpenglow* is available for £50 direct from *www.bentibbetts.com/alpenglow,* compared to an Amazon price of £65.

The Last Great Mountain
The First Ascent of Kangchenjunga
Mick Conefrey
Mick Conefrey, 2020, 315pp, £20

It seemed a sign of the times. When Joe Brown, one of the greatest mountaineers of the 20th century, died last spring the BBC didn't bother to include him in their obituary programme *Last Word*. Nor was any mainstream publisher prepared to take on a masterly new account of the Himalayan climb where Brown had starred so splendidly – the first ascent of Kangchenjunga. In our so-called 'information age' we are actually offered a diminishing supply of ever more predictable fare. Why bother with the world's third-highest mountain when we can feed the punters another story about people queuing and dying on Everest? However, one upside of the digital revolution is that authors with something interesting to say can bypass the bread-and-circuses merchants, and publish their own book. Which is exactly what Mick Conefrey has done.

The 1955 first ascent of the subtitle is a fitting climax, but what really makes this book is the build-up to that ascent, starting with Joseph Hooker's botanical explorations of 1848, the Schlaginweit's explorations and Douglas Freshfield's grand circumnavigation of 1899: all setting the scene for the first climbing attempt by the tiresome Aleister Crowley in 1905. Conefrey deals judiciously with the avalanche accident, which left four dead, concluding that even if Crowley was not actually to blame, he 'had behaved thoughtlessly at best, callously at worst.' The rows and recriminations that beset this first attempt on Kangchenjunga make the minor squabbles on later British Everest expeditions seem very tame. Likewise Conefrey's portrait of the mountain itself, which in the 1930s – as he comments in a rueful sideswipe at philistine publishers – was the most famous mountain in the world. By a quirk of politics, foreigners were allowed occasionally into eastern Nepal, from Sikkim. So, in contrast to the endless trudging up and down the Tibetan side of Everest, Kangchenjunga saw attempts on all three of its mighty faces before the Second World War. Crowley's team looked at the south-west Yalung face in Nepal while Dyhrenfurth's international expedition of 1930, after a prohibitively long approach beset by logistical headaches, attempted the giant terraces of the north-west face. That expedition also ended in disaster with the Sherpa Chettan killed by a collapsing ice cliff.

Both attempts on the Nepali side were ahead of their time. But the most futuristic line of all was the north-east spur in Sikkim, the route chosen by Paul Bauer in 1929 when he was refused entry to Nepal. Conefrey gives a detailed account of the drama, as the Germans and their loyal Sherpas hack, bulldoze and at times *tunnel* their way through giant ice towers, almost reaching the more climbable crest of the north ridge, before a desperate descent and harrowing return through the monsoon-drenched Sikkimese jungle. I was glad to see Conefrey quoting Edward Strutt's fulsome praise of the Germans in the *Alpine Journal*. Later, of course, Strutt would rant against the 'imbecilic' Eigerwand attempts, but for the time being he acknowledged the 'skill, endurance, cold-blooded courage and ... judgement' of the Teutons' 1929 and 1931 attempts on Kangchenjunga. I also enjoyed learning about Bauer's back story. Unlike Dyhrenfurth, the Jewish internationalist who had to escape Germany, Bauer was an ardent nationalist (and later a committed Nazi) who saw mountaineering as a path to German revival after the humiliating defeat of 1918 and subsequent economic chaos. Distasteful perhaps, but, like Strutt, I can't help admiring the sheer verve of the struggle, by a team operating on a fraction of the budget enjoyed by British Everest expeditions.

And so we come to 1955. I'm sure I must have read about it before, but I did enjoy this fresh account. Conefrey is not a climber but after several books and documentaries about polar and mountain exploration he knows enough of the technicalities to be convincing about the climbing, whilst also bringing an outsider's eye to illuminate the more interesting human story. Many readers of this journal will, like me, have met and liked Charles Evans, and this book reinforces the impression of a modest, wise, genial leader. This being a British expedition, the subject of class inevitably crops up and Conefrey relishes the fact that the 1955 team broke the traditional mould, with the two youngest members – working class Joe Brown alongside the toff George Band – chosen for the summit push, on what was supposed just to be a 'reconnaissance' paving the way for a full blown attempt by John Hunt in 1956.

It is perhaps significant that Kangchenjunga has not become a venue for modern commercial guided expeditions. The 1955 route might be the least difficult and dangerous way to the top, but as this account makes clear, it was no pushover. I had forgotten just how precarious that top camp was and how strung out Joe and George were on that long tenuous traverse, culminating in Joe's infamous jamming crack just below the summit. All that's missing from the account is Joe's comment to Tony Streather when he returned to the tiny top camp late that evening: 'I shouldn't bother going to the summit tomorrow, Tony – you'll never manage the rock climbing.' But of course Tony did go, with Norman Hardie, and they found an easy snow gully, neatly bypassing the world's highest sandbag.

Alas the death of Pemi Dorje from an undiagnosed illness at base camp soured the sweetness of success. That tragedy aside, it seems to have been an unusually harmonious expedition. Conefrey concludes nicely by following subsequent careers of the team and by describing briefly the Indian success in 1977 on Paul Bauer's north-east spur and the French-British ascent from the north-west in 1979, bringing full circle the story of 'the last great mountain'.

Stephen Venables

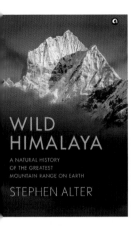

Wild Himalaya
A Natural History of the Greatest Mountain Range
on Earth
Stephen Alter
Aleph, 2019, pp416, £36

On 26 March 2020 I reached chapter 26 of Stephen Alter's very personal take on the natural history of the Himalaya. Entitled 'Oriental Avifauna', the chapter immerses the reader in the jungle of Arunachal Pradesh and a palette of gorgeous colour: the crimson cap and gilded beard of the golden-throated barbet, the scarlet breast of the red-headed trogon, and, in the gloom, a flash of yellow on a chestnut-headed tesia, 'as if someone was trying to light a match in the humid shadow.'

That same spring day, the British public watched their TVs with a mix of fear and incomprehension as the prime minister Boris Johnson imposed his belated lockdown; Covid-19 was taking its deadly hold.

The contrasts were painful: a riot of bird colours and exuberant growth in the 'land of the dawn lit mountains'; a plague cloud building over normal daily life the world over; Alter's lyrical prose; Johnson's cod Churchillian hectoring. Two totally different realities, and one infinitely preferable to the other.

Wild Himalaya became for me a kind of enchantment, a retreat into a realm of rocks and snow, gods and beasts, mountain people and seekers of knowledge and of summits. Thus absorbed I could temporarily forget about rates of infection and mounting death toll. Unfortunately the book's 400 pages proved by no means enough. The return to the Covid nightmare was too abrupt. To preserve the spell I reread Alter's *Becoming a Mountain,* winner of the Kekoo Naoroji Award for Himalayan Literature in 2015.

At first thought, a hefty volume on the natural history of the Himalaya seems a fairly dry, academic prospect. Yes, I do love the birds, beasts and flora of the mountains, but preferably by being out among them, not at a distance, wading through a biology textbook. I need not have worried. *Wild Himalaya* is nothing of the sort. Alter writes with the sensibility of a poet; every page is touched with a certain beauty, though darkly so when he laments man's destructive impact on the Himalaya and the planet as a whole.

The chapter that starts so gloriously among the dazzling denizens of the Arunachal Pradesh jungle ends on a stinking rubbish dump outside Guwahati, Assam. Perched on huge piles of rubbish are hundreds of greater adjutant storks, 'stooped like solemn hunchbacks with bald heads and heavy beaks.' Worse still is the presence there of rag pickers: children scavenging barefoot through broken glass and streams of sewage. The grim, flesh-eating birds look like creatures out of an apocalyptic mirage, Alter writes. 'Reminded of the giant man-eating birds of Sherdukpen folklore,

I can't help feeling that this is how our world may end, a grotesque vision of a polluted land populated by carnivorous storks, who squawk and squabble over rotting skin, entrails and bones.'

To tell the story of the Himalaya from the range's emergence from beneath the Tethys Sea, through rock formation, colonisation by plant and animal life to human settlement, mountaineering and tourism, all the way to the present with its enduring wonders and all manner of degradations, would be a monumental task: literally a task, one might pun, of Himalayan proportions. 'Would be', that is, even if one were only sticking to the scientific, Darwinian version of this unfolding process. Yet Alter offers throughout alternative creation stories and indigenous names and narratives for the myriad beings spread across the 2,500km range.

The Hruso tribe, for example, believe the world was created out of two eggs. One hatched to produce the sky, the other the earth. 'When the Sky made love to the Earth every kind of tree and grass and all living creatures came into being.' Alter is quoting here from Verrier Elwin's *Myths of the North-East Frontier of India*. Studying that sentence though, is it really a myth or simply recognition in poetic form of fundamentals for the very existence of life? *Wild Himalaya* is as thought provoking and beguiling, as it is informative.

The book has a metaphoric base camp, rooted, in and radiating its enquiries from Stephen Alter's home in Mussoorie. The Alters' presence in the Uttarakhand hill station dates back to 1916 and the arrival of his missionary grandparents. In a prologue, Stephen paints a pen portrait of the family home, Oakville, and uses the history of the colonial-era house and its luxuriant grounds to introduce some of the themes of the book. The Gangetic plain is glimpsed between the branches of the deodars, snow and ice of the Himalaya is visible just over a nearby ridge, and the house itself was built of material from the surrounding earth and forest.

The name Oakville comes from the resident *banj* oaks, while among the garden's many blooms is a bright yellow flower known in Garhwal as *phyunli*. Mention of both *banj* oak and *phyunli* is embellished with the kind of folk tales that become a feature of the book. A Garhwali saying compares the tough, but annoyingly knotty banj oak to a cantankerous old man; *phyunli* is a manifestation of a princess homesick for the mountains of her childhood.

Alter is adept at using the personal and particular to discuss the bigger issue, thus a cloudburst overflowing the gutters of Oakville opens the way to reflections on global warming and the droughts, forest fires and floods that beset the Himalaya. Recalling Hindu scripture, he muses on the elusive sacred river Saraswati, said to rise in the mountains and vanish into deserts. 'The disappearance of the Saraswati is an ominous warning to those who believe that rivers are eternal. As glaciers and wetlands disappear and weather patterns change, how many other Himalayan streams may vanish?'

Given the many inferences to Hindu, Buddhist and other indigenous beliefs, it is natural to speculate on Stephen's own spiritual leanings: he is, after all, the scion of Protestant missionaries. In both *Wild Himalaya* and *Becoming a Mountain,* Alter declares himself an atheist, but this smacks of rather more denial than his text suggests. I'm reminded of an answer given by the author Charles Allen at the Edinburgh Book Festival some years ago. Allen was promoting his book *The Buddha and the Sahibs.* Pressed on his own beliefs, Allen thought for a moment, then replied: 'I suppose you could say I am... Buddh-ish.' The reader of *Wild Himalaya* might easily suppose that of Stephen Alter.

The arrival of western climbers in the narrative comes as something of an intrusion. Giants though they may be in the climbing world, Hillary, Buhl, Messner and co are aliens here. Though they are a necessary part of Alter's endeavour, they do not *belong* in these mountains in the same way as the beings described so far, and the pages allotted them do not glow with quite the natural intensity that otherwise illuminates *Wild Himalaya.* Or maybe it is just that climbing history is familiar ground.

Shortly before we get to the mountaineers, there is a wonderful chapter describing how the heroic legends of Garhwal are recited by village bards who accompany their story telling with the percussive beat of a *dhol* and *damaun.* This musical tradition is known as *Dhol Sagar:* an 'ocean of drumming'. It is essentially an aural text, 'part of the ethereal soundscape of the Himalaya', says Alter. *Dhol Sagar* 'evolved out of the first sound in the cosmos, the beating of Lord Shiva's drum.'

After such magic, the next chapter, 'Chomolungma's People', falls a little flat. Alter treks up Khumbu to Kala Pattar; he professes a transcendent moment on the 5,634m summit, despite the presence of 50 other trekkers, yet somehow one feels his heart was not really in this tourist jaunt; that it was a necessary piece of research for the completeness of the book; a personalised device to tell the story of the Sherpas and their material and spiritual attachment to Chomolungma.

Of the mountaineers, the most sympathetically portrayed is Frank Smythe, for his successful combining of a climbing career 'with the avocation of a naturalist'. No surprise then that the most quoted of Smythe's oeuvre is *The Valley of Flowers,* Alter seeming to share Smythe's belief that we go to the hills to experience the beauty of 'a larger freedom', and through the subjugation of the body discover a contentment of spirit. And, Smythe continued, 'through beauty and contentment we gain peace.'

However Alter's own critique of the 'entirely modern' pursuit of mountaineering is a good deal more astringent, refreshingly so. Climbing, he says, is essentially a by-product of the industrial age, not only because it depends on steel implements, nylon ropes and synthetic fabrics, 'but also because it is largely driven by a subliminal sense of discontentment. More often than not, those who climb seek to break free of the oppressive conventions and routines of the mechanised, digitised world we have created for ourselves. Mountaineering promises a release from existential malaise through the physicality of climbing and a rejection of social norms and responsibilities.'

That surely has to be as good a response to the perennial 'why climb' question as you are likely to get. And it is yet one more example of the combination of a clear eye, original mind and prose mastery that makes reading *Wild Himalaya* such a deeply satisfying experience.

Stephen Goodwin

Tales from the Himalaya
Henry Edmundson
Vajra Books, 2019, pp432, £35

This thoughtful and engaging book is an excellent introduction to the history of much of the Himalaya, but for those planning to visit Nepal or Tibet, it should be essential reading. Its primary focus is on the culture, religions and physical geography of the region, most study of the latter originating in the 18th and 19th centuries through intrepid explorers, increasingly and mainly the British as the Raj took control of India. The book is beautifully illustrated throughout with maps and photographs, both current and historic, paintings and illustrations, and geological cross-sections. The style is perhaps best described as an encyclopaedic narrative.

Edmundson divides his 'tales' into four sections: religion, science, politics and society. Clever cross-referencing between these four themes provides links and continuity as the tales unfold in each section, and also moments of 'now I get it!' for the reader. In addition to the four main sections, this reviewer feels there is an undercurrent of three distinct eras reflecting different attitudes both among the local people and the western occupiers (latterly tourists) from the first western incursions to the present day. The first era is expressed in the wonderment of early European explorers, scientists and clerics as they wholeheartedly engaged with this very different world. In early encounters, there is little evidence of the sense of superiority that crept in once the British Empire took control from the East India Company. In those early years, harmonious relations were essential to trade. For the most part East India Company officials wooed maharajas and princes to make the most of good relations and local expertise to further trade, and to gain permission to travel in remote areas, to map and carrying out extensive scientific exploration.

The second era was that of balancing goodwill with the need for a significant military presence to ward off apparent (and mainly imaginary) threats from the Russian Empire, and to suppress rebellion. This period began with the failed attempt to secure Afghanistan through invasion in 1839 and the resulting military disaster. For decades afterwards, there were many small, proxy wars to enable the empire to expand into Hunza, Kashmir and Ladakh, with incursions into Tibet. Many of the territorial disputes began long before the British appeared on the scene and echoes of these conflicts remain with us today. In 1868, William H Johnson mapped the entire Aksai Chin as far north as Ilchi and proposed all of this region was part of Ladakh. But Johnson was at the time working as governor of Ladakh for Maharaja Ranbir Singh and the officials in Calcutta felt he had overstepped the mark. Nehru's later attempt to use the map as India's claim to the area came to nothing since the Chinese had already taken control of the area, and further secured even more it in the 1962 war. What would the current border crisis today be if that expansionist proposal had been acted on by the Raj?

The legacy of Western influence and involvement has shaped, and in some instances inhibited development of the Himalayan countries. This becomes clear as they emerged as independent countries and 'modernised' during the second half of the 20th century. These stories are covered in the last two sections of the book: politics and society. The latter is subtitled 'A Nepalese Story'. It provides a concise history of Nepal from the Gorkha conquest in the 18th century to the present day. These last two sections of the book are also my suggested 'third era'. Although Henry Edmundson does little moralising about the current corruption and turmoil in Nepal, perhaps he might agree with Victor Saunders' summing up of the impact of the west in the Himalaya as having brought three types of pollution: 'environmental, social and cultural'.

Despite Edmundson's concern about the future of Nepal, which is apparent in the final section, the overall impression when reading the book is one of great pleasure and discovery, which I believe the author found in researching, preparing and writing this book. The other side of the coin of a negative western legacy is the positive impact the Himalaya and all its people have had on western science. And not just science, since anyone who has travelled extensively in the Himalaya will appreciate, if not fully comprehend, that there is much we can learn from these complicated, tribal societies, shot through with almost infinite threads of spirituality and religion. These run like tributaries from the Himalayan snows. The fact that Edmundson has managed to capture so much of this in one book is in itself a testament to the power that the Himalaya and its peoples has had over so many of us.

One stunning example of how exploration of the Himalaya has led to major changes in western thinking is found in the section on science subtitled 'The Plates Must Speak'. Starting with the unnerving experience of being caught in the 2015 earthquake while trekking in Solu Khumbu, Edmundson moves backwards in time to recount the records of devasting earthquakes from 1223 and those that have occurred once or twice in nearly every century ever since. These regular catastrophes led to people wanting to find answers as to why the quakes occurred. The East India Company in its early days was fortunate to attract many gifted individuals (all male at that time) who multitasked. While first serving the company on military, engineering, commercial and administrative duties, they then spent time in exploration. This was not exploration for its own sake, but exploration to map and survey and to carry out scientific discoveries in geology, botany and palaeontology before 'natural history' was known as a discipline in its own right.

Many friendships emerged from partnerships that produced ground breaking discovers. For example, Proby Caultey (1802-71) teamed up with Hugh Falconer (1808-65) to spent five years studying the fossils and strata of the Siwalik hills. They discovered 'a complete zoo of extinct mammals,' and using the then emerging nomenclature of geological eras, concluded that the age of the mammal fossils discovered meant that the main Himalaya chain was a young mountain range, much to everyone's surprise. Later in his career, Cautley's main contribution was 'the planning and building of the 350-mile-long Ganges Canal', while Falconer on his return to London became a leading scientific figure who championed his friend Charles Darwin. Falconer detected evidence of evolution in his Himalayan fossil records. At the same time his geological work was 'feted by Charles Lyell', the revolutionary and foremost geologist of the Victorian era. Thus, discoveries in the Himalaya helped support the radical and transformative thinking of the day.

I mentioned earlier that Edmundson cross-references frequently between his four main sections. When learning about Cautley and Falconer, we are also told, 'the name Siwalik derives from a Sanskrit work meaning the tresses of Shiva.' There is an easy erudition to Edmundson's writing, who himself is a geologist. In the final chapter of this section – 'The Eureka Moment' – we are brought into the age of modern plate tectonics. The eureka moment was of course the realisation that the Indian plate was crashing northward into the Eurasian plate, hence the Himalaya and all the earthquakes, and another revolution in geological thinking.

The first section of the book, 'Religion: A Different Type of Reality', provides a potted history of Tibet and the most readable primer on the complexities of Buddhism that I have found. In the west, we sometimes criticise ourselves for spending too much time and effort categorising and defining the physical world and not enough time on the spiritual. But when it comes to categorising the spiritual world, Buddhism (and Hinduism) excel in creating a deity or demon for every human emotion and passion. Edmundson's take on Buddhism (and to a lesser extent Hinduism) reveals a deep understanding and empathy. The history of Tibet and its religions are as entwined as the various strata of rocks that have created the Himalaya.

The concept of a different reality extends well beyond religion and of course, it works both ways. The local people of the Himalaya would have little appreciation of the obsessions of the western explorers for rocks, plants and creating maps. The author at times pokes fun at us all with examples of these differences. In 1913, when Tibet declared itself an independent state, the British called a tripartite conference between China, Tibet and Britain at Simla:

'The main objective was nothing less than defining once and for all the boundaries and legal relations between Tibet and China. Precision on such matters, while second nature to the British, must have seen a novelty to the other two parties.'

And the rest is history, or should we say, the on-going manipulation of history. There is much more to this book than can possibly be covered in a short review, but there is never a dull moment, nor a page without some new gem of discovery waiting. If you have any interest whatsoever in expanding your understanding of the Himalaya and its people, read this book before your next journey.

John Porter

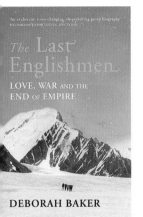

The Last Englishmen
Love, War and the End of Empire
Deborah Baker
Chatto & Windus, 2018, pp382, £25/£11 pb

The Last Englishmen opens on 3 September 1947 with Louis MacNeice, newly arrived in the subcontinent with dinner jacket and summer suit, standing in Lahore Refugee Camp and musing on the seemingly debatable merits of freedom. Two weeks after Independence Day, MacNeice, scripting plays for the BBC, is surveying a blood-soaked nightmare.

And with that we're off on the Baker rollercoaster, looping from the cold, stony banks of the Shaksgam to Calcutta *addas,* Everest, London bedrooms and wartime airfields. Deborah Baker writes with great pace and verve. So much so that at times you're crying 'Hold on! Where are we now?' Then flicking back to pick up the thread.

If you've read Baker's 2008 book *A Blue Hand: the Beats in India,* this pinball style is familiar. It's novelist, ironic and makes for compulsive reading, like no other 'mountaineering' book you've ever read – and the better for it. But then it isn't a mountaineering book at all as such; it's a work of cultural and political history, neatly summarised in that subtitle *Love, War and the End of Empire.* Yet always mountains linger, either to the fore, as with Everest and the Karakoram, or seemingly waiting in a wistful background. Quite rightly, *The Last Englishmen* won the Himalayan Club's 2019 Kekoo Naoroji Book Award.

That this is to be literature staged as a drama is plain from the off with a three-page cast of characters that includes explorers, English writers and the London 'art crowd' of the 1930s and 1940s to Calcutta intellectual circles and politicians and leaders of as varied a stamp as Mohandas Gandhi, Jawaharlal Nehru, the Bengali revolutionary Subhas Chandra Bose, Winston Churchill and Leo Amery, a one-time AC president, though here in his wartime role as secretary of state for India. (Leave a bookmark in this list; you may need it.)

Though Louis McNeice, poet and playwright, is the first of this rich cast to make an entrance, his is only a supporting role. The leading males are John Auden, pioneering geologist of the Himalaya, and surveyor Michael

Spender, first to draw a detailed map of the north face of Everest, both brothers of celebrated writers, and both love rivals in pursuit of the painter Nancy Sharp. Nancy enters the story marrying realist painter William (Bill) Coldstream, has a passionate affair with MacNeice, comes close with John's brother, W H Auden (though his tastes really lie elsewhere), then a dalliance with John himself, and bows out as the widow of Michael Spender.

Entanglements are meat and drink to Baker: *A Blue Hand* stars Allen Ginsberg and his lover Peter Orlovsky roaming India, criss-crossing with Gary Snyder and Joanne Kyger, and watching out for the near-mythical and, today, long-disappeared Hope Savage. Savage had been the muse of Gregory Corso, but neither Corso, nor William Burroughs, nor Jack Kerouac actually get to join the gang in India.

Baker's oeuvre teems with more poets than could cram into a Delhi opium den, something the Beats of course actually did. Calcutta intellectuals and rebels also feature in both books, and mountains even creep into *A Blue Hand*. Snyder – it had to be him – hikes up to about 12,500 feet above Dharamsala on the edge of the Dhauladhar range. He's only equipped with a spiked cane and reluctantly turns back on a snowfield. Snyder and the Dalai Lama hit it off discussing meditation but Ginsberg and Orlovsky find His Holiness less receptive to their obsession with drugs. 'If you take LSD, can you see what's in that briefcase?' asks the Dalai Lama with playful scepticism.

Michael Spender and John Auden both made it a lot higher, but it's hard to say how much of a kick they got out of it. Both led lives of considerable anguish. In the mountaineering world the pair are best known for accompanying Eric Shipton and Bill Tilman on their 1937 exploration of the northern Karakoram: the *Blank on the Map* trip, to use the title of Shipton's classic account. As Stephen Alter puts it in his wonderful *Wild Himalaya* (2019): 'While their siblings were reshaping the contours of modern English verse, J B Auden and Michael Spender were surveying and charting Himalayan terrain. Filling in the blanks.'

Baker treats the four mountaineers, of a species Sara Wheeler dubs 'the beards', with a good deal of irreverence, pointing up their foibles and clashes of character. Tilman had little patience with the 'scientific nonsense' (or Michael Spender for that matter) and regarded the heavy plane table and surveying equipment as an encumbrance to the jolly business of exploring. But a detailed map of the region was what the Foreign and Political Department was most interested in, and in particular the exact location of a pass over the Aghil range, north of the fabled Shaksgam river and regarded by the old Great Gamers as of strategic importance. Fifty years earlier Sir Francis Younghusband had become the first European to cross the Aghil Pass and none had been there since.

In *Blank on the Map* Shipton writes of the party's high state of excitement on reaching the pass (c4800m); northwards lay the rounded snow-capped peaks of the Kun Lun, to the west the limestone sentinels above the Shaksgam. However, having crossed the pass myself in 2012, north to south like

Younghusband, I can vouch that it was Captain Frank who had the better, utterly breathtaking view looking to the heart of the Karakoram: 'tier after tier of stately mountains' … 'untainted snow' … 'glaciers, like some huge dragons, creeping down the valley bottoms'. The pass itself is broad and gentle with a tarn on its north side: not unlike Sty Head in the Lake District.

Regarding the Lake District: it was here that Michael Spender climbed his first 'mountain': Cat Bells at age 10 while on a family holiday at Skelgill Farm in Newlands Valley. And the Audens had a holiday cottage in the tiny hamlet of Wescoe, near Threlkeld. Unfortunately, for all her undoubted research on places elsewhere, Baker, an American, seems a bit hazy on the geography of Cumbria: the north Pennines, and the limestone beloved of both Auden brothers, is not 'only four miles east of Keswick' but a good 24 miles. And the pencil factory was at Keswick, not Penrith.

Both Michael Spender and John Auden were in the frame for Everest in the 1930s but only Michael made it to the mountain, on Shipton's 1935 reconnaissance expedition. Descending for the last time after completing his survey of Everest's north aspect felt for him like a return to life from death, writes Baker, and he 'summoned a dim memory of his arrival at Cat Bells in summer 1917.'

John Auden has the distinction of having taken the first photograph of Everest's southern aspect, while participating in a geological survey of Nepal in 1934 following a major earthquake in the Kathmandu valley. He had joined the Geological Survey of India in 1926 and remained with it until 1953, the last Englishman to step down from the service. His contribution to unlocking the geological mysteries of the Himalaya came from surveys of the Garhwal and from his identification of the Krol Belt of limestone that extends through much of the lower Himalaya. John also has a remote col in the Garhwal named after him. Auden's Col, which he crossed with porters in 1939, stands at 5,490m, some 150km upstream from Rishikesh above Gangotri, and links the Rudragaira valley with the Bhilangana watershed.

The adventures of both John Auden and Michael Spender fed into the play *The Ascent of F6: A Tragedy in Two Acts,* written by W H Auden and Christopher Isherwood and first performed in 1937. Colonial rivalries are echoed in antagonism between the mountaineer hero and his politician brother. The authors dedicated the play to John, who thought the hero silly. 'Michael Ransom' had been modelled on T E Lawrence, a man as emotionally complex (or screwed up) as half the cast of Baker's many-layered tale.

On the dust jacket of *The Last Englishmen* is a photograph taken by Michael Spender on the 1937 Karakoram expedition; five figures insignificant on a vast glacier with a jagged ridge beyond rising into clouds. It is, as the publisher no doubt intended, an image to lure mountaineers; however mountains comprise by no means the whole of this book.

For all the immensity of that Karakoram glacier it represents less confusing terrain for most us than the dispositions of the Calcutta *chatterati* – poets, politicians and revolutionaries – in the turbulent years before independence. Herein is the cast of a parallel drama that is interleaved between the der-ring-do in the hills and is every bit as fascinating. Calcutta (today's Kolkata) was home for John Auden, as it would become decades later for Deborah Baker, who studied Bengali in the city and is married to the writer Amitav Ghosh.

All the main players in *The Last Englishmen* are now dead; John was the last of the Karakoram quartet to go, aged 87 in London. His ashes were cast on the Ganges at Rishikesh in December 1991. 'Though he never succeeded in being the first to climb the highest peaks, no other explorer of his time looked as closely at the mountains of the Himalaya and the rocks they were made of as John Auden,' concludes Baker. Sqn Ldr Michael Spender, an expert in photo-interpretation, died of injuries two days after the plane he was in crashed in a forest in Germany in May 1945. He was 38.

This enthralling book redresses an historical imbalance. Shipton and Tilman eclipsed John Auden and Michael Spender in public memory of the 1937 Karakoram expedition, just as they were in wider life by their younger poet brothers. Deborah Baker is to be thanked for drawing these two pioneers out of the shadows.

Stephen Goodwin

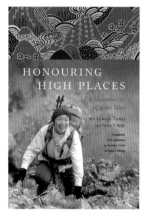

Honouring High Places
The Mountaineering Life of Junko Tabei
Junko Tabei and Helen Y Rolfe
Translated from Japanese by Yumiko Hiraki and Rieko Holtved
Rocky Mountain Books, 2017, pp376, £25

Honouring High Places, winner of the Banff Mountain History Award in 2018, chronicles the remarkable and wide-ranging achievements of the Japanese mountaineer Junko Tabei. From the age of nine, when she was first introduced to the mountains on a trip arranged by her teacher, she experienced 'a joy of achievement I had never felt before,' which fuelled her to do more. Her childhood conviction that mountain climbing was not competitive, unlike school sports where she had always performed poorly, but relied instead on self-discipline to succeed remained with her for the rest of her life.

She carved an improbable niche for herself in the 1960s by joining an all-male climbing club at a time when women were usually excluded from such societies. This provided her with opportunities to progress to rock climbing and winter mountaineering, which quickly became twin obsessions. Her slight frame and small stature belied her strength and her self-effacing nature masked her determination. These attributes were to carry her through a lifetime of high-altitude mountaineering, culminating in the first female ascents of Everest, Annapurna III and the Seven Summits.

Tabei's early life, growing up in patriarchal Japanese society during the Second World War, gave her little opportunity to fan the 'flicker of aspiration' she had felt on her first mountain walks. It was not until she went to Showa Women's University in Tokyo, ironically imagining a gender-stereo-typical female student life in which she would meet 'a nice man', that she discovered the potential for long hikes in the mountains around the city and the realisation that 'the rocky landscape had become a part of me.' In 1969 this conviction eventually led to the formation of the Ladies' Climbing Club, whose members were recruited from the few clubs that accepted women and whose objective became the first ascent of Annapurna III by an all-female expedition. For Junko, this was a far cry from the rigorously held tenets of her early years: blend in and obey the exacting rules that dictated a woman's place in Japanese society.

The success of the Annapurna climb was beset by the habitual problems of strong, ambitious personalities drifting into dissent. When Tabei's book about the expedition was published she wrote with a quiet honesty about the problems the team had faced and the challenges of her position as climbing leader. She regarded anything other than writing candidly about the harsh realities of climbing and the difficulties of group dynamics as 'vanity', and so broke the mould of traditional Japanese summaries of male-only expeditions in which such things were omitted. However, her writing was also suffused with the joy of being in the mountains: the 'unforgiving terrain' was something she loved unwaveringly and which called her irresistibly throughout her life. She combined her dedication to the mountains with the roles of wife and mother, believing that both could be accommodated and thus, yet again, expanding cultural horizons for female mountaineers.

The book's title is apposite: Junko Tabei not only made ground-breaking climbs on the mountains which were in her blood but also worked to maintain them for future generations. After completing an MA in social culture, focusing on the detritus in the Himalaya, she became chair of the Himalayan Adventure Trust, working to ensure that whatever was carried up a mountain was also carried down. Her charitable work in facilitating ascents of Mount Fuji for students and those living in refugee shelters after the Tohoku earthquake of 2011 introduced many people to the mountains who had lost everything but discovered a new interest in life through the beauty of what they saw. Indeed, her last climb with one of these groups was three months before her death from cancer, when she reached 3,010m on the mountain. In addition, she was tireless in opening up the mountain world to women of all ages, giving them the opportunities she had had to work so long to create.

The book contains 32 pages of good quality photographs, a pictorial autobiography, and a detailed timeline of Junko's climbing achievements and personal reminiscences by her friend and climbing partner Setsuko Kitamura, her son Shinya and her husband Masanobu, all of which enrich the narrative from a variety of perspectives.

Honouring High Places paints a picture of an indomitable woman, true to her beliefs, energetic in her climbing life and resolute in her conviction that the mountains she held dear should be accessible to all. What also emerges is her modesty and simple conviction that one cannot give up in the face of difficulties: one step at a time will lead to the summits of whatever challenges present themselves was her maxim and it served her well.

Val Johnson

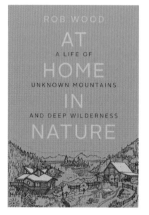

At Home in Nature
A Life of Unknown Mountains and Deep Wilderness
Rob Wood
Rocky Mountain Books, 2017, pp284, £17

After leaving Yorkshire gritstone for the Canadian Rockies, Rob Wood pioneered, with other Brits who had moved to Calgary, waterfall ice climbing and joined Doug Scott's climbs on Baffin Island in the early 1970s. Each of these major contributions to Canadian climbing merit no more than a passing reference in this book. Its focus is on what happened afterwards, especially how personal qualities learned from climbing enabled Rob Wood to literally make a home in nature and continue learning from a deep appreciation of wilderness.

After ascending a 'strenuous and scary' north face in the Rockies (unspecified) four climbers realised that they wouldn't make it to work in the morning and at their bivy ledge just below the summit resolved to give up work in the city to 'find ways to live permanently in the wilds.' All four did just that, but Rob Wood is the only one still alive today. Meeting, in a blind date at Squamish, Laurie Manson, a young woman training to be a rock-climbing instructor, Wood invited her and her four-year-old daughter to join him in setting up home with a group of dropouts who had formed a co-op to buy land on an island between northern Vancouver Island and the remote mainland coast. A series of small clear-cuts on south-facing benches offered the possibility for homesteads built using the plentiful standing timber in this 'beautiful and stimulating place'. Laurie and Rob are still there, on Maurelle Island, British Columbia.

That last phrase, a 'stimulating place' is the key to the theme of this book. Their survival and their thriving are connected at every stage to their awareness of the stimulations of place. This is more about the sea's stimulation from its tides, winds and whirlpools through the Georgia Strait than it is about exploring the mountains unknown to them on the islands and the Coast Range. Wood does climb Mount Waddington (4002m), the 'Mystery Mountain', from his boat and there are casual references to 'many ski mountaineering trips'. They work as wilderness guides for Strathcona Park Lodge on Vancouver Island 'leading hundreds of multi-day hiking journeys through the alpine paradise'. They successfully lead a campaign to resist government-approved mining and logging in Strathcona Provincial Park. Apart from the economic value of tourism, Wood emphasises 'the spiritual, physical and mental health value of wilderness as well as clean drinking water'. So the book keeps returning to the practicalities of dealing with bears, cougars and whales that imply rather than evangelise the spiritual benefits of being cohabitants of a stimulating place.

When serious illness emerges in the lives of first Laurie and then Rob, they reflect, in recovery, that their lives have lost balance. As the original co-op members have left over the passing decades and their grandchildren use their cabins for the summer, Laurie and Rob realise that they have ironically become disconnected from the human species. 'We concluded that far from the conventional idea of rugged and independent individuals, our true self-reliance resided in our connectivity with both our social and natural world. Our new-found conscious intention was to strengthen all the various relationships that make up our field of care, our love'. The tone of this can stand as representative of the whole book: a Yorkshire no-nonsense, honest, practical resolution combined with the unexpected, original and challenging notion of 'our field of care'. One leaves this book feeling, somehow, the better for having read it.

Terry Gifford

Slatehead
The Ascent of Britain's Slate-climbing Scene
Peter Goulding
New Welsh Rarebyte, 2020, pp340, £12

This is an unusual book: not exactly a climbing book but a book about climbing and not climbing as most AC members would know it. Though not fiction, it leads the reader into an alternative world centred on the vast, abandoned Dinorwig slate quarry above Llanberis. Finally closed in 1969 after nearly 200 years of operation and once employing over 3,000 men, the workings, level on level, rise some 1,600ft up the slopes of Elidir Fawr. Visible only from a distance with much of its acres of bare slate remaining hidden, it was forbidden, unexplored and ignored. Climbers, alpine or domestic, long looked askance at slate, typically ice-smooth, friable and untrustworthy; once quarried it might form imposing architecture but it was no substitute for honest rhyolite, granite, limestone or even ice.

The author, a family man in his mid thirties, once a rope-access technician but now an outdoor instructor, lives in deepest Norfolk, belongs to the local climbing club, climbs regularly on the local climbing wall and writes in the first person. When his saga opens in 2014 he is making his first visit to Wales, indeed he is climbing outdoors for the first time. His mates lead him into the quarry where he is captivated not only by the ethos and physicality of climbing on slate but also by the bizarre location. The techniques he perfects during the ensuing four years are little different from those with which he is adept on the Norwich climbing wall and the matrix of the book covers his progression to eventually become a dedicated slate aficionado, a 'slatehead' in fact.

I suspect that many AC members will be unfamiliar with slate climbing, certainly those of my generation. Essentially the technique necessary to climb routes in the quarries, all characteristically thin be they up slab or wall, is first either to explore on a top rope, after which success demands that moves must be learned by falling off them, as often as necessary, until they're wired. Only then can a clean 'redpoint' ascent with no falls be attempted. There is usually no natural protection and the game (indeed survival itself) depends on bolts, 12mm stainless steel now replacing the original rusted-out 8mm variety. The leading protagonists use power drills to place them on potential new routes and scoff at 'trad' climbers who might fall while fumbling to place fiddly stoppers ('smarties') in awkward cracks.

Goulding writes well and he is both philosophical and perceptive in describing his own thoughts and fears as he moves up the rock, or tumbles off it. These detailed first-person descriptions of climbing are among the best and most honest I've read. Nevertheless in due course I found his escapades rather repetitive as he progresses with his special mates Lee and Becky, weekend after weekend, visit after visit, to eventual slatehead-hood, given that they lead to no other denouement.

However, slotted bit by bit into this backdrop is the story of the alternative climbing culture that sprang up in north Wales during the 1970s and 1980s, in Llanberis in particular. Much of it financed by the dole, often drug-fuelled and at its extreme 'anchoring the climbing scene to debauchery', the culture revolved round Pete's Eats, the chip shop, the Llanberis pubs and the Dolbadarn Disco. It also spawned the officially illegal exploration of the quarries and the rapid development of climbing on slate. Goulding introduces many of the leading denizens, rock-jocks such as Al Harris, Stevie Haston, Johnny Redhead, Nick Harms, Johnny Dawes, who invented the 'dyno' move, and the local native Ian Lloyd-Jones among others. The tale is spiced with the futile efforts of the quarry owners, the First Hydro Company whose power station lies inside the mountain, to prevent trespassers.

Dominating this alternative world is Dinorwig Quarry itself, a vertical post-industrial wasteland, tier upon tier of out-of-this-world rock architecture, of towering walls and slabs, of profound voids, bottomless pits, strange tunnels and weird water-filled holes, scattered with roofless sheds, broken machinery and traversed by rusting cables. The slate climbers see it as a Tolkienesque mountainscape complete with hanging glaciers of scree, cornices of poised boulders, of crevasses, arêtes, avalanches of loose rock and rumbling rock falls. Goulding himself notices the colours and textures of the rock and relishes the recently emergent vegetation, oasis of green amid the shattered greys, blues and blacks. He hears the voices of the long dead quarrymen too. And writes of their history.

I enjoyed the book, describing as it does a scene I had briefly encountered but of which I knew little. The well-researched history is buttressed

with lavish notes, references, Welsh glossaries and an excellent index. It is
no surprise to know that *Slatehead* won the prestigious 2019 Rheidol Prize
for Writing with a Welsh Theme.

John Cleare

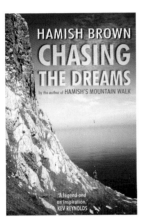

Chasing the Dreams
Hamish Brown
Sandstone Press, 2019, pp305, £9

With the subtitle 'a traveller remembers', one of the
UK's most prolific outdoor writers dips his hand
into a bran-tub that contains hundreds of his magazine and newspaper articles covering some 60-odd
years of adventuring, and pulls out a wide-ranging
selection of tales to relate in this companion to his
previous collection, *Walking the Song*.

A traveller remembers ...

Well, yes, now in his eighties, Hamish Brown
might be forgiven for surveying a lifetime's activity
in the hills through the rosy glow of selective memory. But these are tales
told at the time: accounts of journeys made, people met, peaks climbed,
camps and bivouacs shared, attacks by midges, disasters dodged, not with
the relish of hindsight but with a sense of the here and now stolen from
a journal entry, a letter home, or an account first published decades ago.

'Dreams have to be chased,' he says. 'It is the chasing that is life.' Then
he goes on to quote Robert Service: '… it isn't the gold that I'm wanting,/
So much as just finding the gold.'

So Hamish Brown is a prospector among the world's mountains,
although it's not gold that he's searching for, just the riches of a life to live
well. If you're after summits, you'll find plenty in this book, but it's the
getting from here to there, and what he finds on the journey that counts. In
a way he's a Shipton, a romantic, ever on the move: prospecting, exploring
the world's countless riches and sensing all its wonder.

In one narrative he treads in Shipton's footsteps through the intimidating Rishi Ganga gorge to reach the fabled Nanda Devi Sanctuary. And
there, overwhelmed by the mountain herself, he writes as Shipton himself
would have written: 'Everyone has now retreated to tents. Candles glow
and *odd conversations are muted by the river. I wouldn't be anywhere else in the
world.'* (My italics.)

That, to me, is more meaningful than the survival of any stormbound
epic on a major 'expedition' peak, for it's something many of us can relate
to. It's what going to the mountains is all about. It's what this book is
about. Not great achievements in the overall scheme of things, but gathering joyful moments when chasing the dreams.

Scotland features heavily, of course. From a man who has been an unofficial ambassador for walking and climbing there, this is hardly surprising,

but it's when he records travels, climbs and encounters further afield that his 'prospecting' gains momentum. With some pithy comments we learn that he doesn't think much of professional guides in the Swiss Alps who (in the 1960s) seemed less interested in giving their clients a memorable day out, than treating them as baggage to haul up and down their chosen peak in as short a time as possible. It's here that his narrative comes alive, and continues to grip with Africa-themed traveller's tales that make light of the Drakensberg and a tease of those 'splendidly wild, seldom-visited Mulanje Mountains' as he travels from the Cape to Kilimanjaro.

Hamish's second home is to be found in Morocco's Atlas Mountains which he first visited in 1965 and to which he has made countless return visits. *(The Mountains Look on Marrakech,* the account of his epic end-to-end traverse of the range, was shortlisted for the Boardman Tasker Prize.) But it's as much the Berbers who live there as it is the mountains that draw him back. 'In the Atlas I found a people and a culture I could admire, a simplicity of life, still rooted in family, culturally rich, the very antithesis of our cramped, rat-race, broken culture of the West.' Echoes of Shipton? Maybe, and I can think of no greater compliment than that.

Perhaps the title of this book should be 'Living the Dreams,' for the author's dreams are those that many of us aspire to, but rarely capture, while the tales he tells here when chasing them are well worth reading.

Kev Reynolds

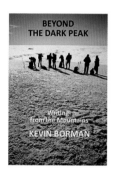

Beyond the Dark Peak
Writing From the Mountains
Kevin Borman
FeedARead.com Publishing, 2019, pp406, £10

Kevin Borman was never an alpinist, but a fell runner, hill walker, poet, bothy botherer, Sheffield geography teacher, writer and book reviewer for *High* magazine, traveller and incorrigible journal writer. From his retirement home in the Almeria region of south-eastern Spain he has published two books about exploring the trails and culture of that area, *Flamingos in the Desert* (2014) and *Where Hoopoes Fly* (2017). But each February he still joins a long-established group of friends for hill days in Scotland. He is, he says, 'an ordinary guy with the mountain bug'. At the end of this book he admits that he still cannot resist a run up the hill behind his house, although the old goat confesses that these days there's more walking than running up the Sierra Cabrera. 'If I was one of those people who keeps records, I'd know that I've made 602 ascents so far.' Fell runners, Munroists and geography teachers are incorrigible record keepers. So the 'Dark Peak' of Borman's book title is both the Dark Peak Fell Runners club and the moorland back garden of the city of Sheffield, whilst the 'Beyond' is both other mountain regions and beyond record keeping. In *Beyond the Dark Peak* Borman has revisited all the various forms of his writings about

Sam Brown on the Pembroke classic *New Morning,* one of many stunning new photos in a contemporary update from Vertebrate Publishing of Ken Wilson's classic *Hard Rock.* Edited by Ian Parnell and priced £40, the book features several new essays alongside classics from Ed Drummond, Al Alvarez and Chris Bonington. *(Emma Alsford)*

mountains to produce a cleanly written collection of often muddy mountain experiences that are at times hilarious, moving, poetic, informative and always warmly personable.

Writing about the worst section of running in Tanky's Trog, the Marsden to Edale Fell Race, Borman says, simply, 'Underfoot it is sodden. Overhead it is sullen.' Visiting the crash site where his lodger, Victor Radvils, died along with other British climbers and guides in the PIA Kathmandu plane crash of 1992, Borman writes: 'A scarred slope, tatters of fabric hanging like streamers from the remains of trees, bits of metal. The memory of being there is sharp but the detail of what I saw isn't; there's just a blur.' The fact that he's made that journey three months after losing his friend is testimony to the commitment to friendships shown in this book. But the piece begins by describing a walk on Bleaklow, in the Dark Peak, to Higher Shelf Stones to visit the remains of an American aircraft that crashed there in 1948. Here walking is a means of seeking solace for what remains raw years later. Days in the mountains offer a mirror for our reflections. Mostly unspoken in this book is the inner life of 'an ordinary guy' looking out, as he moves through the mountains, with extraordinary alertness.

Terry Gifford

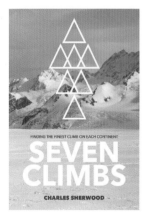

Seven Climbs
Charles Sherwood
Vertebrate Publishing, pp192, £14.95

'The whole thing,' Charles Sherwood writes, 'is little more than a delightful ruse for having a very good time.' This is the real raison d'être of this book's quest, an attempt to find the best climb on each continent, eschewing the traditional Seven Summits challenge, which is to simply reach the highest point. That round was first completed by Americans Dick Bass and Frank Wells in April 1985 and ever since, climbers being climbers, there has been dispute about the 'real' seven-highest peaks, particularly in Australasia or Oceania. Myriad books have been written about this challenge, starting with its originators and including Reinhold Messner, and there are any number of companies queuing up to help you, although you'll need access to big bucks to take it on.

This author is having nothing to do with that list. No. Charles Sherwood decided to put his own stamp on summit collecting, beginning with the north face of the Eiger by the 1938 route. It was on that ascent he decided to undertake his own seven-summits challenge, to be achieved in a five-star way having a good time throughout.

Sherwood began climbing as a student at Cambridge, including the traditional night ascents of its buildings. He has since climbed widely in the UK, the Alps and Himalaya, ski toured avidly and participated in a range of other outdoor adventure sports, including paragliding, diving (he is a qualified PADI dive-master) and cave diving. On top of that he has various post-grad qualifications from Harvard and the LSE, a wife, three children and a 30-year career in the risk capital industry.

As I said, his first 'fine climb' was the north face of the Eiger, which took two attempts and 10 for his guide Mark Seaton, who has lived and worked out of Chamonix for over two decades, and who is also a children's author, writing as 'Mark the Guide'. Their first attempt ended somewhat embarrassingly when Mark, desperate for a pee, relieved himself in oncoming bad weather, got caught in a spindrift avalanche and suffered frost-nip in his most sensitive regions. It was an education to me how Charles and his guide kept in contact with each other by way of a two-way radio, and how easy it was to summon a helicopter with a mobile call. Once deposited safely in Alpiglen and confronted with a charming young Swiss female paramedic, Mark opted to be flown directly to hospital in Interlaken rather than suffer an embarrassing on-the-spot examination. A year later, in September 2007, they were back and after four days of struggle, with hard but stable conditions, they completed the route. I guess few who have done this route spent a night high on the face discussing Sartre and existentialism, moving onto Kierkegaard, Nietzsche and Dostoevsky.

His second climb, the south-west ridge of Ama Dablam (6856m), is done as a client on a well-organised commercial ascent. In the 1990s I led three commercial trips in the Karakoram but never enjoyed such luxuries as warm showers at base camp, wifi and mobile coverage. Ama Dablam is a beautiful mountain but remains for me the resting place of George Fraser and Mike Harris, who I climbed with the weekend before leaving to attempt the first ascent and who disappeared high on the mountain.

Number three on the list is the Nose of El Capitan. His leader is Andy Kirkpatrick who we might refer to as 'Mr El Cap', having made so many ascents of the wall, although perhaps surprisingly this was his first of the Nose. Sherwood's fourth climb is set in the Cordillera Blanca of Peru, via the south-west face of Alpamayo, once voted in a 1966 poll of readers of the German magazine *Alpinismus* as the most beautiful mountain in the world. He describes the mountain's history, how it was first climbed in 1957 from the south by a German party led by Gunter Hauser, who wrote a fine book *White Mountain Tawny Plain* about this ascent. He also describes attempts to climb it from the north and how a British party finally succeeded in 1966, a party, which I led. (Our film of the climb won at Trento in 1967.) The south-west face had seemed to us impregnable in 1966 but an Italian team proved us wrong in 1975 and now it is a classic ascent, on the itineraries of many of the commercial operators. The one the author joined, led by American guides, seems to have been well led but another surprise for me was the age range of participants: on Sherwood's trip the youngest was 16, while he was the senior at 54. There were other commercial groups on roughly the same route and it seems the hills are alive with well-heeled clients, who wish for a lower level of risk, home comforts but who obviously love the experience. The whole scene is so changed from 1966. Had you told us when we climbed Alpamayo in 1966 that some years down the road many clients would be taken up its south-west face each year we would not have believed it. It is as Lao Tzu advised: 'the only certain thing in life is change.'

The author's fifth climb is Mount Kenya, the traverse of Nelion (5188m) and Batian (5199m), again in the company of Mark Seaton. Having lived there, and as a former member of its mountain club, so many of the names Sherwood mentions resonate with me: Ian Howell, Rusty Baillie and Phil Snyder, who first climbed the *Diamond Couloir,* alas no more with global warming were once my rope-mates. We would have been amazed at someone turning up with a cook and porters. We used to drive up to Naro Moru after finishing work on a Friday night, sleep there and go up through the forest at first light. I was on the mountain once with my wife and met two Germans at the end of the day. They insisted on descending through the forest that evening: a dangerous thing to do in the dark and they were trampled to death by elephants. Traversing Mount Kenya is a tremendous outing, which Sherwood carried out in exemplary fashion over a long day.

His sixth climb is Aoraki-Mount Cook (3754m) in New Zealand. Initially he was not certain whether to climb Titea-Mount Aspiring (3033m) since its south-west ridge is such a classic ice climb. (Sherwood explains how dual Maori and English names for these mountains became officially mandated in the 1998 Ngai Tahu settlement.) So he did them both, Aoraki by its equally classic Linda glacier route. For the first he teamed up with Canadian guide Eric Ostpkevich from the Bugaboos and the latter he took local guide Dean Staples, a veteran of more than 20 expeditions to peaks over 6,000m including nine ascents of Everest.

The author's final pick was to sail to Antarctica for a coast-to-coast traverse of the Salveson range in South Georgia on a trip organised by Skip Novak and Stephen Venables in 2018. This seventh choice was more about adventuring than peak bagging. A couple of easy mountains were climbed, but it was the 12-day journey across the island, which made it so memorable and earned its place as his final choice.

Seven Climbs is well ordered and well illustrated, with some topos to orientate the reader. It is a fun read but maybe it will start a new craze for others to seek out their seven favourite routes, one on each continent? If mountaineers can in fact ever travel freely again, hemmed in by the coronavirus and the need to overcome the challenges posed by climate change.

Dennis Gray

• Proceeds from the sale of *Seven Climbs* are being donated to the Himalayan Trust UK, supporting the mountain people of Nepal.

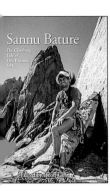

Sannu Bature
The Climbing Life of Des Rubens, SMC
Edited by Geoff Cohen
FastPrint, 2019, pp360, £17

I am sure many members have a collection of mountain-eering books. The books consist of an enormous range of categories: biographies, autobiographies, accounts of expeditions, history, musings on the 'Meaning of it All' and so on. Some may also have a small number of books that would never have been produced by main-stream publishers because the likely sales would be too small. For example, after Robin Hodgkin's death his son Adam was able to print his letters home from the Sudan during the Second World War and up to independence. Robin was a family friend and his memories from the 1950s, a time I can barely remember, are suddenly made available. It has been possible for books to appear about Pete Livesey and Dick Isherwood, collections of their magazine articles and of recollections by their friends. None would be possible without enterprises like 'printmybook.com'; these are among the books I most value.

And now I have another such book to treasure: a book subtitled 'The Climbing Life of Des Rubens, SMC'. Des was born near Perth, was at school in Dundee, then university in Edinburgh; he had the good fortune to meet his wife Jane in 1971 in his first year. The city was the base for his family life and for his life as a teacher, at first of physics and then in outdoor education. He climbed much in Scotland and put much energy into the SMC, writing about the exploits of its members and becoming its president. I rarely see their club journal but Des' note in the *SMCJ* 1986, 'The Single Transferable Munro System', made me laugh out loud.

Some of the content of the book is from writings by his climbing com-panions; most is from his own writing. He kept a fairly complete climbing diary from the earliest days, his writing as an 18 year old being clear and naïve (virtues in a diary). Here is the mouse in the bothy: 'it had bitten through two layers of paper to consume a substantial part of our chocolate supply. Tonight its preference was for sausages and it consumed part of a paper bag, a cellophane wrapper and some sausage skin in order to gratify its desires. In doing so it made an incredibly loud noise for such a small beast.'

In the diaries and articles he does not just list the routes but tells a story, the story of incidents and setbacks, feelings of anxiety and the beauty, or otherwise, of the location. But it is never unalloyed fear or unblemished beauty. For example, this is Yosemite Valley: '… we felt we couldn't leave the Valley without attempting a route in the area with the world's second-finest granite crags. The routes we did proved great classics, though lacking the grass, loose rock, wet moss and grimy cracks of some of the better Scottish crags.' He is good on those small moments we all recognise.

After a long day and then a good sleep, he experiences 'the luxury of stretching in a sleeping bag after the heat of the morning sun wakes you.' Or the small moments of despair, 'the commonplace impossibility of reconciling the guide description with the rocks of reality.' And I nodded with familiarity at: 'we were informed, as I have found common in parts of the world not too usually frequented by Westerners, weather of this unpleasantness was unusual hereabouts.'

Just a few of his tales are from the *Alpine Journal* because he became an AC member in his last decade. There is a phrase from 'Return to Zanskar 2012' (*AJ* 2013) that often comes to mind (mainly when I get out of bed in the morning): 'Nothing could stop us now except age and decrepitude (factors not to be readily dismissed in men of our age and with a not-far-below-the-surface-of-the-skin reservoir of ailments).' That is a very accurate analogy: one hopes that none of the ailments quite floats to the top to spill over.

Writing this review in the depths of a plague I wonder whether Des' years of climbing (1970-2016) will be seen as a golden age of ever cheaper, ever easier travel, not to be seen again. Des seems to have enjoyed visits to most continents and most flavours of climbing, from bolts or frozen waterfalls close by roads to long trips to unvisited regions. Some of the trips were pretty desperate. His Pakistan trip in 1980 was only written about in 2010 and the two photographs of the bivouac on K7 West back up that impression, only spoiled by the grin on Des' face as he abseils down to the bivy. And some seem to have been pleasure all the way, for example the trip to Cordillera Vilcanota in 2004 with good weather, a compatible team and plenty of routes for pioneers.

Photographs are a large part of the book, 150 of them in 350 pages. Some of the earlier colour images, scanned from slides, are quite dim: a reminder of what photos were like pre-digital. Some are wonderful compositions. I particularly liked Dave Broadhead's picture of Piz Cengalo's east ridge, so very three-dimensional, and the composition of base camp with Mount Waddington by Des.

Oh, and the title? It's explained at the end of Geoff Cohen's introduction. It's a Hausa phrase, that Des and his friends adopted while in Nigeria to mean, 'how are you, my friend?' Indeed.

Simon Brown

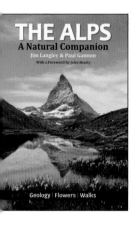

The Alps: A Natural Companion
Geology Flowers Walks
Jim Langley & Paul Gannon
Foreword by John Beatty
Oxford Alpine Club, 2019, 300pp, £20

This is a welcome, and possibly unique contribution to Alpine literature (at least in English). It's a concise, largely accessible, comprehensive and well produced guide to the natural history of the Alps. Both the authors and the publishers (the Oxford Alpine Club, est 1876 and so mere whippersnappers) deserve commendation for bringing this to market. As John Beatty, no stranger to wild nature says in his experiential foreword '... Jim Langley and Paul Gannon piece together the fragments that help us understand the sheer diversity and wealth of our alpine world.' He's not wrong.

The book covers the main bases and does so well: its structure maintains interest and has a thoughtful progression to it. For example, most geology texts start with the time column and its familiar roll call of eras and periods. In their section on geology, this is only introduced after we learn about how the Alps came about, their geography, creation and (mostly) slow erosion. The blurb claims that 'technical language is kept to a minimum ... everything is explained in straightforward language.' It is certainly well written and I spotted no typos (a minor miracle in modern publishing) but there are times when plainer language could have been found. 'Churning maw', to describe tectonic plates being mashed in the mountain-building zone, I can just about forgive as poetic (if old school) but describing a tottering rock overhang (Photo 6.2, p51) as an 'oversteepened slope' was pushing it. There is also a slightly pedantic completism about area names that could be confusing to many, with overlapping geological and geographical terms, sometimes admixed with language variants. Happily the terms are used consistently, though I did see the terms 'Northern Alps' and 'Central Alps' creep into one diagram (13.1, p140), which were not used elsewhere.

A section ('Area Notes') follows on the different parts of the Alps, which read better: concise, with a good mix of technical, human and locational information. Who knew that the height of Mont Blanc varies each year? Or that the border between Italy and France in that area is disputed? Or that the Matterhorn is composed of African rock? Future AC pub quizmasters, this book is for you. The section on the Dolomites is amazingly all on one page, which hints at a conciseness that could have been applied elsewhere. The next two sections take us into the biological world with a good tour of plant ecology, the Alpine environment and the medicinal uses of plants, followed by an excellent flower identification guide, based simply on the colour of the flowers with other key characteristics thrown in. Completist tendencies emerge again with some plants being given their legal conservation status; even as a professional conservationist, I'm not sure what this brings to the party, save telling us most orchids are rare?

The final section is a wide-ranging selection of twenty walks: a connoisseur's pick of areas and Alpine phenomena, each with an easy-to-follow description and map. From an esoteric afternoon wander to the well-known, multiday Tour of Mount Blanc, there's something for everyone. Excellent glossaries for botanical and geological terms follow, a bibliography and a general index plus an index of flowers. Again, testament to a well planned and executed book.

Indeed it is the production values that give this book its added value and mark it out: huge numbers of excellent photographs, often annotated to illustrate features. Clear and simple diagrams that help convey often complicated themes. This will have been a labour of love for both the authors and the OAC publishing team. For those wanting to know more about the Alps' natural environment, it will be useful pre-trip reading and then again in camp, van or hotel (depending on your dirtbag quotient). A tad big for the back pocket though.

Andy Tickle

Crazy Sorrow
The Life and Death of Alan Mullin
Edited by Grant Farquhar
Atlantis Publishing, 2019, pp264, £28 pb / £8 e-book

Unless you were keyed in to the Scottish winter climbing scene of the late 1990s, it's possible you didn't catch Alan Mullin's fiery but short-lived trajectory across the firmament of climbing stars. Blink, and you could have missed him. And yet, as this fragmentary memoir and biography makes clear, he had an explosive impact, detonating a change of culture and a rapid rise in standards, not only in terms of grade but also commitment and ambition. Forget the apprenticeship, in two years Mullin reached the top of the tree, at least in terms of mixed climbing, becoming, according to Simon Richardson (and he should know) 'the best winter climber of his day'.

Initially self-taught, in 1997 he began a partnership with a talented but low-key winter climber called Steve Paget and in the following years, either with Paget or alone, Mullin pulled off a series of mind-boggling new routes, including in 1998 the first winter ascent of *The Needle* on Shelter Stone in a continuous 17-hour push, the first to be graded IX. The following year they went one better, climbing another Shelter Stone classic, *The Steeple,* regarded by many as a last great problem of Scottish winter climbing. Simon Richardson judged this 'without question the most sustained technical winter route climbed in Scotland to date.' Climbing alone, Mullin did the first winter ascent of *Rolling Thunder* (VII,8) on Lochnagar in the middle of a full-on blizzard, with gullies avalanching around him. In late 2002 he climbed another Lochnagar route, an E3 called *Crazy Sorrow,* which gave the Scottish winter route *Frozen Sorrow,* the first ground-up grade X but an ascent mired in controversy and left out of the guidebook, a crescendo of the criticism Mullin had drawn throughout his new-routing career. He was, as Andy Kirkpatrick once put it, 'one of climbing's greatest disruptors.' After that Mullin was gone, his career ended by the worsening of a knee injury sustained during his army service years earlier. 'If I can't climb really hard,' he once told an interviewer, 'then I don't want to climb at all.'

Life without climbing proved insufferable for Mullin. His German-born wife Marion watched as he became withdrawn and his tendency to depression worsened markedly. He was admitted for the first time to the local psychiatric ward in June 2004 and later that summer was diagnosed as bipolar. The various drugs he was using, both recreational and the opiate he relied on for the pain of a slipped disc can't have helped. Soon after he was discharged from hospital, Mullin wrote to his friend, the US-based climber Kevin Thaw. I think it's fair to say that the three expeditions to Patagonia Mullin shared with Thaw were among the happiest and most fulfilled periods of his life.

I just have to try and learn to stop hating myself so badly, and then maybe I will get much better. I suppose the truth is just a point of view, but it's scary when you become so vacant as a soul.

Mullin remained an outpatient until May 2005 but then lost contact with the hospital. He stopped taking his anti-psychotic drugs because of their side effects and tried instead to find meaning in the world, in particular the meaning of himself in the world. He studied philosophy and psychology at the Open University (hence the ubiquity in the text of Nietzsche quotes, which always unnerves me), trained as an alcohol counsellor and enrolled on an anthropology course at Aberdeen University. Nothing stuck and Mullin spent more and more time at his computer in an upstairs office, staying up for days as he searched the Internet for answers and his descent into mental illness accelerated. Early in 2007 he made a serious attempt at ending his life (standing in front of a car on the A9) and after a misguided police intervention at his home ended up in prison in Inverness, the last place he should have been and, as it turned out, the last place he was alive. Because on 9 March, after more than three weeks in prison, on the first occasion he was left alone in his cell, Alan Mullin hung himself with the flex from a radio.

The circumstances of his death were so dreadful that I ended up writing a newspaper article about it, which is how I came to meet Mullin's wife Marion, in a state of grief and also guilt at her decision to seek the police's help in dealing with her psychotic husband. Eighteen months later there was an enquiry; the family was represented by Joanna Cherry QC, now a Scottish Nationalist Party member of parliament. It transpired that the procurator fiscal had phoned Mullin's consultant psychiatrist, who told him that Mullin was exhibiting antisocial personality disorder. 'Do you mean the old Scottish psychopath?' the procurator fiscal asked. The psychiatrist agreed and on that basis the procurator fiscal concluded that Alan Mullin, a man who had announced to his family he was Jesus, had slashed his own wrist and then sat on a bible on the kitchen floor to ward off an imaginary killer, was in fact 'bad not mad' and despite having hurt only himself was made the subject of a criminal prosecution. It occurred to me after I left Alan Mullin's old home that had he not been a top climber then I wouldn't have known of him and wouldn't have written about his suicide. So many others suffering similar fates disappear without trace and little has happened in the last 13 years to improve their situation.

What I hadn't understood before I met Marion was how contradictory Mullin's character was. I'd met Alan a few times, found him quick-witted but intense, even aggressive. I'd seen a little of the online fury he could provoke, his apparent indifference to the delicacies of an introverted climbing scene. He could seem arrogant, often said he couldn't care less about what others thought of him but gave every indication that recognition is what he craved most. Marion told me about another man, one who was fiercely committed to his family, capable of kindness and empathy, thoughtful and reflective, someone powerfully different to his image in the climbing world. What I still lacked was a full understanding of the circumstances behind that apparent contradiction, something this biography provides.

It is a harrowing read. If you want climbing writing to be about inspiration or escapism, or if you have a low tolerance for profanities then this book is not for you. (Think Irvine Welsh on a gloomy day after a sleepless night on speed.) It is also at times chaotic in its execution, although its qualities far outweigh its defects. The account opens with an introduction from Alan's brother Kevin, and then an essay from Simon Richardson laying out the history of Scottish mixed climbing, giving the reader a grasp on where Alan Mullin fits in and the revolutionary impact he had. We then move on to Alan's account of his own downwardly mobile upbringing, first in Kilwinning on the outskirts of Glasgow and then, after his father walks out, the sink estate of Stevenston, at which point he 'really goes off the rails' as his mother subsides into alcoholism. Mullin, small but already bristling with aggression, also switches from a Protestant upbringing to a Catholic school, bringing a sectarian dimension into an already dismal equation. In Mullin's words, this is a world of violence or else the threat of violence.

The only thing that keeps him going is the prospect of joining the army and getting out, not a wildly popular decision in a Catholic community. Then, when he does join, he chooses the Royal Green Jackets, an English regiment, where his background marks him out as an untrustworthy 'feinian Jock'. Far from being a hindrance, his aggression-drenched childhood seems to have been a real advantage as a young soldier. 'After almost a year of training,' he recalled, 'I had transformed from a scrawny young recruit into a finely tuned psycho with a thirst for violence: exactly what the army was looking for.' (If you think this an exaggeration, bear in mind that one of those who attempted to bully Mullin during his service was later convicted of the rape and manslaughter of a young Danish travel rep during a tour of duty on Cyprus.) Mullin endures a miserable tour of Northern Ireland, where he wrecks his knee, and a happier posting to South Georgia where he suffers the second major injury of his army life, the squashed disc, an injury compounded by the reckless indifference of his commanding officer. No wonder Alan was intolerant of authority.

Invalided out of the army at 23 after almost eight years and now married to Marion, with two children from her first marriage (her first husband died in a helicopter crash) and their young son, Mullin and his family are struggling to find their feet as this first-person narrative ends. We then have an account of his climbing career through published articles from Mullin himself and contemporaries, a section that is patchier and uneven but at least allows some light into what is otherwise a pitch-dark story. Then the injuries take their toll, the climbing ends and Mullin begins his final descent. The book concludes with the aftermath of his suicide from the book's editor Grant Farquhar, a psychiatrist and climber who is well placed to offer an incisive and compelling account of Mullin's mental illness and the disastrous impact of the state's authority on his prospects.

Crazy Sorrow raises powerful questions about the climbing world and wider society. As far as the latter's concerned, I've already touched on the grim circumstances of Mullin's upbringing and the more brutal aspects of his military service. The failures around his arrest and detention were aired in court. People often have a strong reaction to suicide and will pick out the reasons they believe lie behind it. More often than not such explanations say more about how they perceive human nature than about suicide itself. For what it's worth, I think Mullin's childhood and early exposure to the army were toxic environments for a developing mind and that the sudden loss of self-esteem he took from climbing, the one place he'd felt fulfilled, tipped him into depression. I also don't believe his suicide was inevitable, so while many weren't surprised at this early death, the failures of the system can't be ignored.

There are also questions for the climbing 'community', which, as Andy Kirkpatrick rather acidly points out, is not as supportive as it sometimes likes to think it is. With the advent of the Internet and social media, opportunities for doing random damage to the psychological wellbeing of others have increased at about the same rate as the apparent need for some people to be seen and recognised. The hyper-individualism of today is very different from the more communitarian era many older climbers will recall. In the past, a friend would take you to one side if you were being an idiot. Now strangers rant online, inviting others to pile on. When Mullin joined the climbing glitterati he had admired from afar, they seemed to him brittle and self-absorbed, not the sort of company to offer your inner frailties. The few moments of comfort in this unsettling book come in the compassion of those of his friends who were mature enough to offer support, like Kevin Thaw. But in the sea of troubles Alan Mullin faced, they were never enough to bail him out.

Ed Douglas

Crack Climbing
Mastering the Skills and Techniques
Pete Whittaker
Vertebrate Publishing, 2020, pp288, £25

The ability to climb cracks is at the core of a climber's craft and this weighty tome provides a single point of reference for all crack-climbing techniques, regardless of the grade you climb. Author Pete Whittaker is one half of the Wide Boyz duo with Tom Randall, a brand that has become synonymous with hard crack climbing. He has taken techniques learnt on his local crags and applied them with great effect all over the world, most notably on the huge roof cracks in the desert areas of Utah, and on the big walls of Yosemite. In 2014 Pete flashed the classic *Freerider* (5.12d) on El Capitan, Yosemite, and in 2016 he became the first person to make a solo-free ascent of El Capitan in under 24 hours. On his local gritstone, Pete's major first ascents include *Bigger Baron* (E10 7a) and *Sleepy Hollow* (E10 7a), while further afield, he has made first ascents of *Century Crack* (5.14b), the world's hardest offwidth crack and *Lamb of God* (5.14b), his hardest crack to date, all in Canyonlands National Park, Utah.

Drawing on his years of experience, Whittaker demonstrates the many different crack techniques and when, why and how to use them. The book is split into sections on techniques for different widths of cracks, including finger cracks, hand and fist cracks, off-width cracks and chimneys. Pete looks at the basics, including the hand jam, the essential technique in any crack climber's repertoire, right through to such esoteric innovations as the sidewinder and the trout tickler. Step-by-step information is supplemented with tips and tricks alongside illustrations from Alex Poyzer and lavish photographs. Additional chapters cover how to tape up, as well as essential gear and equipment. Pete has also interviewed some of the world's top crack climbers, including Lynn Hill, Alex Honnold, Barbara Zangerl and Peter Croft.

Martin Kocsis climbing the immaculate thin hands and finger crack of *Scarface* (5.11a) on the Wingate Sandstone at Indian Creek, USA. Everything you will ever need to know about crack-climbing technique and much more besides is the subject of Pete Whittaker's new book.

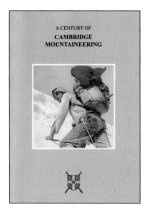

A Century of Cambridge Mountaineering
Edited by Henry Edmundson
CUMC, 2019, pp179, £10

This delightful compendium of articles by former members of the Cambridge University Mountaineering Club will be of interest to members, and in fact quite a few AC members past and present appear, including past presidents. The book was the suggestion of Alex Corio, the then editor of the CUMC journal, *Cambridge Mountaineering,* as a way to celebrate the centenary of the club in 2005. Some work was done, but the project lapsed. It is to the credit of the CUMC and the Cambridge Alpine Club, the complementary body largely made up of Cambridge graduates, that the project was resuscitated in 2017 and completed.

There is a treasury of memories and useful history in this volume with a list of contributors as distinguished as it is long. George Band is on good form describing his early Alpine days with Chris Brasher. Roger Chorley recalls John Streetly's 'bigger and stronger' brother Arthur, a novice climber, shouting down from the crux of *Central Buttress* when he got stuck for advice. 'Layback,' came the reply. 'What's a layback?' Streetly replied, but he did it anyway. There's an affectionate piece from John Barry on the brilliant Cambridge mathematician Al Rouse and the fateful sequence of events that took him to K2 in 1986. I also hugely enjoyed pieces from Rupert Roschnik on Nick Estcourt and some of his narrow escapes. Audrey Salkeld and Terry Gifford offer pieces on famous Cambridge stars, the latter on 'Noyce's Cambridge Mountaineering Poets', and the former on George Mallory. There are reports too from Cambridge expeditions, a piece from Martin Moran, and regular *Alpine Journal* contributors, including John Harding, Dick Isherwood, Rob Collister and Charles Clarke. Isherwood opens his piece uncertain that he wants to be an alpinist and when the president limps on stage at the start of a lecture he wonders: 'My God, he must have fallen off a climb.' As it turns out, he had been run over at the annual beer party by a fast-rolling barrel. Great fun.

Ed Douglas

• *A Century of Cambridge Mountaineering* is available direct from Henry Edmundson

Flying over the Himalaya
Tamotsu Nakamura
Nakanishiya Shuppan, 2019, pp234, £60

When thinking of aerial views of the Himalaya, another Japanese Himalayan photographer sprang to mind: Koichiro Ohmori, whose sumptuous *Over the Himalaya,* published by Ken Wilson's Diadem, appeared more than a quarter of a century ago. While *Flying over the Himalaya* doesn't match the photographic quality of Ohmori's book, with the cover being among the weaker shots, it more than compensates with its practical usefulness. Herein is an (almost entirely) aerial annotated view of the Karakoram and Himalayan chain to aid and inspire expedition climbers. Not surprisingly, given Tom Nakamura's longstanding interest in the eastern Himalaya, that end of things is far more comprehensively provided for than the western end. The Karakoram section is somewhat cursory, ditto the western end of the Himalaya. There are no shots of Zanskar, and not much of Himachal Pradesh either. Kamet, the first peak attempted in the Himalaya by foreign climbers, is absent. But there are mouth-watering objectives in glorious detail from further east, and on that basis this book is immensely useful. Finding a copy, on the other hand, might prove difficult. It is not currently available on amazon, although copies are available elsewhere on the Internet.

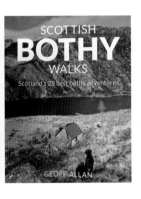

Scottish Bothy Walks
Scotland's 28 Best Bothy Adventures
Geoff Allan
Wild Things Publishing, 2020, pp256, £17

This is a sequel to Geoff Allan's popular and award-winning *Scottish Bothy Bible,* published in 2017, and describes 28 sensational walking adventures to Scotland's finest bothies. Choosing his favourite bothies as the focal point, Geoff Allan guides the reader on a mix of day walks and multi-day excursions, highlighting the incredible mountains, wildlife, geography and history that you will find along the way. Some include challenging mountain walks and summits, including the traverse of the Rum Cuillin from the Dibidil bothy. Others are more straightforward outings, a way to experience the coast or make multi-day trips. Each of the 28 entries offers a taste of what makes the specific area special, from its unique geology, wildlife and flora, to history and culture. The chosen bothies stretch from the Orkneys to the Borders. I would hesitate to call this a guidebook; it's format and sumptuous illustrations make its route information more useful photographed than carried. But its fresh layout and passion make it welcome inspiration. Allan extols the virtues of the Mountain Bothies Association and one can only hope that the increasing popularity of these remote shelters doesn't weaken their appeal or sustainability.

Tour du Mont Blanc
Kingsley Jones
Vertebrate Publishing, 2020, pp140, £17

The Tour du Mont Blanc is among the most iconic circular long-distance trails, not only in the Alps but the world, and this guidebook promises customised itinerary planning for walkers, trekkers, 'fast packers' and trail runners. Written by Tour du Mont Blanc expert Kingsley Jones, this guidebook includes customised timings depending on your approach to allow accurate itinerary planning. There's a wealth of information to plan your Tour du Mont Blanc, including travel information, navigation, accommodation options, equipment and safety, food and drink, as well as useful extra information such as wild swimming locations and trekking tips. The route description appears with the relevant 1:40,000-scale maps. Route variations are also included. It was a bit surprising to see wet wipes included in the recommended gear list but there is at least a section on environmental awareness and sound advice on bivouacs. There was also no mention in a list of notable 'characters' from the Tour du Mont Blanc of Lizzy Hawker, who has won the race five times: a curious omission. The book is light enough to slip into your back pocket, a welcome change from the current trend.

And if even that proves too much for your lightweight principles, then Vertebrate have produced an excellent accompanying 1:40,000 map that is waterproof, durable and with all the necessary information. The map includes a GPX file download as well and is £12 from their website.

Obituaries

Plate 20. *'Jumnotree [Yamunotri], the source of the river Jumna [Yamuna]'*

In Memoriam

As usual, the editor will be pleased to receive obituaries for any of those above not included in the following pages.

Alfred Alvarez
1929 - 2019

It was early morning when we drove off the ferry at Zeebrugge.

'You drive,' Al said. 'I'm going to sleep. Don't go over the red mark on the rev counter. Oh, and by the way, the brake cylinder's leaking. You've got only one big stab on the brakes then you'll have to pull over and top it up. There's a can of brake fluid in the trunk.'

Then he stretched out on the passenger seat of the Lotus Elite and was soon fast asleep. Having explored the controls I set off apprehensively on the long drive down the autobahn towards the Brenner pass. The Lotus was Al's pride and joy and I'd never driven such a hot sport car before. This was trust. But that was Alvarez: stimulating company but laid back when appropriate, a gentle guy who enjoyed life and encouraged others to do the same.

'Climbing was part of who I was.' Al Alvarez follows Pete Crew on the second ascent of *MPP*, Dinas Mot. *(John Cleare)*

Frequently seen at Harrisons, Ynys Ettws or the Bosigran Count House, Al was a popular figure in 1960s and 1970s climbing circles, often in the company of his close buddy and Hampstead neighbour, that larger-than-life character Ian McNaught-Davis. With a shared sense of humour, each proved a foil for the antics of the other. Indeed, in their younger, wilder days when both owned distinctive white Mini Coopers, it was said that on Welsh mountain roads they would delight when approaching each other from opposite directions in passing on the wrong side or the road. Al certainly enjoyed driving fast and owned a sequence of performance motors including a Cooper Climax, giving rise to the quip among his literary friends: 'Have you seen Al's climax?' He also had an E-Type Jaguar before family responsibilities demanded less exuberant transport, although no less classy.

Al Alvarez was that rare person, a genuine intellectual, although it was said that thanks to his time spent in America, his mode was more affable gunslinger than stuffy Oxbridge academic. By profession a man-of-letters, he was a poet, essayist, author, novelist and critic; by inclination he was a rock climber, poker player and lover of classical music. He looked the part too, with his high forehead, broken nose and moustache, his neat beard and kindly eyes.

He was proud of being 'a Londoner heart and soul – if not quite an Eng-lishman' for his ancestors, Sephardic Jews from Spain, had settled in Lon-don merely four centuries before. Born in 1929 into a well-heeled family living in some style in Hampstead, he was reared by a strict nanny before being sent off to school at Oundle, which he hated. Initially a persistent rule-breaker and something of a weedy boy with a damaged leg, he held his own by playing good rugby and learning to box and meanwhile enjoying his first rock climb. Just missing wartime conscription, Al killed time teach-ing at a prep school before going up to Oxford in 1949 to read English at Corpus Christi where he took a rare first – and joined the Climbers' Club. Now a research fellow but still a rebel, he declared that English, as currently studied at university level, was 'a discipline for the clever rather than the brilliant', while his antipathy for convention and 'high-table chat' caused something of a rumpus in the staid fields of poetry and literary criticism. He was attracting attention.

The big break came when he was invited to present a series of seminars at Princeton, where he immediately took to the more laid-back American scene and made much of the opportunity to climb with university colleagues in the Shawangunks. Following the publication of his first two books, deal-ing respectively with Elizabethan and modern British and American poetry, he took up a D H Lawrence Fellowship at the University of New Mexico. As it happened, Al had become a keen disciple of Lawrence's work and in 1956 he married Frieda Lawrence's granddaughter Ursula Barr but their union was short-lived and their son Adam died in 2016. Al abandoned aca-deme for Hampstead, and via an enjoyable stint on the North Sea oilrigs, he settled into the uncertain career of a freelance writer.

He soon met with success, editing Penguin's Modern European Poets series and becoming the poetry and film critic for the *Observer* during that paper's great days, while doing much to establish the reputation of his friends Ted Hughes and Sylvia Plath and of the American poets John Berryman and Robert Lowell. He wrote regularly for top-flight British and American journals and magazines and over the years published more than 20 books, among them *The Savage God,* a meditation on suicide – he had once tried it himself – and in due course an engaging autobiography *Where Did It All Go Right?* In 1966 he married Anne Adams, a Canadian child psychotherapist, to become, as his friend John le Carré wrote 'an impassioned husband and a family man', meanwhile keeping fit by swimming in all weathers in the nearby Hampstead Heath ponds, insisting that 'cold water delays the ageing process.'

Al's interest in poker had been kindled during his time in America; the game intrigued him, he became an adept and in London he played regularly, often for high stakes, claiming that poker taught him patience. Chris Bonington, himself a keen poker player, wrote that playing with Alvarez, though very exciting, could be quite terrifying. An assignment on poker in Las Vegas for the *New Yorker* became the nucleus for his book *The Biggest Game in Town,* and periodically Vegas lured him back for a session. True to form, Al asserted 'serious poker is no more about gambling than rock climbing is about taking risks.'

As a climber his interest was in rock rather than snow, ice or high mountains. A self-confessed adrenaline junkie, being close to danger was important; a climb, Alvarez wrote, 'is like playing chess with your body ... every move has to be worked out by a kind of physical strategy in terms of effort, balance and consciousness.' If not the most elegant climber, he was very capable, strong and moved with a purposeful muscularity, happily following the best leaders in the game – he knew most of them – on many of the harder routes.

Alvarez had been enlisted to help host the 1960 Russian party, the first to climb in Wales. Both he and one of the guests broke bones in bad falls but at Bangor Al's ankle had been badly set, thereafter giving gradually worsening trouble that by his sixties was seriously curtailing his climbing.

In 1964 I had invited Al to contribute the text to *Rock Climbers in Action in Snowdonia,* just commissioned by Secker & Warburg, but the paltry advance was dwarfed by the fee offered for a *New Yorker* article and he reluctantly declined. But a year later the *Observer Magazine* commissioned us to produce a major feature on the current climbing ace, the computer wizard Pete Crew. Al made the second ascent of *MPP* with him, then considered one of the more fearsome routes in the Llanberis Pass, though not without liberal use of the f-word, a favourite expletive for which Al was well known.

Bosigran was his favourite cliff where he often climbed with his close friends Pete and Barrie Biven and the artist Cliff Fishwick. With Pete he made the second ascent of Pete's intimidating *Moonraker* on Torbay's Berry Head, and also with Pete, the first ascent of the superb *Last Exit to Torquay:* Al had appeared as a defence witness during the obscenity trial of *Last Exit to Brooklyn.*

His first serious mountain had been in 1958, an early ascent with American friends of the spectacular Shiprock in the Four Corners desert of New Mexico. But as something of an Italophile, Al's happiest hunting ground became the Dolomites. On a first visit in 1962 with the London climber Graham Hughes, he ticked off the regular Lavaredo classics, the *Preuss Chimney* and the *Dibona Ridge* on the Cima Grande, returning the following year to the Sella Towers where he climbed his first grade VI. In 1964 we drove out to Cortina together, shredding the Lotus' silencer on the mule track to the Lavaredo hut, to meet up with John Wharton, a fellow Princeton alumni and his Ogwen Cottage colleague Mo Anthoine.

Al had set his heart on the *Comici* route on the north face of the Grande, but Wharton and I had both done the route previously so after warming up on the Spigolo Giallo, Al set off with Mo up the *Comici* despite rather dubious weather. They were still climbing the overhanging section when a storm arrived and eventually reaching the merely vertical wall above, now plastered in wet snow, they were forced to bivouac with neither sustenance nor extra clothing. In the early hours the sky cleared, the snow melted and their ledge became a waterfall. Then it froze. Later Al wrote: 'I concluded that our luck had run out and that we too would soon be frozen.'

At dawn Wharton and I climbed the regular route to the summit with dry clothing, hot drinks and food to offer what support we could. When they emerged Mo casually described the night as 'a bit parky' and although both were exhausted and frostbitten, they were none the worse for the experience. Indeed, Al was exuberant. It was the epic he had long desired and would never forget, and it had a profound influence on both his climbing and his writing. In his 1988 book *Feeding the Rat* in which he profiled his rope-mate Mo, Al declared: 'My own preference for warm rock, warm food and a warm bed – as well as my plain lack of ability – ensured that I would never make the big time in mountaineering.'

Not to be put off, Al climbed on the Civetta the following season with Gunn Clark and Tony Smythe, while in 1966 he enjoyed a long holiday in Yosemite during which he partnered Chuck Pratt on El Cap's *East Buttress* (5.10, A2). Subsequently warm limestone won the day and for the next decade Al climbed regularly in the Apuan Alps, an Apennines sub-range in Tuscany, sometimes with Mo but usually with local Italian climbers, being especially proud of his ascent in 1983 of the intimidating 2,500ft north face of Pizza d'Ucello with Damasco Pinelli. Al returned to cold northern climes in 1985 when Mo Anthoine led him with George Band and party up the Old Man of Hoy. Now, feeling perhaps that it was time to recall epics rather than face them, Al was proposed by Roger Chorley and elected to the AC. But Hoy was hardly a swansong: he continued climbing for almost a further decade, albeit hobbling to the foot of lesser crags such as Harrisons Rocks. As he was later to write 'climbing was part of who I was.'

Eventually, in 2008, there was a stroke and now wheelchair-bound but still full of humour, Al remained at home in Hampstead. A last book, *Pondlife: A Swimmer's Journal* was published in 2013. He died on 23 September 2019, from viral pneumonia, aged 90. He leaves Anne, his son Luke – a CC member for many years – a daughter Kate and two grandsons who are learning to climb.

John Cleare

Trevor H Braham
1922 - 2020

To most of the present generation of climbers, Trevor Braham, who died on 2 March 2020 shortly before his 98th birthday, is largely unknown. Reference works such as George Band's *Summit: 150 Years of the Alpine Club* only mentions Braham as the author of an Alpine history book. Colin Wells' *Who's Who* is a blank. Yet Braham was a leading British Himalayan explorer and significant mountaineer, most active during the third quarter of the 20th century including the post-Everest Himalayan 'Golden Age'. He had a wide knowledge of mountaineering history, which he shared in three major

Trevor Braham in Sikkim, 1949. To his left is Ang Tharkay, to his right Sonam and Ajeeba. *(Trevor Braham)*

Braham and his guide Arthur Lochmattter on the summit of Monte Rosa in 1951. *(Trevor Braham)*

Trevor Braham in Switzerland. *(Swissinfo)*

books and many articles in mountaineering journals. He organised and took part in 15 Himalayan expeditions and many more 'small trips' to largely unknown areas. His preferred modus operandi was based on independent small-scale expeditions, very much in the style of Tilman and Shipton.

Braham spent much of his boyhood in India, during the fading years of the British Raj, alternating between Calcutta and Darjeeling, where, in the mid 1930s, he attended St Joseph's as a boarder for four years. Living within sight of the magnificent spectacle of Kangchenjunga and its satellite peaks exerted a strong influence upon him, arousing later ambitions: 'The view [from Observatory Hill] never failed to arouse a mixture of excitement and desire: from Nepal in the west across Tibet and Bhutan in the east, 200 miles of snow-covered ranges, filled the horizon with Kangchenjunga as the centrepiece.' By chance, in April 1942 and just turned 20, Braham joined a short trip making up a party of four from Darjeeling to the Singalila range. The seed was sown. He later recalled he knew he had discovered something permanent and he would have to return.

In his first book, *Himalayan Odyssey* (Allen & Unwin, 1974), Braham shared with his readers 30 years of personal involvement with the wider Himalayan ranges extending from Afghanistan in the west to Assam in the east that separate the Indian subcontinent from the great central Asian landmass to the north. He claimed that the book was neither a biography or about mountaineering, but was about his personal involvement with mountains. Furthermore, and perhaps too modestly, he laid no claim to respectability by the criterion of some singular achievement or success.

The day seems to have passed when the amateur or the idealist practised his pastime in his own individual way. Mountain climbing, like most other activities, is becoming increasingly professional, demanding, whether we like it or not, many of the symbols of professionalism. I have approached the mountains with the amateur's undemanding indulgence. There was never a question why: I simply had to.

Over these 30 years we are taken from Sikkim to Kangchenjunga, Kumaon and Garhwal, Kullu and Spiti, to the Karakoram, Swat and Indus Kohistan, Nepal, Chitral and Kaghan. The 1949 trek to Sikkim was notable because it included a Czech skier, Miroslav Hruska, who had no previous mountaineering experience. Hruska's photographs and memories are archived (and available) at Athabasca University, with rare images of Braham and also the Sherpa Ang Tharkay of whom Braham had a high opinion, not least for his hot buttered scones. The magnificent peak of Chombu (6362m) was distantly observed, a peak still unclimbed despite attempts in 1993 by a Japanese party and in 1996 Doug Scott who described it as 'the Matterhorn of Sikkim', and, as described in this edition of the *Alpine Journal,* two attempts in 2019 by Mick Fowler and Victor Saunders.

The Kangchenjunga reconnaissance occurred in 1954, when John Kempe led a party comprising Tucker, Jackson, Lewis, Braham and medical officer, Mathews. They explored the upper Yalung glacier with the intention to discover a practicable route to the great ice-shelf that runs across the southwest face of Kangchenjunga. This reconnaissance (*HJ* 19, 1956) led to the route used by the successful 1955 expedition, when Band and Brown made the first ascent.

Together with Peter Holmes, a young Cambridge University geologist, he made the second ascent of Guan Nelda (6303m) from the barren plateau of Spiti in 1955. Rinzing, a 20-year-old Ladakhi, 'a natural leader' was edged to the front for the final steps to the summit.

In 1958 Braham joined a small group, Warr, the leader, Hoyle and Shipley to attempt Minipin peak, now called Diran (7257m) in the Karakoram. Travellers familiar with the upper Indus and Gilgit would not be surprised by the trials and tribulations Braham encountered: the bureaucracy, uncomfortable travel, dangerous roads, even more dangerous vehicles and drivers, spectacular flights, recalcitrant porters, the oasis charm of Hunza and the magnificent peaks on both sides of the valley now traversed by the Karakoram Highway as it climbs to the Khunjerab pass on the Chinese border. Although later in the expedition, and after Braham had left early due to work constraints, two members were killed, their route pointed the way to eventual success by an Austrian party in 1968, following three more failed attempts in the intervening years. It is worth noting that during the 1958 Minapin attempt, Rakaposhi finally succumbed to Banks and Patey of the British Pakistani Forces Expedition. In 1996 an ice axe was found high on Minapin by Japanese climbers. The story of its identification and how it was eventually reunited with the daughter of Warr, one of the climbers lost, was told by Shigeharu Inouje *(AJ* 1996, pp190-9), an account that also included notes by Braham on the 1958 expedition.

Throughout this period, Braham lived and worked in India, first with his father in Calcutta, then in Pakistan in the employ of a cotton company. He joined the Himalayan Club in 1946, becoming its regional secretary based in Calcutta in March 1949, the Swiss Alpine Club in 1948 and the Alpine Club in 1951. He was vice president of the Himalayan Club (1958-65), honorary editor of the *Himalayan Journal* (1957-9) and in 1980 an honorary member of the Himalayan Club. He spent many seasons in the Alps. In 1947 he visited Geoffrey Winthrop Young in London to ask for advice on Alpine climbing. He recalled 'a sombre room, bookshelves, a table scattered with mountain magazines in several languages, and a distinguished-looking white-haired man seated in an armchair with a stick at his side – he had lost his left leg during World War I ...' and his advice: 'Whatever you do, don't climb the ordinary Swiss route on the Matterhorn. The Z'mutt ridge is much more interesting.'

In 1971, at the somewhat mature age of 49, he married Elizabeth Höflin before moving to Switzerland with his wife and sons Anthony and Michael in 1974. Shortly after *Himalayan Odyssey* was published. There followed a career in commodity trading based in Lausanne, many trips in the Alps and after retirement in 1997 he published his remarkable second book: *When the Alps Cast Their Spell: Mountaineers of the Alpine Golden Age* (In Pinn, 2004).

In his review for the *Alpine Journal,* Stephen Venables had no doubts *(AJ* 2005, pp371-2): 'We have had quite a few new books recently on our Victorian climbing ancestors. The trouble with these overviews is that they often tend towards the facile, regurgitating second-hand preconceptions, with the odd inaccuracy thrown in for good measure. So – what a joy to open Trevor Braham's treasure box of glittering surprises and correct some of my *own* preconceptions.' In the *American Alpine Journal,* Clinch agreed: 'When the judges gave the 2004 Boardman-Tasker Award for the best mountain literature to *When the Alps Cast Their Spell,* they knew what they were doing. It is a gold mine of scholarship about a critical period in the history of mountaineering.'

Braham starts with a succinct but thorough chapter on the beginnings of mountaineering but the heart of the book are chapters on seven mountaineers, five of whom epitomised the Golden Age: Alfred Wills, John Tyndall, Leslie Stephen, A W Moore and Edward Whymper. Braham then reviews subsequent developments through chapters on A F Mummery and Emmanuel Boileau. Braham covers alpinists who may have otherwise been omitted in the chapter 'There Were Many Others', which includes leading ladies, eminent Europeans, and great guides. There is also an excellent bibliography and a thorough, accurate list of Alpine first ascents from the 13th to the 19th centuries. If this is not enough, one can read the chapter endnotes, a treasure trove of obscure but fascinating information.

Those familiar with this history will recognise many of Braham's stories but he combined well-known material with original research, making this an important book even for those who think they know the history and an invaluable one for climbers unfamiliar with our rich traditions. The book is infused with Braham's acute observations and judgments. 'Whatever might be the future of mountaineering,' he concludes, 'it is to be hoped that certain essentials will remain. Such as the first spellbound moment of a youthful spirit stepping across the threshold into an awareness of the mountain world, and the birth of a desire to preserve what it has discovered."

Braham third's book, *Himalayan Playground: Adventures on the Roof of the World, 1942-72,* appeared in 2008. 'Having crossed the Rubicon of my eighth decade, I find myself out of harmony with some aspects of the evolution of mountaineering. Boundary lines, re-drawn about three decades ago, are now devoid of limits as to what is feasible and admissible technically, ethically, and physically. Clearly, advancing age has distanced me from practices now considered to be perfectly acceptable. Also, alas, diminishing capacity has begun to deprive me of the pleasures of wandering freely across cherished mountain regions. I have no doubt that a direct relationship exists between the two.' These thoughts are condensed from 'The Effects of Change on Mountaineering Ethics' *(AJ* 1997, pp161-8).

Doug Scott provided an enthusiastic, sympathetic and insightful foreword:

> *How wonderfully fresh and adventurous it must have been for the 20-year-old Braham travelling through the Himalaya in 1942 as a young soldier on leave during the Second World War and how wonderful to have Sherpa companions whom he had read about in the pre-war Everest expedition books. It is reassuring to find a climbing author not entirely consumed with himself while acknowledging not only whom he was with but also the vital contributions played by those who went before. ... He has the gift to be able to evoke images of Himalayan landscape and bring the people therein to life. Trevor Braham found himself in association with such luminaries as Hillary, Lowe and Riddiford from New Zealand, got to climb with the leading Swiss climbers of the day René Dittert, André Roch and Alexander Graven climbing Kedarnath Dome in the Gangotri. He also travelled and climbed with the Sherpas and Bhotias – Tenzing, Ang Tharkay and other indigenous climbers who had become almost as well known to the British public as the sahibs on whose expeditions they greatly assisted. In fact one of the strengths of the book stems from the time Trevor Braham spent with the local people. He reminds us just how important the Sherpas were to Himalayan exploration and climbing – men like Pasang Dawa Sherpa who climbed Chomolhari in 1937 with Spencer Chapman and later reached a high point with Wiessner of 8,385 metres on K2 in 1939. In the footsteps of Dr A M Kellas he spent long periods with the Darjeeling Sherpas throughout Sikkim and beyond. Trevor Braham had the capacity to spend long*

periods happy with his own company as well as that of local people. … He was right there at a time of great change in the region and was actually in the holy town of Badrinath on the day when 'with pride and joy India's independence was being colourfully celebrated'. He looks back to those times 60 years later with deep appreciation for all that the mountains have given him. He went to the mountains not to seek material objectives or accolades but for those 'rewards that only mountains possess the power to grant ... free from the clamour and complexities of everyday life'. The vast majority, if not all mountaineers to some extent, will readily identify with this wellspring to adventure, even those pushing out beyond the limits that Trevor Braham set for himself.

Braham continued to have an active life until at the age of 95, when a bad fall at home followed by pneumonia left him unable to walk and hardly able to speak. His last couple of years were spent in a nursing home in Gimel. His room overlooked the Alps with, on a clear day, a magnificent view of Mont Blanc. At his memorial service, constrained by Covid-19 restrictions, tributes were read from the Himalayan Club, a representative of the Alpine Club attended and a video conferencing link enabled his many family and friends in the UK to participate.

During his oration at the service his son Anthony, said of his father, 'He has been described as an icon, a legend and even a hero by people who knew him from his mountaineering days. Those who knew him socially in his later years described as the quintessential English gentleman. Of course, to me he was just Daddy, and the only hint at his mountaineering time were the rows of mountaineering books in his study – and occasionally, the visits to our home by those I realised afterwards were 'famous' mountaineers. His modesty – not just to his family – was a trait that was I think rather typical of his generation.'

Roderick A Smith

Richard Brooke
1927 - 2020

In the mid 1950s, Richard Brooke completed a unique hat-trick of landmark expeditions to both north and south polar regions and to the Himalaya, including the British North Greenland Expedition, the Commonwealth Trans-Antarctic Expedition led by Vivian Fuchs and the Combined Services Expedition that made the first ascent of Rakaposhi in 1958.

Richard first went to the Alps in 1947 on leave from the navy and had three more seasons, quickly building his experience and climbing many routes, including the *Kuffner* on Mont Maudit and the *Ryan-Lochmatter* on the Plan, both big undertakings at the time. He was one of the last surviving British climbers from this post-war period, having climbed in the 1950s with such brilliant mountaineers as Wilf Noyce, Geoff Sutton, Tom Patey, Mike Westmacott and Mike Banks. This group started to repeat the harder

Richard Brooke.

existing Alpine climbs; Richard and Mike Banks for example climbed *Route Major* on Mont Blanc in 1951, the first guideless ascent since its first ascent in 1928 by Frank Smythe and T Graham Brown. They climbed it by moonlight, an experience well described in Mike's book *Commando Climber.* In August 1955 Richard climbed the Couturier couloir on the Aiguille Verte with Noyce and Sutton. This was before the days of curved-pick axes when the route was still an undertaking. He described his traverse in April 1956 of the Bernese Oberland with Chris Stocken in *AJ* 1956 pp334-9. Around this time Richard was elected as a leading alpinist to the Alpine Climbing Group. And he spanned the generations, taking a very young Nick Estcourt up the Marinelli couloir of Monte Rosa.

Richard had gone to Dartmouth Naval College during the Second World War at the tender age of 13 because, as he said, 'the magic of the sea inspired me and there was a sense of adventure.' He joined the battleship Warspite about a month before D-Day, seeing action manning a four-inch gun off the landing beaches. In 1948 he joined the ship John Biscoe, taking stores from the Falklands to bases in Graham Land. Three years later he joined a naval reconnaissance expedition to Greenland, a precursor to the major British North Greenland Expedition of 1952-4, which Richard joined and where he made his first dogsled journeys. He was away for two years and awarded the Polar Medal. Mike Banks was on the same expedition, described in his account *High Arctic,* and they became lifelong friends. It was on this expedition that Mike saved Richard's life after spilt fuel from a petrol-stove set their tent alight. Mike rescued Richard by cutting open their tent with an ice axe. Later, under the pretext of surveying, Richard and Mike Banks climbed five virgin peaks in the Barth Mountains, including a Greenland Matterhorn.

In 1956 Richard joined the Commonwealth Trans-Antarctic Expedition, which finally achieved Shackleton's goal of crossing the frozen continent via the South Pole, but mainly by using motorised vehicles *(The Crossing of Antarctica,* Fuchs and Hillary, 1958). Richard was attached to the New Zealand dog teams laying depots, spending much time on remote dogsled journeys surveying and climbing mountains to make survey stations. He even had a mountain named after him, Mount Brooke, climbed with Murray Douglas at the head of the Mackay glacier. Another achievement was the first ascent of Mt Huggins (3800m) during a 1,000-mile dogsled trip.

Many years later Bernie Gunn, who was a fellow expedition member, wrote of Richard: 'he was prepared to travel hard, perhaps harder than any Polar explorer before or since.'

Richard had been away for 16 months yet somehow persuaded the navy that he should join the Combined Services Expedition to attempt the unclimbed Rakaposhi (7790m) in the Karakoram. Richard joined the expedition via New Zealand on his way home from Antarctica. Tom Patey and Mike Banks reached the summit with Richard and Dicky Grant carrying supplies to the high camp at 7,300m. An old and unreliable tent thwarted Richard's own summit attempt a few days later *(AJ* 1958, pp159-68). Patey recalled how during the course of the expedition they narrowly avoided disaster when a wind-slab avalanche swept down the face he and Brooke were climbing. Richard, with typical sangfroid, simply said: 'this place is distinctly dangerous. I propose that we turn back.'

Richard married Valerie in 1965, later having two sons, David and Patrick. He finally left the navy, having been passed over for promotion to commander, probably due to his many expeditions. He briefly took over the Mountaineering Association, a training body that used some well-known instructors like Hamish MacInnes and Ian Clough. Richard realised the MA was in financial trouble so left to take up a post with the Electricity Council, where he remained until retirement. His responsibilities never came between Richard and the hills. Before an important board meeting in South Wales, Richard took the opportunity to do a long run over the Brecon Beacons but during the meeting got cramp, leaping up with a howl of pain. 'Been up mountains again, Brooke?' his CEO drily inquired.

I first met Richard in 1974 after expressing an interest in joining the Club. In those days the AC was still regarded as rather elitist, full of men with Oxbridge accents wearing suits. We met at the Wyndcliffe, a steep crag in the Wye valley where a lean and fit-looking Richard greeted me warmly: he was then 47 and 22 years older than I was. We did some great climbs around the VS level and I must have passed muster. Richard and I subsequently climbed together in the Alps and the UK for many more years, remaining friends until he died. Richard always wrote wonderful detailed letters that I still have, after every Alpine, climbing or walking trip, often analysing our performance. He was a kind, modest man and never boasted about his incredible achievements.

After our first meeting Richard asked if I would join him and Mike Banks on a winter climbing trip to Scotland in early 1975. I brought my friend Dave Viggers and we had a fantastic week that included *Observatory Ridge, Comb Gully* and *NE Buttress* in a fast time allowing the oldies Richard and Mike, with a combined age of 100 years, to descend *Tower Ridge,* an impressive effort. Later that year, the same party, but with Jeremy Whitehead replacing Mike Banks, went to the Alps. Richard wanted to attempt the Hirondelles ridge (D+) on the Grandes Jorasses. After acclimatising with the north ridge of the Grivola, we based ourselves at the Gervasutti bivouac hut above Courmayeur from where we climbed the Petites Jorasses (TD) and two days later the Hirondelles after two attempts. We reached the summit in an electrical storm, gear and axes buzzing, and started the unfamiliar, long and complex descent, staggering into the Boccolatte hut exhausted after more than 20 hours of climbing. This route in particular reinforced my impression of Richard's steely determination, fitness, steadiness and good decision-making *(AJ* 1976 pp196-203).

In the following years we climbed together in the Scottish winter, including classics like *Crowberry Gully* and *Glovers Chimney.* In the 1960s, Richard had climbed with Tom Patey, including first ascents of *South Post Direct, Last Post* and *Post Horn Gallop* on Creag Meagaidh, all done cutting steps. The pair also made a spirited attempt to traverse the Cuillin ridge in winter. Richard was also a solid leader on rock, always modest but capable of leading at HVS and above. His footwork was a joy to watch, probably because he had started climbing in nailed boots when careful footwork was a necessity. We climbed together on rock for 20 years visiting virtually every climbing area in Britain.

We had an excellent Alpine season in 1979, warming up on the *Frendo Spur* of the Aiguille du Midi and then attempting the two-day traverse of the Rochefort Arête and west ridge of the Grandes Jorasses via the Canzio bivouac. All went well until after the Aiguille Rochefort and the Dôme de Rochefort. Descending towards the Canzio we followed the wrong line of abseils, too far to the west. Totally committed, we had no option but to continue down steep ice into France with only one axe each and no ice screws. At the bergschrund I watched terrified with no belay as Richard downclimbed carefully towards me. His calm competence under difficult circumstances was always impressive.

Despite this failure, and only two days later, we felt ready to try Richard's long-held ambition of another major climb on Mont Blanc. Richard was now well into his second half-century and felt this was his last chance for a really big route. We chose the Peuterey ridge of Mont Blanc via the Aiguille Blanche (D+), described in the guidebook as 'the epitome of all Alpine routes'. Intending to make only one bivouac, we left the valley in the afternoon, crossed the chaotic Freney glacier and bivouacked near the top of the Schneider ledges. After a cold night with little sleep we traversed Pointe Gugliermina along loose ledges on the Brenva flank. The weather looked superb and as the sun rose, it turned the rocks a magnificent red colour. Having miraculously reached the ridge at the correct spot, we traversed snow ridges across the summits of the Aiguille Blanche until we overlooked the Col Peuterey. Having abseiled down, we followed the rocky edge of the Eckpfeiler towards Mont Blanc de Courmayeur but progress was slow: it was not until after 5pm that we reached the foot of the final snow ridge leading to the summit of Mont Blanc de Courmayeur. Richard led, while I was just glad to follow in his steps.

Over the cornice it was a different world: wind, snow and swirling cloud with a dark and threatening sky to the west but Richard was pleased as punch, holding out his hand in congratulation. The desperate cold brought

Richard Brooke climbing Eagle Ridge on Lochnagar.

us back to reality. We found our way over Mont Blanc to the Vallot hut in poor visibility, arriving at 8.30pm. We had taken 16.5 hours from our bivouac. At last in the hut we could relax and in a euphoric mood fell into a deep sleep despite the storm raging outside. Richard wrote how the Peuterey 'gave me more pleasure to look back on than any other climb I have done and that includes *Route Major (AJ 1980, pp16-21).*' In subsequent years, instead of the Alps, we had several summer trips to Scotland climbing most of the routes in Ken Wilson's *Classic Rock.*

Richard continued to enjoy ski-mountaineering expeditions, traversing the Jura in 1983 with Mike Banks. He went twice with Alan Blackshaw and others to Sweden and Norway, writing: 'I am completely hooked on this type of ski touring which reminds me strongly of the Polar regions.' He went on four more such trips with David Ford, quite often in epic weather conditions and covering large distances. In 1985 Richard decided to show me the joys of Nordic skiing in a snowy north Wales. The A5 was blocked before Corwen so we bivouacked in the car, digging it out in the morning. The road was deserted and we skied along it, stopping at the Berwyn Arms before heading into the hills. Richard thought he would ask the landlord if he would serve us coffee. From an upstairs window he told us to bugger off. 'I think coffee is off,' Richard said. We soon discovered the strong wind was blowing snow off the Berwyns' tracks so we moved south to the Long Mynd, getting some odd looks skiing up High Street in Church Stretton with large rucksacks. It was desperately cold and windy when we camped on the ridge: even our camping gas froze. In the morning we struggled on to the north edge and I noticed Richard's nose had turned white. Richard mumbled he had last suffered this in Greenland.

Aside from climbing and ski touring, Richard's other great talent was for fast long-distance walking, relying on his phenomenal stamina and perseverance. For example, in an organised 47-mile walk over the Brecon Beacons in 1981, he finished an hour ahead of the field. Similarly, he soloed the round of Lake District 3,000ers in 16 hours in 1984 and later ran the Dorset Doddle, 33 miles along the Jurassic coast in five and a half hours.

In 1985 Richard completed his first 100-mile nonstop walk organised by the Long Distance Walkers Association and including the highest peaks in Yorkshire. The weather was atrocious but Richard finished in 37 hours, albeit with trench foot. He did two more 100-mile walks, one covering most of south Wales and the last when he was 60, through much of north Wales from Llanrwst to Porthmadog, Harlech, Ffestiniog and back to Llanrwst. This included 3,700m of ascent achieved in 32 and a half hours. Richard also enjoyed mountain marathon events, competing in the Saunders Marathon in 1988 with David Ford when they finished 12th in the expert class. With John Daniels, Richard competed in six Karrimor Mountain Marathons between 1981 and 1988, winning the veteran race in Snowdonia in 1987.

In 1989 Richard, John and myself had another Alpine holiday, Richard, now 62, leading his son David and a friend. We climbed Mont Dolent from Courmayeur, followed by Ciarforon and the Gran Paradiso, with Richard still climbing strongly. Richard's last Alpine season was in 1990 with his old friend Mike Banks, when they climbed several mountains around Arolla. In 1991, despite reservations, Richard joined a 'golden oldies' Himalayan expedition to Jaonli (6630m) in the Garhwal, sponsored by Saga. It included Mike Banks, Mike Westmacott, Jim Milledge, Joss Lynam and Paddy O'Leary, all aged well over 60. Their high point was around 6,100m when they stopped following a huge earthquake that made their mountain unstable (*AJ* 1996, pp103-107).

In 1993 I was surprised to get letter from Richard, now 66, to say he was giving up serious rock and ice climbing. His reasons were many but he felt he was not as fit and had various back, knee and shoulder injuries. He was more conscious of the dangers and felt he owed it to Val, his wife, to spend more time together. He was also deeply committed to his local church, studying to become a lay reader. He wrote: 'I find this difficult to write because inside I am torn both ways. The urge to climb is no longer there and other things have taken precedence in my life.' We had climbed together for almost 20 years so I was deeply saddened but understood his reasons.

Despite this, Richard continued walking in the hills for many more years with John Daniels and less frequently myself. Richard and John also enjoyed several weeklong mountain holidays in Scotland, still with some strenuous days. Even in his 90s Richard continued walking around his home in Bath and the local hills. Only a few months before he died, we enjoyed a slideshow of our earlier Alpine holidays, rekindling old memories.

Richard died on 29 June following a stroke. He leaves his wife Val and sons David and Patrick and their families. After 46 years of friendship it seems almost inconceivable that he is no longer here. I will miss him deeply.

Colin Beechey

Richard Brooke with John Harding in April 1969 on the Haute Route overlooking the Plateau de Trient.

John Harding writes: As befitted a former Royal Navy lieutenant commander, Richard Brooke had a heart of oak and an equally durable physique. Whether on or off a mountain, he was courageous, imperturbable and utterly dependable. A devout Christian who in his later years became a lay reader, his innate modesty (though his climbs were anything but) and blameless character mirrored a faith that was as unflinching as it was lightly worn.

I first met Richard in the late 1960s when we did some of the classic rock routes in north Wales together. In April 1969, after a two-day ridge-hopping traverse of the Brecon Beacons to get ourselves fit, we set off from Chamonix bound for Zermatt by the Haute Route. Our start had been delayed by three days owing to an injury I had sustained while skiing the Vallée Blanche. It was typical of Richard to insist that we should carry on to do at least part of the route, even though I would inevitably have to bow out early as my leave had run out. At the Col du Chardonnet, we paused for a moment to glance back at the tremendous sight of the sunlit Aiguille Verte, with the Couturier couloir a dark-shadowed gash splitting the face, which Richard had done in 1955 with the peerless Noyce and Sutton. After summiting, they were descending the Whymper couloir when a pair of French climbers, who had been following them throughout, slipped on the ice and fell to their deaths.

We had seen no other ski tourers all day, but that evening at the Trient hut we were joined by a bumptious group of young Frenchmen. Knowing that I would have to return home after reaching the next staging point at Orsières, I suggested to the Frenchmen that Richard might join them to enable him to finish the course. Staring askance at the weatherworn Richard, they shrugged off the idea with Gallic disdain. Had they known anything about Richard's mountaineering record, their attitude might have been different but it changed radically early next morning when we were hit by a tremendous storm when descending the key passage down the Combe d'Ornay. The French had started long before us but were now in disarray and only too glad to be ferried down to Orsières where they implored Richard to join them. He did so with characteristic grace, but two days later their bid to reach Zermatt had to be abandoned when an avalanche shattered Richard's skis and French morale.

Richard generally regarded ski mountaineering as essentially a means to climb mountains. However, he was a sound skier and always generous in sharing his mountaineering expertise and experience that extended from the Alps, New Zealand, Antarctica to the Himalayas. In 1978, when the recently widowed Beryl Wilberforce Smith was looking for a couple of experienced ski mountaineers to lead the ninth and final stage of the historic ski traverse of the Alps that she and her recently deceased husband Peter had started eight years earlier, Richard and another AC stalwart Fred Jenkins volunteered to lead what turned out to be a demanding but successful stage taking in the Zillertal, Venediger and Gross Glockner ranges. This was typical of Richard and I remain indebted to him not only for his staunch companionship but also for putting me in touch with New Zealand's climbing fraternity and for his suggestion that the traverse of Mont Blanc via the Aiguilles de la Bérangère and Bionassay was a worthwhile expedition.

Over the years, Richard and I had done a good many tramps together in the hills of south Wales, but his last few were spent selflessly nursing his sick wife Valerie who survives him with their two sons David and Patrick. I will always revere the memory of this exceptional man.

Joe Brown CBE
1930 - 2020

He's like a Human Spider
Clinging to the wall
Suction, Faith and Friction
And nothing else at all
But the secret of his success
Is his most amazing knack
Of hanging from a hand-jam
In an overhanging crack.

So wrote Joe Brown's close friend Tom Patey. Tom died in 1970 *(AJ* 1971, pp331-6), the year that Joe turned 40, and his complete 'Ballad of Joe Brown', of which this is just one of many verses, is essentially the early story of the most significant climber Britain has ever produced. For many years it rang out on Saturday nights in climbing pubs all around Britain. The refrain runs:

We've sung it once, we've sung it twice
He's the hardest man in the Rock & Ice
He's marvellous – he's fabulous
He's a wonder man is Joe!

By 1970 and for long after Joe was indeed the icon of every climber in the country and had gained an international reputation. He was already 'The Master' or 'The Baron', acknowledged as among the world's leading rock climbers, well known to Fleet Street, the BBC and the general public. Not surprisingly a letter once reached him in Llanberis addressed simply to 'The Human Fly, North Wales'.

Rock climbing was then an esoteric game that had always evaded public attention. However, in the early 1950s rumours circulated in climbing circles that two young Manchester fellows with baboon-like arms, steel fingers and prodigious talent were sweeping through Derbyshire and Snowdonia putting up dozens of routes of such difficulty that they were unrepeatable. The mist cleared in 1954 when the same pair reached the Alps to amaze the Alpine establishment with their speed and ability. Brown and Whillans had arrived.

He crossed the sea to Chamonix
And to show what he could do,
He knocked three days off the record time
For the west face of the Dru –
On the unclimbed face of the Blaitière
The crux had tumbled down –
But he cracked the crux by the crucial crack
Now known as the fissure Brown

The Fissure Brown was for some years considered to be the hardest rock pitch in the Alps.

No wonder the Alpine Club took notice. Charles Evans was organising a reconnaissance expedition to the still unclimbed Kangchenjunga and invited Joe, the more urbane of the duo, to join the team, most of them already Himalayan veterans.

'Twas young Joe Brown that hurried down
To rally to the call

John Cleare's iconic photo of Joe Brown on Spider's Web, Gogarth.

But when Evans mentioned that while all expenses would be paid, £20 pocket money might be useful for the voyage, Joe was taken aback. That sort of ready cash was beyond his reach. Nevertheless he soon found his feet and with his rope-mate George Band, an Everest 1953 climber, he made the first ascent of the mountain, having himself led the crux rock pitch immediately below the summit. Coming so soon after the Everest success, the ascent of the world's third-highest peak was a national event and like it or not, Joe – an ordinary working man – became a public figure.

> *In the cold, cold Karakoram*
> *Where crags are five miles high,*
> *The best in France had seen the chance*
> *To pass us on the sly.*
> *You may talk of Keller, Contamine,*
> *Magnone, Paragot*
> *But the man of the hour on the Mustagh Tower*
> *Was known by the name of Joe.*

Now self-employed with his own property repair business and still living with his mother, Joe was invited in 1956 to join a four-man, shoestring attempt on the Mustagh Tower: 'built on the lines of the Matterhorn but infinitely more grand' according to Charles Bruce. Ian McNaught-Davis and Tom Patey were prominent ACG members while the organiser John Hartog had been fixated on the peak since childhood. After a difficult climb up the north-west ridge, Joe and Mac reached the summit, Tom and John, the latter badly frostbitten, followed next day. Six days later the crack French team Tom sung about summited via the south-east ridge.

> *With Colonel Hunt on the Russian Front*
> *He paved the Paths of Peace*
> *And helped to bridge the gulf that lay*
> *Between the West and East*
> *That Climbers all might Brothers be*
> *In the Kingdom of the Snow*

In 1962 a joint AC and SMC expedition led by John Hunt and Malcolm Slesser was invited to the Pamirs, then in Soviet Tajikistan. It was not a happy expedition. Wilf Noyce and Robin Smith were killed descending Pik Garmo while Joe and McNaught-Davis made an epic if ultimately successful ascent of Communism Peak (now Ismoil Somoni Peak).

The British found Russian bureaucracy tiresome, the weather frustrating and the rock dangerous, while the Russian climbers continually berated their guests for smoking and for their lackadaisical unfitness. Later Joe told how descending the tedious moraines on the long Garmo glacier with Mac, tired and suffering from piles, they located by luck a particular glacial trough giving easy going. Their fitness-freak Russian counterparts meanwhile, having stumbled their way down a different and more gruelling route, were amazed to find their guests stretched out in the sun and smoking. After the second such occurrence the bemused Russians demanded to know how fast Joe could travel when he was fit.

Joseph Brown was born into a poor but respectable family in a poor part of Manchester where his widowed mother worked hard to support seven children, of whom he was the youngest. Bombed out, his home destroyed in the Manchester blitz of 1940, bored by organised games and expelled from the Scouts for refusing to attend church parade, he was something of a rebel as a youth and happiest messing about outdoors with a small group of other adventurous youngsters: fishing, hiking, camping and scrambling around on the craggy moorland where the fringes of the Peak District approach the city.

Apprenticed to a builder at 14, he was paid 10 shillings (50p) a week but his generous boss allowed him time off when not busy and paid for his first hiking boots. Joe had devoured Colin Kirkus' seminal book *Let's Go Climbing* and realised that climbers used ropes – but how? Attempting to climb up Kinder Downfall with his chums one day equipped with his mother's legendary washing line, the lads encountered a real climber who showed them a proper hemp climbing rope, how to use it, and most importantly how to belay.

> *He first laid hand upon a crag*
> *In the year of Forty-nine*
> *He'd nowt but pluck, beginners' luck*
> *And his mother's washing line.*
> *He scaled the gritstone classics*
> *With unprecedented skill –*
> *His fame soon reached the Gwryd,*
> *Likewise the Dungeon Ghyll.*

In due course it certainly did, but not quite yet. Joe soon fell in with other young Peak District climbers, making his first visit to Wales at Christmas 1947 and climbing the regular routes on the Idwal Slabs. John Barford's classic paperback *Climbing in Britain* inspired hitch-hiking to Ben Nevis at Easter 1948, to No3 Gully and a blizzard, while that summer he tried harder Welsh climbs, notably notorious *Lot's Groove* on Glyder Fach – still Hard VS today – which he sailed up using hand jams, a technique which came to him naturally but in those days was rarely exploited. Back on gritstone new routes fell to him thick and fast, including the long feared *Right Unconquerable* on Stanage Edge which Joe led in 1949 shortly before national service caught up with him; two years as an Royal Army Ordnance Corps storeman in Singapore proved rather tame.

Back home again, the small group of lads with whom he now climbed dubbed themselves the Rock and Ice Club. It wouldn't become properly recognised as a club for some years but its antics and achievements, especially

The 'team of all talents' on Hoy in 1967. From left to right: Joe Brown, Dougal Haston, Chris Bonington, Ian McNaught-Davis, Tom Patey and Pete Crew. *(John Cleare)*

those of Joe and his now frequent rope-mate Don Whillans, soon gathered a legendary reputation. Joe was creative, not only with routes but with names, and when in 1952 he and Don climbed *Cemetery Gates* on Dinas Cromlech, the destination seen on a Chester bus that evening seemed an appropriate name for this desperate line between *Cenotaph Corner* and *Ivy Sepulchre;* it was another year before Joe climbed the famous corner itself, four years after his first abortive attempt, and in socks. Normally Joe climbed in nails or plimsolls, but socks where sometimes necessary. He first used Vibrams on Kangchenjunga.

Not content with the Three Cliffs in Llanberis, the Rock and Ice boys dominated Clogwyn Du'r Arddu for nearly a decade, Joe himself making six hard new routes in six weeks in 1952. It was a similar picture some 12 years later when Craig Gogarth was discovered; Joe had married Valerie Gray in 1957, fathered two daughters and by now had settled in Llanberis where he opened his mountain emporium in 1966 and could go climbing whenever he wished. Often now partnered by Peter Crew, he played a major part in developing this huge sea cliff, pioneering nearly 50 new routes in the ensuing three years. His autobiography *The Hard Years,* authored with Crew and Robin Collomb, was published by Livia Gollancz in 1967, rather prematurely given that Joe was still in his prime.

It was film and television that endeared Joe to the general public. Recruited to work on a climbing documentary, Joe horrified the BBC crew by sliding at speed down the Snowdon railway tracks on a conveniently shaped stone, a Rock and Ice stunt originally employed by railway navvies using shovels during track construction in the 1890s. Tom Stobart, the 1953

Joe Brown on *Creagh Dhu Wall* at Craig y Castell with Julie Collins. The climb was 'training' for a filmed ascent of Vector, brainchild of Ned Kelly, then a senior producer at TWW TV in Bristol, who had done a previous broadcast of Coronation Street. *(John Cleare)*

Everest film maker, cast Joe for his now classic steel industry information film *Safety,* shot mostly on the Spigolo Giallo in the Dolomites, which gave Joe an opportunity to make a second attempt on the *Cassin* route on the Cima Grande with Don Roscoe. They failed, frustrated by a fierce storm, but managed to make the first successful descent down the overhanging face. In fact, Joe never really liked the Dolomites, writing later after a more successful season: 'I'd had enough of the Dollies, I was fed up with the similarity of the climbing. I longed to return to Chamonix and some snow and ice.'

Elected to the elite ACG in 1954, Joe returned to Chamonix frequently, notably the next year to the Dru again, also with Whillans, only to retreat in a storm from the very route that a few days later was to become the *Bonatti Pillar.* Then with Tom Patey in the 1960s he climbed several fine new lines including the *Central Pillar* on the Plan's west face – via the Fissure Brown-Patey – and the north-west spur of the Aiguille sans Nom.

Joe worked with Stobart again in 1961 in the remote Valley of the Assassins in Iran's Elbruz mountains where he climbed crumbling conglomerate rock and used complex rope techniques to reach otherwise inaccessible caves, unfortunately missing a large gold horde which archaeologists uncovered nearby just months later. The next year in Petra the rock was better and the climbing as difficult. Even more complex rope-work was necessary to reach hidden tombs and discover old skeletons and pottery shards but by then Joe had started a formal job as an instructor under Eric Langmuir at Derbyshire's White Hall Outdoor Pursuits Centre and such irregular jaunts were not welcomed.

Nevertheless teaching climbing at White Hall provided Joe a useful opportunity to analyse his own climbing technique and also to master canoeing and skiing, but one particular incident is worth recording from when the British gymnastics squad for the 1964 Olympics came to White Hall to train. The gymnasts were taken aback to discover that whereas Joe could easily repeat much of their routine, they were unable to match some of his informal 'gymnastic' feats. Indeed, their coach remarked to Langmuir that should Joe take up proper gymnastics he was a potential Olympic medallist.

In 1963 Joe had featured with McNaught-Davis, Whillans and the French climber Paragot in a disappointing BBC live broadcast in poor weather from Clogwyn d'ur Arddu, a return match for a French broadcast from the Aiguille du Midi aborted in a snowstorm. However, by 1966 the BBC had managed to master the difficult art of televising live climbing, having realised that a difficult climb amid dramatic scenery was not enough: decent weather was axiomatic, climbers were essentially actors and humorous repartee was obligatory. Joe's smooth, unflustered movement, his ability to be climbing the right move at the right moment and his wicked sense of humour, especially when teamed with such an ebullient character as his frequent rope-mate McNaught-Davis, made Joe a must-have performer for live television. Good weather was more likely on a sea cliff and a live broadcast from Craig Gogarth in 1966 with Joe leading *Red Wall* proved a great success. Following the now historic two-day broadcast the following year from the awesome Old Man of Hoy, during which he led the first ascent of the south face after 'training' on the curious Castle of Yesnaby sea stack, Joe was known to every television viewer, and when colour TV arrived in 1970, the spectacular live broadcast from *Spider's Web,* a great natural arch on Craig Gogarth, assured his public fame.

About this time the BBC became interested in the possibilities of a climb on St Kilda and in the height of winter Joe, Tom Patey, Pete Crew and I were storm-bound on the island for many days: most of the time Joe and Pete were content to remain indoors playing poker while Tom and I felt compelled to brave the snow and thoroughly explore the island. Eventually rescued by an intrepid Harris fisherman, the wild 10-hour voyage back to civilisation was mitigated with fresh lobster, good malt whisky and Joe's tall stories.

Thereafter, whenever a climber was required, Joe was the man: on television, in films or stills. He climbed so smoothly, always relaxed, flowing up the pitch to make every move appear straightforward, but while this was perfect for moving pictures, when shooting stills it was not always easy to portray a climb to be as desperate as I knew it really was.

On one educational film I shot with him the script called for a demonstration of the qualities of a good climbing helmet. Joe produced an ancient, battered continental helmet, and explaining to camera that such gear was actually dangerous, proceed to thwack it with a peg hammer, expecting it to shatter immediately. The hammer bounced simply off. We shot take after take, Joe thwacking the helmet harder and harder to no effect. Though humorous at first, the situation soon became frustrating and the invective rich. We stopped, re-hung the script and proceeded to the next shot, to demonstrate how a modern helmet, one of the new Joe Brown brand, really did protect the head. One tap and the thing shattered. In fact, only the outer coloured fibreglass layer had shattered, but on film this was enough to suggest total failure. We scrubbed the entire sequence and stalked off to the Padarn pub.

By the 1970s, the BBC had tired of live climbing broadcasts on a national scale. 'No more jockstrap television!' as one London BBC executive was heard to declare. But there was still film work. Several times Joe found himself doubling for celebrity actors on major feature films, in Fred Zinnemann's last film *Five Days One Summer* and Roland Joffé's *The Mission*.

> *You should see him grin where the holds are thin*
> *On an overhanging wall*
> *He's known to everybody*
> *As the Man who'll Never Fall.*

Actually Joe did have his share of mishaps and fighting retreats and survived two major falls, one on Cloggy during an early Rock and Ice attempt on *Vember* (named for the daughter of Mrs Williams at the Halfway House) when his hemp rope was all but severed, and then on the Ben when shattered ice and a failed belay resulted in a major fall from *Point Five Gully,* leaving Joe shaken badly enough for his wife to declare 'Joe Brown, you're a dud on ice!' He also broke a leg while scree running in Wales.

> *Some say Joe Brown is sinking down*
> *To mediocrity*
> *He even climbs with useless types*
> *Like Dennis Gray and me*

Now more relaxed as he faded gradually from the public eye, but still hard as nails and more active than ever, Joe was always happiest exploring and climbing something new, although he did take special pleasure in plying his original profession during frequent forays to Hamish MacInnes' bolt-hole in Torridon. With MacInnes and other chums he was now regularly enjoying small, low-key expeditions, most of which escaped publicity, among them a trip to climb the grotesque Drongs sea stacks off Shetland, but the 1973 ascent of the Nose of Roraima, a 17-day tropical epic on Guyana's bizarre 'Lost World', did attract considerable media attention.

Most noteworthy was the first ascent with three friends of the Nameless Tower of Trango (6240m) in 1976, probably the most difficult technical rock climb then accomplished at that altitude. But success was not as important as the climbing itself, as being involved. There were forays to Everest's north-east ridge, to Cho Oyu and to interesting peaks in the Andes, and in the 1980s to Thalay Sagar in Garhwal with Mo Anthoine. More esoteric perhaps were trips with chums such as MacInnes, the American climber Yvon Chouinard and others 'nosing' around the Andes, prospecting in the Amazon, or yeti hunting in remote Nepal. Well into his mid seventies, Joe took annual winter holidays making new routes in the Moroccan Anti-Atlas, while at home he continued to enjoy steep rock until arthritis finally closed in and the AC elected him to honorary membership and the Queen invested him CBE for services to mountaineering.

Although by the 1980s a younger generation of gifted climbers had entered the lists, and even harder routes were being climbed, Joe's eye for a line and his uncanny rock sense remained exceptional. But the game and how it was played were changing. Ethics and style were important to him. He'd made his name in the days when protection was minimal and long runouts the norm, and he believed that if one couldn't climb a route cleanly, it should be left for someone who could. An unassuming man, never courting publicity – though it arrived willy-nilly – he was always good for a laugh or a game of darts, and with his natural courtesy and big, slow smile, Joe Brown was known in Llanberis as a good neighbour.

He had been ill for a while and died on 15 April, leaving his wife, Valerie, two daughters Helen and Zoe, herself a climber, four grandchildren and a host of legends, in Patey's phrase, 'the Last of the Grand Old Masters'.

John Cleare

Mike Bullock
1939 - 2020

I first met Mike in 1962 when he participated in a Yeti Club meet in Snowdonia with a group from our Midlands section. He was a strong walker and we rapidly became close friends. Mike's love of the mountains was principally expressed through fell and hillwalking although in our early days he climbed with me on a number of rock routes and snow gullies in both north Wales and the Lake District. There always seemed to be plenty of snow, back in the days before the effects of climate change became apparent.

He invited me on a walking weekend with a number of friends at Wasdale Head in January 1965. In all there was 13 of us. The Saturday was a classic Lakeland wet winter day but we crossed via Sty Head to Borrowdale, returning up Honister, Ennerdale and Black Sail. After dinner and an interesting evening in the bar we still managed to walk over Burnmoor to the Boot Inn Eskdale the following day. Thus began our informal walking group the 'Wasdale 13' which has met annually in January ever since. Between us, Mike and I attended more than a hundred meets and it was a consequence of our visits that I became the owner of the Wasdale Head Inn for 26 years.

I remain indebted to Mike for his original invitation, though there were times when I quietly cursed him.

Mike also organised a number of hillwalking trips mainly in Scotland, bagging a number of Munros including those on the Cuillin Ridge. For more than 25 years he and his wife Frances normally took two weeks walking holiday in the Pennine Alps area of Switzerland, where they my wife often joined them.

Mike grew up in Rutland, his family having evacuated from Birmingham in the early part of the war. He won a scholarship to Oakham School from where he joined Barclays Bank before being called up for national service, commissioned into the Royal Corps of Signals. He then returned to his career with Barclays in the Midlands region. By 1962 he was security clerk in the Chapel Ash branch, before progressing rapidly through the ranks of management to become a senior local director in the international section. After taking early retirement he had more time for his beloved mountains and travel.

He studied for an MLitt from Birmingham University and then wrote two books: *Missed Signals on the Western Front,* co-authored with an American, Larry Lyons, which detailed the prejudice of the army against wireless communications in the First World War; and *Priestley's Progress,* a biography of Sir Raymond Priestley who went with Shackleton and Scott on the *Nimrod* and *Terra Nova* expeditions to Antarctica. Both books he researched in depth. Surprisingly, this was the first biography of Priestley, who in Cambridge after the First World War played a leading role in the establishment of the Scott Polar Research Institute, followed by appointments as vice chancellor of the Universities of Melbourne and then Birmingham.

Mike also sang in the Worcester Cathedral choir. He was a fellow of the Royal Geographical Society and attended many of the London lectures. In 1965 he married Frances Cubitt. Fran and their three children, Helen, David and Robin all survive him.

Ed Hammond

Julian Davey
1946 - 2020

I met Julian Davey in the late 1990s on an ice-climbing trip. We were matched together by Victor Saunders, beginning over twenty years of friendship and adventure. I cannot remember too much about that trip, other than we climbed in Chamonix and then did some ice routes in the Aosta valley. In the couple of decades that followed we were fortunate enough to build joint memories during summer and winter trips to the Alps, and outings in the Lake District and Scotland. Looking back, our current Club president had set us up on an amazing 'blind date'.

Julian was born after the war and introduced to the British hills on family holidays. He went to school in Kingston upon Thames, then after a gap year

Julian Davey in the Julian Alps, Slovenia.

with Voluntary Service Overseas went up to Selwyn College, Cambridge. There he joined a Commonwealth expedition (Comex) and drove a bus to India. Julian was also the expedition banker and tasked with exchanging currencies as they drove through Europe and Asia. He put his analytical mind to the task of getting the most optimal exchange rates, even when this included using the black market.

After university he joined the British Council; his first posting was to Ethiopia. Julian also served for many years in Malaysia, where his lifelong involvement with the Hash House Harriers began. Ultimately he became regional director for finance in the Far East, based in Hong Kong. When he left the British Council he was able to spend more of his time mountaineering, skiing and rock climbing.

In retirement Julian joined several expeditions to the Greater Ranges, including a trip to Island Peak with Community Action Nepal. After qualifying as a European Mountain Leader he began to lead school expeditions. These trips provided young people with rewarding challenges, and personal development in adventurous environments. Julian was a staunch advocate for expanding educational opportunities, and he was especially proud when his daughter Julia entered the teaching profession.

Julian also enjoyed skiing and mountaineering trips with his wife Kate, and together they visited places as far afield as Greenland and Antarctica. I think that during one of our many late night génépi sessions he told me that he was most proud of his winter ski ascent of Mont Blanc. Julian had a broad range of interests outside of mountaineering that included potholing, wild swimming, classical music, singing and furniture making. He was a trustee of the Theatre By The Lake in Keswick, founding chairman of Hesket Newmarket Brewery Cooperative, and a volunteer adviser at Penrith Citizens Advice Bureau. In recent years Julian delighted in introducing his granddaughter to the outdoors, and built her a customised Wendy house cum indoor climbing wall.

Julian was an interesting conversationalist and great company. A self-confessed turophile (cheese lover), on climbing trips he was always on the lookout for a truckle of something obscure. It is right and proper that Julian should be remembered for his achievements and for his zeal and alacrity, but he should also be remembered for his generosity and kindness.

Vernon Gayle

Yvonne Holland
1957 - 2020

Yvonne Holland was born in north Wales and no doubt developed an early taste for the mountains through her parents being for a short while guardians of the Idwal Cottage Youth Hostel. I met her when we were both students at Manchester University and we were almost inseparable for the next 12 years. It was climbing and particularly mountaineering that was our great passion.

We had such great adventures, driven by Yvonne's tireless enthusiasm. Like many young and relatively poor climbers at that time, every summer we caught the climber's coach from Victoria coach station to Chamonix. One summer we went too early and the Chamonix valley was still in post-ski season shutdown, the lifts and the Saint Gervais tramway were not operating and the trails were still buried in snow. But we wanted to climb Mont Blanc, so set off anyway, up the trails from the valley floor, struggling through deep snow and getting to the Tête Rousse hut, where we finally gave up. Six weeks later, undeterred, we caught the coach from London again and this time the weather was glorious. We went straight up to the Goûter hut and the day after to the summit, with throbbing headaches and retching from our lack of acclimatisation.

There were many other great trips climbing Alpine peaks: Mont Dolent, Tour Ronde, Aiguille d'Argentière, Monte Rosa, Castor and Pollux, Alphubel, Weisshorn, Dent Blanche, Mont Blanc (again) and many, many others. Then we set our sights on the Himalaya, going first to Mera in Khumbu, back in the day when commercial ascents of trekking peaks was just starting out, and we then organised our own expedition, to Baruntse (7162m). On that trip, soon after our arrival in Kathmandu, we went to the Mountain Travel compound to meet our sirdar and check on our equipment to find that their other major client that season was one Reinhold Messner, who had a huge mountain of equipment taking up most of the compound, whereas our tiny pile of gear was under a tarpaulin way off to one side.

Yvonne Holland mid flight on a river crossing in northern Pakistan. *(A Wigley)*

We had an enjoyable expedition but failed to summit and back in Kathmandu, Yvonne had big plans for more travel and mountain adventures. She wrote home about the hair-raising journey that followed: "We arranged a bus and train journey to Delhi and boarded a bus in Kathmandu at about 7pm. At about midnight our 'luxury' bus had broken down in the middle of nowhere along the sun Khosi river valley. There are many buses travelling that way every night, so it was a case of trying to get on another one. Of course, all the busses are packed like sardines so we ended up travelling on the roof of one with about 20 other people and all the baggage! We were just all heaped up in a big pile. I was sitting at the edge with my feet braced under a bar to stop me falling off. Although it was dark I could just see the river roaring below a precipitous drop – I was terrified." But we made it to Delhi and then made our way back into the mountains, to the Indian Himalaya this time, up to Srinagar and over the passes to Ladakh and Zanskar for more climbing and exploratory adventures.

And we carried on around the world, climbing in the Sierra Nevada in California and walking the John Muir trail, and then bought a car and drove to Mexico where we climbed Popocatépetl, Iztaccíhuatl and Pico de Orizaba. It was a fantastic trip that epitomised Yvonne's love for adventure, for travel and her passion for the mountains. Yvonne went on to ever-greater exploits and adventures in the mountains, summiting Khan Tengri and Denali and many others, and an attempt on Everest.

Yvonne will be remembered for her strong character and her independent spirit, but there was another side to her also. A loving, caring person who was happy sharing good food and a glass of wine with friends or spending time with family. During the last 10 years or so Yvonne organised and took her non-climbing sister Louise and her husband on no less than six long-distance treks: two to the Pyrenees, one to the Dolomites, a trek in the Maritime Alps and a trip to Peru to visit Machu Picchu followed immediately by a second Peruvian trek. As Yvonne put it: 'Well, if you're going to Peru you may as well do two treks while you're there!' That was typical of her enthusiasm. Yvonne made the treks more appealing for her little sister by booking refuges along the route and they travelled to places they never would have dreamt of going to without Yvonne's suggestion.

Thank you, Yvonne, for inspiring us all with your endless enthusiasm and inexhaustible sense of adventure. You are sorely missed.

Andy Wigley

Yvonne had a love of all mountains but had a special fondness for the Scottish Highlands and the Pyrenees. We had two trips to the Pyrenees together, the first about 10 years ago and the second in 2017. Towards the end of the first trip, which had been very successful, I managed to get my arm broken by a loose boulder while ascending a gully. I will always be grateful that Yvonne was there to go down to the nearest hut to raise the alarm.

Yvonne was close to completing her second round of Munros as well as doing the Corbetts and Grahams. While she was in remission, one very memorable trip was based at a bunkhouse near Inverlael. We did the Beinn Dearg 'four' one day and then three of the Fannichs the next day. The weather was glorious and the views stunning, I was hard pushed to keep up. Happy memories.

Jeff Harris

In the 15 years I knew her, Yvonne talked almost exclusively of mountains, music (mostly the Neil Young variety), food (vegetarianism), Buddhism and men: usually in that order. Almost every weekend or holiday was a trip to some mountain region or other, whether in the UK or abroad. Yvonne loved walking in the company of friends, but if no one was available she was just as happy to go on her own, often camping in the wild along the way. She prided herself on her fitness, speed and competence, all of which were outstanding.

One of the best days we had together was traversing Striding Edge to Helvellyn one snowy November. Yvonne was recovering from an operation to remove the cancer and was determined to regain her mountain fitness. It was a relief to me that she was a little slower than usual as it gave me a chance to keep up. Stragglers were not tolerated well. It was a perfect winter's day and, at the time, she felt full of hope for a future that, sadly as it turned out, was not to be.

Several years earlier Yvonne and I had been on expeditions to Bolivia and then to Peru. It was on these trips that I experienced first-hand her ease in the mountains. Many lasting mountain memories are full of drama and intrigue, but my memories of climbing with Yvonne are of her calm confidence. She was also pretty determined and able to dig deep to achieve her goals, which included some serious mountain summits. On my trips with her in the Alps and Greater Ranges she climbed Monte Viso, Pequeño Alpamayo, Illimani, Ishinca and Yanapacha. These were but a few of her considerable achievements.

I can't really say I knew what drew Yvonne to the mountains. It just seemed to be a necessity. A sort of life force. I think I can say that Yvonne was a 'true' mountaineer and should be remembered as one of the best.

Adèle Long

Martin Moran
1955 - 2019

On 26 May 2019, Martin Moran died in an accident on unclimbed Peak 6447m in the Nanda Devi region, together with his six clients and their Indian liaison officer. It was a tragic end to an exceptional life in the mountains.

Martin was born in 1955 and was brought up on North Tyneside. His parents had a love for the hills and holidays were taken in the Scottish Highlands and the Lake District. Martin spent his teenage years exploring the Cheviots and camping with the Scouts. He studied geography at St Catherine's College, Cambridge and became a chartered accountant, but the hills and mountains continued to draw him. He made his first winter visit to the Scottish mountains in December 1978 and three years later he had climbed the north face of the Eiger. Martin was always a fast learner. His mind was now made up: he would become a mountain guide. In 1982 Martin joined the British Mountain Guides training scheme having negotiated three months leave of absence from his accountancy job.

During the winter of 1984-5 Martin put himself on the map with the first winter round of the Scottish Munros. Supported by his wife Joy, Martin walked over 1,000 miles over 83 days and made 150,000m of ascent to complete the 277 summits. Apart from the Cuillin on Skye, the Munros do not involve technical climbing, but in winter they are a serious mountaineering proposition. To put the achievement into context, a winter Munro round has only been completed twice since.

Martin qualified as a British and IFMGA mountain guide in March 1985 and six months later he set up his guiding business with Joy in Lochcarron, in the north-west Highlands. The winter Munros had caught the public imagination and he immediately attracted clients. Guiding in the north-west Highlands was tough with longer approaches than Glen Coe or the northern Cairngorms, but Martin was interested in attracting a more adventurous brand of client. His brochure advertised 'visits to remote corries with potential for new routes' and that promise was fulfilled with the first ascent of *Crown Jewel* (IV,5) on Beinn Alligin with Nigel Adey and Mick Guest in March 1986. Martin went on to record dozens of new routes with other course attendees.

In the mid 1980s the north-west Highlands had not been thoroughly explored as a winter climbing venue and there were countless opportunities for new routes. As Martin's business grew he took on other guides and mountaineering instructors. Not surprisingly, Andy Nisbet, the most prolific Scottish winter climber of all time, took the remit of exploring new ground to heart, making many first ascents with clients on Martin's courses. I first met Martin on his local mountain Fuar Tholl one glorious Saturday afternoon in February 1994. Dave Hesleden and I had just completed a new ice climb on the rarely in condition South-East Cliff and bumped into Martin on the summit. Martin introduced himself and asked what we had just climbed. He knew the line, of course, but said he'd 'forbidden' Andy to climb it,

Martin on the summit of Panwali Dwar (6663m) in Garhwal, with Nanda Devi in the background, on the first guide and first alpine-style ascent in 1993.

intending to have a go himself later in the week. For many climbers having a line plucked from their home ground would have been a considerable disappointment but Martin acted with grace and charm and warmly congratulated us on our ascent.

Martin's contribution to Scottish winter climbing was enormous. He climbed well over a hundred new routes, many at the highest grades. 'There are many impressive winter cliffs in the Torridon Highlands,' he wrote, 'but only three can be described as truly awesome: Fuar Tholl's Mainreachan Buttress, the West Central Wall on Beinn Eighe and the Giant's Wall on Beinn Bhan. All are places where a significant grip factor is added to the intrinsic difficulties of the climbs.'

It is on these three walls that Martin's most celebrated Scottish new routes lie. In 1989 he climbed *Reach For the Sky* (VII,6) on Fuar Tholl, and in 1993 succeeded on *Blood, Sweat and Frozen Tears* (VII,8) on Beinn Eighe. But a new line on Beinn Bhan's huge Giant's Wall on the left side of Coire nan Fhamhair eluded him until March 2002, when he breached the impressive unclimbed terrain between *Gully of the Gods* and *Great Overhanging Gully* with Paul Tattersall. Moran first spotted the great corner splitting the upper section of the cliff thirty years before when he visited the corrie as a 17-year-old scout on a camping trip. *The Godfather* (VIII,8) provided a huge struggle, especially when both headtorches failed as they were climbing into the night, but it has now seen several repeats and has become one of the most prized routes in the northern Highlands.

A notable aspect of Martin's new routing was his creativity. In March 1989 he soloed *Das Rheingold,* a girdle traverse across Beinn Bhan's four corries. With over 2.8km of sustained climbing up to grade V across poorly understood terrain, it was a bold step into the unknown. Other notable successes include the first ascent of *Storvegen* (VI,8), a spectacular 200m ramp-line on the big cliff behind the Old Man of Storr on Skye, and the first winter ascent of the continuously overhanging *Hung Drawn and Quartered* (VIII,8) on the north face of Am Basteir.

Martin's winter climbing showed no sign of slowing down with age. In late 2010 he had a superb run of routes resulting in two new VIIIs and a IX. His campaign started with the first ascent of *Omerta* (VIII,9) in Coire an t-Sneachda with Pete Macpherson. Soon after, the pair made the fifth ascent of *The Secret* on Ben Nevis (VIII,9) before making the second ascent of *The God Delusion* (IX,9) on Beinn Bhan, widely regarded as the hardest route in the northern Highlands. Later that December he teamed up with Murdoch Jamieson and Francis Blunt to make the first winter ascent of *Feast of The East* (VIII,9), a summer E1 on the Eastern Ramparts of Beinn Eighe. A few days later he was with Jamieson again to climb *The Wailing Wall* (IX,9) on the awe-inspiring left side of Haystack Gully on An Teallach. This was one of the first Scottish grade IX first ascents to be climbed on sight.

Martin moved with extraordinary speed in the mountains. In June 1990 he set a new 3h 33m record for the Cuillin Ridge, beating the previous time by an astonishing 17 minutes. This fitness translated to the Alps where he climbed many *grandes courses* like the *American Direct* on the Dru, the north face of Les Droites and a very fast 36-hour ascent of the *Peuterey Integrale.* He climbed several routes alone notching up solo ascents of the Nant Blanc face of the Aiguille Verte, the *Gervasutti Pillar* on Mont Blanc du Tacul, the *Cordier Pillar-Roc-Grepon* enchainment and the *Cassin* on the Badile. In July 1985, he added a new route *Échec et Mat* (TD+), to the steep north-west face of the Peigne.

Without doubt, Martin's outstanding Alpine achievement took place in the summer of 1993, when he climbed the 75 major 4,000m peaks in a single journey with Simon Jenkins. They covered over 1,000km on bike and foot and made over 70,000m of ascent in 52 days. In my view this is one of the greatest British achievements in the Alps. Think Whymper on the Matterhorn, or Bonington, Whillans and Clough on the Central Pillar of Frêney, for undertakings of comparable significance. On his return, Martin wrote to say that he had seen my name in the Canzio bivouac hut log book where Guy Muhlemann and I had spent the night whilst traversing the Jorasses and Rochefort after climbing the Walker Spur. This was so typical of Martin. Our achievement was insignificant compared to his, yet he still found time to congratulate us.

Martin's guiding operations extended to the Alps and he ran summer Alpine mountaineering courses initially based in Argentière and then in Evolène. Many British guides broadened their experience and enhanced their craft instructing on these courses and benefitted immensely from Martin's knowledge and tactical awareness of where to go for the best conditions. Many tributes paid to Martin are from British guides who deeply valued his friendship and his role as a mentor.

In 2005 Martin started running ice-climbing courses in Hemsedal in Norway. Martin had noted that the flight from Aberdeen to Bergen took only an hour, which meant that Norwegian icefalls could be reached in less time than it takes to get to the foot of Ben Nevis. Guiding big ice climbs is exacting, but inevitably Martin was drawn to the biggest challenges. One day off in 2010 he made an early repeat of the legendary 275m Vettifossen, Europe's highest single-drop waterfall, with Martin Welch. Further north, Martin took groups to Lofoten and the Lyngen Alps, not for the easy option of summer rock climbing and ski touring but for serious mountaineering on challenging peaks such as Rulten and Jiehkkevarri. Reading between the lines, one senses that these mountains were amongst the most challenging of Martin's guiding career.

In 1983, Martin made his first visit to the Indian Himalaya where he made the first ascent of the west ridge of Bhagirathi I (6854m) in the Garhwal with Charlie Heard and John Mothersele. Tragically Heard died whilst descending this magnificent and elegant 2,000m route when an abseil anchor failed. His death overshadowed a line compared to the *Peuterey Integrale.*

The following year Martin retuned to make the first ascent of the 600m *Sunrise Pillar* (TD) on Kedarnath Dome's east flank. These two trips ignited a passion for the Indian Himalaya, and Martin visited over 20 times, often with clients, resulting in dozens of first ascents. Highlights in India included the first ascents of the south face of Nanda Kot (6861m) in 1995, and the west ridge of Nilkanth (6596m) in 2000. In 2009 he attempted Nanda Devi East (7434m) and returned to try a new route on the same mountain in 2015 with Mark Thomas, where they reached a high point of 6,865m on the spectacular and unclimbed 2,000m north-east ridge.

Martin wrote in a fluid and entertaining style and authored several books. His magnum opus was *Scotland's Winter Mountains,* a thoroughly researched treatise on how to survive, walk, climb and ski in the Scottish mountains in winter. He also wrote an excellent Alpine Club guidebook to climbing the 4,000m peaks, where his detailed knowledge shines through on every page, and *Higher Ground,* an account of his life as a mountain guide. I suspect that *The Munros in Winter* is his most popular book, but I continually return to *Alps 4000,* the account of his 4,000m Alpine odyssey. Any single chapter, such as the western Zermatt skyline (Bishorn-Weisshorn-Zinal Rothorn-Obergabelhorn-Dent Blanche-Dent d'Hérens-Matterhorn), is the stuff of dreams. To achieve just one of the many link ups described in the book would be the culmination of an Alpine career.

In 2016 Martin and Ian Dring made the first ascent of the *North Spur* (ED) of Marikula Killa in the upper Miyar valley. This 1,300m route is the

Martin Moran and Simon Jenkins during their epic round of the Alpine 4,000ers during the summer of 1993. They climbed 75 peaks and 70,000m in 52 days, covering 1,000km on foot and by bike.

Indian Himalaya's version of the Walker and took seven days to climb. It was a remarkable achievement for a man now into his seventh decade and Martin modestly likened it to an extended *Gervasutti Pillar,* commenting that a faster team could do it in three or four days now the bivouac ledges were in place. Martin was still setting the pace just months before his accident: in February 2019 he made the first ascent of *Scarred for Life* (VIII,9) on Beinn Eighe with Robin Thomas. This route lies on the rarely visited north face of Sgurr Ban and was arguably the most adventurous pioneering climb of the Scottish winter season.

Martin's achievements, whether hill walking, fell running, winter climbing or as an alpinist, were ground breaking and inspirational. Nobody will ever know exactly what happened on that fateful day on Peak 6447m, but it is possible that a cornice collapse triggered the massive avalanche that swept away Martin and his seven companions. One thing is for certain: the world had lost one of its most influential mountaineers, a man of huge enthusiasm, wisdom and drive.

Martin is survived by his wife Joy, their son Alex and their daughter Hazel.

Simon Richardson

Alan Pope
1943 - 2019

Alan enjoyed a life of mountaineering in his native Ireland, the Alps and the Greater Ranges. Born in Dublin, he attended the High School. When he left school, he went into articles and became a chartered accountant. Amongst his friends were members of Dublin University Climbing Club and he joined them on climbing trips. His appetite whetted, he joined the Irish Mountaineering Club where he made lifelong friends.

He got married in 1969 and three daughters came along in due course. He dabbled in rock climbing and often climbed with Frank Winder in Dalkey. Frank (1928-2007) was an Irish professor of biochemistry, a naturalist, and one of Ireland's leading rock climbers in the 1950s and 1960s with many quality first ascents to his credit.

Alan Pope.

Alan visited the Alps on many occasions. In 2003 he experienced a major rockfall, triggered by a heat wave, on the descent from the Matterhorn. Ninety climbers had to be taken off the mountain by helicopter, which Alan photographed as he descended. In the same year he was elected to the AC as an aspirant member.

He climbed Mont Blanc, the Mittellegi ridge on the Eiger and the north ridge of the Piz Badile. He also had forays to Bolivia and Peru, climbing in the Cordillera Real and the Cordillera Blanca. He had an interest in ski touring and went on various trips including the Haute Route. In later years he went on several solo trips to via ferrata in the Dolomites and to the Picos de Europa. Further afield he went to Meru and Mount Kilimanjaro. He had an understated steely determination to keep on going to the places that he loved and was always acutely aware of the finite time we are given.

He had a collection of climbing books from the 1950s and 1960s to which he added modern books from time to time. He gave several lectures on alpine climbing, using his library for historical context. He was a keen sailor for 42 years, taking part in races 'round the cans' in Dublin Bay as well as offshore events. When he gave up racing, he took up cruising. He painted in oils, a talent inherited from his mother. The main subject matter was mountains and getting it just right caused him endless frustration. He was an excellent cook and loved cooking for special events.

Quiet and self-effacing, throughout his life Alan accomplished a great deal but did not parade his achievements. A great, much loved human being, he died suddenly of a heart attack in his beloved Wicklow mountains in March 2019.

Thelma Pope & Roderick A Smith

Robin Henry Lister Richards
1938 - 2019

Robin Richards.

Robin Richards was born in Cape Town in 1938 and spent his early years in Zimbabwe. After leaving Diocesan College School in Cape Town, he spent two years as a national serviceman in the Royal Navy before gaining a degree in natural sciences at Worcester College, Oxford. He then joined Dublin brewers Arthur Guinness, working there for many years before returning to South Africa where he founded a Cape Town-based asset management company.

Yet Robin was always at heart a mountaineer. He climbed many of the major peaks in the Alps and participated in five Himalayan expeditions. His love affair with the Alps started in Hochsholden, which in 1956 had only one lift. Robin's first ski lessons therefore led to a tour across to the Braunschweiger hut and, since the guide surprisingly saw fit to include this inexperienced youngster in his party, the first Alpine peak Robin climbed was the Wildspitze. This was followed a month later by an ascent of the Olperer and others in that area.

While Robin and Alan Wedgwood were national servicemen together, they journeyed to Scotland whenever possible to explore the mountains there, and from time to time Robin managed leave from his ship to climb in the Lake District. Once established at Oxford, long vacations allowed more climbing opportunities. He hired a guide to attempt the Dreiherrnspitze above the Zillertal and was intrigued to find the guide taking altimeter readings all the way up a very crevassed glacier. The weather had appeared perfect, but within minutes of reaching the Zsigmondyspitze, heavy snow started to fall. They began to retreat and Robin never forgot the guide's foresight in marking his route by spot heights. He subsequently always regarded his altimeter as more important than his compass in high mountains.

Many Alpine adventures followed, some with guides, some with Alan and Janet Wedgwood, and Colin and Jane Taylor. The Bernese Oberland was a favourite area of his. Robin made his first visit to Zermatt in 1960, climbing the Rimpfischhorn and Alphubel with two university friends. In those days he stayed at the Hotel Bahnhof, hosted by Bernhard Biner and his sister Paula, well known to so many climbers. It was a thrill for him to return in 2007 for the 150th anniversary of the founding of the Club and to book for the occasion at the prestigious Monte Rosa Hotel. He had joined in 1976 and deeply appreciated that the organisation to which he now belonged had the same ideals and love for mountains as he did.

Robin was particularly proud of his ascent of the Cresta Santa Caterina on the Monte Rosa by the Marinelli couloir above Macugnaga on July 20th 1969, the very same day that Neil Armstrong first walked on the moon. A 12-day, self-guided Haute Route tour in April 1971 was another highlight of Robin's mountaineering days. The route from Chamonix to Saas Fee ran through Zermatt so the travellers, Robert West, Angela Faller, Dick Sykes and Robin enjoyed the comfort of a night at the Bahnhof, warmly welcomed by Paula Biner. Their next focus would be to climb Castor and spend a night at the Monte Rosa hut.

Robin managed another few Alpine seasons: in Chamonix, with ascents of Mont Blanc, the Aiguilles du Chardonnet, du Géant and Verte; the Silvretta group and the Monte Rosa group. But family life and the world of work were beginning to curtail his opportunities for mountaineering. After the family moved to the southern hemisphere, the Mountain Club of South Africa introduced Robin to the joys of rock climbing on Table Mountain. And the Ski Club of South Africa had a hut on the Matroosberg, only three hours way from home, where all the family learnt to ski among the boulders.

It was to mark the Mountain Club of South Africa's centenary that Robin first found himself in the Karakoram. The mountains were certainly high and challenging enough and he relished the isolation and the remoteness of the areas he visited, but he acknowledged they could never replace the Alps in his heart. Occasionally, Robin was able to join Pam and Alastair Andrews' ABMSAC meets at Madonna di Campiglio and other venues. He then became a regular skier in the Trois Vallées and other Alpine resorts, which, up to a point, satisfied the lure of the high mountains.

Robin only very recently retired from the ski slopes and resigned himself to taking holidays at sea level. But the snow still drew him and his favourite cruise was to Spitzbergen, Greenland and the Arctic fiords. His retirement in Hermanus was enhanced by the friendships shared on mountain walks and the intellectual stimulus of the Hermanus U3A. He leaves his wife Deirdre, three children and six grandchildren.

Deirdre Richards

Ernst Helmut Sondheimer
1923 - 2019

In his outlook towards mountains my friend Ernst was a traditionalist. With a love of every aspect of the world's high places, he was a peaks, passes and glaciers man, as happy when crossing a grassy alp in search of an elusive flower, as he was when plodding up the final snow slope to a 4,000m summit.

He made no first ascents but was content to follow established routes; the majority of his climbs in the Alps were guideless, several of which were made

The endlessly curious, 'gentle, generous and modestly wise' Ernst Sondheimer on Maderia. *(K Reynolds)*

with his son Julian, and he often claimed that his ascent of Piz Badile's north ridge was the slowest on record. Not that it mattered, of course; it was being among the mountains that counted. Sadly I never saw him in his physical prime, nor did we ever share a rope, but to spend a day in his company discussing mountains (or any other of his passions) was one of life's joys, and he retained a boyish enthusiasm for them well into late old age.

Ernst Sondheimer was something of a polymath, a man of high intellect and broad interests, knowledgeable about everything from the art of Emil Nolde to classical German literature via bridge, opera and the Himalayan plant hunters. Widely read, his bookshelves groaned beneath heavyweight biographies, scientific tomes, books on art and exploration, collections of poetry and a splendid library of mountaineering books too. Beyond the cerebral he was gentle, generous and modestly wise; a man who grabbed life with both hands, whose presence could light a room, and who had the ability to relate to anyone, no matter what their background, education, culture or creed, as I discovered on our very first meeting.

Maya Angelou once remarked that people may forget what you said, they may forget what you did, but they will never forget how you made them feel. Ernst made those who knew him feel blessed.

Ernst Sondheimer was born into a comfortable middle-class Jewish family in Stuttgart, where his father Max ran the family glue factory, founded in Oberdorf by his paternal grandfather. His other grandfather was a banker in Wertheim am Main. The family were not observant Jews, although Ernst once confessed that he'd had his bar mitzvah because he knew he'd receive lots of presents. His father was a good patriot who had fought on the Western Front in the First World War, and in its wake thought that 'this Nazi nonsense' would not last long. But in 1935, after he and his wife were detained and interrogated by the Gestapo, he rightly saw this as a warning of things to come and began to look for a place of safety for his family. The following year he sent the 13-year-old Ernst to a small boarding school in Bournemouth, where he was extremely homesick for a while. Returning to Stuttgart in 1937 for what he thought was a family holiday, Ernst and his younger brother Franz were taken by their parents to Switzerland. Once safely within Swiss borders they discovered there would be no return to Germany. Instead, the whole family came to England, thereby avoiding Kristallnacht and the ensuing Holocaust.

Although he had no English when he first arrived as a refugee, Ernst learned quickly and after sitting for his higher certificate at University

College School in Highgate, he went up to Cambridge in 1941, intending to study chemistry. However the director of studies told him the country needed physicists, so he changed course and after passing his final exams in December 1943, was taken on by John Rendall to work in a reserved occupation, before returning to his studies in theoretical physics under Alan Wilson.

Thankful that he and his family had escaped the horrors of Auschwitz, after the war Ernst became naturalised as a British citizen, taking an oath of allegiance to King George VI. 'If you have had good fortune such as mine you must be grateful,' he said. 'Being British means a lot to me, more than if I just happened to be born into it.'

It was during his time at Cambridge that he met Janet Matthews across the bridge table. The Anglican niece of the Bishop of Truro, Janet was a fellow of Girton College where she'd gained her PhD in history. She and Ernst married in 1950, spent their honeymoon in the Dolomites, raised two children and continued to play bridge together until Janet died in 2007.

The newly married Ernst was offered a lectureship at Imperial College in 1951 then became a reader in applied mathematics at Queen Mary College before accepting the post of professor of mathematics at Westfield College in 1960. And there he stayed for more than 20 years. By his own admission he enjoyed teaching and maintained contact with former colleagues and some of his students long after he took retirement in 1982.

His love of mountains had taken root on pre-war family ski holidays in the Black Forest and the Jura, and was revived during his Dolomites honeymoon when his enthusiasm for the Alps really took off. It led to ascents of such peaks as the Gran Paradiso, Monte Rosa (when he made the classic error of stabbing himself in the calf with one of his crampons), the Weissmies, Zermatt Breithorn and Nadelhorn, a failed attempt on the Zinalrothorn, but successes on Piz Cengalo and Badile (twice), the graceful Monte Disgrazia, two routes on Piz Bernina, the Spallagrat and Biancograt, as well as such lesser-known peaks as the Rheinwaldhorn and Piz Terri.

As you can see, his climbing was not restricted to the honeypot areas, for he found equal pleasure among the mountains of Ticino, the Glarus and Uri Alps, the Graians, Silvretta and Alpstein massifs. He also climbed in Norway with Fred Jenkins, added Kilimanjaro to his list, went to the Atlas and Corsica with Hamish Brown's parties, and frequently joined Hamish's famous Hogmanay gatherings where he developed a love of Skye and claimed the In Pinn as his first Munro.

Ernst was elected to the Club in 1974 giving a list of his climbs dating from 1963, his proposer being Mike Baker. He became a committee member in 1984 and from 1987-92 edited the *Alpine Journal*. Thanks to his editorship, his net of contacts was cast ever wider, which was a great boon to me when researching a variety of writing projects. Through him a number of mutual friendships developed. Did I need information about the Carpathians or Caucasus? Ernst knew just the man. Norway? Ditto. The Julian Alps? Ernst had a friend in Ljubljana. He'd pick up the telephone or send a note abroad and back would come a response. Everyone wanted to help him.

He was everyone's friend. And his knowledge of mountains worldwide grew, especially the Alps, which he knew so well from the numerous journeys he'd made among them.

Ever inquisitive about the wider world, he loved to travel, and for a year or two after Janet died it seemed he was barely at home. He rode the trans-Siberian railway from Moscow to Vladivostok, visited South Africa and Italy, went to Spitzbergen and Greenland.

Some years earlier he had bought a copy of John Cleare's *Trekking: Great Walks of the World* in which Colin Monteath had contributed a chapter on New Zealand's Routeburn Track. That was it. His appetite was whetted. Ernst being Ernst, he flew to New Zealand, spent four days walking the route in the Southern Alps north-west of Queenstown then flew home again. He was gone for just over a week.

Although we never shared a rope and for the first 20 years of our friendship we never even looked at a mountain together (other than on film, in books or via the thousands of dusty slides projected across his cluttered study), every few weeks throughout the year we'd go walking among the hills of Kent or Sussex. I'd meet him off the train and he'd be on the last carriage, taking forever to make his way along the platform. There'd be a wave of the hand, a bright smile on his face and a rucksack on his back big enough for a month in the Himalaya. What did he have in it? Well, waterproofs, I guess, and a book or two, his camera and a gift for my wife – and his predictable picnic food: it was always boiled eggs and bagels. Then we'd spend the day wandering. Those walks were sedate rambles, for Ernst had – how shall I put it? – an unhurried, thoughtful pace that never varied. Uphill or down. And there were so many distractions: a fox breaking cover, a deer, a rabbit or a squirrel to capture his attention. Most likely it'd be a flower. Ernst loved wild flowers. Especially alpines.

He explained this in an article he wrote for the *Himalayan Journal:* 'As my climbing powers, such as they were, diminish with advancing age, my interests have turned more and more to the mountain flora.' So he became a member of the Alpine Garden Society, and with the expert help of Jeannie Simmons, created a splendid alpine garden on the steep terraces behind his house in Highgate. It attracted visitors from as far away as Japan and Sweden, and for several years he opened it to the public under the National Gardens Scheme. Livia Gollancz, who lived in a house opposite Ernst for half a century – and was no slouch of a gardener herself – would sometimes wander over to offer sage advice.

Combined with his love of mountains, his passion for alpines led to his joining plant-hunting parties to the Spanish Pyrenees and the Picos de Europa. He went to Ireland and Croatia, and my wife and I once accompanied him to Madeira. Most notable were his visits to the Himalaya, to the mountains of Bhutan in 1993 and twice to south-east Tibet, Namche Barwa in the late spring of 1996 and the remote and now forbidden Tsari region three years later.

At the age of 72 on the Namche Barwa trip, he crossed the Doshong La in foul weather and was excited to discover plant hunter Kingdon-Ward's fabled 'daffodil primula' that is endemic there. Once over the pass the rain was relentless, but such was the party's devotion to their task that they continued to botanise regardless. Meanwhile a lot of fresh snow had fallen on the pass. When it was time to return, had it not been for the assistance of his young Tibetan guide, Ernst doubted he would have made it. 'I still wonder,' he wrote some time later, 'what would have happened to me if I got stuck down there on the far side – we had no permission to travel further south, and no provisions either.'

Such concerns soon fade from memory and in 1999 and now 75 years old he returned to Tibet where he fell in love with the rich flora of Tsari. The Tsari valley lies close to the Indian border and, being a politically sensitive area, permission to go there was not easy to obtain. Furthermore, once in Tibet a series of 5,000m passes had to be crossed to reach what Ernst referred to as 'the promised land, with its streams, flowers, forests … [all] framed by mountains – a beautiful place indeed.'

After four nights the party set out for the Bimbi La where they discovered countless alpine gems before descending through hillsides ablaze with yellow and pink rhododendrons, followed by a walk alongside the Bimbi chu where they found clumps of a beautiful blue member of the buttercup family growing among cliffs close to the track.

It was his Himalayan swansong and writing about it later in the *Himalayan Journal,* his sense of wonder and delight shone through. He wrote of Tsari's 'incredible beauty, its gentle, friendly people, the religion which shows no signs of being exterminated and, of course, what we had really come for, the wonderful plants, alpines, rhododendrons and the rest. Those primula meadows below the Bimbi La – can there be anything more beautiful on our planet?'

These are the words of a true enthusiast: a man who lived life at full pitch. A man who loved the wild places in all their rich diversity. And they echo his first editorial for the *AJ* all those years ago:

'Whilst men and women are preoccupied with their puny doings, the hills remain, in their infinite variety and the richness of their offering – if we let them speak to us with humility and a receptive heart.'

Ernst Sondheimer did just that.

Following a botched hospital procedure in 2011 Ernst became virtually housebound but was lovingly cared for by Jan Ronnenbergh heading a team of other helpers. She encouraged his bridge playing and would often take him to the theatre and to Sunday concerts at the Wigmore Hall, feeding his interests and extending his life with a fresh vitality. My wife and I would make regular visits, and the hour we'd spend with him every four or five weeks was guaranteed to be uplifting. Even when his memory had faded to little more than a fog, he was a delight to be with, for he radiated a glow of serenity. Knowing much of his life story, we were able to light some of the dark corners of his mind from which distant climbs, journeys and faces of friends long gone would emerge, if only for a few brief minutes. But those moments were priceless.

Ernst died peacefully on 9 June 2019 at the home in Highgate in which he'd lived for over 60 years. He is survived by son Julian and daughter Judith, three grandchildren and one great grand-daughter.

Kev Reynolds

OFFICERS AND COMMITTEE FOR 2020

PRESIDENT .... Victor Saunders
VICE-PRESIDENTS .... Richard Nadin, Melanie Windridge
HONORARY SECRETARY .... Sherry Macliver
HONORARY TREASURER .... Trevor Campbell Davis
HONORARY EDITOR OF THE *ALPINE JOURNAL* .... Ed Douglas
HONORARY LIBRARIAN .... Barbara Grigor-Taylor
CHAIRS OF SUB-COMMITTEES:
CLIMBING & EVENTS .... Nicholas Hurndall Smith
INFORMATION TECHNOLOGY .... Mike Fletcher[1]
MARKETING, MEMBERSHIP & RECRUITMENT .... Melanie Windridge
CHAIR OF THE ALPINE CLUB LIBRARY COUNCIL .... Philip Meredith
COMMITTEE, *elected* .... Jim Fotheringham, Tom Livingstone,
Chris Martin, Marjan Schoeke
COMMITTEE, *co-opted* .... John Porter

OFFICE BEARERS

MEMBERSHIP SECRETARY .... Sherry Macliver
LONDON LECTURE ORGANISER .... Derek Buckle
SOUTH-WEST LECTURE ORGANISER .... Tony Westcott, Chris Storie
PEAK LECTURE ORGANISER .... Martin Wragg
LAKES LECTURE ORGANISER .... Anna Lawford
EDINBURGH LECTURE ORGANISER .... Tim Elson, Zoe Strong
NORTH WALES LECTURE ORGANISER .... Peter Frost
WINTER DINNER CONVENOR .... William Newsom
CHAIR OF THE CLIMBING FUND SUB-COMMITTEE .... Malcolm Bass
CHAIR OF THE FINANCE SUB-COMMITTEE .... John Dempster
CHAIR OF THE MEMBERSHIP APPLICATIONS SUB-COMMITTEE .. Richard Nadin
CHAIR OF THE PROPERTY SUB-COMMITTEE .... Victor Saunders
STUDENT LIAISON OFFICER .... Richard Ive
UIAA REPRESENTATIVE .... Steve Goodwin
CIRCULATION MANAGER OF THE ENVIRONMENT PANEL .... Ed Douglas
HONORARY LIBRARIAN EMERITUS .... Jerry Lovatt
HONORARY ARCHIVIST .... Glyn Hughes
HONORARY KEEPER OF THE CLUB'S ARTEFACTS .... Nigel Buckley
HONORARY KEEPER OF THE CLUB'S MONUMENTS .... Charlie Burbridge
HONORARY KEEPER OF THE CLUB'S PAINTINGS .... Simon Pierse
HONORARY KEEPER OF THE CLUB'S PHOTOGRAPHS .... Bernie Ingrams
ASSISTANT EDITOR OF THE ALPINE JOURNAL (OBITUARIES) .... Rod Smith
NEWSLETTER EDITOR .... Adele Long
WEBSITE EDITORS .... Jeremy Gould, David Lund
WIRED GUIDEBOOKS REPRESENTATIVE .... Mike Mortimer
OFFICE MANAGER .... Stephen Grey
LIBRARIAN .... Nigel Buckley

ALPINE CLIMBING GROUP

PRESIDENT .... Tom Livingstone
HONORARY SECRETARY .... Tim Elson
COMMITTEE .... Ian Parnell, Paul Ramsden

1. Stepped down from post during year

Alpine Club Notes

Plate 7. *'Bheem ke Udar'*

JOHN PORTER

President's Valedictory Address

Read before the Alpine Club on 30 November, 2019

In the autumn of 2016, Lindsay Griffin phoned to ask if I wanted to be the next president of the Alpine Club. It was one of those 'what me?' moments. I thought about it for a few days. I had my doubts if I was the right person. If even a quarter of my generation had survived our Himalayan exploits, the question would never have come my way. So many talented and able friends back in the 1970s and 1980s were lost, and lost to the Alpine Club: Pete, Paul, Alison, Alex, Roger, Joe, Julie, Pete again, Alan. I do not need to add the surnames. They are remembered.

I say this not for any sentimental reasons, but to remind us that what we 'have' is not our only heritage. What we don't have, yet is well remembered is equally important. In an age of the 'perpetual present' driven by social media, one of the AC's challenges is to provide a filter on what might be important in the future to our members. We could easily lose what we don't have by not making the effort now to record the present. I'll come back to that later.

After the dinner three years ago, my wife Rose happened to be standing with a small group of members when someone asked her: 'do you have any idea who John Porter is?' Had she known then what was to follow, she should have replied: 'I have no idea. But whoever he is, he must be mad to take on this job.'

Yet being the president of the Alpine Club has been an honour, and doubly so since I am the first American in the job. It reminds me that I have been President Porter once before, of the climbing club at the University of Oregon in 1967. The vice president's surname was Coolie. Porter and Coolie, a hardworking pair, like Stupart and Porter over these past three years. Now, many decades later, I find myself on the last stage of a much more complex and important portering role, carrying the ethos and well-being of the world's first and most prestigious climbing club from one point in time to another: from the AGM three years ago to this moment, now.

Stephen Venables warned me that the three-year term falls into three distinct periods: the first year enthusiastically scoping out where the club is at and what is needed; the second year working to put new ideas and plans in place; and the third despairing when all the good intentions seem to lead to nothing. My experience has been a mirror image of Stephen's and a rather dark mirror at times: from despair in the first year to increasingly constructive and positive current happenings and future plans.

Most of my first year was occupied in trying to avoid the club imploding over the BMC question, trying to find a consensus on the role of the Alpine Club. Do we in the 2010s have any responsibility for the direction and management of the BMC, and if so, what is it since the BMC is a wholly separate company with its own objectives? Is the BMC even relevant to the future of the Club and alpinism?

These questions occupied an inordinate amount of my time and that of the AC Committee in meeting after meeting. They were the result of a Motion of No Confidence in the BMC's management lodged by a vociferous group, which included a number of AC members including two ex-presidents. Most AC members stayed neutral and gentlemanly in discussion with the rebels but there was also much emotional debate and the club's image was badly damaged by a few social media trolls. Ignoring valid concerns about the BMC structure and management, many shared internally by the BMC, the trolls described the MONC as an attempted takeover by group of old elitist and colonialist AC members. Some of that stuck and more than a score of members resigned. They were mainly active BMC volunteers who felt the BMC was doing well enough and it was no business of the Alpine Club. At the same time, some senior AC members who had signed the MONC became the target of scurrilous attacks for their views. It was not a happy time.

Endless discussions brought home to me that the clearest message from our members and the AC Committee was that the Club is about climbing, not politics, and that we should focus on what we do best. Regardless of what direction the BMC took, the Alpine Club will still be here in a hundred years' time with a healthy ethos of adventure alpinism. This was confirmed first at an Extraordinary General Meeting in April 2017 at the Club HQ. Increasingly, I was encouraged to take a measured approach in discussions with Club members and yet be proactive in discussions with the BMC on issues of common concern. But the atmosphere remained toxic on social media throughout the year. I found myself embroiled in endless emails and on-line debates that exhibited the same entrenched and ill-informed views that characterised the Brexit debate.

Behind the surface turmoil, senior officers in the Club became critical friends to the BMC. We shared too many common interests not to do so. AC members took part in the BMC's organisational review, providing both welcome and unwelcome analysis and suggestions leading to the proposal for a Tier 1 not Tier 3 affiliation with Sport England. The work of Crag Jones, John Booth and Jonathan White was critical in supporting the importance of members' views. The fact that Jonathan is now a BMC director shows that his work was valued.

Enough said: the BMC review is on going and fraught with uncertainty and knotty issues. The reality is we need the BMC to be our representative body. The wider world of mountain activities is tarnished by competitions, commercial and commodified interests, but that is the world that we as well as the BMC live in. Their priorities inevitably are different from the AC's.

Alpinism is of interest to a tiny percentage of BMC members. Few BMC members have the skills or inclination for alpine adventures. Some even believe adventures can be bought and sold. But all AC members know that the joy of alpinism is taking personal responsibility for the risks that come when playing on rock and ice high up in the sky.

Behind all the BMC hoo-ha, there was much else going on in year one. We recruited our excellent office manager Stephen Grey. His expertise meant that running and managing of our primary asset – Charlotte Road – became much easier. The BMC Young Alpinist Group initiative led by Tom Livingstone and Ian Parnell took root, and discussions began of how we could create pathways to offer wider experience through the AC. Malcolm Bass, Paul Ramsden and Nick Colton were also heavily involved, and during my second year, the Alpine Climbing Group was re-invigorated as one of those pathways. At the same time Nick Smith and his meets team ensured that the aspirant route into the AC, with meets designed to gain skills to become full members, remained the welcoming cornerstone of the Club's attraction for new young members. By my third year the ACG and the mainstream membership approached full integration with some meets between AC and YAG shared.

The most important event during my second year was the strategic weekend held at the Blencathra Centre in November 2018. The impetus for this gathering was in part Mick Fowler's comment in his 2013 valedictory speech: 'the Alpine Club has a habit of re-inventing itself.' To avoid this, the Committee set its sights on preparing the Club for what would be needed when it is 175 years old in 2032. Clearly the issue of climate change will be much more prominent then. Over 80 AC members took part and many others unable to attend contributed their thoughts before and after. We discussed the forward plan for the Club's members' services, Charlotte Road and the operational requirements of the Club and the Alpine Club Library. Building on the achievements of the most recent Committees under Mick and Lindsay Griffin, we felt a written forward plan would help prevent re-invention. This plan will be presented in draft at the January AC Committee in 2020 and distributed for member consideration later that year.

The new structure of the Club approved at the 2019 AGM will help us deliver a wide range of member services including many more meets, better use of the Club's amazing collection both through exhibitions and online, improved communications and access to the wealth of information held by the club. With Nigel Buckley joining the ACL as Librarian, we now have someone as important to the future of the AC Collections as Stephen is to the smooth running of the AC Office.

Some things that have rolled out from Blencathra are already being reported in the newsletters, website and on social media. A new Environmental Panel was set up by Rob Collister and advises and proposes means to minimise our environmental impact. The Montane AC grants panel (along with the MEF and BMC) will be considering how some conditions attached to grants can help expeditions monitor and reduce their environmental and cultural impact.

As we entered 2019, the work of our large and enthusiastic group of volunteers from all age groups and from all parts of the country became more evident in the quality of everything the Club does, from international meets to the expanded regional lectures. Without all the volunteers there would be no activities.

The international activities of the Club have also become more evident. Last year, we held meets with the Poles and the French and in the coming year we have another meet planned with the Marseille section of CAF, the Italian Alpine Club, and the Lecco Spiders with plans for exchanges with the American Alpine Club, other sections of CAI and the Kenyan Mountain Club being discussed. We are supporting the International Scottish Winter meet in February 2020, as we supported the international Rendez-vous Hautes Montagnes in Langdale last summer. While working in India and Korea earlier this year, I met with the Himalayan Club, the Maharashtra Association of Clubs and the Korean Alpine Club. Potential collaborative projects on climbing exchanges, publishing and work with the UIAA are underway. Our presence at the Piolets d'Or continues year on year as climbers and organisers. In 2018, the AC Spirit of Mountaineering panel recognised Polish climbers for their role in the winter rescue of Elizabeth Revol, and the pilots of the Pakistani Fearless 5 Squadron for their part not only for the Nanga Parbat rescue but in several other dramatic rescues in the past two years, four involving AC members.

Now back to the future: Mt Everest. Our honorary secretary Charles says the Club's international esteem allows us 'to punch above our weight.' Here is an example. Over the past few years the office received an increasing number of questions from the media regarding accidents on Everest. They assumed that the AC would be involved or provide an answer. We had a stock statement to the effect: 'not me guv'. But that is not good enough given the Club's long association with Everest and Nepal.

To answer the question 'What is happening?' and propose solutions, we first had to recognise all the underlying causes. Doug Scott led the way with his statement in Kathmandu in June. Building on that, Ed Douglas and I gathered in opinions from many climbers and organisations that know Nepal well and understand the interlocking complexity of the situation. We have written a set of proposals based on a sense of a duty of care both to the legacy of Everest and to Nepal as a whole. Now completed, it covers a range of things that need to be addressed: from workers' rights to helicopter scams, from guiding standards to freedom of access, and a need to deal with some clear examples of corruption.

Fortunately, the BMC supported the proposals through their International Committee and helped gain the support of the UIAA and in turn the IFMGA. Even the Nepal Mountaineering Association voted in favour of the proposals at the UIAA Congress at the beginning of November 2019. With the BMC and with the signatures of the UIAA and IFMGA, the proposals were lodged with the Nepal Ministry of Tourism. It was heartening to receive votes of thanks to the AC from clubs and federations from around the world. The proposals will need to be resourced and agencies will have to come on side to agree standards of safety and management. We expect it will take a generation for results. Time is always on the AC's side.

And what is the ethos of the AC? For me it is quite simple. It is the knowledge gained through the exploration of high places and the connections that can be made with people, places and the unknown, both within and without during our short existence. How we share this becomes our heritage, reflected in the writing, paintings, philosophical musings and photographs of our members from 1857 until this moment. But how do we filter what is important for the future from the thousands of weekly instagrams and tweets, and chaotic commercial mountain festivals like Kendal? We have to take part, and that is what our younger members in particular are doing well.

Mountain adventure is being squeezed at both ends of our commodified sport, at one end by gymnastic competitions, now in the Olympics, and at the other, by the equivalent of a Bob Graham Round of the 8,000ers completed by Nims in just 190 days a few weeks ago. We recognise the incredible athleticism and stamina involved in these activities, but I'd like to think that alpinism is more than just a sport, and that climbing an 8,000er is more than an ultra-marathon or a high-hazard industry, which is what Everest tourism has become. Within the mountain world, there are physically still more unclimbed 6,000m peaks than those that have been climbed, and for those taking part, many more adventures taking place than we know about.

Coming together as members, to climb together and share stories, we are part of the filter that adds value to an activity that many might say is useless or of value only on a resumé. As Paul Nunn once said, 'the most important aspect of climbing is taking responsibility for putting one foot in front of another for as long as you are able knowing that you will still be responsible for each step when and if you return.' And as a goal for 2032, I quote another old friend Roger Baxter Jones who advised us all to 'a: come back, b: come back friends, and c: get to the top, in that order.' Perhaps now we should add one thing more: 'give something back.'

I started by saying that as a porter I had a load to carry but during my stint as president I have been one of many in a long line who contributed to the wellbeing of the Club over the last three years. In particular, I thank Charles Stupart our honorary secretary for his incredible work to ensure we are compliant with regulations, from databases to meets guidelines, and to Sherry MacIver his deputy who takes over in the New Year. Rob Collister steps down as vice president this year but will remain active on the Environment Panel. Richard Nadin takes his place. Richard also heads the panel that vets new members. I am pleased to say that despite those resignations I mentioned as a result of the BMC feud, and the inevitable loss of members to time, we have a small net gain in member numbers over the past three years. I have already mentioned Nick Smith, but if you have been on the meets, you will know what a great job Kate Ross, Tim Elson, Giles Roberson, Paul MacWhinney and the other meet co-ordinators have done.

Philip Meredith and the other ACL trustees, whose excellent annual reports today illustrates how the ACL and AC objectives have come together over the past two years, has been ably assisted by Barbara Grigor-Taylor. Thanks to the contributions from the rest of the Committee, to Melanie Windridge, Marjan Schoeke and Ed Douglas for their social media development. And finally, to the finance team, to John Dempster as chair of the Finance Subcommittee and to our honorary treasurer Trevor Campbell Davis for very sage advice over the past three years, and for keeping us financially in a strong position. And now we welcome Victor Saunders as our new president, who not only is a brilliant climber and the Club's first British mountain guide president, but who also knows what it means to carry heavy loads over long distances. You have a great team to work with on the route forward.

The Rendez-vous Hautes Montagne Visits Langdale

In 1967, Baroness Felicitas von Reznicek's book *Von der Krinoline zum sechsten Grad* ('From the Crinoline to the 6th Grade) was published. In it she describes the history of female mountaineering. A year later, in May 1968 the baroness decided to organize a unique women's mountaineering meeting at Engelberg, Switzerland for the purpose of 'mutual learning'. It was a success, with seventy mountaineers and climbers from different countries climbing together for a week. At this meet the Rendez-Vous Hautes Montagnes was born and since then women mountaineers and climbers from many countries have met at least once a year in different mountain places to share friendship, enthusiasm and climbing together. The 61st Meet of the Rendez-vous Hautes Montagnes (RHM) was held in Great Langdale from 13 to 21 July 2019.

One of the purposes of the meets was, through official invitations, to allow female climbers from eastern bloc countries to make trips to the west, something they may not otherwise have been allowed to do at that time. Each participating country had a representative, whose task was to pass the word around about forthcoming meets. In the eastern bloc, the representative sometimes had the job of selecting the climbers to come on the meet. The RHM then and now has never been a club but rather a network of female climbers with representatives helping to spread the word about the opportunity to join up with other women climbers.

I first heard about the RHM in 1979 when a friend showed me a small entry in an Alpine Club newsletter. It invited women climbers who led grade IV to join other female alpinists at the 11th meet of the RHM held that year at Serre Chevalier, France. My first climbing trip to the Alps had been just the year before and having led IV+ I hoped to meet the standard required. I wrote to the French organiser, Mirielle Marks, to ask if I might come along. I received a warm reply in which she said I was the first British girl to be going for a long time and that Baroness Felicitas, now the president of the RHM, would be pleased about that.

I was privileged to meet well-known French climbers like Loulou Boulaz, Jeanne Franco, Suzy Peguy, Christine de Colombel and Simone Badier, and also Wanda Rutkiewicz from Poland, the first woman to climb K2. This meet had taken Mireille Marks a whole year to organise and involved all sorts of grand receptions, a final banquet and lots of climbing on the mountain peaks of the Dauphiné.

I've attended many RHM meets since then: several in Switzerland at Handegg, Meiringen, Goschenen, Melchsee; in former Yugoslavia at Paklenica; in the Tatra mountains of Slovakia; two in the Czech Republic; and in Sardinia, to name a few. The ranks of Britons attending grew year on year and we were able to host a successful meet in north Wales in 1989. Since then there have been three more summer RHMs in the UK, including the 2019 Langdale meet. There are now also annual ice-climbing and ski-mountaineering meets in other parts of Europe. The summer meets are now often in sport-climbing venues, although the Langdale meet was, of course, traditional.

Charlotte Steinmeier (Germany) topping out on Raven Crag, Langdale.
(Cathy Woodhead)

There are other changes. The pomp and ceremony of the early meets has gone to a large extent, the Internet has made communication far easier for everyone, the English language has also become much more widespread and there is no longer a problem for climbers from the old eastern bloc to visit western Europe. But its essence, of women mountaineers and climbers of many countries meeting in different mountain places to share friendship and enthusiasm climbing together, continues unabated.

The 61st meeting was based at the National Trust campsite in Great Langdale and the meet was a huge success, thanks to the hard work of organisers Stella Adams, Jo Barnes, Fiona Sanders and Rya Tibawi, and many others. The week started officially with a welcome reception. Information was provided on the main climbing areas, and thanks to the FRCC, guidebooks were available to buy at a discounted price. Along with other clubs the Alpine Club had kindly donated money towards the costs of the meet, which included the hire of a marquee, the purchase of special t-shirts (this year red with the RHM logo with the place and year of the meet) and food and drinks for the reception. Anna Lawford of the AC, Lynn Robinson, president of the BMC, Vic Odell, president of the CC and Nina Stirrup of FRCC all attended the reception as representatives. The Pinnacle Club, which was also a sponsor, was well represented amongst the UK women present.

About 70 women attended all or part of the meet with the youngest participant being only four months and the oldest aged 92. There were women from Germany, Switzerland, Italy, Austria and the Czech Republic

RHM participants on the final evening at Sticklebarn, Langdale. *(Keith Sanders)*

and over 40 attending from all over the UK. Regulars from other countries exhorted all these new attendees to make the effort to travel to future RHM meets outside the UK promising the same warm welcome they themselves received in Langdale. Climbing partnerships were made daily. Crags climbed on during the week included Gimmer, Pavey Ark, Dow, Bowfell, Raven, Kettle, and Long Scar. For many attendees it was their first experience of traditional climbing. The weather was typical of the Lakes with good weather for the first four and a half days followed by lengthy downpours of rain during which we explored Cathedral Cavern in Little Langdale, went to Kendal Climbing Wall, or travelled out of the Lakes to find dry climbing opportunities. Even when it rained spirits were high and Mandy Glanvill introduced our visitors to the delights of scrambling up greasy, mossy, water courses: a great hit. Anne Salisbury did some belaying instruction, which was very helpful for those who were not confident about climbing purely on trad gear.

There was a buzz, energy, enthusiasm and a sense of fun throughout the meet and the final evening was no exception as we gathered for a final dinner at the Sticklebarn, where the venue for next year's meet was announced. It will be in Slovenia in July 2020 and, of course, all women climbers will be welcome. See *https://www.rhm-climbing.net/* for more information.

Cathy Woodhead

Catherine Destivelle, awarded the 12th lifetime achievement award from the Piolets d'Or, on Shishapangma in 1994. *(Érik Decamp)*

Piolets d'Or 2020

Once again made at the Ladek Mountain Festival in Poland, this year celebrating its 25th anniversary, four outstanding ascents from 2019 were awarded a Piolet d'Or. The year 2019 turned out to be a very rich one, with a substantial number of significant first ascents from all over the globe. The protagonists were alpinists of wide diversity. There were notable ascents by the 'old guard' of highly experienced high-altitude climbers, but also fine achievements by a promising new generation of 'young guns'. The eight-member international technical jury had the difficult task of making a choice, the intention being not to discard any remarkable climbs, but to choose a few significant ascents as emblematic of modern, alpine-style mountaineering. In the end the jury chose what they believed to be a consistent selection of four climbs.

The four ascents comprise two from Nepal and two from Pakistan. Most had seen previous attempts and were on the radar of number of strong parties. All climbed to rarely visited, or in one case virgin summits. They include, in no particular order, the north-west face and traverse of Chamlang (7321m), climbed between 17 and 23 May by Marek Holeček and Zdeněk Hák from the Czech Republic. When Holeček and Zdeněk Hák arrived in Nepal, it was obvious the face had little snow and a lot of hard water ice. Outflanking objective dangers in the lower section would prove to be one of the keys. From a bivouac at 5,300m on the glacier below the face the two Czechs headed up more or less directly below the summit. On the fourth day they reached the upper east ridge and bivouacked 80m below the top. On 21 May they crossed the summit and spent the rest of the day trying to navigate the original *Japanese* route on the south ridge. This proved more

The Czech route *UFO* on the north-west face of Chamlang.

difficult than expected. Two more bivouacs without food and difficult down climbing and rappelling in often poor visibility were needed to reach the valley. The route was named *UFO* (2,000m, WI5, M6) as a tribute to Reinhold Messner and Doug Scott, who in 1981, with Sherpas Ang Dorje and Pasang, were the first to climb on the north side of the Chamlang massif to reach one of the middle summits. The pair was puzzled to see a box-like object hovering above them and shining in the midday sun.

Alan Rousseau and Tino Villanueva climbed the west face of Tengi Ragi Tau (6938m), starting from a glacier camp below the face on 13 October and returning on 17 October. In 2012, on their first expedition to the Himalaya, Rousseau and Villanueva made the first ascent of Langmoche Ri on the north ridge of Tengi Ragi Tau in Nepal's Rolwaling. Walking below the west face of Tengi Ragi Tau they were mesmerised by its sheer magnitude and fine ice runnels through beautiful granite. They returned in 2014 to attempt a direct line, climbing to around 6,500m in less than ideal weather before retreating. Five years on and the face had attracted the attention of several strong parties. After crossing the Tashi Laptsa pass and camping on the Drolambo glacier, the two Americans climbed the initial dry-tooling pitches to access the snowy face and then made three bivouacs before reaching the summit. A tricky rappel descent was made down the line of ascent. With a multi-pitch ice crux high on the route, followed by steep flutings of unprotectable snow, this technical and elegant line on one of the most outstanding unclimbed faces of the Rolwaling was just reward for the perseverance of these two experienced alpine guides. They called their route *Release the Kraken* (1,600m, AI5 M5+). Their ascent was only the second of this difficult mountain and the first in alpine style.

Another American team comprising Mark Richey, Steven Swenson, Chris Wright and Graham Zimmerman made the first ascent of Link Sar (7041m) in east Pakistan, another much coveted objective and reported on at length elsewhere in this edition of the *Alpine Journal*. Finally, the Japanese team of Kazuya Hiraide and Kenro Nakajima climbed the south face and south-east ridge of Rakaposhi (7788m), more than 4,000m from base camp, starting on 27 June and returning on 3 July. Whilst the south side of the mountain, leading to the crest of the great south-east ridge, had been reconnoitred in the past, it remained untouched with climbers unable to find a feasible route. An ascent from this less visible side of the mountain would be highly exploratory. From a 3,660m base camp at the snout of the glacier, and in generally unstable weather, Kazuya Hiraide and Kenro Nakajima climbed

The Japanese route on Rakaposhi.

the south face to 6,100m, both to acclimatise and confirm that their chosen line would go. On their second outing they took three days, strenuously climbing through often deep soft snow, to reach a camp at 6,800m on the south-east ridge, where they were forced to wait two days in bad weather. After this they climbed to the summit and back in a single long day, and on the following reversed their line of ascent all the way down to base camp. Although the route does not feature the high technical difficulties of the three other awarded ascents, its huge length, and the commitment and style of Hiraide and Nakajima's determined ascent on a rarely climbed mountain, makes it of equal merit for a 2020 Piolet d'Or.

Announcing this year's Piolets d'Or, the organisers took the opportunity to acknowledge the passing of Jan Kiełkowski, one of the world's great chroniclers of alpinism, and author of many guidebooks to the Greater Ranges. His death on 5 April 2020 was a shock to the Polish mountaineering community but poorly publicised outside his home country. Born in 1943, Kiełkowski was a talented alpinist, with many new lines in the Polish Tatras. He created six new routes on Kazalnica, the highest wall of the Tatras, more than any other individual climber. He also climbed in the Cordillera Huayhuash, Caucasus, Pamir, Hindu Kush and Himalaya. But his biggest contribution to world climbing was his documentary work. Starting with *Mount Everest Massif* in 1985, he published over 20 guidebooks for alpinists on areas of the Himalaya, Karakoram and Andes, including 11 volumes of the well-known 'Mountaineering Series' between 1995 and 2015.

Together with his wife Małgorzata he was the main editor and co-author of seven volumes of *Wielka Encyklopedia Gór i Alpinizmu* (Great Encyclopaedia of Mountains and Alpinism), published from 2013 to 2017. This work, currently only available in Polish, is the world's biggest resource of its type.

The 12th Walter Bonatti Piolets d'Or Lifetime Achievement Award was presented to Catherine Destivelle. Destivelle started making a name for herself in the climbing world during the 1980s, at a time when sport climbing was exploding in popularity and grades were rising rapidly. Shortly after discovering climbing at Fontainebleau at the age of 12, Destivelle was tackling big routes in the Mont Blanc massif. However, by the mid 1980s she was participating in sport-climbing competitions and her success in these, and the fact she became the first woman to redpoint 8a, turned her into a rock-climbing star. Few people knew that as a teenager she climbed some of the biggest routes in the Alps. In 1990, the rock star made her mountain comeback with an impressive solo ascent of the *Bonatti* on the Petit Dru. This finally gained her recognition as an alpinist. She went on to put up her own new route on the west face of the Petit Dru over 11 days, before completing a solo winter trilogy: the north face of the Eiger in 1992, the Walker spur on the north face of the Grandes Jorasses in 1993, and the *Bonatti* route on the north face of the Matterhorn in 1994. The latter is still rarely climbed today. It was her second big Bonatti route and the first time a woman had climbed at such a high standard in the Alps. Catherine didn't just want to be known as an accomplished female climber, she wanted her performances to be measured against those of any alpinist, no matter their gender.

Alpine Club Library Report 2019

Hywel Lloyd retired as chair of the Library Council and as a Library trustee at the 2018 AGM after 13 years at the helm. The volunteers' party last December provided a fitting opportunity to celebrate Hywel's outstanding work for the Library and the Club over many years. Vice president Steve Goodwin presented Hywel with an engraved plaque on behalf of the AC, while Philip Meredith presented him with a framed and inscribed print on behalf of the ACL. This is therefore my first annual report. Happily, there are plenty of positive activities to report and there have been plenty of positive folk to help out.

Because I was elected as new chair of Council to replace Hywel, we needed a new ACL Council secretary, and I am delighted to report that Nigel Buckley, our professional librarian, was appointed to that role at the beginning of the year. Since Nigel is also the new keeper of artefacts he is going to be kept very busy. Peter Rowland stepped down as keeper of photographs in the spring after eight years in that post. We thank Peter for all his efforts in improving and enhancing the photograph collection, photographing much of the artefact collection and for driving forward the digitisation programme. Peter is ably succeeded as keeper by Bernie Ingrams. Bernie has been involved with the photograph collection for many years, and especially with the digitisation programme, so I am sure we can look forward to continuity and a smooth transition.

In this year of change, John Fairley also stepped down as keeper of pictures, again after eight years in charge. John transformed the storage of the picture collection, completely replaced the hanging system in the lecture room to a modern and adaptable system, and oversaw the selection and conservation of the more than 80 pictures loaned to Chamonix for the fantastically successful exhibition celebrating the 150th anniversary of the 'Golden Age of Alpinism' in 2015. We are delighted that the AC has appointed Simon Pierse as the new keeper of pictures; Simon is an acclaimed artist and senior lecturer emeritus in fine art at Aberystwyth University. He is a member and former vice-president of the Royal Watercolour Society and a fellow of the Royal Society of Arts. Notable amongst his many publications is *Kangchenjunga: Imaging a Himalayan Mountain,* jointly published by the Alpine Club and with a foreword by George Band. I think it is fair to say that responsibility for the picture collection will remain in safe hands for the foreseeable future. In a further enhancement to the custodianship of the pictures, the Club has appointed Janet Johnson as assistant keeper of pictures. Janet is also a well-known artist, and she has already taken on responsibility for the hanging of all exhibitions in the Clubhouse lecture room and for liaison with Art UK, more of which later. We warmly welcome Janet to the team.

As part of the ACL's regulations, we have to rotate three trustees off the Council each year although they are eligible for re-appointment. We are pleased to record that Jerry Lovatt and Philip Meredith have been re-appointed as trustees by the AC, and that Kimball Morrison has been re-appointed by the BMC as its trustee.

Last year we reported on a major step forward in updating the Library structure to meet the original intention when it was established in its present form in 1971, by the appointment of ACL members. In addition to all the keepers, assistant keepers and the honorary archivist, the AC Committee has also nominated Sue Hare, Hywel Lloyd, John Porter and Peter Payne as members, and these have all been ratified by the ACL Council. The Library very much welcomes this development and the new members. Now that all AC keepers are also all ACL members, we can look forward to an age of smooth and seamless custodianship of the Club's heritage collections.

The New Alpine Club Library Catalogue

Not everyone is aware that the Library is much more than books. Library is used as a catch-all, since the Library actually houses and takes responsibility for all the AC and ACL collections, comprising over 30,000 books, magazines, journals and expedition reports, 40,000 photographs and slides, around 700 paintings, prints and drawings, the Alpine Club document archive and the collection of around 300 historical artefacts. Highlights include Maurice Wilson's diary, George Band's 1953 Everest diaries, Michel Paccard's notebook, and much more. There are 1,500 Mount Everest Foundation (MEF) reports on the database; most are currently available to download, and the remaining few will be added shortly. *Alpine Journals* from 1930-2018 can now also be accessed online.

Over the past year, Nigel Buckley has been working tirelessly to implement the Koha cataloguing system to replace our obsolescent AdLib cataloguing software. Koha provides a fully integrated system that can incorporate images in each library record. It enables cross-referencing between all items in the database and thus allows a much simpler and user-friendly search facility. The first implementation of the system is now live, and you can search it all in the new library catalogue available on the Library page of the Club's website at: *http://www.alpine-club.org.uk/ac2/ac-media/library.*

Pre-Meet Planning
Nigel Buckley has started a new section of our guidebook collection in the Library specifically targeted to support the club's climbing meets. These will be available to borrow and use as regular ACL loans. If any member wants to use the Library and its resources to organise a pre-meet planning session, please feel free to contact Nigel, who will make relevant maps, guidebooks and reports available .

Art UK
The AC is now a member of Art UK, a cultural education charity that allows online access to virtually every public art collection in the UK. These artworks are housed in museums, universities, town halls, hospitals and other civic buildings across the country, and over 80% are not normally on public view. As an initial step, the ACL has put 70 of the finest pictures from the AC collection online through Art UK, with more to follow. In addition to viewing the pictures, with their associated metadata, prints can be purchased in a range of sizes and for modest prices from the Art UK shop. This will not only provide a resource for members but also a source of income for the ACL to use for restoration purposes. Visit *https://artuk.org* for more details, to view the pictures and to purchase prints.

Fundraising Strategy
The ACL relies greatly on financial donations and legacies, as well as gifts of books, photographs, pictures and artefacts. The honorary librarian, Barbara Grigor-Taylor, issues lists of donated duplicate books for sale to members, raising a significant annual sum to help support Library activities. Additionally, the Library is always seeking to identify possible external sources of funding to support its work and activities in an increasing competitive world. This activity has been significantly enhanced through a very generous, anonymous donation from a senior AC member that has allowed us to increase Nigel's hours to five days per week, with the extra day focussed on increasing external support.

A fundraising strategy has been developed and approved by the Library Council, and there have already been some successes. In August, the Library won a TownsWeb Archiving Digitisation Grant (£3,000 worth of services) for a project to digitise important archival collections, including: Alpine Club Committee minutes (1857 onwards); Alpine Club qualification papers;

Ruskin's watercolour 'Vevey, Sunrise', part of the highly successful exhibition 'John Ruskin: The Power of Seeing'.

The art of Riccarda de Eccher.

From the Simon Pierse exhibition. Pierse is the Club's new keeper of pictures.

Alpine Climbing Group qualification papers; Ladies' Alpine Club minutes (1907-75); and Ladies' Alpine Club membership records. This material is unique to our collection, and not available elsewhere. We propose both to digitise the material and to catalogue it at a granular level, making these historic papers much more accessible. The official papers of the Alpine Club receive a lot of demand for use, and this project will allow digital facsimiles to be made available online via our recently launched public catalogue. Earlier in the year, we also made a successful application to the Sporting Heritage and Armed Forces Digitisation Project to scan and catalogue our Everest archives. In this bid, we highlighted both the extent of our material and the high number of Everest team members from 1921-53 who had served in the armed forces.

Visitors and Enquiries
It has been another busy year for visitors and enquiries, with 209 people visiting the Library and 205 research enquiries received and answered via email. Highlights included a visit by Lynn Robinson, BMC president and an exhibition and talk by Nigel and Barbara to sixth form students studying German at St Paul's Girls' School reading Harrer's *Die Weisse Spinne.* An exhibition of documents and artefacts on mountain medicine covering mountain sickness (Longstaff, 1906), nutrition on Everest (Warren, Humphreys, 1933-6) and oxygen on Everest and Kangchenjunga (Pugh, Ward, 1936-55) was received with amazement by a group of visitors from the Royal College of Nursing. Nigel had a surprise visit in November by designers from Adidas, whose design team was in London and interested in old mountain clothing: how it was designed and made, if it was effective, and if Adidas could learn from

that and inform their future designs for its clothing range. The item most inspired them was Frank Smythe's cotton cagoule used on Everest in 1936. After showing them other clothing from our collection, Nigel gave them a tour and showed some highlights from the rest of the collections.

Exhibitions
A highlight of the year was the exhibition 'John Ruskin: The Power of Seeing', held at Two Temple Place in London from January to April to mark the bicentenary of the birth of John Ruskin in 1819. Four of Ruskin's painting from the AC and ACL collections were exhibited, including the watercolour 'Vevey, Sunrise', which was also selected as the image for the 2019 AC Christmas card. The exhibition received rave reviews, and subsequently moved to the Millennium Gallery in Sheffield as 'John Ruskin: Art & Wonder', from May to September. I am happy to report that all our Ruskin paintings have now been safely returned to Charlotte Road.

During the year, John Fairley and Janet Johnson organized a number of exhibitions in the lecture room. These included 'Montagna: the Art of Riccarda de Eccher', an exhibition by Simon Pierse, our new keeper of pictures, entitled 'Icebergs & Northern Lights', and an exhibition of acrylic and mixed media paintings and charcoal drawings, 'Amongst the 4000ers', by Barbara Swindin, author of *All But One,* her memoir about her quest to climb the 52 highest mountains in the Alps.

Nigel also curated an exhibition of library and archive material in the lecture room related to the Victorian scientist, mountaineer and intellectual John Tyndall, to coincide with Roland Jackson's lecture, based on his biography *The Ascent of John Tyndall,* published in 2018.

Collections
The ACL is an active library and not a book museum, so we aim to enhance the collection with all interesting new books on climbing and mountaineering. Nigel has made an outstanding effort with publishers to obtain complimentary copies of most newly published books, and has also worked successfully to upgrade the guidebooks section. All of this requires extra space. So, a major effort has therefore been made during the year, led by Barbara and Nigel, to dispose of unwanted material (mostly old magazines and old furniture) to tidy up the basement and create more and better storage space. Barbara has overseen the use of the Chorley bequest to repair and conserve a number of valuable books, archive material and unframed artwork. She and Richard Nadin completed the first comprehensive valuation of all AC Collections and, with volunteers, Barbara has also undertaken a total inventory of all books in the Library, recording donors' names and authors' inscriptions, which are being recorded in the Library catalogue.

Pictures
In addition to the exhibitions listed above, John Fairley organised an exhibition of material from our own collections in Spring 2019, entitled 'Alpine Club

The meeting at the Gorphwysfa Hotel at Pen-y-Pass in 1913 from the Club's newly conserved scrapbooks.

The plaque to Maurice Simond outside the Bar National.

Collection: Paintings and Artefacts from the Golden Age of Alpinism'. A major activity during the year has been selecting the initial 70 pictures to be put online through Art UK, and ensuring that we had high-resolution digital images to make available through the Art UK shop. In this initial phase, we selected only pictures by artists who have been deceased for over 70 years so that all the images are out of copyright.

The new keeper of pictures is in the process of listing his picture conservation priorities for the coming year. Repair of around 60 damaged frames will be started, and improvements to the storage of the paintings will be made so that they are less prone to damage in the future.

Photographs

Sally Westmacott has donated four boxes of Mike Westmacott's lecture slides of the following expeditions: 1953 Everest; 1956 Huaguruncho, Peru; 1964 Arrigetch in the Brooks Range, Alaska; and 1968 Hindu Kush. Peter Payne has finished scanning the best of Frank Smythe's 35mm slides: a quite daunting task.

After a lot of work, a large number of images from the photo collection are now available to members. Notable amongst these are: the Harish Kapadia collection, comprising 1,700 images and a catalogue; the Tom Nakamura 'Himalayan Flight' collection of 78 images with a catalogue; and the Sella portfolio of 50 images and a catalogue. The first two collections will be particularly interesting to members who are planning climbs in the Himalaya, as well as researchers. The Sella collection includes images rarely seen before, and shows the Alps and alpinism as it was in the 1890s.

Artefacts

We expect to complete the task of photographing the entire artefact collection during the coming year. Over the summer, Nigel made a great effort to improve the storage of the club's artefacts. Archival storage boxes have been bought for clothing and ropes, and a new ice axe storage rack has been built to provide better storage for the historical ice-axe collection; each axe now has a permanent storage location and they are all catalogued. This also makes retrieval much easier.

Archives

Alfred Wills' diaries and letters have been given into our care, comprising some 28 volumes of unique and historically important material. Not surprisingly, these have attracted much attention, not least from members of the Wills and Norton families, and from Roland Jackson, the biographer of John Tyndall, who is interested in correspondence between Tyndall and Wills.

During the year, we purchased Simon Pierre Benoit's guide carnet of 1863-74. Many of Benoit's clients were members of the AC. We now have 50 original guides carnets, but this is the first addition to that collection since 1950. This purchase has made us more aware of the value of carnets as primary sources of information on early Alpine climbing. They are already listed in the online catalogue, but that only records the guides' names and dates of ascents. There is no information on the clients and the routes that they climbed. Honorary archivist Glyn Hughes has therefore made a start on extending the catalogue to include this extra information.

Unusually, we own two copies of the scrapbooks that record the gatherings organised by Geoffrey Winthrop Young at the Gorphwysfa Hotel, Pen-y-Pass, between 1896 and 1947, but they were in poor condition. We have therefore commissioned Museum Conservation Services of Duxford to clean and flatten one set using their humidification chamber. They also photographed all the individual sheets and provided us with digital copies. Our binder, Cyril Titus, has now been asked to make a set of special conservation-grade storage boxes to hold them and keep them flat.

Monuments

Charlie Burbridge, keeper of monuments, visited the Hinchcliffe memorial on Riffelalp whilst attending the aspirants meet in August and reports that it is in good condition but no longer enjoys a commanding view of the Matterhorn because it is now obscured by trees. An attempt will be made to see if these trees can be removed. He also visited the plaque to Clinton Dent on the wall of the Britannia hut. This is not an official AC monument, but the AC contributed to the cost of the construction of the Brittannia hut along with the LAC and the ABMSAC, hence the name of the hut. The existence of the plaque is not common knowledge and the hut staff needed an extensive search to find it, but it is in good condition.

Finally, Charlie also arranged for the Maurice Simond memorial plaque on the outside wall of the Bar National in Chamonix to be cleaned. This is also not an official AC monument, but its erection was arranged by former AC president Tut Braithwaite. Furthermore, since the AC is the main body that represents British alpinism, it was felt that we should contribute to its upkeep. This amounts simply to elbow grease and Brasso.

Finally, I cannot end this report without expressing gratitude to everyone in the Library team and to all the volunteers who gave their time so ungrudgingly throughout the year. Without your efforts the ACL could not function. Thank you.

Philip Meredith

Boardman Tasker Award 2019

This year the award resulted in 32 entries from five countries: the UK, USA, Canada, Italy and New Zealand. Continuing the high number of submissions, this is the fifth year in a row we have had more than 30 entries. The 2019 Judges were Roger Hubank, Katie Ives and Tony Shaw. They produced a shortlist of six authors: Mick Fowler for *No Easy Way* (Vertebrate Publishing); Kate Harris for *Lands of Lost Borders* (Dey Street Books); Geoff Powter for *Inner Ranges* (Rocky Mountain Books); David Smart for *Paul Preuss* (Rocky Mountain Books); Jeff Smoot for *Hangdog Days* (Mountaineers Books); David Wilson for *The Equilibrium Line* (The Poetry Business).

The Award was presented at the Kendal Mountain Festival with Stephen Venables interviewing all the authors. Readings were taken from all six books and were warmly received by a large audience. The chair of judges Roger Hubank gave an extensive speech outlining the merits of the shortlisted books and then announced 2019's winner as Kate Harris for *Lands of Lost Borders,* a gripping account of an epic journey made by the writer and her partner following the Silk Road through many different countries. Hubank said:

> Readers of mountain books of my generation were brought up on the great epics: the Germans and Austrians on Nanga Parbat, the French on Annapurna, the Americans on K2, the Brits on Everest. Lands of Lost Borders, which has nothing to do with the 8,000m peaks, nevertheless reads like an expedition epic. It offers a gripping account of a challenging journey, fraught with many difficulties and dangers, following the old Silk Road. Each day a plunge into the unknown. As one of my fellow judges said, 'The writing is suffused throughout with a sense of exuberance and joy in the present moment, and illuminated with such keen-eyed observations that its images linger long in the readers imagination.'
>
> I myself was put in mind again and again, of the question put by the great 19th century explorer Sir Martin Conway: 'What truth is it lies behind those mountain walls that is a lie here in the world beyond?' Certainly Land of Lost Borders might very well, in the words of the rubric, 'Challenge and inspire readers to look at the world in a different way.' It is truly a life-affirming book.

Full details of all submissions, the shortlist and of the event including film of Roger Hubank's speech are available at *www.boardmantasker.com.*

Steve Dean

Contributors

Plate 19. *'Byramghattee [Bhaironghati]'*

Contributors

ROBIN CAMPBELL has held every office in the Scottish Mountaineering Club for which administrative competence is not required, including a long stint as editor in the 1960s and 1970s, and as archivist since 1997. Retired from a desultory career as an academic child psychologist, he now wastes his time and money in collecting and studying old drawings and watercolours, particularly those depicting mountains before they were trampled into familiarity by the boots of mountaineers.

JOHN CLEARE has been a freelance professional photographer for over 50 years but a climber for rather longer. Business and many expeditions have taken him all over the world, while he has several dozen books, several films and live TV broadcasts, more than a few new routes and several virgin summits to his credit. An ex-vice president of the AC and an ex-president of the Alpine Ski Club, he lives in remote Wiltshire.

ROB COLLISTER is a retired mountain guide who lives on the edge of the Carneddau in north Wales but still enjoys leading ski tours in the Alps. PETER FOSTER is a retired consultant physician. He has been a member of the Alpine Club since 1975. His biography of T Graham Brown was published in January 2019.

MICK FOWLER worked for Her Majesty's Revenue and Customs, injecting as much memorable adventure and excitement into his climbing holidays. He has climbed extensively in the UK and led expeditions to the Greater Ranges for three decades. He has written two books, *Vertical Pleasure* (1995) and *On Thin Ice* (2005). Mick served as president of the Alpine Club from 2010.

TERRY GIFFORD was director of the annual International Festival of Mountaineering Literature for 21 years. Former chair of the Mountain Heritage Trust, he is the author of *The Joy of Climbing* (Whittles, 2004) and *Al Otro Lado del Aguilar* (Oversteps Books, 2011). Visiting professor at Bath Spa University's Centre for Writing and Environment and *profesor honorífico* at the University of Alicante, he celebrated his 70th birthday appropriately on *Wreckers' Slab*.

JERRY GORE was a Royal Marines officer and is now a businessman and expedition mountaineer. Jerry was diagnosed as a type-1 insulin-dependent diabetic in 2001. Each year he organises mountain challenges like the Eiger climb included in this year's *Journal,* to raise monies for his charity Action4Diabetics.org (A4D) to help young people with diabetes in emerging countries across south-east Asia.

DENNIS GRAY started climbing on Yorkshire gritstone in 1947. Secretary of the ACG, first national officer, then general secretary of the BMC, Dennis has visited over 60 countries, most recently travelling widely in China. He has written two autobiographies, two books of stories, a novel and a volume of poetry, plays the banjo and sings on three CDs of climbing themed songs.

JIM GREGSON has climbed widely in the Alps since 1972. He is also a telemark ski mountaineer who makes regular trips to Norway. He first visited the Arctic in1991 and has returned many times, often as an expedition leader, and is one of Britain's leading Arctic mountaineers. His book *Exploring Greenland* documents many of his trips and showcases his photography.

LINDSAY GRIFFIN lives in North Wales, from where he continues to report on developments in world mountaineering. An enthusiastic mind still tries to coax a less than enthusiastic body up pleasant bits of rock and ice, both at home and abroad. He remains the world's leading chronicler of mountaineering achievement.

DAVID HAMILTON has been a leading high altitude guide and expedition leader for more than 30 years with numerous successful ascents of 7000m and 8000m peaks. When not working in the greater ranges he has a passion for long European ski journeys, and aims to be the first person to make complete ski crossings of the Alps, Pyrenees and the mountains of Scandinavia.

MATT HELLIKER grew up in south-west England, discovering his passion for climbing on sea cliffs and at Cheddar Gorge before discovering mixed climbing in Scotland. An IFMGA guide, he's redpointed 8c, climbed trad E9 and on-sighted Scottish IX,9, and climbed in South America, Alaska and the Himalaya, with the goal of new routes in alpine style, garnering several Piolets d'Or nominations.

GLYN HUGHES is a some-time hon secretary of the Alpine Club, but now carries out the equally important roles of hon archivist and barman: or as the AC quaintly puts it, 'chairman of the Wine Committee'. In 2014 he took on the near-impossible task of following Bill Ruthven as hon secretary of the Mount Everest Foundation.

TOM LIVINGSTONE has a penchant for trad, winter and alpine climbing: the bigger and harder the better. Among his recent successes are ascents of Latok I, *Divine Providence* (ED3), and a winter ascent of the *Walker Spur* (ED3), but he's still hungry for more. He works as an outdoor instructor, holding the Mountain Leader and Single Pitch Award, and as a rope access technician.

DONALD ORR is a member of the Scottish Mountaineering Club and recently retired from a career in theology and fine art, which does beg questions. He now spends his time climbing and writing, and being irresponsible with his grandsons. His writings on mountaineering and the mountain environment have contributed over the years to the *Scottish Mountaineering Club Journal.*

SIMON RICHARDSON lives in Aberdeen. Experience gained in the Alps, Andes, Patagonia, Canada, the Himalaya, Caucasus, Alaska and the Yukon is put to good use most winter weekends whilst exploring and climbing in the Scottish Highlands.

C A RUSSELL who formerly worked with a City bank, devotes much of his time to mountaineering and related activities. He has climbed in many regions of the Alps, in the Pyrenees, East Africa, North America and the Himalaya.

VICTOR SAUNDERS was born in Lossiemouth and grew up in Peninsular Malaysia. He began climbing in the Alps in 1978 and has since climbed in the Andes, Antarctica, Papua, Rockies, Caucasus and across the Himalaya and Karakoram. Formerly a London-based architect, he is now an IF-MGA guide based in Chamonix. His first book, *Elusive Summits,* won the Boardman Tasker Prize. In 2007 he received an honorary MA from the University of Stirling for services to Scottish mountaineering.

MARCELO SCANU is an Argentine climber who lives in Buenos Aires. He specialises in ascending virgin mountains and volcanoes in the Central Andes. His articles and photographs about alpinism, trekking, and mountain history, archaeology and ecology appear in prominent magazines in Europe and America. When not climbing, he works for a workers' union.

DAVID SEDDON is a physician in Nottingham. He has walked, climbed and skied in some unusual places often in the company of John Harding or Derek Fordham. On a good day he might even climb a mountain. He has an ongoing interest in the life and art of T H Somervell.

RODERICK A SMITH began his fascination with mountains following the first ascent of Everest in 1953. He has travelled to the Himalaya, Svalbard, Greenland, Arctic Canada, Japan and the Alps but always returns to his favourites in the Lake District. A lifetime's enjoyment has not been hampered with overweening ambition, but he is proud of his first ascent of a peak in the Stauning Alps and that he can still enjoy climbing and skiing at a modest level, despite the onset of decrepitude.

STEVE SWENSON served as president of the American Alpine Club from 2009 to 2012 and recently published a memoir of his long experience of climbing in Pakistan, Karakoram: Climbing Through the Kashmir Conflict. In 2012, Swenson made the first ascent of Saser Kangri II with Mark Richey and Freddie Wilkinson for which he was awarded the Piolet d'Or, as he was in 2020, at the age of 66, for the ascent of Link Sar.

BEN TIBBETTS is a photographer, artist and IFMGA guide based in Chamonix and the UK. He studied Fine Art to postgraduate level and spent almost two years working in the Antarctic and over four months in Greenland. In Europe he is usually preoccupied with climbing long Alpine routes of different styles and difficulty or looking for interesting lines to ski. Over the last few years he has been working on a large format photographic guidebook on the finest routes on the 4,000m peaks of the Alps.

ERIC VOLA is a French climber who lives in Chamonix and Marseille. He spent three years at University College, London, and climbed in the early 1960s with Chris Bonington, Nick Estcourt, Don Whillans and other Brits. In recent years he has translated British mountaineering books, including a selection of Chris Bonington's best stories and Andy Cave's *Learning to Breathe*.

IAN WALL worked at Plas-y-Brenin in the 1960s. Since then he has climbed extensively throughout the UK, the Alps and in Norway. He was involved with the first round of the Kendal Mountain Film Festival in 1980. He has led treks in Africa, Ladakh, Tibet and Nepal, where he now lives and acts as an advisor to the Kathmandu International Mountain Film Festival, Kathmandu Environmental Education Project and in developing and training the Nepal Mountain Leader programme working closely with the Nepal Mountaineering Association.

NOTES FOR CONTRIBUTORS

The *Alpine Journal* records all aspects of mountains and mountaineering, including expeditions, exploration, art, literature, geography, history, geology, medicine, ethics and the mountain environment.

Articles Contributions in English are invited. They should be sent to the Hon Editor *The Alpine Journal*, Alpine Club, 55 Charlotte Road, London EC2A 3QF, UK. (**journal.editor@alpine-club.org.uk**) Articles, including images, can be sent as an email attachment, on a disk or memory stick. File-sharing services are also acceptable, by prior arrangement with the editor. With files created in Microsoft Word please confine formatting to italics and bold. A typical article is 2,500 words **and may be edited or shortened at their discretion**. Longer pieces should be discussed with the editor.

The Alpine Journal is unable to offer a fee for articles published, but authors who are not AC members receive a copy of the issue of the *Journal* in which their article appears.

Maps and diagrams These should be well researched, accurate and show the most important place-names mentioned in the text. If submitted electronically, maps and route diagrams should be originated as CMYK .eps files in Adobe Illustrator, Freehand or similar ensuring embedded images are at 300dpi resolution and CMYK. Hard copy should be scanned as a Photoshop compatible 300dpi tiff at A4 finished size. This can be arranged through the editor if required.

Photographs Image files should have unique names or serial numbers **that correspond to the list of captions** appended to the article, as a separate document, or in an email. They should be large jpgs or tiff files. Captions must include the photographer's name. Colour transparencies should be originals. Pre-scanned images should be **300dpi** Greyscale or RGB, tiffs or maximum quality jpegs at A4 final size or larger.

Copyright It is the author's responsibility to obtain copyright clearance for text, photographs, digital images and maps, to pay any fees involved and to ensure acknowledgements are in the form required by the copyright owner.

Summaries A brief summary, listing team members, dates, objectives attempted and achieved, should be included at the end of expedition articles.

Biographies Authors are asked to provide a short autobiography of about 50 words, listing noteworthy highlights in their climbing career and anything else they wish to mention.

Deadline Copy and photographs should reach the editor by **1 February** of the year of publication.

Index

Plate 11. *'Gangotri, the holy shrine of Mahadeo [Shiva]'*

Index 2020

THE BEST ALPINE START YOU CAN GET

Climbing packs the way we want them

For more than fifty years Mountain Equipment has been at the forefront of Himalayan and alpine climbing. We've now taken that experience, passion and opinion to the design of our new range of climbing packs. Lightweight, durable and highly weather resistant, the Tupilak series of packs have been developed specifically for climbers and mountaineers needing the very best in simple, functional design. Excelling on rock, ice and mixed ground, they provide uncompromising functionality for alpinism's leading edge.

MOUNTAIN
EQUIPMENT

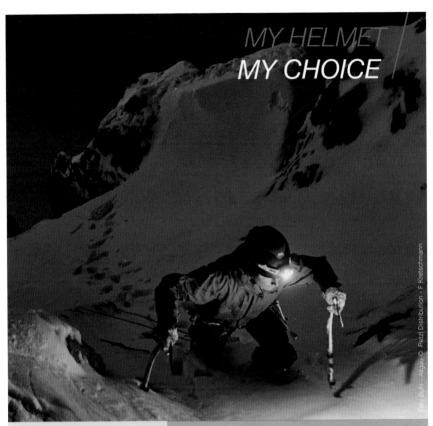

DAVID GOETLLER,
CHAMLANG, NEPAL

THE
NORTH
FACE

SUMMITSERIES™

ADVANCED
MOUNTAIN KIT™
THE PINNACLE OF MOUNTAINEERING

Available **Spring 2021** from
Ellis Brigham, Covent Garden, London
& ellis-brigham.com/thenorthface